14.95

D0521215

A FINE KETTLE OF FISH

AND OTHER FIGURATIVE PHRASES

A FINE
KETTLE
OF FISH

AND OTHER FIGURATIVE PHRASES

LAURENCE URDANG

WALTER W. HUNSINGER • NANCY LaROCHE

DETROIT   CHICAGO   WASHINGTON, D.C.   LONDON

A Fine Kettle of Fish
and Other Figurative Phrases

Published by Visible Ink Press,
a division of Gale Research Inc.
835 Penobscot Building
Detroit, MI 48226-4094

Visible Ink Press is a trademark of Gale Research Inc.

ISBN 0-8103-9406-5

Art Director: Arthur Chartow
Cover Design: Cynthia Baldwin
Interior Design: Mary Krzewinski, Bernadette Gornie
Illustrations: Terry Colon

Printed in the United States of America
All rights reserved

10 9 8 7 6 5 4 3 2 1

Contents

Introduction   vii

Table of Thematic Categories   1

The Expressions   11

Index   355

Introduction

When a situation left you **high and dry,** did you realize that expression referred to boats in dry dock? Did a **point-blank** question ever remind you of that term's origin in ballistics? When inclined to **take a gander** have you ever felt like an inquisitive goose? What are the **cockles of your heart?** And what does a **shambles** have to do with a footstool?

Our language is rife with figurative expressions whose familiarity has obscured their peculiarity. Seldom do we pause to wonder about the origins or to note the often bizarre literal implications of phrases we hear and use daily. A contest may be won **with flying colors,** or it may be **nip and tuck** all the way. Some speakers always **beat around the bush,** while others **call a spade a spade.** An older person may be considered **long in the tooth** but still feel like he is in his **salad days.** Where did these expressions come from, and how did they become part of our language?

Many such expressions have only recently made their way into our dictionaries, where they are defined but rarely explained. Others have yet to acquire lexicographical legitimacy. *A Fine Kettle of Fish and Other Figurative Phrases* includes nearly 2500 examples of such phrases. Entries are defined, their origins explained, and the approximate date of their appearance in the written language cited whenever possible. The editors have in some cases acknowledged the difficulty of pinpointing the origin of a phrase with any degree of accuracy. In such instances, sometimes we offer probable theories; other times we acknowledge a well-worn etymological myth—but question its plausibility or disprove its authenticity. Where appropriate, entries include comments on connotations or usage, as well as illustrative quotations.

Inside This Book

Selection Criteria

Phrases found in *A Fine Kettle of Fish* have entered the general language from a variety of specialized fields: sports, politics, games, finance, the world of entertainment, the events of history, and the customs of long ago have all contributed a wealth of words and sayings. As might be expected, the Bible and other major literary works are the source of a significant number of expressions. In dealing with this plethora of material, our principles of selection were simple in nature and two in number: variety and interest. *A Fine Kettle of Fish* includes both newly coined and vintage phrases. The slang and the literary, the commonplace and the esoteric have been placed side by side, as have the crude and the overly nice. In selection and treatment, the editors have tried to avoid both obscurity and obviousness. Despite a few self-evident expressions whose ubiquity or colorfulness demanded their admission, most words and phrases found on the following pages required some degree of explanation, offered particularly interesting origins, or simply surprised us by their longevity in the language. The editors have tried to make *A Fine Kettle of Fish* a reference work that is both useful and enjoyable.

Using This Book

A Fine Kettle of Fish and Other Figurative Phrases is designed to serve as a browsing book for word fanciers, as a reference book for language students, and as a resource book for writers. This unique third purpose required a unique arrangement of entries. Expressions have been grouped according to thematic categories, a system that allows for use of the book as a thesaurus.

To use *A Fine Kettle of Fish* as a browsing book, browse.

To use *A Fine Kettle of Fish* as a dictionary-style reference book, go first to the **Index** to find whether the phrase about which you seek information is included in the book. The **Index** lists all entries and variant forms in alphabetical order, and gives for each the page number where the expression can be found.

To use *A Fine Kettle of Fish* as a thesaurus, determine a likely category for the concept you wish to express (e.g., CERTAINTY or STATUS). An alphabetical list of the 120 or so thematic categories, under which all entries are organized in the text, can be found in the **Table of Thematic Categories,** along with ample cross references. To facilitate greater access to this thematic organization, more than 300 synonyms (also listed in the **Table of Thematic Categories**) refer the user from terms not used as categories to related terms that are categories in *A Fine Kettle of Fish,* under which desired information may be found. All categories and synonyms, with their cross references, are shown in the text as well.

Organization

All entries, whether single words, phrases, or sentences, follow strict letter-by-letter alphabetization, both under their thematic categories and in the **Index;** exceptions to this principle are made for initial articles (*a, an,* or *the*), the *to* of verbal infinitive forms, and all words shown within brackets or parentheses. In all cases, the editors have sought to give an entry in the form in which it is most frequently encountered. Thus, phrases usually used negatively, for instance, may begin with *not* or *neither,* e.g., **not worth a hill of beans.** Variant forms are included within entries and are listed in italics in the **Index.**

Entries that could be considered to belong to more than one category are treated in full only once, with cross references in other categories to the full entry. For example, **loaves and fishes** appears fully under MONEY, but the expression itself is also listed under the category ABUNDANCE, where the user is referred to the entry at MONEY.

Final Advice

The editors sincerely hope readers will find much **grist for the mill** between these covers, so rather than **champ at the bit,** why don't you **get the ball rolling,** if possible **in one fell swoop,** and have a **field day** with *A Fine Kettle of Fish.* You may find it **takes the cake.**

Table of Thematic Categories

In the following table, categories used throughout the text and synonyms that are cross-references to categories are combined in one alphabetic order.

ABANDONMENT
Abeyance
    See TEMPORIZING
ABILITY
ABUNDANCE
Acceptance
    See APPROVAL
Accomplishment
    See COMPLETION; SUCCESS
Accuracy
    See PRECISION
Acquiescence
    See DEFERENCE;
    RESIGNATION
Adolescence
    See YOUTH
Advantage
    See OUTDOING
Affectation
    See OSTENTATIOUSNESS;
    PRETENSE
Affluence
    See MONEY
AGE
    See also YOUTH
Aid
    See ASSISTANCE
Alcohol
    See DRUNKENNESS; FOOD
    AND DRINK
Alertness
    See PERCEPTIVENESS
Amalgamation
    See MIXTURE
Amorousness
    See LOVE

ANGER
    See also VEXATION
Annoyance
    See VEXATION
Anxiety
    See FEAR; IMPATIENCE
Appearance
    See PHYSICAL APPEARANCE;
    PRETENSE
APPROVAL
Arrogance
    See HAUGHTINESS
Assay
    See TEST
ASSISTANCE
Astuteness
    See PERCEPTIVENESS
Augmentation
    See EXACERBATION
Auspiciousness
    See OPPORTUNENESS
AUTHORITATIVENESS
Automobiles
    See VEHICLES
Avarice
    See DESIRE
Award
    See REWARD
AWKWARDNESS
Beginnings
    See INITIATION; STARTING
Bewilderment
    See CONFUSION
Bias
    See PREJUDICE

Bothersomeness
　　See VEXATION
Bribery
　　See PAYMENT
CANDIDNESS
Capability
　　See ABILITY
Capacity
　　See ABILITY
Censure
　　See CRITICISM; REPRIMAND
CERTAINTY
Cessation
　　See COMPLETION;
　　TERMINATION
Challenge
　　See DIFFICULTY
Chaos
　　See DISORDER
Closeness
　　See FRIENDSHIP
Clumsiness
　　See AWKWARDNESS
COERCION
Commendation
　　See APPROVAL; REWARD
Competence
　　See ABILITY
COMPLETION
　　See also TERMINATION
Complication
　　See DIFFICULTY
Comprehensiveness
　　See INCLUSIVENESS
Compulsion
　　See COERCION
Concealment
　　See SECRECY
Conclusion
　　See COMPLETION;
　　TERMINATION
Condemnation
　　See REPRIMAND
Confidence
　　See CERTAINTY
Confidentiality
　　See SECRECY
CONFUSION
　　See also DISORDER

Conglomeration
　　See MIXTURE
Consent
　　See APPROVAL
Continuation
　　See RESUMPTION
CONTROL
　　See also MANIPULATION
Conviction
　　See CERTAINTY
Cooperation
　　See ASSISTANCE;
　　RECIPROCITY
Cordiality
　　See FRIENDSHIP
Corpulence
　　See PHYSICAL APPEARANCE
Correctness
　　See CERTAINTY; PRECISION
Cost
　　See PAYMENT; SELLING
Countenance
　　See VISAGE
Craving
　　See DESIRE
Craziness
　　See IRRATIONALITY
Criterion
　　See TEST
CRITICISM
　　See also REPRIMAND
Culmination
　　See COMPLETION;
　　TERMINATION
CURIOSITY
DANGER
　　See also VULNERABILITY
Deceit
　　See MENDACITY
Deception
　　See MENDACITY; PLOY;
　　PRETENSE; TRICKERY
Decisiveness
　　See IRREVOCABILITY
Defeat
　　See FAILURE
Defenselessness
　　See VULNERABILITY
DEFERENCE

Defiance
    See REBELLIOUSNESS
Dejection
    See GRIEVING
Delaying
    See TEMPORIZING
Delight
    See ENJOYMENT
DENIAL
    See also REFUSAL
DEPARTURE
Derision
    See INSULT
Desertion
    See ABANDONMENT
DESIRE
Destitution
    See POVERTY
Destruction
    See DOWNFALL
Determination
    See PERSEVERANCE
Diction
    See LANGUAGE
Differentiation
    See PERCEPTIVENESS
DIFFICULTY
    See also IMPEDIMENT
Diligence
    See EXERTION
Disadvantage
    See VULNERABILITY
Disappointment
    See FAILURE
Disapproval
    See CRITICISM; INSULT
Disarray
    See DISORDER
Discernment
    See PERCEPTIVENESS
Discomfort
    See DIFFICULTY; ILL HEALTH
Disdain
    See HAUGHTINESS
Dishonesty
    See MENDACITY;
    UNSCRUPULOUSNESS
Dishonorableness
    See UNSCRUPULOUSNESS

DISORDER
    See also CONFUSION
Disorientation
    See CONFUSION
Domination
    See CONTROL;
    MANIPULATION
DOWNFALL
    See also FAILURE
Drinking
    See FOOD AND DRINK
DRUNKENNESS
    See also FOOD AND DRINK
Duration
    See ENDURANCE; TIME
Duress
    See COERCION
ECCENTRICITY
    See also FATUOUSNESS
Effort
    See EXERTION
Elation
    See ENJOYMENT
ENDURANCE
    See also PERSEVERANCE
ENJOYMENT
Entirety
    See INCLUSIVENESS;
    TOTALITY
EQUIVALENCE
ERRONEOUSNESS
Escape
    See DEPARTURE
Evil
    See UNSCRUPULOUSNESS
EXACERBATION
Exactness
    See PRECISION
Exaggeration
    See MENDACITY
Excelling
    See OUTDOING
EXCESSIVENESS
EXCLAMATIONS
    See LANGUAGE; RETORTS
EXERTION
EXPLOITATION
Expulsion
    See REFUSAL

3

Extemporaneousness
   See SPONTANEITY
Extortion
   See COERCION; PAYMENT
Extravagance
   See EXCESSIVENESS
Facial Appearance
   See VISAGE
FAILURE
   See also DOWNFALL
Fallaciousness
   See ERRONEOUSNESS
Familiarity
   See FRIENDSHIP
FATUOUSNESS
   See also ECCENTRICITY;
   IGNORANCE
Faultfinding
   See CRITICISM; REPRIMAND
Favoritism
   See INJUSTICE; PREJUDICE
Fawning
   See OBSEQUIOUSNESS
FEAR
Finality
   See TERMINATION
Finance
   See INDEBTEDNESS; MONEY
Flamboyance
   See OSTENTATIOUSNESS
Flattery
   See OBSEQUIOUSNESS
FOOD AND DRINK
   See also DRUNKENNESS
Foolishness
   See FATUOUSNESS
Force
   See COERCION
Frankness
   See CANDIDNESS
Frenziedness
   See DISORDER;
   IRRATIONALITY
FRIENDSHIP
   See also LOVE
Furtiveness
   See SECRECY
Fury
   See ANGER; VEXATION

FUTILITY
Gibberish
   See LANGUAGE; NONSENSE
Good Luck
   See SUPERSTITION
Graft
   See PAYMENT
Greed
   See DESIRE
GRIEVING
Harassment
   See VEXATION
HAUGHTINESS
Health
   See ILL HEALTH
Help
   See ASSISTANCE
Hindrance
   See IMPEDIMENT
Hopelessness
   See FUTILITY
Horror
   See FEAR
Hypocrisy
   See PRETENSE
Idleness
   See INDOLENCE
IGNORANCE
   See also FATUOUSNESS
ILL HEALTH
Ill Temper
   See ANGER
Illness
   See ILL HEALTH
Immediacy
   See INSTANTANEOUSNESS
Immoderation
   See EXCESSIVENESS
IMPATIENCE
IMPEDIMENT
   See also DIFFICULTY
Impropriety
   See UNSCRUPULOUSNESS
Inability
   See FAILURE
Inaccuracy
   See ERRONEOUSNESS
Inactivity
   See INDOLENCE

Inanity
See FATUOUSNESS
INCLUSIVENESS
See also TOTALITY
INDEBTEDNESS
See also POVERTY;
VULNERABILITY
Indecision
See VACILLATION
Indecisiveness
See VACILLATION
Independence
See SELF-RELIANCE
Indigence
See POVERTY
INDOLENCE
Industriousness
See EXERTION
Inebriation
See DRUNKENNESS
Ineffectuality
See FUTILITY
Influence
See MANIPULATION
Infrequency
See TIME
INITIATION
See also STARTING
INJUSTICE
See also PREJUDICE
Inquisitiveness
See CURIOSITY
Insanity
See ECCENTRICITY;
IRRATIONALITY
INSIGNIFICANCE
Insolvency
See INDEBTEDNESS
INSTANTANEOUSNESS
INSULT
Intensification
See EXACERBATION
Intoxication
See DRUNKENNESS
Introduction
See INITIATION
Intrusiveness
See CURIOSITY
IRRATIONALITY

Irreversibility
See IRREVOCABILITY
IRREVOCABILITY
Irritation
See ANGER; VEXATION
Lamentation
See GRIEVING
LANGUAGE
See also PROFANITY
Laziness
See INDOLENCE
Leave-taking
See DEPARTURE
Licentiousness
See PROMISCUOUSNESS
Locomotion
See VEHICLES
Longing
See DESIRE
Looks
See PHYSICAL APPEARANCE
Looseness
See PROMISCUOUSNESS
LOVE
See also FRIENDSHIP
Lunacy
See IRRATIONALITY
Lust
See DESIRE;
PROMISCUOUSNESS
Lying
See MENDACITY
MANIPULATION
See also CONTROL
Mastery
See CONTROL
Maturity
See AGE
Meaninglessness
See NONSENSE
Meddlesomeness
See CURIOSITY
MENDACITY
Miscellaneousness
See MIXTURE
Mistakenness
See ERRONEOUSNESS
MIXTURE

MONEY
    See also PAYMENT
Mourning
    See GRIEVING
Mutuality
    See RECIPROCITY
Nakedness
    See PHYSICAL APPEARANCE
Neglect
    See ABANDONMENT
Newness
    See AGE
NONSENSE
Nourishment
    See FOOD AND DRINK
Nuisance
    See VEXATION
Objection
    See CRITICISM
Obscenity
    See PROFANITY
OBSEQUIOUSNESS
Obsolescence
    See AGE
Obstacle
    See IMPEDIMENT
Old Age
    See AGE
Oldness
    See AGE
Openness
    See CANDIDNESS
OPPORTUNENESS
    See also TIME
OSTENTATIOUSNESS
OUTDOING
Overshadowing
    See OUTDOING
Overwork
    See EXERTION
Parity
    See EQUIVALENCE
PAYMENT
    See also MONEY; REWARD
PERCEPTIVENESS
Perplexity
    See CONFUSION
PERSEVERANCE
    See also ENDURANCE

Persistence
    See PERSEVERANCE
Personages
    See STATUS
PHYSICAL APPEARANCE
    See also VISAGE
Physical Stature
    See PHYSICAL APPEARANCE
Pleasure
    See ENJOYMENT
Plenty
    See ABUNDANCE
PLOY
    See also TRICKERY
Politeness
    See DEFERENCE
Pomposity
    See HAUGHTINESS;
    OSTENTATIOUSNESS
Postponement
    See TEMPORIZING
Potential
    See ABILITY
POVERTY
    See also INDEBTEDNESS
Precariousness
    See DANGER; VULNERABILITY
PRECISION
Predicament
    See DANGER; DIFFICULTY;
    IMPEDIMENT; INDEBTEDNESS;
    VULNERABILITY
PREJUDICE
    See also INJUSTICE
Preparation
    See STARTING
PRETENSE
Pretentiousness
    See OSTENTATIOUSNESS
Pride
    See HAUGHTINESS
Priggishness
    See PRUDISHNESS
Prize
    See REWARD
Procrastination
    See TEMPORIZING
PROFANITY
    See also LANGUAGE

Proliferation
    See ABUNDANCE
PROMISCUOUSNESS
Propitiousness
    See OPPORTUNENESS
Propriety
    See PRUDISHNESS
Prosperousness
    See ABUNDANCE; SUCCESS
Protest
    See REBELLIOUSNESS
Provocation
    See VEXATION
PRUDISHNESS
Quickness
    See INSTANTANEOUSNESS
Racism
    See PREJUDICE
Rank
    See INSTANTANEOUSNESS
REBELLIOUSNESS
Recantation
    See DENIAL; REVERSAL;
    VACILLATION
RECIPROCITY
REFUSAL
    See also DENIAL
Rejection
    See ABANDONMENT; DENIAL;
    REFUSAL
Rejoinder
    See RETORTS
Renewing
    See RESUMPTION
REPRIMAND
    See also CRITICISM
Reproach
    See CRITICISM
RESIGNATION
    See also SUBMISSION
Resistance
    See REBELLIOUSNESS
Resolve
    See PERSEVERANCE
Restarting
    See RESUMPTION
Restlessness
    See IMPATIENCE
RESUMPTION

RETALIATION
RETORTS
Retribution
    See RETALIATION
Revenge
    See RETALIATION
REVERSAL
REWARD
    See also PAYMENT
Ridicule
    See INSULT
Risk
    See DANGER; VULNERABILITY
Ruination
    See DOWNFALL
Sameness
    See EQUIVALENCE
Sanction
    See AUTHORITATIVENESS
Scolding
    See REPRIMAND
SECRECY
    See also SILENCE
SELF-RELIANCE
Self-sufficiency
    See SELF-RELIANCE
SELLING
Semblance
    See PRETENSE
Servility
    See OBSEQUIOUSNESS
Showiness
    See OSTENTATIOUSNESS
Shrewdness
    See PERCEPTIVENESS
Sickness
    See ILL HEALTH
SILENCE
    See also SECRECY
Silliness
    See FATUOUSNESS
Similarity
    See EQUIVALENCE
Sincerity
    See CANDIDNESS
Skepticism
    See SUSPICIOUSNESS
Snobbishness
    See HAUGHTINESS

Solicitation
　　See PAYMENT
Speechlessness
　　See SILENCE
Speeding
　　See INSTANTANEOUSNESS
SPONTANEITY
STARTING
　　See also INITIATION
STATUS
Stupidity
　　See FATUOUSNESS;
　　IGNORANCE; NONSENCE
SUBMISSION
　　See also RESIGNATION
Submissiveness
　　See DEFERENCE;
　　OBSEQUIOUSNESS;
　　SUBMISSION
Subordination
　　See STATUS
Subservience
　　See OBSEQUIOUSNESS
Subsistence
　　See POVERTY
SUCCESS
Sufferance
　　See ENDURANCE
Suitability
　　See WORTHINESS
Superfluousness
　　See ABUNDANCE;
　　EXCESSIVENESS
SUPERSTITION
Surpassing
　　See OUTDOING
Surrender
　　See SUBMISSION
SUSPICIOUSNESS
Sustenance
　　See FOOD AND DRINK
Swindling
　　See TRICKERY
Talent
　　See ABILITY
TEMPORIZING
Tenacity
　　See PERSEVERANCE

TERMINATION
　　See also COMPLETION
TEST
Thoroughness
　　See INCLUSIVENESS;
　　TOTALITY
Thwarting
　　See IMPEDIMENT;
　　TERMINATION
TIME
　　See also OPPORTUNENESS
Timeliness
　　See OPPORTUNENESS; TIME
Timidity
　　See FEAR
Tippling
　　See DRUNKENNESS; FOOD
　　AND DRINK
Toil
　　See EXERTION
TOTALITY
　　See also INCLUSIVENESS
Transportation
　　See VEHICLES
TRICKERY
　　See also PLOY
Triviality
　　See INSIGNIFICANCE
Troublesomeness
　　See DIFFICULTY
Turnaround
　　See REVERSAL
Uncertainty
　　See CONFUSION;
　　VACILLATION
Unconventionality
　　See ECCENTRICITY;
　　FATUOUSNESS
Unfairness
　　See INJUSTICE;
　　UNSCRUPULOUSNESS
Unimportance
　　See INSIGNIFICANCE
Unrest
　　See DISORDER
UNSCRUPULOUSNESS
Uselessness
　　See FUTILITY
VACILLATION

Validation
See AUTHORITATIVENESS
Validity
See AUTHORITATIVENESS
Value
See WORTHINESS
VEHICLES
Vending
See SELLING
Vengeance
See RETALIATION
VEXATION
See also ANGER
Victimization
See EXPLOITATION;
MANIPULATION
Virtuousness
See WORTHINESS
VISAGE
See also PHYSICAL
APPEARANCE

Vulgarity
See PROFANITY
VULNERABILITY
See also DANGER;
INDEBTEDNESS
Wavering
See VACILLATION
Wholeness
See TOTALITY
Words
See LANGUAGE
Work
See EXERTION
Worsening
See EXACERBATION
WORTHINESS
Worthlessness
See INSIGNIFICANCE
Yielding
See DEFERENCE
YOUTH
See also AGE

The Expressions

ABANDONMENT

brain drain—Emigration of highly skilled, professional people; the loss of scientists, trained technical personnel, and university professors to another country or organization. This expression was coined by the British immediately following World War II in reference to the extensive loss of their country's professionals and skilled workers to other countries, especially to the United States, which offered higher salaries and better working conditions. However, the term soon took on a more universal aspect as many of the industrialized nations of the world increased their capacities for production and entered the game of luring top people into influential positions. Thus was born the inverse term *brain gain*.

> For the recipient countries the emigrants produce the opposite of the brain drain, a brain gain. (Andrew H. Malcolm, *The New York Times*, November 7, 1977)

dead as Chelsea—Useless; no longer of value. Chelsea, England, was the location of a military hospital for severely injured soldiers. Since many of these soldiers had lost limbs or were otherwise disabled, they were of no further value to the military effort. According to one source, this expression was first used during the Battle of Fontenoy (1745) by a soldier whose leg had been shot off by a cannonball.

empty nester—A parent whose children have grown and left home to be on their own. This expression alludes to the annual ritual of birds' building a nest, rearing their young in it, and then abandoning it after the young have flown away. Both terms have been in use since the early 1960s.

> Like their grown children, the empty nesters are intent on living well. (*Maclean's*, July 1976)

Some parents seize upon the opportunity to establish a new life for themselves, while others sink into a melancholy state. Psychiatrists have coined an expression for the latter condition, *empty nest syndrome*.

11

We knew, of course, about the empty nest syndrome but were not perceptive enough to recognize it in ourselves. (*McCall's*, January 1973)

left high and dry—Left in the lurch, abandoned, forsaken, rejected, deserted, stranded. The allusion is to a vessel in dry dock or grounded on the shore.

> Meanwhile, Dr. Flood's successor had been appointed, and Dr. Flood was left high and dry without preferment owing to an undoubted breach of faith on the part of Duckworth. (E. W. Hamilton, *Diary*, 1881)

Both literal and figurative uses of this expression date from the nineteenth century.

left in the basket—Abandoned; neglected. The allusion in this phrase is to the practice of leaving abandoned babies at the doorsteps of hospitals or private homes. At one time the practice was so common that some foundling institutions actually left baskets outside their doors to receive such infants. Hence, the implication that one *left in the basket* has been rejected.

left in the lurch—To be deserted while in difficulty; to be left in a dangerous predicament without assistance. *Lurch* is derived from the French *lourche* 'discomfited,' implying that someone left in the lurch is likely to find himself in the uncomfortable position of facing a threatening or perilous situation alone.

> The Volscians seeing themselves abandoned and left in the lurch by them, ... quit the camp and field. (Philemon Holland, *Livy's Roman History*, 1600)

In medieval times, a *lurch* was a lurking place where poachers would hide as they placed illegal animal traps. If a poacher were deserted by his companions when the authorities approached, he was *left in the lurch*. *Lurch* was also the name of an ancient, backgammon-like game in which the objective was to leave the other players as far behind as possible. *Left in the lurch* also describes the predicament of a cribbage player whose opponent wins before the player has even "turned the corner," i.e., moved his pieces halfway around the board.

ABEYANCE
SEE TEMPORIZING

ABILITY

all is fish that comes to his net—A proverbial phrase describing the luck of one for whom nothing ever goes awry because of a seemingly innate

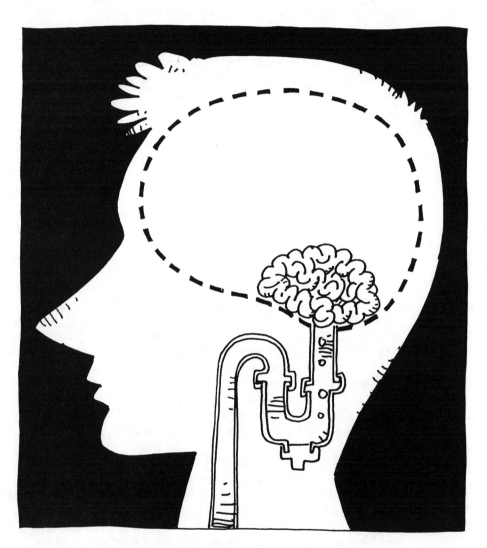

BRAIN DRAIN

ability to turn everything to profit. Most fishermen expect to discover undesirable animals or debris in their nets, but the fortuitous fisherman's net overflows with valuable fish only. The expression is used of one with an extraordinary capacity to develop invariably successful schemes and make consistently lucrative financial investments.

anchor man—The man who runs or swims the last leg in a relay race; the rear man on a tug-of-war team; the newscaster who coordinates a radio broadcast or television program. In sports jargon the *anchor man* runs or swims the *anchor leg*; he is usually the fastest or strongest member of the team. In broadcasting, as with sports, the *anchor man* is usually the strongest member of a news team. His function, however, is to operate from a control center and direct the gathering and dissemination of the news from various spots about the nation or the world.

> In the fall, NBC moved David Brinkley to Washington, as permanent anchor there for the news of the nation's capital. (John Gunn, *The Americana Annual*, 1978)

In the sports world the term *anchor man* has been in use since the late 1800s; in broadcasting it came into use in the 1930s and was shortened to *anchor* in 1956, thus eliminating any sexual identification.

double in brass—To obtain income from more than one source; to be versatile; to serve two purposes; to play two roles; to be capable of doing more than one thing well. This phrase probably had its genesis in the theatrical world, most likely the circus, where it was often necessary for a performer to be able to play a musical instrument in the band along with his regular duties in the ring, *in brass* being short for *in the brass section*. Another practice common to the circus, which may have contributed to the popularity of the term, was to have some performers march along with the band and fake playing in order to make the band appear larger. Today the term is only heard figuratively to indicate doubling up.

get the hang of—To get the knack; to get the significance; to be able to do; to come to understand the operation of something. This American expression, in common use since at least 1839, derives its meaning from a colloquial application of the word *hang*, 'familiar knowledge' or 'knack,' which, in turn, has its roots in the craft of the tailor or seamstress; one must get the proper hang of coats, skirts, drapes, curtains to satisfy the customer.

> Suggs lost his money and his horse, but then he hadn't got the hang of the game. (Johnson J. Hooper, *Simon Suggs*, 1845)

green thumb—An above-average ability to grow plants; the knack of successfully cultivating and propagating plants. This phrase and its variant *green fingers* date from the early 1900s. A *green thumb* is like a magic touch which encourages rapid growth. Although the phrase is usually heard in the context of gardening, it can apply to any innate ability to make things grow and prosper.

> "Success with money is often accidental," she sighed. "One needs 'green fingers' to make it grow." (*Daily Telegraph*, April 26, 1969)

jack of all trades—This expression refers to a person who can turn his hand to almost any trade but is not especially proficient in any one of them. The term is often used contemptuously to indicate one who pretends to be knowledgeable in many areas, one with a smattering of learning, a pretender. The phrase has been in common use since at least 1618.

> "How comes it that I am so unlucky? Jack of all trades and master of none," said Goodenough with a sneer. (Maria Edgeworth, *Popular Tales*, 1800)

keep [one's] hand in—To keep in practice, to dabble in, to maintain one's proficiency in a certain activity. The expression usually implies sporadic or intermittent interest and activity.

lynx-eyed—Keen of vision; having acute sight; sharp-eyed; having the ability to distinguish objects at a great distance. This expression is derived from the mythological figure Lynceus, a member of Jason's crew on the Argo, who had vision so sharp that he could see precious metals buried deep in the earth. It has erroneously been associated with the cat-like animal, the lynx, which has, in fact, rather poor vision.

> The lynx-eyed agent of some loan society. (*The Nineteenth Century*, May 1883)

not just another pretty face—This expression, which came into greater prominence as a favorite catchphrase of the women's liberation movement, is a warning or putdown directed at men who view women merely as sexual objects, without any appreciation for their intellectual potential or ability. In essence the woman using this phrase is telling her male antagonist that she has ability and that her looks are not part of her qualifications. It is also used among men in speaking of women.

> "She's not just a pretty face," Philpott went on, "she's clever, too." (Miles Tripp, *Woman at Risk*, 1974)

In recent years the tables have been turned, and women often apply the term jocularly to men. It has also received broader metaphoric currency in reference, for example, to a piece of machinery that has been attractively designed yet, perhaps surprisingly, is able to accomplish its work effectively.

play a straight bat—To know what you are doing, to know your business. This Briticism comes from the game of cricket.

to the manner born—See STATUS.

wear different hats—To perform more than one function simultaneously; to play two or more roles; to fulfill two positions concurrently. This expression alludes to someone who can perform two or more responsible duties while operating from the same position, with reference to the practice of wearing a distinctive hat that indicates one's occupation. A common variant is *wear two hats*.

> Except for Chairman Wheeler, each of these men wears two hats: one as topbraid officer of his service, the other as a member of the Joint Chiefs. (*Time*, February 5, 1965)

ABUNDANCE

at rack and manger—In extravagance; reckless abundance; in the midst of plenty; wanting for nothing. This British expression, dating from at least 1378, alludes to the life of domestic beasts. They stand in a rack, protected from the elements, have their food placed before them in a manger, and never have to give any thought to the acquisition of their own provisions. *Live at rack and manger*, a variant, means 'to live without worry about the future.'

> John Lackland . . . tearing out the bowels of St. Edmundsbury Convent . . . by living at rack and manger there. (Thomas Carlyle, *Reminiscences*, 1866)

cloud of witnesses—A great number of observers; a host of onlookers; a multitude who will swear to what they saw. This expression is directly attributable to the Bible; it appears more than once in the King James version, but appears first in Hebrews 12:1:

> Seeing we also are compassed about with so great a cloud of witnesses.

corn in Egypt—Anything in abundance that can be purchased from a supplier; something waiting for a buyer to come along. This phrase has its origin in the Old Testament:

> And he said, Behold, I have heard that there is corn in Egypt; get you down thither, and buy for us from thence; that we may live, and not die. (Genesis 42:2)

The original innocence of the Biblical expression has given way to a more sardonic application in modern usage: the product is available if the money is plentiful.

> There is corn in Egypt while there is cash in Leadenhall. (Charles Lamb, *Letter*, c. 1830)

fat city—An extremely satisfactory condition; a comfortable situation; sitting pretty. *Fat* in this American slang expression is obvious in its reference to abundance or plenty. *City* seemingly derives from the post-World War II use of -*sville*, a slang suffix added for emphasis, as in *dullsville*, meaning 'extremely dull.' *City* appeared in the early 1960s, and was popularized by a New York City propaganda campaign to promote tourism, in which the city advertised itself as *fun city*.

> "I've put it behind me," Stockdale says of his long ordeal. "I think of it as just another tour of duty. In so many ways I'm in fat city." (*Newsweek*, February 25, 1974)

forty acres and a mule—An illusion of plenty; an optimistic expectancy of future blessings; pie in the sky; a dream or fantasy of a future without want. On January 16, 1865 General William Tecumseh Sherman of the United States Army gave the following special field order.

> Every family shall have a plot of not more than forty acres of tillable ground.

It was probably this order which was responsible for many Southern Blacks believing that upon their emancipation after the Civil War that their masters' plantations would be confiscated and divided among them. From about 1862 the fantasy had been *ten acres and a mule*, which undoubtedly accounted for the *mule* in the new version, *forty acres and a mule*. In England a similar cry of hopefulness arose during the 1880s, *three acres and a cow*. See also three acres and a cow, below.

loaves and fishes—See MONEY.

my cup runneth over—Any state of abundance, profusion, or excess; a run of luck or good fortune. This phrase from the well-known Twenty-third Psalm ("The Lord is my shepherd") is now commonly used in a secular sense, though in its original context it referred to the plentitude of God's goodness and spiritual gifts.

> Thou preparest a table before me in the presence of mine enemies:
> Thou hast anointed my head with oil;
> My cup runneth over.
> Surely goodness and mercy shall follow me all the days of my life;
> And I shall dwell in the house of the Lord for ever.
> (Psalms 23:5-6)

spring up like mushrooms—To proliferate; to appear in great quantity all at once. Mushrooms, a type of fungus, grow rapidly and abundantly following the slightest rainfall.

three acres and a cow—Excessive optimism; an illusion of a future free from want; pie in the sky. Daniel Defoe had suggested as early as 1724 in *Tour through the Whole Islands of Great Britain* that each farmer should be allotted at least *three acres and a cow*. That may have been the source of the phrase, but it became current from a song popular in the 1880s. At any event, Jesse Collings, a leader of the Liberal party, picked up the phrase and used it as a campaign slogan (1887–1889). The phrase became so closely associated with Collings and his radical agrarian politics that he became known as *Three Acres and a Cow Collings*.

An honest man who had worked long and well should have "three acres and a cow." (Dean Hole, *Then and Now*, 1902)

widow's cruse—A seemingly inexhaustible supply; a meager supply of food that is, through clever management, made to last through several meals. In II Kings 4, Elisha comes to the rescue of a destitute widow who is about to lose her two sons as bondmen to her dead husband's creditor. Upon learning that the only thing she has in her house is a small amount of oil, he tells her to gather all the empty containers she can find in the village and bring them to her house. He then tells her to start pouring the oil from the cruse into the containers. Her small supply of oil miraculously multiplies as she pours, allowing her to fill all the containers, to sell the oil to pay off her debt, and to save her sons.

ACCEPTANCE
SEE APPROVAL

ACCOMPLISHMENT
SEE COMPLETION; SUCCESS

ACCURACY
SEE PRECISION

ACQUIESCENCE
SEE DEFERENCE; RESIGNATION

ADOLESCENCE
SEE YOUTH

ADVANTAGE
SEE OUTDOING

AFFECTATION
SEE OSTENTATIOUSNESS; PRETENSE

AFFLUENCE
SEE MONEY

AGE
See also YOUTH

before [one] had nails on [one's] toes—See TIME.

brand-new—Entirely or completely new; unused; absolutely or perfectly new; also *bran-new*. This term, in use since 1570, is said to have come from the Anglo-Saxon word *brand* 'torch' and formerly denoted metals or metal articles fresh from the fire or furnace. A synonym is *fire-new*, used by Shakespeare in *Richard III:*

> Your fire-new stamp of Honor is scarce current. (I,iii)

chair days—Old age; the evening of life. The reference is to that time in a person's life when he is old, and perhaps feeble, and passes much of his time in the ease and comfort of a chair. Shakespeare made use of the phrase.

> Wast thou ordain'd, dear father
> To lose thy youth in peace, and to achieve
> The silvery livery of advised age,
> And, in thy reverence and thy chair-days, thus
> To die in ruffian battle?
> (*Henry the Sixth, Part 2,* V,ii)

geezer—An eccentric old person; an unknown old man; a senior citizen. This slang expression, usually used in a derogatory manner, is probably a corruption of *guiser*, a masquerader or a mummer. The *OED* lists the first written use as:

> If we wake up the old geezers, we shall get notice to quit without compensation. ('Corin,' *Truth about the Stage*, 1885)

last leaf—Very old; the last of a generation; one who clings to life; one who has lived past his time. This expression appeared in its figurative sense in the Oliver Wendell Holmes poem, *The Last Leaf* (1831). In the poem Holmes writes of Major Thomas Melville, a survivor of the Boston Tea Party, as one who, like the *last leaf*, finds himself still clinging to the tree in the spring when the new buds are bursting out all about him.

> And if I should live to be
> The last leaf upon the tree
> In the spring,
> Let them smile, as I do now,
> At the old forsaken bough
> Where I cling.

lay [one's] nuts aside—To lay aside one's frivolities; to give up boyish extravagances; to become mature. The ceremony to which this expression alludes was practiced in old Roman wedding rites. As the bridegroom led his new wife home, he strewed nuts through the crowd to symbolize his newly found maturity.

long in the tooth—Old; showing signs of old age. Although currently used of people, this expression originally applied exclusively to horses. It refers to the seemingly longer length of an older horse's teeth, due to gum recession.

To be honest I am getting quite long in the tooth and this is a method of bringing children into my Christmas. (*Sunday Express*, December 24, 1972)

over the hill—Past the time of greatest efficiency or power, past the prime of life, too old, aging; also, past the crisis, over the hurdles. The expression's latter meanings may be derived from a traveler's achievement of crossing a hill, after which the going is easier. The phrase's more common meanings, however, allude to a hill as being the high point, or apex, of one's effectiveness and authority, after which the only course is downhill. In contemporary usage, the phrase most often describes a person of advancing age.

As they say about boxers who are getting on in years, she is over the hill. (I. Cross, *God Boy*, 1957)

AID
SEE ASSISTANCE

ALCOHOL
SEE DRUNKENNESS; FOOD AND DRINK

ALERTNESS
SEE PERCEPTIVENESS

AMALGAMATION
SEE MIXTURE

AMOROUSNESS
SEE LOVE

ANGER
See also VEXATION

bent out of shape—Vexed, irritated, annoyed. This phrase, of recent vintage, has yet to find its way into our lexicons. The implicit analogy between an object's physical shape and an individual's mental state suggests that the latter condition has a specific cause, a temporary nature, and contrasts with one's "usual self."

cross as two sticks—Angry, vexed, out of humor; irritated; in high dudgeon. This British pun alludes to the image of crossed sticks in the shape of an "X." The image of two sticks "passing or lying athwart each other" *(OED)* gives rise to associations of contrariness, opposition, and adversity.

He has been as cross as two sticks at not having been asked to dinner at Court. (R. M. Milnes Houghton in *Life, Letters, and Friendships*, 1855)

fit to be tied—Incensed, enraged, livid, irate, very angry. This expression probably comes from the hospital practice of restraining patients who pose a danger to themselves or others. In its contemporary hyperbolic usage, *fit to be tied* refers to anyone (not just a patient) who is extremely angry or who is acting irrationally, implying that if this person were in a hospital, he would be tied down for his own protection as well as for the protection of others.

> It threw the place into a tizzy. ... The boss is fit to be tied. When he gets hold of you .... (C. Simak, *Strangers in the Universe*, 1956)

hot under the collar—Angry, mad, infuriated; hot and bothered, distraught, upset, agitated. The allusion is to the red or "hot" color of an enraged person's neck and face due to the rush of blood to those areas.

> After years of this sort of puling imbecility one gets hot under the collar and is perhaps carried to an extreme. (Ezra Pound, *Letters*, 1918)

The expression dates from at least 1895.

in a snit—In a tiff, peeved; agitated, in a fuss or stew, all worked-up. *Webster's Third* cites the following usage from *Information Please Almanac*:

> Wall Street brokers were in a snit because nobody bought stocks.

In an obsolete, literal sense *snit* was 'the glowing part of the wick of a candle when blown out,' perhaps the source of the figurative meaning of the word today.

in a tiff—In a fit of anger; in a huff; with a slight outburst of temper. The origin of this phrase is obscure, but it may be imitative in nature, from the sound of a puff of escaping steam. It has been in common use since the early 18th century.

> Abrupt Captain Anthony being in some tiff of his own ... (Thomas Carlyle, *Letters to Mrs. Carlyle*, 1871)

little pot is soon hot—A small person is quickly provoked; a little person is easily roused to anger. A small pot, which naturally contains less water than a larger one, comes to a boil more quickly. *Little* in this expression apparently means both small in size and small in mind. Shakespeare alludes to the proverb in *The Taming of the Shrew* (IV,i):

> Now, were not I a little pot and soon hot, ...

Use of the expression dates from at least 1546.

mad as a baited bull—Extremely angry; infuriated; in a rage; incensed; livid. Thomas Fuller in his *The Worthies of England* (1662) attributes the source of this phrase to:

> ... as mad as the baiting bull of Stamford.

According to the account, one Earl Warren gave the town of Stamford a meadow to use as a public park, with the proviso that each year the townspeople provide a mad bull for baiting for six weeks before Christmas.

Baiting consists of restraining the beast in some way, by chains, by ropes, or by confinement, and then tormenting it with dogs. Related terms are *mad as a baited bear* and *mad as a baited boar*.

mad as a hatter—See IRRATIONALITY.

mad as a tup—Out of humor; vexed; distraught; hot and bothered. In *Shropshire Folk-Lore* (1883), Charlotte Burne maintains that the entire saying is *mad as a tup in a halter*, which helps to explain the expression, for a tup is a ram and rams were usually allowed to run freely with the ewes. Therefore, to place a ram in a halter would certainly be cause for his becoming irritated.

> In Derbyshire . . . there is no commoner saying to express anger shown by anyone than to say that he or she was 'as mad as a tup'. (*Notes and Queries*, December 21, 1901)

mad as a wet hen—Very angry, furious, enraged. Chicken farmers maintain that this popular simile has no basis in fact, since hens do not get particularly excited when wet. These female fowl are, however, known for their angry clucking and pecking when provoked.

> The chicken farmers of Quebec . . . are mad as, well, a wet hen. (*The Wall Street Journal*, July 1971)

mad as hops—Extremely angry; livid, infuriated, incensed; enraged, furious. This expression is probably a twist on *hopping mad*, implying that a person has become so angry that he hops about in a frenzied rage.

> Such a grin! It made me mad as hops! (*Harper's Magazine*, October 1884)

mean as hungry Tyson—Extremely disagreeable; ignoble; beyond contempt. The allusion in this Australian phrase, dating from the late 1800s, is to a legendary farmer named Tyson who, out of his miserliness, cut back so severely on his family's food supplies that they were constantly in a state of hunger that made them extremely testy.

out of countenance—Visibly abashed, ashamed, confounded, or disconcerted; upset, annoyed, perturbed. When a person is flustered or upset, the feeling is usually registered on his face. The phrase dates from the 16th century.

take it in snuff—To become angry; to take offense at; to demonstrate indignation. The *OED* proposes that the original reference may have been to the irritating smell from the odor proceeding from a snuffed candle. *Brewer's* propounds that the phrase derives from the irritating quality of snuff powder, a tobacco derivative. However, a more likely explanation is that it derives from the act of sniffing as an expression of disdain or contempt. In *Retaliation* (1774) Oliver Goldsmith makes use of the term to create a double entendre about Sir Joshua Reynolds' greatness:

When they talked of their Raphaels,
Correggios, and stuff,
He shifted his trumpet, and only took snuff.

The expression has been in use since the 16th century.

towering rage—Extreme anger; such an intense state of fury that violence is conceivable. This expression apparently has its roots in the medieval practice of falconry. The word *towering* is used figuratively for extreme height or intensity, adapted from the practice of falcons or other birds of prey towering, i.e., soaring at their maximum height before attacking. Combined with the word *rage*, which means violently angry, a *towering rage* indicates the possibility of a murderous attack at any moment.

vent [one's] spleen—To let loose one's anger, malice, or ill-humor on another; to release one's emotions in a fit of temper. The spleen, a flat, ductless, vascular organ lying near the stomach, was once regarded as the seat of various emotions: melancholy, ill-temper, and spitefulness. Therefore, to *vent one's spleen* was to release all these horrible emotions in one vehement tirade.

To vent their spleen on the first idle coxcomb they can find. (Thomas Peacock, *Headlong Hall*, 1816)

ANNOYANCE
SEE VEXATION

ANXIETY
SEE FEAR; IMPATIENCE

APPEARANCE
SEE PHYSICAL APPEARANCE; PRETENSE

APPROVAL

amen corner—A coterie of fervent believers or ardent followers, so-called from the place in a church, usually near the pulpit, occupied by those who lead the responsive "amens." A person in the amen corner is, figuratively speaking, a disciple or devotee; often a yesman or sycophantic toady. The expression is now thoroughly American, but it may well derive from the Amen Corner of London's Paternoster Row, the supposed point at which the Corpus Christi procession reached the "Amen" of the "Pater Noster."

applaud to the echo—To applaud so energetically as to produce echoes; to demonstrate high acclaim or enthusiastic approval. In *Macbeth*, V, iii,

Approval

Macbeth informs his physician that if he can discover the sickness that infects the country and cure it:

I would applaud thee to the very echo
That should applaud again.

The expression has been in use since the early 1500s, although in *The Devil's Dictionary* (1906), Ambrose Bierce takes a rather darker view of the subject.

Applause is the echo of a platitude.

get the nod—To receive approval or affirmation; to be selected. In this expression, *nod* 'a slight, quick inclination of the head as in assent or command' is used figuratively more often than literally. A variation is *give the nod*.

Paul L. Troast got the G.O.P. nod, beating his nearest rival . . . by more than 53,000 votes. (*The Wall Street Journal*, April 23, 1953)

in [one's] books—In favor with one; in one's good esteem; have one's approval. At one time the word *book* meant any written piece, whether one page or many; hence, a list might be called a book, and to be *in one's books* was to be on one's list of friends. The expression dates from about 1500. A variant, *in one's good books*, is a more recent form.

Kentish fire—Protracted applause; a prolonged volley of applause. This expression is said to have originated with the extended salvos of applause and cheering given to those who spoke in Kent in 1828–29 in opposition to the Catholic Emancipation Bill. *Brewer's Dictionary of Phrase and Fable* cites Lord Winchelsea, proposing a toast to the Earl of Roden on August 15, 1834:

Let it be given with Kentish fire.

ARROGANCE
SEE HAUGHTINESS

ASSAY
SEE TEST

Assistance

ASSISTANCE

boy scout—One who comes to the assistance of another; one who is overly helpful or insists on helping when no help is needed; a naive fellow who has much growing-up to do. The organization known as the *Boy Scouts* was founded in 1908 in England by General Sir Robert Baden-Powell to promote good citizenship through usefulness to others. One cardinal rule, that each member should do a good deed each day, soon became a butt for humorists: there is the familiar allusion to the little old lady being helped across a street by a zealous boy scout when she did not wish any help.

Thus, the modern slang connotation for someone overly helpful arose about 1910, and the connotation for someone young and overly naive arose about 1920. As a slang term, the expression is most frequently heard today as a form of derision. The derision is undisguised in this English music hall song.

On Sunday I walk out with a soldier,
On Monday I'm taken by a tar,
On Tuesday I'm out with a baby Boy Scout,
On Wednesday an Hussar.
(Arthur Wimperis, *I'll Make a Man of You*)

candle-holder—An abettor; an assistant or attendant. The reference is to the Catholic practice of having someone hold a candle for the reader during a religious service. In everyday language, the expression applies to anyone who helps out in some small way, but who is not a real participant in the action or undertaking. Shakespeare used the term in *Romeo and Juliet*:

I'll be a candleholder and look on.
(I,iv)

give a leg up—To lend a helping hand; to give someone assistance through a difficult or trying time. This expression, originally meaning to help someone mount a horse, now carries the figurative sense of assisting another over life's obstacles or helping someone advance through the ranks.

She was now devoting all her energies to give them a leg up. (William E. Norris, *Misadventure*, 1890)

good Samaritan—A compassionate person who selflessly helps those in need; a friend in need; also simply a *Samaritan*. The allusion is to the Biblical parable (Luke 10:30–37) which tells of a man who had been beaten by thieves. He lay halfdead by the roadside while his neighbors, a priest and a Levite, passed him by. It was a Samaritan, his supposed enemy, who finally showed compassion for the man and took care of him. This expression dates from at least 1644.

I wish some good Samaritan of a Conservative with sufficient authority could heal the feuds among our friends. (Lord Ashburton, *Croker Papers*, 1846)

go to bat for—To support actively, to stick up for or defend; to intercede for, to go to the assistance of. This American slang expression owes its origin to baseball—specifically the role of the pinch hitter. In the mid 1800s, *go to the bat* was used; by the turn of the century *go* or *come to bat for* gained currency. Now *go to bat for* is heard almost exclusively.

The daughter of old man Brewster who owns the *Evening Tab*, my meal ticket, came to bat when my show was ready to close. (J. P. McEvoy, *Show Girl*, 1928)

help a lame dog over a stile—Help one in trouble; offer a helping hand; comfort one troubled in spirit. This expression, dating from at least the 1500s, alludes to the obstacles one encounters in life, whether physical or spiritual, and the comfort one feels when he holds out a helping hand to someone in distress.

> Let me display a Christian spirit And try to lift a lame dog o'er a style. (John Wolcott, *Works*, 1788)

Of course, one cannot always expect to be rewarded for displaying a virtuous conscience.

> I once knew a man out of courtesy, help a lame dog over a stile, and he for requittal bit him by the fingers. (William Chillingworth, *The Religion of Protestants*, 1638)

Jack at a pinch—One who offers a helping hand during a time of need; one called upon in an emergency, especially a stand-in clergyman. The first listing for this entry in the *OED* is James Mabbe's translation of *Alemans Guzman de Alfarache* (1622):

> When there was need of my service, I was seldom or never wanting; I was Jack at a pinch.

Originally this term was used to designate a clergyman who had no parish, and who, as a result, would substitute for a fee in any church where his services were needed. Eventually it came to mean any person who lent a hand during an emergency situation. The term is seldom heard today except as a localism.

ka me, ka thee—See RECIPROCITY.

pelican crossing—A pedestrian-controlled lighted crossing. Unlike the *zebra crossing*, named for the broad black and white stripes which mark zones for pedestrians to cross the street, the *pelican crossing* is named from the initial letters of the phrase *pe*destrian *li*ght *con*trolled (with a slight spelling change) and indicates a street crossing where the citizen activates the light. *Zebra crossings* have existed in Britain since 1952, and *pelican crossings* since 1968.

> One particular concern is the pelican crossing: old people tend to distrust them, fearing the lights will change before they can reach the other side of the road. (*London Times*, February 19, 1976)

pinch-hit—To substitute for a regular worker, player, speaker, or performer, especially in an emergency; to take another person's place. In this expression, *pinch* refers to an emergency, a time of stress, and *hit* refers to a successful, or hopefully successful, attempt. A person called upon in such a predicament is called a *pinch-hitter*. Though it originated and is most commonly used in baseball to describe the substitution of a batter for the regularly scheduled one, usually at a crucial point in the game, *pinch-hit* has been expanded to include many other situations and contexts.

> In his absence, he has called upon three good friends, also authors of daily columns, to pinch-hit for him and give his readers a "change of pace." (*Lubbock* [Texas] *Morning Avalanche*, February 1949)

yeoman service—Efficient, loyal aid, as from a faithful servant; good, useful assistance; unflagging support to one's employer or master.

> I once did hold it as our statists do,
> A baseness to write fair and laboured much
> How to forget that learning, but, Sir, now
> It did me yeoman's service.
> (Shakespeare, *Hamlet*, V,ii)

Yeoman, probably a shortening of *young man*, was originally applied to those superior grade servants in English households who performed many tasks. These young servants applied themselves so faithfully, so energetically, that the term *yeoman service* has been extended in meaning to include any outstanding continuing service.

ASTUTENESS
SEE PERCEPTIVENESS

AUGMENTATION
SEE EXACERBATION

AUSPICIOUSNESS
SEE OPPORTUNENESS

AUTHORITATIVENESS

arrow of Acestes—The making of one's point in an authoritative manner; a dogmatic presentation of an argument. The allusion in this phrase is to the great force with which Acestes discharged his arrow. Portrayed in the *Aeneid* as the son of a river god and a Trojan woman, Acestes, while involved in a trial of skill, released his arrow from his bow with such force that it caught fire in flight. The expression is used to characterize an orator, or other public speaker, who presents his argument with fiery vehemence.

chapter and verse—An authority that gives credence and validity to one's opinions or beliefs; a definitive source that can be specifically cited. The phrase derives from the Scriptures, which are arranged in chapters and verses, thus facilitating easy reference to particular lines. In non-Biblical contexts, *chapter and verse* is frequently a challenge to produce incontrovertible, detailed evidence for one's opinions. Figurative use dates from the early 17th century.

> She can give chapter and verse for her belief. (William Makepeace Thackeray, *The Adventures of Philip on His Way Through the World*, 1862)

ex cathedra—Authoritatively, dogmatically, officially; Latin for 'from the chair.' *Cathedra* itself refers to the chair or seat of a bishop in his church. Most specifically, it refers to that of the Bishop of Rome, the Pope, who according to church doctrine is infallible when speaking *ex cathedra* since he is not speaking for himself but as the successor and agent of Saint Peter. More generally *cathedra* means any seat of office or professorial chair. Anyone speaking from such a seat of power or knowledge would naturally speak with great authority. The phrase dates from at least 1635.

from the horse's mouth—On good authority, from a reliable source, directly from someone in the know; often in the phrase *straight from the horse's mouth*. The allusion is to the practice of looking at a horse's teeth to determine its age and condition, rather than relying on the word of a horse trader.

> The prospect of getting the true facts—straight, as it were, from the horse's mouth—held him . . . fascinated. (P. G. Wodehouse in *Strand Magazine*, August 1928)

in black and white—In writing or in print—black referring to the ink, white to the paper; certain, verifiable. Written opinion or assertion is assumed to carry more weight than a verbal one. The phrase has been in use since the time of Shakespeare.

> Moreover sir, which indeed is not under white and black, this plaintiff here . . . did call me ass. (Shakespeare, *Much Ado About Nothing* V,i)

take for gospel—To take as truth without question; to accept as infallibly true; to believe as absolutely accurate. The allusion here is to the first four books of the New Testament, which are considered the Christian Gospels. Since the Bible is supposedly the word of God, it follows that a true believer must accept the Gospels as absolutely truthful. The phrase has been in common use in English since the Middle Ages. A related phrase, *gospel truth*, carries the same connotations.

> All is not gospel, out of doubt,
> That men say in the town about.
> (Geoffrey Chaucer, *The Romance of the Rose*, 1365)

write the book on—To be the final authority; to have all the answers. This expression assumes that one who has written a book on a subject is about as knowledgeable on it as can be; therefore, he must be the final authority,

A BULL IN A CHINA SHOP

the one in the know. The phrase is modern, having come into common usage during the 1970s.

> Merrill Lynch writes the book on IRA investments. (Advertisement in *New Yorker*, November 15, 1982)

AUTOMOBILES
SEE VEHICLES

AVARICE
SEE DESIRE

AWARD
SEE REWARD

AWKWARDNESS

all thumbs—Awkward, inept; clumsy, butterfingered. A forerunner of the current expression appeared in John Heywood's *Proverbs* in 1546:

> When he should get ought, each finger is a thumb.

The phrase as we know it was in use by 1870:

> Your uneducated man is all thumbs, as the phrase runs; and what education does for him is to supply him with clever fingers. (*The Echo*, November 16, 1870)

awkward squad—A squad of inept military recruits; a group unskilled in their roles or functions. This expression, dating from the 1700s, has its roots in the military. However, in today's usage, it refers to any group who are clumsy or ungraceful in their performance. The term generally implies derogation; however, it is occasionally applied in a jocular sense.

> The household regiments of Versailles and St. James would have appeared an awkward squad. (Thomas B. Macaulay, *Critical and Miscellaneous Essays*, 1842)

bear's service—Mistakenly causing a person a serious problem while trying to be helpful to him; clumsiness; awkwardness. This expression has its origin in an old Russian fable which appeared for many years in children's schoolbooks. A man who lives in solitude in a barren place becomes lonesome and befriends a lonely bear. The bear wants to be helpful, so when the man rests after lunch, the bear sits beside him and chases the flies away. One fly returns and returns until the bear becomes angry, whereupon he grabs a huge stone, throws it at the fly and kills it, crushing the man's skull in the process.

bull in a china shop—A careless person whose clumsiness produces devastation; a bungling oaf. The earliest recorded literary use of this phrase seems to have been in Marryat's *Jacob Faithful*, written in 1834. "I'm like a bull in a china shop." An article in the May 1929 issue of *Notes and Queries* suggests that the source of the expression may be in the following:

> This morning an overdrove bullock rushed into the china shop of Miss Powell, opposite St. Andrews Church, Holborn, where he frightened the lady into a hysterical fit, and broke a quantity of glass and china. (*London Packet*, March 17, 1773)

butterfingers—One who lets things, especially a ball, slip or fall through his fingers; one who drops things easily; a clumsy or awkward person. This expression alludes to one who has been handling butter, or some other slippery substance, and whose hands have thus become so greasy that he cannot grasp whatever is handed or tossed to him. The term is common in English-speaking countries throughout the world, and the adjective form, *butter-fingered* has been in use since at least the early 17th century.

> When the executioner had come to the last of the heads, he lifted it up, but, by some clumsiness, allowed it to drop; at this the crowd yelled out, 'Ah, Butterfingers!' (William M. Thackeray, *Miscellanies*, 1857)

catch a crab—To make a faulty stroke in rowing that causes one to lose one's balance in the boat. The explanation of this phrase has been a matter for some speculation. The allusion seems to be to encountering a crab so large that it can grab the oar and hold it in place in the water. The *OED* suggests that the expression refers to getting one's oar caught deeply in the water so that the resulting resistance drives the handle against the rower's body and pushes him out of his seat. The expression has also been used to indicate a missing of the water completely with one's oar and toppling backward; the *OED*, however, calls this "an improper use by the uninitiated." A variant, which is seldom heard today, is *cut a crab*. The image in the phrase suggests that the fault lies either in momentarily losing one's hold on the oar so that it falls in the water and is difficult to recover, owing to the force of the water as the boat moves, or in accidentally hitting the water with the oar on the backstroke, causing a sudden, unexpected resistance that can cause loss of balance and of one's hold.

have two left feet—To be unusually clumsy; uncoordinated, maladroit. The expression does not constitute an image of deformity, but an emphasis on the negative concepts of *left* as 'gauche, awkward, clumsy.'

> Mr. Dawson . . . gave it as his opinion that one of the lady dancers had two left feet. (P. G. Wodehouse, *Psmith Journalist*, 1915)

hog in armor—One who is stiff and clumsy; one who cuts a ridiculous figure because of his fine, but awkward manner of dress. This expression, which is seldom heard today, made its appearance in England during the Middle Ages. Its source is uncertain, but *Brewer's Dictionary of Phrase and Fable* suggests that it might be a corruption of *hodge in armor, hodge* being a condescending term for a farm worker.

Awkwardness

He did not carry his finery like a hog in armour, as an Englishman so often does, when an Englishman stoops to be fine. (Anthony Trollope, *The Three Clerks*, 1857)

BEGINNINGS
SEE INITIATION; STARTING

BEWILDERMENT
SEE CONFUSION

BIAS
SEE PREJUDICE

BOTHERSOMENESS
SEE VEXATION

BRIBERY
SEE PAYMENT

Candidness

CANDIDNESS

above-board—In full view, in open sight; honestly, unsurreptitiously. The most widely held theory claims the phrase for card playing; gamblers were wont to engage in chicanery when their hands were out of sight and under the table (or board). Another source also attributes the term to the practice of gamesters, but to those who controlled wheels of fortune by means of a treadle hidden beneath a counter.

call a spade a spade—To speak plainly or bluntly; to be straightforward and candid, sometimes to the point of rudeness; to call something by its real name. The ultimate source of this expression is Erasmus' translation of Plutarch's *Apophthegmata*. According to the *OED*, the phrase in question was mistranslated from the original Greek. The expression has been popular in English since Nicholas Udall's 1542 translation of the Erasmus version. An early example is in Humfrey Gifford's *A Posie of Gilloflowers* (1580):

I cannot say the crow is white, But needs must call a spade a spade.

flat-footed—Direct, to the point; firmly resolved, uncompromising; often heard in the phrase *come out flat-footed* 'to make a direct and firm statement of one's opinion or preference.' This American colloquial expression most likely derives from body language—a firm stance with legs slightly apart and both feet flat on the ground as a sign of determination and will. Both *flat-footed* and *come out flat-footed* have been in use since the mid 19th century.

Mr. Pickens . . . has come out flatfooted for the Administration, a real red-hot Democrat, dyed in the wool. (*New York Herald*, June 30, 1846)

get something off [one's] chest —To relieve oneself by expressing what one feels; to confess; to unburden oneself. In the Middle Ages the heart was believed to be the seat of the emotions; therefore, when one alleviated himself of a pressing emotional problem, he believed that he was literally getting it off his chest. Although modern man no longer believes that the heart is the center of the emotions, he continues to employ the phrase in its original sense.

> "I've got to get it off my chest," said he. I want to tell you that I've been every end of a silly ass." (W.J. Locke, *Simon the Jester*, 1910)

let [one's] hair down—To relax; to act or speak informally; to speak candidly or intimately; to behave in an uninhibited, unrestrained manner, particularly in a situation requiring dignity and reserve. This figurative expression alludes to the fact that until fairly recently, a woman was expected to maintain a very staid and formal public image, and as a result, often wore her hair pinned up on the top of her head. In the privacy and relative comfort of her own home, however, such a woman usually felt free to relax and would let her hair down. It was in these informal moments that her true personality would be revealed.

> You can let your hair down in front of me. (Jerome Weidman, *I Can Get It For You Wholesale!*, 1937)

A related expression is *hairdown* 'an intimate conversation.' In recent years, *let [one's] hair down* has largely been replaced by, and may in fact have given rise to, expressions such as *hang loose, loosen up,* and *let it all hang out*.

let it all hang out—To be uninhibited; to let one's hair down; to be open and frank; to tell all the facts without holding anything back; to make a full confession. This expression, probably an allusion to the male sex organ, originated as a slang expression during the 1950s. However, the phrase was popularized by extensive media exposure during the Watergate proceedings in the early 1970s, for it was a favorite term of some of the principals in the case.

> As the current saying goes, NCR has it all hanging out. (*Forbes*, July 15, 1973)

make a clean breast—To give a full confession, especially one that relieves guilt and anxiety; to make a complete disclosure. One explanation of this term lies in the ancient custom of branding a sinner on the breast with a symbol appropriate to his sin. The confession redeemed him and the punishment made a clean breast. A more reasonable allusion attributes the term to the heart as the seat of emotion; thus, confession cleanses the heart of any evil stains that might be lodged in the breast.

> The pagan Aztecs only confessed once in a lifetime...then they made a clean breast of it once for all. (Long, *Essays in Literature*, 1891)

make no bones about—To be outspoken, to deal with someone directly and openly; to go along with, to acquiesce without raising any objections. Variants of this expression appeared in print as early as the 15th century. A number of theories have been suggested to explain its origin, the most plausible being that it grew out of the literal *find bones in*, referring to the bones in soup which are an obstacle to its being safely swallowed. Thus *find bones in* became *make bones about*, meaning 'to scruple, to raise objections, to offer opposition.'

> Do you think that the Government or the Opposition would make any bones about accepting the seat if he offered it to them? (William Makepeace Thackeray, *The History of Pendennis*, 1850)

Currently the expression is heard almost exclusively in the negative.

> On the other hand, Dr. Libby makes no bones about the catastrophe of a nuclear war. (*Bulletin Atomic Science*, September 1955)

naked truth—Plain, unadorned truth; unvarnished truth. According to an ancient fable, two goddesses, Truth and Falsehood, were bathing. Falsehood came out of the water first and adorned herself in Truth's clothes. Truth, not wishing to wear the trappings of Falsehood, decided to go naked. Thus the expression.

not to mince the matter—To be plain or outspoken; to speak frankly or bluntly; to be truthful about something; to get to the point. This expression was originally devised in the positive sense, *to mince matters*, and meant 'to put things delicately or moderately.' The allusion is to the mincing of meat to make it more readily digestible. However, the term is more commonly heard today in the negative sense.

> A man's speculative view depends—not to mince the matter—on the state of his secretions. (Willkie Collins, *Dead Secret*, 1857)

point-blank—Direct, straightforward, explicit; blunt, frank, unmincing. In ballistics, a weapon fired point-blank is one whose sights are aimed directly at a nearby target so that the projectile travels in a flat trajectory to its destination. By extension, then, a point-blank comment, question, accusation, etc., is one which is direct and to the point, one which does not mince words.

> This is point-blank treason against my sovereign authority. (Samuel Foote, *The Lame Lover*, 1770)

Quaker bargain—A take it or leave proceeding; a yes or no bargain; a straightforward deal. This expression alludes to the honesty for which members of the Quaker sect are known, and for their no-nonsense directness in dealing with others in any aspect of life.

skin the bear at once—To come straight to the point, to waste no time getting down to brass tacks.

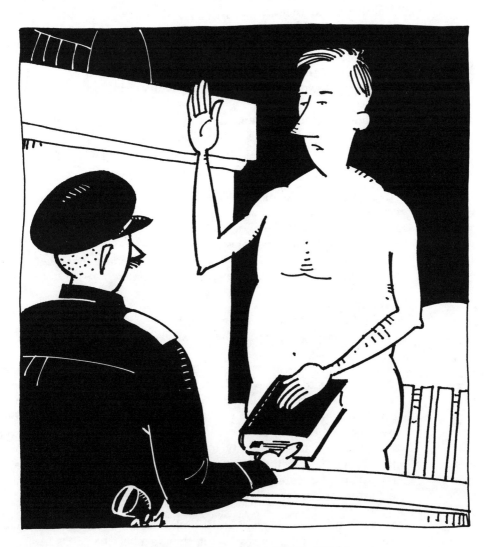

THE NAKED TRUTH

But now, to skin the *bar* at once, can you give me and five other gentlemen employment? (*The New Orleans Picayune,* September 1844) This U.S. colloquialism, the opposite of *beat around the bush,* refers to the skinning of an animal immediately after it is slain because the hide is more easily removed then.

speak by the card—To express oneself in a clear and concise manner; to carefully select one's words; to speak honestly. This expression appears in Shakespeare's *Hamlet:*

We must speak by the card, or equivocation will undo us.
(V,i)

This phrase refers to a compass card, on which every point has its own precise and unambiguous designation.

I speak by the card in order to avoid entanglement of words. (Benjamin Jowett, *Plato,* 1875)

straight from the shoulder—Frankly; candidly; truthfully; directly. This expression originated as a boxing term for the delivering of a direct, full-force punch. Today, the phrase retains its figurative meaning of the voicing of a forthright, unembellished comment.

A man that talks old-fashioned American Democracy straight from the shoulder. (R. D. Saunders, *Colonel Todhunter,* 1911)

talk turkey—To speak frankly or plainly, to talk seriously and straightforwardly, to get to the point.

Let's talk turkey about this threat to your welfare. (*Florida Grower,* February 1950)

Legend has it that an American Indian and a white man out hunting together bagged a turkey and a crow. When the time came to split the catch, the white man said, "You may have your choice, you take the crow and I'll take the turkey, or if you'd rather, I'll take the turkey and you take the crow"; whereupon the Indian replied "Ugh! you no talk turkey to me a bit." Although this bit of etymological folklore should be taken with a massive dose of salt, it does serve to point out the importance of the turkey as food and therefore as serious business, a fact which may have given rise to the expression as it is used today.

unvarnished tale—A plain and simple recounting; a story told without any attempt to soften or disguise it; the unembellished facts. Another one of the many expressions attributed to the pen of Shakespeare, this phrase appears in *Othello* (I,iii). The Moor is trying to convince his superiors that he used no witchcraft to win Desdemona, whom he has taken to wife:

Yet, by your gracious patience,
I will a round unvarnished tale deliver
Of my whole course of love, what drugs, what charms,
What conjuration.

A common related term with the same connotation is *unvarnished truth*.

warts and all—With no attempt to conceal blemishes, weaknesses, failings, vices, foibles, etc. Portrait painters, particularly those commissioned by the powerful and prideful, were wont to depict their subjects in a favorable and flattering light. In doing so, they frequently completed canvases bearing but slight resemblance to the original, their artist's scalpel having excised warts, moles, scars, and other such blemishes; they also smoothed wrinkles, straightened bones, and otherwise played the plastic surgeon. The phrase *warts and all* has come to describe a visual or verbal portrait which aims at a realistic picture of its subject by presenting his "ugly" as well as his commendable side. According to William Safire's *Political Dictionary* (1978), the British statesman Oliver Cromwell (1599–1658) is reputed to have directed his portraitist:

> Use all your skill to paint my picture truly like me, and not to flatter me ... remark all those roughnesses, pimples, warts, and everything as you see me; otherwise I will never pay one farthing for it.

Occasionally the phrase is extended to intangibles such as plans, intentions, etc., when liabilities as well as assets are clearly communicated.

CAPABILITY
SEE ABILITY

CAPACITY
SEE ABILITY

CENSURE
SEE CRITICISM; REPRIMAND

CERTAINTY

bet [one's] boots—To be absolutely sure or certain of something. The reference is to a gambler (perhaps a cowboy, whose boots are among his most important possessions) so sure of winning that he will bet everything he owns, including his boots. The phrase appeared in 1856 in *Spirit of Times*. Similar expressions are *bet [one's] life* and *bet [one's] bottom dollar*.

dead to rights—Indisputably, unquestionably; positively, assuredly; usually in the phrases *have someone dead to rights* or *caught dead to rights*, in which it is equivalent to 'in the act, redhanded.' Attempts to explain the origin of this American colloquial expression are frustrating and futile. *Dead* appears to be used in its meaning of 'absolutely, utterly'; but the equivalent British expression *bang to rights* suggests something closer to 'directly, precisely.' The context of wrongdoing in which the phrase always appears in early citations indicates that *to rights* may relate to the rights of the guilty party, but the theory does not withstand careful analysis. The

OED suggests a connection between the *to rights* of the phrase and the obsolete *to rights* 'in a proper manner,' but no citations contain analogous syntactic constructions. Despite its refusal to yield an elucidating explanation, *dead to rights* has been a commonly used expression since the mid 1800s.

dollars to doughnuts—A sure thing, a certainty; usually in the phrase *bet dollars to doughnuts*, in use since 1890. Although the precise origin of this expression is unknown, it obviously plays on the value of a dollar contrasted with the relative small worth of a doughnut, which once cost 5¢. Anyone willing to wager dollars to doughnuts is confident of winning his bet. One use of the expression apparently referred to the declining value of the dollar:

> Dollars to doughnuts is a pretty even bet today. (*Redbook*, 1947)

eat [one's] hat—To admit willingness to "eat one's hat" is to express certainty and confidence, and to be ready to abase oneself should things not turn out as one had anticipated. Should such cocksureness prove ill-founded, *eating one's hat* would be analogous to *eating crow* or *eating one's words*. The first use of this expression is attributed to Charles Dickens in *The Pickwick Papers* (1837).

> If I knew as little of life as that, I'd eat my hat and swallow the buckle whole.

Of British origin, *eat [one's] hat* is currently popular in the United States as well.

eggs is eggs—Surely, definitely, absolutely, without a doubt. Usually used as an interjection or in the phrase *sure as eggs is eggs*, this British colloquialism is probably a humorous twist or an ignorant mispronunciation of "X" in the familiar algebraic equation, "X is X."

> [After examining me] the doctor shook his head and said, "Eggs is eggs." (Johnny Carson, on *The Tonight Show*, NBC Television, 1978)

far and away—Absolutely, incomparably, easily, undoubtedly; by far. Used to increase the intensity of a superlative adjective, this expression implies that there are no competitors or contenders within reach of this description.

> You are far and away the greatest scoundrel I ever saw. (William E. Norris, *Thirlby Hall*, 1883)

hat to a halfpenny—An exclamation of affirmation, said in the form of giving high odds on a wager, to assure others that one speaks the truth. In medieval times, when this expression was coined, a hat was an expensive and highly valued item in a man's wardrobe; therefore, to be willing to bet one's hat against a halfpenny was the equivalent of being certain in one's convictions.

My hat to a halfpenny, Pompey proves the best Worthy. (Shakespeare, *Love's Labour's Lost*, V,ii)

in spades—Definitely, emphatically, to the utmost degree; without restraint or qualification; no ifs, ands, or buts. This expression connoting extremeness derives from the fact that spades are the highest suit in some card games. *In spades* is used as an intensifier, as in the following citation from *Webster's Third*:

[I] have thought him a stinker, in spades, for many years. (Inez Robb)

in the bag—Assured, certain. The most plausible and frequent explanation holds that the reference is to game which has been killed and bagged, i.e., put in the gamebag. One source claims a cockfighting origin for the term; since a live gamecock is literally brought to the pits in a bag, for the owner confident of victory, "It's in the bag."

lead-pipe cinch—An absolute certainty; a certain success; something that is easily accomplished; a piece of cake. In this expression, *cinch* refers to a saddle girth, the beltlike strap used to secure the saddle on a horse. If the cinch were tight enough, the rider did not have to worry about the saddle's slipping; in fact, it was a certainty that the saddle would stay in place. Although the rationale for the inclusion of "leadpipe" in this expression is unclear, it is possible that the relative ease with which lead for (waste) plumbing could be worked (compared with cast iron) gave rise to *lead-pipe* as an intensifier.

It is a doublebarrelled leadpipe cinch that you'll be more anxious to get it back than you ever were about a $10 loan overdue. (*Outing*, July 1921)

shoo-in—A candidate, athlete, team, or other competitor considered to be a sure winner; the favorite. This expression employs the verb phrase *shoo-in* 'to cause to go into' as a noun.

In the [Republican presidential] preferential poll, Taft looked like a shoo-in over Stassen. (AP wire story, May 13, 1952)

sure as shooting—Certainly without a doubt, most assuredly. This colloquialism of American origin appeared in print by the mid-1800s. It was probably a cowboy expression referring to one's need for *sure*, i.e., 'accurate' shooting to avoid being shot dead in turn.

Sure as shootin'...one of these days one of my customers will be coming in and telling me he caught a fish with one of your jackets. (*Field and Stream*, June 19, 1947)

that's flat—An expression used to specify that one has just spoken the undeniable, absolute truth; defiant expression stating one's resolve to do or not to do something; a statement of bold rebelliousness. This expression is frequently heard as an emphatic conclusion to a preceding remark.

It's the greatest bogg of Europe . . . that's flat. (*A Survey of the Affairs of the United Netherlands,* 1665)

This expression, can also be used to demonstrate one's determination to take a stand even though one faces possible disciplinary action for taking such a position. Falstaff, in Shakespeare's *Henry IV, Part 1,* decides rather suddenly and defiantly to refuse to go into battle with the ragtag army which he himself has assembled to bilk the crown of money.

I'll not march through Coventry with them, that's flat. (IV,ii)

The term has been in use since the mid-16th century.

CESSATION
SEE COMPLETION; TERMINATION

CHALLENGE
SEE DIFFICULTY

CHAOS
SEE DISORDER

CLOSENESS
SEE FRIENDSHIP

CLUMSINESS
SEE AWKWARDNESS

COERCION

Duke of Exeter's daughter—The name given to the rack in the Tower of London. John Holland, the Duke of Exeter, served as Constable of the Tower of London in 1420. He is credited with introducing the rack to the Tower as an instrument of torture or punishment. As a result of its birthright, the instrument became known as the Duke of Exeter's daughter.

They threatened to make me hug the Duke of Exeter's daughter. (Sir Walter Scott, *The Fortunes of Nigel,* 1822)

An allied term, *Skeffinger's daughter* or *Scavenger's daughter,* another instrument of torture, was named for Leonard Skeffington who, along with his father, Sir William Skeffington, Lieutenant of the Tower of London in the 16th century, invented the device. The contrivance doubled a person's body so the head was brought against the legs with such great pressure that blood was forced from the nose and ears.

One of the instruments of torture, called the Scavenger's daughter, was employed in the Tower on Catholics. (William Andrews, *Critical Review of Foxe's Book of Martyrs,* 1826)

Another related term is *gunner's daughter,* a term for the gun to which sailors were lashed before they were whipped.

I was . . . made to kiss the gunner's daughter. (Frederick Marryat, *Peter Simple,* 1833)

force [someone's] hand—To pressure someone into taking a stand or revealing his beliefs or intentions; to compel someone to act immediately and against his will. In print since the mid 19th century, this expression perhaps derives from card games in which one player forces another to play a particular card and thereby reveal the contents of his hand. Another possible theory is that *force [someone's] hand* is like *twist [someone's] arm*, suggesting that the present figurative use derives from actual physical force.

jawbone—To apply pressure from a position of influence; to use upper echelon arm-twisting. The modern sense of this term developed sometime during the 1960s. Today in Washington it is still used to denote strong unofficial pressure brought by an important government official upon labor and business, frequently with the intention of imposing government guidelines on spending, prices, and wages. Its popularity is often attributed to President Lyndon B. Johnson, who was especially fond of the term and used it frequently.

knobstick wedding—The forced marriage of a pregnant, unwed woman; a shotgun wedding. Churchwardens (lay officers who dealt with the secular affairs of the church and who were the legal representatives of the parish) formerly used their authority to ensure such marriages. The term *knobstick* 'a knobbed stick, cane, or club used chiefly as a weapon' refers to the churchwarden's staff, the symbol of his office, used as an instrument of coercion, or cudgel.

put the screws to—To compel action by exercise of coercion, pressure, extortion, blackmail, etc. The expression derives from an early method of torture involving the use of thumbscrews to extract confessions.

put the squeeze on—To pressure another for one's own purposes; to demand payment or performance by means of harassment or threats.

> She hired me to put the squeeze on Linda for a divorce. (Raymond Chandler, *High Window*, 1942)

ram down [someone's] throat—To force one's point of view upon another; to declare forcefully without allowing opportunity for rebuttal; to deliver an opinion to another as if it were dogma. This phrase, along with its variations using the verbs *cram*, *thrust*, or *shove*, has been employed since the early 1700s. The allusion is to feeding someone ideas and opinions as one forcefeeds food. The expression is common today, especially in the world of sales.

> . . . Quha rammed and crammed,
> That bargain down their throats.
> (Allan Ramsay, *Vision*, 1724)

41

Coercion

shanghai—To kidnap a person and press him into service, especially as a seaman; to maliciously deceive someone. This term, apparently coined on the San Francisco waterfront in the early 19th century, is believed to have originated from the frequent voyages between that city and Shanghai, China. Since many sailors were reluctant to sign on for long voyages, the practice of *shanghaiing* arose. A sailor would be sated with drugs or drink until he passed out; he would awake at sea, a crew member on a vessel headed for Shanghai or some other distant port. In many instances those who procured able-bodied men by such means were paid a premium for each victim.

> Before that they would have been drugged, shanghaied, and taken away from all means of making complaint. (*New York Tribune*, March 1, 1871)

By extension the word has come to signify any deceiving or misleading of another person.

shotgun wedding—Any union, compromise, agreement, etc., brought about by necessity or threat; originally a wedding necessitated or hastened by the bride-to-be's pregnancy, a forced marriage; also *shotgun marriage*. The allusion is to an irate father attempting to protect his daughter's reputation by using a shotgun to threaten the man responsible for her condition into marrying her. Use of the expression dates from at least 1927.

> Werdel...characterized the Brannan plan as a "shotgun wedding between agriculture and labor." (*California Citrograph*, January 1950)

when push comes to shove—See EXACERBATION.

COMMENDATION
SEE APPROVAL; REWARD

COMPETENCE
SEE ABILITY

Completion

COMPLETION
See also TERMINATION

finishing touch—That which completes an enterprise or endeavor; the final skillful or artistic stroke; the final detail or effort given to anything. This phrase originally applied to painting and to those final strokes the artist applied to the canvas to alter or to smooth out any rough details in his work. By transference it came to mean any final detail in any line of endeavor, especially writing. The expression has been in use since about 1700.

> We tire of the painter's art when it wants those finishing touches. (Horace Walpole, *Anecdotes of Painting*, 1771)

go through-stitch—To go through with; to finish or conclude; to follow through. This expression alluding to the work of a tailor was popular in the 17th century but is no longer heard today.

> For when a man has once undertaken a business, let him go through-stitch with it. (*The Pagan Prince*, 1690)

in for a penny, in for a pound—Once involved in a matter, however slightly, one must carry it through whatever the consequences. The metaphor comes from the monetary units of Great Britain: formerly, the penny was ½ of a shilling and the pound 20 shillings or 240 pence; since decimalization, the pound is 100 new pence.

sign off—To complete or end a performance, project, or other matter; to terminate; to withdraw. In the 9th century and for several hundred years thereafter, a person could change his religious affiliation simply by *signing off*, i.e., by signing a legal paper that ended his membership in one religious organization and, if he so desired, enrolled him in another.

> The revolution . . . broke up the State Church and gave to every man the liberty of "signing off" as it was called, to any denomination that pleased him. (Harriet Beecher Stowe, *The Poganuc People, Their Loves and Lives*, 1878)

Beginning in the late Middle Ages, *sign off* usually referred to a creditor's releasing a debtor from financial obligation by *signing off*, i.e., by affixing his signature to a document to that effect. A contemporary variation that refers to this practice of canceling a debt or amortizing an asset is *write off*.

> The company wrote off the loss as a bad debt. (*Law Times*, 1891)

Since the 1930s, *sign-off* (as a noun) most commonly applies to a radio or television station's ending its broadcast day.

> Because of the earlier sign-off required by the Federal Communications Commission . . . (*ABC Radio*, 1949)

tie up the loose ends—To conclude or settle matters; to answer all questions and account for any seemingly superfluous details. *Loose ends* in this expression refers to the last bit of unfinished business, the apparently irrelevant or contradictory details of a plan, arrangement, project, etc. This figurative use may derive from the practice of tying the ends of thread that hang loose after a cloth is woven or a garment is knitted.

COMPLICATION
SEE DIFFICULTY

COMPREHENSIVENESS
SEE INCLUSIVENESS

COMPULSION
SEE COERCION

CONCEALMENT
SEE SECRECY

CONCLUSION
SEE COMPLETION; TERMINATION

CONDEMNATION
SEE REPRIMAND

CONFIDENCE
SEE CERTAINTY

CONFIDENTIALITY
SEE SECRECY

Confusion

CONFUSION
See also DISORDER

all balled up—Confused; disorganized; perplexed; all mixed up; tangled. When horses were the principal means of transportation, one of the hazards of taking them out in winter was the formation of hard and uncomfortable balls of snow or ice under their hooves. These balls of snow sometimes caused horses, especially a team pulling a sleigh, to flounder and fall, resulting in a scene of complete confusion; hence, the expression *all balled up*. The term has been in use as a figurative expression since the late 1700s.

> His childhood had been tragically balled up by circumstances which had branded him with such a passionate bitterness as I have seldom seen in a man. (*Century Magazine*, March 1923)

at loose ends—Unsettled, undecided, lacking direction or goal; uncommitted to one's present position and uncertain of one's future status. A loose end is anything that is left hanging or not properly attached, as a piece of fabric or a seemingly superfluous detail. A person is "at loose ends" when his life lacks coherence or a sense of direction as exemplified in the following fragment quoted in *Webster's Third*:

> ... feeling himself at loose ends—no job, no immediate prospects. (Dixon Wecter)

See also **tie up the loose ends**, COMPLETION.

at sea—Confused, perplexed; without direction, design, or stability; in a state of uncertainty. Figurative use of this expression dates from the mid 18th century and is based on an analogy to a ship lost at sea, having no bearings and out of sight of land. *At sea* can refer to a person or state of affairs. *All adrift* is an analogous nautical expression with a similar figurative meaning 'aimless, confused.'

bear garden—A place of confusion; a site of turmoil and agitation. Bears were kept and baited for public entertainment in establishments known as *bear gardens* during the latter years of the Tudor and the early years of the Stuart monarchies. In London these *bear gardens* were located on the south side of the Thames and became notorious for their scenes of chaotic disorder. Shakespeare moved to that area in 1597, at the time a district of rapid growth.

> ... he was residing in the theatrical district on the Bankside, not far from the Bear Garden and near the site of the Globe. (Louis B. Wright, *Shakespeare for Everyman*, 1964)

A related term, *bear-garden language*, was a figurative expression for the foul and blasphemous language associated with this crude sport.

> He's as great a master of ill language as ever was bred at a Bear-Garden. (Edward Ward, *London Terraefilius*, 1707)

Chinese fire drill—Any scene of great confusion or complete disorder. The origin of this phrase is uncertain. The most plausible explanation attributes the expression to British troops who served with the Chinese during World War II. Apparently these troops found the Chinese way of doing things confusing and disorderly; hence, the pejorative sense in such terms as: *Chinese national anthem*, any harsh, clangorous noise; *Chinese three-point landing*, a crash; and *Chinese landing*, one made by a *Chinese ace*, One Wing Low. Another plausible explanation attributes the term to the early 1950s and the Korean War specifically. Because the Chinese backed and eventually fought for the North Koreans, they were out of favor with the Western powers at that time. When the Chinese first entered the Korean War, their attacks were great cacophonies accompanied by thousands of troops rushing forward, blowing bugles, and screaming. Such an image of confusion could account for any disorderly situation being associated with the Chinese.

come unhinged—To become extremely nervous; to become unstable; to be reduced to a state of confusion. The allusion in this term is to the condition of a door or window shutter that has lost one of its hinges and hangs in disarray. Dating from the late 16th century, the expression is most often heard today in its figurative sense.

> As for those wingy mysteries in divinity, and airy subtleties in religion, which have unhinged the brains of better heads, they never stretched the *pia mater* of mine. (Sir Thomas Browne, *Religio Medici*, 1643)

A variant, *come unglued*, dates from about the same period, and probably refers to a piece of furniture coming unglued, creating an unstable condition.

flutter the dovecotes—To throw into a state of agitation or confusion; to upset the serenity of a society. A dovecote is a house for doves or pigeons that will accommodate a number of birds simultaneously; hence, to *flutter* *the dovecote* is to upset the equanimity of the entire social structure. The expression has been in use since at least 1600.

> If you have writ your annals true, 'tis there
> That, like an eagle in a dove-cote, I
> Fluttered your Volscians in Corioli.
> (Shakespeare, *Coriolanus*, V,vi)

God writes straight with crooked lines—Sometimes the will of the divine is a mystery to mankind; one doesn't always understand life's foibles. There is some controversy over the source of this expression. Some attribute it to St. Augustine, which would set the date of its origin at about 400, while others attribute it to an old Portuguese proverb from about 1400. Three correspondents to *American Notes and Queries*, in a series of articles between December 1964 and April 1965, conclude that the proverb is Portuguese, for, they maintain, the St. Augustine theory came about through an error in translation. Whatever the case, Paul Claudel, the French dramatist and poet, used the expression as the theme of one of his plays, *The Satin Slipper* (1931).

knock for a loop—To disorient someone by saying or doing something shocking or unexpected; to strike a blow and cause one to lose balance and fall. The *loop* in this modern slang expression derives from the aeronautical term for the mid-air maneuver of an airplane. To knock someone for a loop is to hit that person hard enough to make him do a somersault. The feeling of dizziness and disorientation is carried over into the more common figurative use.

> That little charade of hers had knocked him for a loop. (D. Ramsey, *Deadly Discretion*, 1973)

Also current is *throw for a loop*.

> I was really confused. That memorandum threw me for a loop. (E. Ambler, *Intercom Conspiracy*, 1969)

lose [one's] bearings—To become lost; to lose all sense of direction; to become hopelessly disoriented, confused, or bewildered. In this expression, *bearings* carries the literal meaning of reference points or directions in relation to one's position; thus, the term's use to describe a person who is lost or disoriented.

not have the foggiest (idea)—Not to have any notion at all; to be bewildered, perplexed; to find something cloudy, blurred, indistinct. The allusion in this expression is to the lack of clarity one experiences in the midst of a dense fog; one may lose all sense of direction, for even familiar objects become indistinct or obscure.

> Uncle: Wonder who she is?
> Niece: Haven't the foggiest. Must be pre-war.
> (*Punch*, August 22, 1917)

not know if [one] is afoot or on horseback—So completely confused as to not know what one is doing, thoroughly befuddled or mixed-up; not to know whether one is coming or going. This self-evident American colloquialism dates from the late 19th century.

> "Fay Daniels!" gasps the girl, which don't know if she's afoot or horseback—and neither did I. (*Collier's,* October 1927)

not to know if [one] is coming or going—Not to know what one is doing; extremely confused or mixed-up; not to know which end is up; ignorant, stupid.

> There's nobody at the Town Hall could take it on. Town Clerk doesn't know whether he's coming or going. (J. B. Priestley, *Fest. Frabridge,* 1951)

Use of the phrase dates from at least 1924.

not to know which end is up—See IGNORANCE.

rattle [one's] cage—To joggle one's thoughts; wake someone up; confuse; embarrass; disconcert. This American slang expression refers to the inhumane practice of shaking a cage to awaken or excite a captive animal. The resulting reaction is entirely unpredictable; it may be one of confusion, of irritation, or of absolute fury.

razzle-dazzle—An act to create a confusion or bewilderment; tricky maneuvers intended to astound another person; a flurry of rapid activity. Dating from the late 1800s, the roots of this American slang expression lie in the much older word *dazzle*, which means 'to overcome with an excess of bright lights.' The *OED* indicates that *dazzle* first appeared in Caxton's *The History of Reynard the Fox* (1481), and that the first written example of *razzle-dazzle* is:

> I'm going to razzle-dazzle the boys ... With my great lightning change act. (Archibald Gunter, *Miss Nobody,* 1890)

In modern usage the expression seems to be restricted to sports and gambling jargon.

send to Dulcarnon—The key word in this phrase is *Dulcarnon,* a word derived from the Arabic meaning 'possessor of two horns,' hence, to *send to Dulcarnon* is to place upon the horns of a dilemma, to put into a state of perplexity. Dating from at least the 14th century, the expression appears in Chaucer's *Troilus and Criseyde*

> I am, til God me bettre mynde sende
> At Dulcarnon, right at my wittes ende.

A variant, *be in Dulcarnon,* means 'to be on the horns of a dilemma.'

slaphappy—See FATUOUSNESS.

up a stump—Confused; embarrassed; at a loss; in a perplexing position. This American slang expression has been attributed to two different situations, each one involving the stump of a tree. The first ascribes the term to the fact that a person on a stump can't climb any higher; therefore, he is at a loss as to what to do next. The other explanation, and seemingly the more plausible, alludes to the political speaker who, delivering a speech from a tree stump, finds himself confined and surrounded by strange, often unfriendly, faces. He frequently becomes confused and embarrassed, and occasionally feels trapped. Whatever the case, the term has been in common use since the early 1800s.

> You're up a stump, ain't you? (Mark Twain, *Tom Sawyer*, 1876)

when the dust settles—When the confusion has ended; when order has returned after a great commotion. The allusion is to a great cloud of dust created by vigorous activity, dust so irritating that seeing or breathing becomes difficult and one must wait for it to settle before one can continue to work.

> Most important, when the dust settled, it did seem that more often than not, votes were cast based on candidates' qualifications rather than their race, sex, or personal life. (*Time*, November 21, 1983)

CONGLOMERATION
SEE MIXTURE

CONSENT
SEE APPROVAL

CONTINUATION
SEE RESUMPTION

CONTROL
See also MANIPULATION

Aaron's serpent—An all-controlling force; a power so great that it can overcome any other power. The reference in this expression is to Aaron's demonstration of God's power to the Pharaoh of Egypt in the book of Exodus. Obeying the Lord's instructions, Aaron cast down his rod before the Pharaoh, and it became a serpent. The Pharaoh then called forth his wise men and sorcerers, who did likewise, but Aaron's serpent swallowed up all the other serpents, thus proving the power of the Lord. The expression is still in use to demonstrate unusual power.

> And hence one master passion in the breast,
> Like Aaron's serpent swallows up all the rest.
> (Alexander Pope, *Essay on Man*, 1733)

A variant is *Aaron's rod*.

body English—An attempt to control the movement of an object, as a billiard ball, bowling ball, pinball, etc., by contorting the body, without touching the object. This American expression, dating from the mid 1800s, probably has its roots in the game of billiards. In American billiards *English* is the spin given to the cue ball by striking it to the right or left of center; in other games, especially bowling, *English* is applied by spinning the ball at the moment of release. The British word is *side*. *Body English* is not restricted to game participants; it is often practiced by spectators as well.

carry the ball—To assume responsibility for the progress of an undertaking; to be in charge and bear the burden of success or failure. This metaphorical expression stems from the role of the ball carrier in American football.

corner the market—To possess, have access to, or be in control of something which is in demand; from the financial practice of attempting to secure control over particular stocks or commodities. This U.S. expression, dating from the mid 19th century, was originally heard only in financial contexts; however it is now heard in noncommercial contexts as well. In financial terms, a *cornering* involves one party buying all of one kind of stock or commodity, thereby driving potential buyers and sellers into a corner because they have no option but to acquiesce to the price demands of those controlling the stock.

flag down—To catch the attention of and signal to stop; to cause to stop; to hail, as a taxi. This expression, used almost exclusively today in regard to automobiles, derived from the old railway practice of displaying a flag in order to stop trains at small stations that would normally be passed without even slowing down. The terms *flag stop* and *flag station* came to be used of small, jerkwater towns, while *flag down* was extended in use and has remained as a standard expression in the general language.

get the deadwood on—Get someone in one's power; to have control over another; hold the upper hand. This phrase arises from the game of ten pins where, in the early days of the sport, deadwood, as the fallen pins were called, was allowed to remain. Such a situation gave the bowler greater control, for he could use the deadwood to sweep the standing pins from the alley. With the advent of mechanical pin setters, the deadwood was automatically swept from the alley; however, the deadwood is still allowed to remain in the game of candlepins.

> If they ask a man an embarrassing question, or in any way have placed him in an equivocal position, they will triumphantly declare that they have got the deadwood on him. (Louise Clappe, *The Shirley Letters from California*, 1851)

have a handle on—To have a method of control; to be able to direct or guide. This phrase, which gained currency in the early 1970s, is obvious in its meaning; if one has a handle to hold or guide something by, he has much better control.

> Carter's State of the Union speech failed to convince foreign moneymen that the Administration has a handle on the economy's problems. (*Time*, January 30, 1978)

In contrast, to *lose the handle* means to 'drop the ball,' to lose control of a situation.

hold the fort—To take charge, often to act as a temporary substitute; to remain at one's post, to maintain or defend one's position. This expression is attributed to General Sherman, who in 1864 is said to have signaled this message to General Corse. In modern use, *fort* can refer to a place or a philosophical position.

> Elizabeth and her archbishops... had held the fort until their church had come... to have an ethos of its own. (A. L. Rowse, *Tudor Cornwall*, 1941)

hold the line—To try to prevent a situation from becoming uncontrollable or unwieldy; to maintain the status quo. This Americanism probably comes from the game of football. It is frequently heard in an economic context, as in "to hold the line on taxes" or "to hold the line on prices."

hold the purse strings—To determine how much money shall be spent and how much saved; to regulate the expenditure of money. *Purse strings* refers literally to the strings at the mouth of a money pouch which can be tightened or loosened, thereby controlling the amount of money put in or taken out. By extension, this term also refers to the right to manage monies. To *hold the purse strings* is to be in charge of the finances.

in the driver's seat—To be in control of a vehicle; to be in a position of authority or superiority; to be able to control a situation. This expression, dating back to at least the 16th century, is obvious in its meaning; anyone who is in a position to control a vehicle is in control of his own destiny as well as that of those who accompany him. And since he is in such a position of trust, he must be prepared not to *steer [one] wrong*, both literally and figuratively.

> And the hardware's been designed to do the same. They won't steer you wrong. The trained salespeople... realize that you may never have been in this particular driver's seat before. (*New Yorker*, November 15, 1982)

in the saddle—In control; in a position of authority; in readiness. This expression derives from the image of authority that is suggested by a good rider on horseback. Contributing to this sense is the fact that during the

Middle Ages only the affluent could afford a horse; consequently, those of wealth came to be *in the saddle*. Furthermore, a man afoot is in no position to dispute with a man on horseback. Today the term is heard only in its figurative sense.

> Let us put Germany, so to speak, in the saddle! you will see that she can ride. (Otto von Bismarck, *To the Parliament of the Confederation*, March 11, 1867)

muzzle the ox—To place restrictions upon those whom one should trust; to deprive a person in one's employment of those little extra considerations he might expect. A provision of old Jewish law instructs that one must have faith in those whom he employs.

> Thou shalt not muzzle the ox when he treadeth out the corn. (Deuteronomy 25:4)

In Biblical times domestic animals were usually muzzled to keep them from grazing in the open farm lands; hence, the instruction to unmuzzle the ox which is working in one's fields and allow him a few well-earned perquisites. The expression is occasionally heard today.

> Isn't there a proverb about not muzzling the ox that treads out the corn? (Ethel White, *Fear Stalks the Village*, 1942)

put a bold face on—Control one's countenance; repress a feeling outwardly. This phrase, although occasionally used to indicate impudence, is most commonly used to indicate a person who is trying to bear up under a disagreeable situation without showing his feelings to the public. The origin of the expression is uncertain; it has been in use since the 1600s. A synonymous phrase is *set one's face* while to *put on a bold front* is to display impudence or cheek.

run a tight ship—To maintain good order and firm discipline; to manage a project or organization so that its interdependent parts and personnel function smoothly together, with machine-like efficiency and precision. A literal tight ship is one which is both water-tight and well-run, in that officers and crew carry out their respective roles with an absence of friction. Though *run a tight ship* may have connotations of martinetlike strictness, it is usually used positively to compliment an efficient administrator.

[the one] who pays the piper calls the tune—An adage implying that a person has control of a project or other matter by virtue of bearing its expenses. The figurative use of this expression is derived from its literal meaning, i.e., someone who pays a musician has the right to request a certain song.

> Londoners had paid the piper, and should choose the tune. (*Daily News*, December 18, 1895)

CONVICTION
SEE CERTAINTY

COOPERATION
SEE ASSISTANCE; RECIPROCITY

CORDIALITY
SEE FRIENDSHIP

CORPULENCE
SEE PHYSICAL APPEARANCE

CORRECTNESS
SEE CERTAINTY; PRECISION

COST
SEE PAYMENT; SELLING

COUNTENANCE
SEE VISAGE

CRAVING
SEE DESIRE

CRAZINESS
SEE IRRATIONALITY

CRITERION
SEE TEST

Criticism

CRITICISM
See also REPRIMAND

blue-pencil—To delete or excise, alter or abridge; to mark for correction or improvement. Used of written matter exclusively, *blue-pencil* derives from the blue pencil used by many editors to make manuscript changes and comments.

damn with faint praise—To praise in such restrained or indifferent terms as to render the praise worthless; to condemn by using words which, at best, express mediocrity. Its first use was probably by Alexander Pope in his 1735 *Epistle to Dr. Arbuthnot:*
Damn with faint praise, assent with civil leer.

dip [one's] pen in gall—To write with bitterness and spite; to malign another. Gall is the bile, the bitter organic secretion produced by the liver, hence, the bitter connotation of this expression.
In the *Contemporary Review* an anonymous writer dips his pen in gall in order to depict the German Emperor. (*Review of Reviews,* 1892)
The *OED* suggests that a pun inherent in the word *gall* may be the source of this phrase, for *oakgall*, an excrescence produced by oak trees, is employed

in the manufacture of ink. Shakespeare certainly used it in punning fashion in *Twelfth Night*:

> Let there be gall enough in thy ink, though thou write with a goose-pen, no matter. (III,ii)

A related term, *gall of bitterness*, meaning the very bitterest of grief, has been in use since at least the Middle Ages.

don't come the uncle over me—Do not criticize me too severely; do not exceed your right to censure me. This ancient expression dates from Classical Rome and is rooted in the Roman concept that an uncle's function was to point out a nephew's shortcomings. Nephews looked upon uncles as severe critics; hence, the figurative use of the word *uncle* in the expression.

> Don't criticize too severely, as uncles are apt to do with nephews. (Erasmus, *Adagia*, 1500)

I knew him when!—A caustic comment used of an ex- friend who has become successful to the point of being self-important; an expression to describe an acquaintance who has risen to such a level of prominence that he is no longer approachable. The phrase is an ellipsis for *I knew him when he was only a cab driver*, or some such similar expression of humble origin. During the 1930s the satirist-poet Arthur Guiterman utilized this expression in a poem which appeared in his *Prophets in their Own Country*.

> Of all cold words of tongue or pen,
> The worst are these, 'I knew him when.'

The lines are, of course, a parody of the well-known lines from John Greenleaf Whittier's *Maud* (1856):

> For all sad words of tongue or pen
> The saddest are these: 'It might have been.'

jump down [someone's] throat—To criticize severely; to berate sharply; to attack in words angrily. This expression, obvious in its figurative meaning, has been in use since the early 1800s. The *OED* also lists an application of the phrase which is seldom heard, to 'give oneself up absolutely to another person,' and offers the following citation:

> I might have jumped down this gentleman's throat in my foolish admiration for his powers of equitation. (Mrs. Nina Kennard, *The Right Sort*, 1883)

peanut gallery—See INSIGNIFICANCE.

pot shot—A random, offhand criticism or condemnation; a censorious remark shot from the hip, lacking forethought and direction. *Webster's Third* cites C. H. Page's reference to:

> subjects which require serious discussion, not verbal potshots.

Pot shot originally referred to the indiscriminate, haphazard nature of shots taken at game with the simple intention of providing a meal, i.e., filling the pot. By transference, the term acquired the sense of a shot taken at a defenseless person or thing at close range from an advantageous position.

slings and arrows—Barbed attacks, stinging criticism; any suffering or affliction, usually intentionally directed or inflicted. The words come from the famous soliloquy in which Hamlet contemplates suicide:

Whether 'tis nobler in the mind to suffer

The slings and arrows of outrageous fortune,

Or to take arms against a sea of troubles

And by opposing end them.

(III,i)

As commonly used, the expression often retains the *suffer* of the original phrase, but usually completes the thought by substituting another object for *outrageous fortune*, as in the following:

En route to the United States the enterprise has suffered the slings and arrows of detractors as diverse as George Meany and Joseph Papp. (Roland Gelatt, in *Saturday Review*, February 1979)

stop-watch critic—A hidebound formalist, whose focus is so riveted on traditional criteria or irrelevant minutiae that he fails to attend to or even see the true and total object of his concern. Laurence Sterne gave us the term in *Tristram Shandy*.

"And how did Garrick speak the soliloquy last night?"

"Oh, against all the rule, my lord, most ungrammatically. Betwixt the substantive and the adjective, which should agree together in number, case, and gender, he made a breach, thus—stopping as if the point wanted settling; and betwixt the nominative case, which, your lordship knows, should govern the verb, he suspended his voice in the epilogue a dozen times, three seconds and three-fifths by a stop-watch, my lord, each time."

"Admirable grammarian! But in suspending his voice was the sense suspended likewise? Did no expression of attitude or countenance fill up the chasm? Was the eye silent? Did you narrowly look?"

"I looked only at the stopwatch, my lord."

"Excellent observer!"

write [someone] down—To make a negative criticism of another; to disparage another's actions or character in writing; to make a list or a mental note of another's misdeeds. This expression, another of the many more familiar by its use in Shakespeare, appears in *Much Ado About Nothing* (IV,ii). Dogberry, a clownish constable, conducts an investigation, in which he has Verges, his assistant, write everything and everybody down. At the end of the scene Dogberry comes to the conclusion:

FLY ON THE WALL

O that he were here to write me down an ass! But, masters, remember that I am an ass; though it be not written down, yet forget not that I am an ass.

The term is occasionally heard today, most commonly in the figurative sense.

CULMINATION
SEE COMPLETION; TERMINATION

CURIOSITY

eavesdropper—One who clandestinely listens in on private conversations; a fly on the wall, a snoop or spy. It was formerly the practice of such persons to listen in on private conversations by standing under the eaves of the dwelling in which they occurred. The *dropper* part of the term seems to have some connection with rain dripping off the eaves and onto the listener standing under them, as indicated by the following passage describing the punishment prescribed by the Freemasons for a convicted eavesdropper:

> To be placed under the eaves of the house in rainy weather, till the water runs in at his shoulders and out at his heels.

The term dates from 1487.

fly on the wall—An eavesdropper, an unseen witness. In this expression, the implication is that a small, inconspicuous fly that has settled on a wall is able to witness events without being noticed. The phrase is nearly always heard as part of a person's expressed desire to see and hear certain conversations or goings on ("I'd love to be a fly on the wall"); rarely is it used in contexts implying actual clandestine behavior. This same concept, that is, a small, unobtrusive insect acting as a witness, may have given rise to *bug* 'a concealed recording device or microphone.' However, it is more likely that *bug* was used to describe the tiny microphone, which resembles an insect.

play the bird with the long neck—To be out looking for someone or something; to look at someone or something out of curiosity. This expression is closely related to *go gandering* or to *take a gander*. All three phrases refer to the natural curiosity of the male goose and his habit of stretching his long neck to observe what goes on about him.

rubberneck—A person who gapes and gawks; one who stares intently at something or someone; a curious observer; a tourist. This expression alludes to the elasticlike neck contortions of one trying to view everything in sight. Although the phrase sometimes carries a disparaging implication of unjustified curiosity, *rubberneck* is more often applied humorously to conspicuous sightseers in an unfamiliar locale who gaze wonderingly at scenes taken for granted by the natives.

> They are the nobility—the swells. They don't hang around the streets like tourists and rubbernecks. (G. B. McCutcheon, *Truxton King*, 1910)

take a gander—To glance at; to look at out of curiosity. This expression, derived from the inquisitive male goose, enjoys widespread use in the United States and Great Britain.

> Take a gander at the see-through door below. See that corrugated piece of steel? (*Scientific American*, October 1971)

DANGER
See also VULNERABILITY

Bellerophontic letter—A letter containing material dangerous to the person who delivers it; a document prejudicial to the bearer. This expression has its origin in Greek mythology. Bellerophon, the son of Sisyphus, while a guest at the home of Proteus, king of Argos, was accused by Proteus's wife of compromising her honor. Bellerophon, who was innocent of any such charges, which had been made out of revenge for his rejecting her advances, was sent to Iobates, king of Lycia, with a letter requesting that Bellerophon be killed. Iobates, loath to have him killed in cold blood, assigned many dangerous tasks to Bellerophon, who succeeded in carrying them all out triumphantly. Finally wearying of trying to kill him, Iobates gave him his daughter's hand in marriage and made him heir to his kingdom.

beware the ides of March—See SUPERSTITION.

cat ice—Flimsy ground, precarious condition. Cat ice is extremely thin ice formed on shallow water which has since receded. It owes its name to the belief that it could not support even the weight of a cat. The phrase has been in use since 1884.

dirty work at the crossroads—Foul play; skullduggery; deceitful dealing. This expression was probably coined in the 1880s by Walter Melville, who used it frequently in his music-hall melodramas. Since robbers found crossroads a convenient place to practice their trade, much dirty work did take place at crossroads. Furthermore, it was common practice in Victorian England to bury suicides in graves at crossroads, with a stake driven through their hearts. In modern usage, the term is most commonly heard in a jocular sense, as:

> She's pregnant? There must have been some dirty work at the crossroads!

57

notch in his tail—A phrase that refers to an extremely dangerous horse that is hard to handle. This expression, a descriptive term used by American cowboys for a man-killing bronco, draws a parallel to the notches that gunfighters of the Old West would cut in their gun handles for each man they had killed. The term, now figurative, is still heard around rodeos.

nourish a snake in [one's] bosom—To show kindness to one who proves ungrateful. The allusion is to the Aesop fable in which a farmer, finding a snake frozen stiff with cold, placed it in his bosom. The snake, thawed by the warmth, quickly revived and inflicted a fatal bite on its benefactor.

I fear me you but warm the starved snake,
Who, cherished in your breasts, will sting your hearts.
(Shakespeare, *II Henry VI*, III,i)

pad in the straw—A hidden danger; a lurking peril; a snake in the grass. *Pad* in this phrase is short for *paddock*, 'a toad.' Toads were once represented as embodiments of attendant spirits to witches and other malignant creatures. For example, in *Macbeth* the second Weird Sister's attendant spirit is Paddock, a toad. The term, in use as early as 1530, became a jocular warning to young lovers to be careful of the invisible evil that lurks in the straw.

Take heed, wench, there lies a pad in the straw. (William Haughton, *English-Men for My Money*, 1605)

side winder—A dangerous person; one who might strike at any moment; a villain. This American expression, in regular use since the early 1800s, has its origin in the old west and owes its modern popularity to grade "B" cowboy films. A favorite epithet for the villains of these movies, the term alludes to *sidewinder*, the term for a small rattlesnake that strikes with a sideways motion.

The trouble never actually reached the 'Draw, you sidewinder!' phase, but it had some unique angles. (*Omaha World-Herald*, May 15, 1949)

snake in the grass—A sneak, dastard, skulker; a suspicious, treacherous, or disingenuous person; a traitor or craven; any lurking danger. This expression is derived from a line in Virgil's *Third Eclogue* (approx. 40 B.C.), *Latet anguis in herba* 'a snake lurks in the grass,' alluding to the potential danger posed by a poisonous snake that is hidden in the grass as if in ambush.

There is a snake in the grass and the design is mischievous. (Thomas Hearne, *Remarks and Collections*, 1709)

sword of Damocles—The threat of impending danger or doom; also *Damocles' sword*.

Little do directors and their companies know of this sword of Damocles that hangs over them. (*Law Times*, 1892)

The allusion is to the sycophant Damocles, invited by Dionysius of Syracuse to a lavish banquet. But Damocles could not enjoy the sumptuous feast because Dionysius had had suspended over his head a sword hanging by a single hair. He dared not move lest the sword fall and kill him.

tiger by the tail—An extremely precarious situation; the horns of a dilemma; a risk; flirtation with danger. The situation alluded to here is obvious; if one lets go, he's in grave danger, but if he holds on, he may be in more danger.

And all his life Jelly Roll held a tiger by the tail . . . all he had was the music of the Storyville bordellos—it was his tiger, and he bet his life on it. (Alan Lomax, *Mister Jelly Roll*, 1950)

A related Chinese proverb states *he who rides a tiger is afraid to dismount.*

DECEIT
SEE MENDACITY

DECEPTION
SEE MENDACITY; PLOY; PRETENSE; TRICKERY

DECISIVENESS
SEE IRREVOCABILITY

DEFEAT
SEE FAILURE

DEFENSELESSNESS
SEE VULNERABILITY

DEFERENCE

after you, my dear Alphonse—This popular catch phrase is the first half of the complete expression "After you, my dear Alphonse—no, after you, my dear Gaston." It first appeared in the Hearst (King Features) comic strip *Happy Hooligan* written by F. Opper. The strip ran throughout the 1920s and for part of the 1930s. The characters Alphonse and Gaston were two extremely debonair Frenchmen who were so polite that they would jeopardize themselves in times of danger by taking the time to courteously ask each other to go first. Today, when two people go to do the same thing at the same time, one might humorously say to the other, "After you, my dear Alphonse."

cap in hand—Submissively; with a deferential air or manner. The phrase alludes to the image of a rustic or servant who selfconsciously and humbly takes off his cap and holds it, usually against his chest, while speaking to someone of higher social status.

courteous as a dog in the kitchen—Submissive; with cap in hand. This expression alludes to the perfect behavior a dog exhibits when near a source of food, hoping for a handout.

give the wall—To yield the safest place; to allow another to walk on the walled side of a street. This expression is derived from an old custom which compelled pedestrians to surrender the safer, inner path bordering a roadway to a person of higher social rank. Modern social etiquette still requires a man to walk on the streetside of a female when walking along a sidewalk. A related expression, *take the wall*, describes the adamant perambulator who assumes the safer path closer to the wall. The inevitable friction between "givers" and "takers" is discussed by James Boswell in his *Journal of a Tour of the Hebrides* (1773):

> In the last age . . . there were two sets of people, those who gave the wall, and those who took it; the peaceable and the quarrelsome . . . .
> Now it is fixed that every man keeps to the right; or, if one is taking the wall, another yields it, and it is never a dispute.

hat in hand—With a respectful or a deferential air; in a courteous manner; with regard for another. This expression alludes to a gentleman who removes his hat in the presence of ladies or to show respect for another gentleman. In contrast to *cap in hand*, the action of an underling to indicate servility or obsequiousness, *hat in hand* connotes an action of one's own free will to signify respect or courtesy. The phrase has been in use since at least the Middle Ages.

> A man's hat in his hand never did him any harm. (Samuel Palmer, *Moral Essays on Proverbs*, 1710)

strike sail—See SUBMISSION.

DEFIANCE
SEE REBELLIOUSNESS

DEJECTION
SEE GRIEVING

DELAYING
SEE TEMPORIZING

DELIGHT
SEE ENJOYMENT

DENIAL
See also REFUSAL

did not lay a finger on—To have avoided striking someone, even in the very slightest way. This phrase is very commonly used in the negative, as "I didn't lay a finger on him," or in the conditional, "if you dare lay a finger on him. . . ." The *OED* lists the first written use of the term as:

He wished he'd never laid a finger on him to save his life. (Robert S. Hawker, *Prose Works*, 1865)

DEPARTURE

any more for the Skylark?—Last chance; last call; now or never. Among the small excursion boats at English resort areas, almost invariably one was named *Skylark*. Generalizing from this situation, the practice arose among attendants of any of these boats to announce, "Any more for the Skylark?" shortly before departure, to solicit more passengers. Sometime in the early years of the 20th century, the phrase came to be used in British English as a summons for any situation requiring last-minute action, such as:

I'm driving into the village in a moment; any more for the Skylark? The phrase is heard less frequently today.

bail out—To make a hasty exit as from an airplane about to crash; to depart precipitously. This American slang expression alludes to the hasty departure one makes from an airplane in an emergency. The aeronautical sense derives from the nautical, 'to empty a ship of water.' In use since the 1940s, the term is usually heard when one wishes to discard a project, depart from a relationship which is unsuccessful, or to make an abrupt departure to avoid impending trouble, as:

I could see that a fight was about to break out in the tavern, so I bailed out of there.

cut and run—To leave as quickly as possible; to take off without further to-do; in slang terms, to split or cut out. These figurative meanings derive from the nautical use of *cut and run* which dates from the 18th century. According to a book on sailing entitled *Rigging and Seamanship* (1794), *cut and run* means "to cut the cable and make sail instantly, without waiting to weigh anchor." By extension, this expression can be used to describe any type of quick getaway.

The alternative was to go to jail, or as the phrase is, to cut and run. (H. H. Brackenridge, *Modern Chivalry*, 1815)
Both nautical and figurative uses are current today.

cut [one's] stick—To be off, to go away, to depart, to leave; also *to cut one's lucky*, although the sense here is more to decamp, to escape. This British slang expression, which dates from the early 19th century, is said to have come from the custom of cutting a walking stick prior to a departure.

61

do a Dunkirk—Evacuate under pressure; depart hastily; abandon; cut and run. The allusion in this expression is to the hasty abandonment of Dunkirk, France by British troops in 1940. The evacuation, from the shores of France to the British Isles, was completed with the assistance of thousands of British citizens operating small pleasure and commercial craft, most of which had never before been taken from the inland waters of Britain. Under constant bombardment by German aircraft, the British Navy, abetted by these little boats, rescued hundreds of thousands of British and allied troops. Winston Churchill, prime minister at the time, called the operation a "miracle of deliverance." Today the term is used figuratively to indicate a rather abrupt or an emergency leave-taking.

French leave—Sudden flight or departure, often leaving behind unpaid bills; leave taken secretly or without prior notice. This expression has its origin in the Parisian etiquette of the 18th century. Arriving guests were received lavishly, passing down a long receiving line which included all guests who had preceded them to the party. However, upon departure the guest simply left without any thank yous or farewells to anyone, including the host and hostess. Apparently this abrupt departure was designed not to interrupt the party.

> My only plan was to take French leave, and slip out when nobody was watching. (Robert Louis Stevenson, *Treasure Island*, 1883)

The French call such a precipitous exit taking *English leave (filer à l'anglaise)*.

hightail it—To depart hastily; to run at full speed; to escape, especially by running away; to rush away in fright. This American slang expression was coined during the early 1800s by the trappers who roamed the American West. The allusion is to the practice of some wild animals, especially deer, of raising their tails as they rush away when startled or alarmed.

> Often they'd scatter like a bunch of antelope, and hightail it in any direction excepting the right one. (Will James, *Cow Country*, 1927)

Today the term is most commonly applied to a hasty exit or getaway, on foot or in a vehicle.

> We hightailed it for the hangout. (Hal Moore, *Flynn's*, April 19, 1930)

hoist the blue peter—To indicate or advertise that departure is imminent. A "blue peter" is a flag of the International Code of Signals for the letter "P," used aboard vessels to signal that preparations are being made for departure. A blue flag with a white square in the center, it is a signal for hands on shore to come aboard and for others to conclude business with the crew. It dates from about 1800. By 1823, figurative use of *hoist the blue peter* gained currency, as exemplified in the following quotation from Byron's *Don Juan* (1823):

> It is time that I should hoist my "blue Peter,"
> And sail for a new theme.

Blue peter is also the name for a move in whist in which one plays an unnecessarily high card as a call for trumps.

hop the twig—To depart suddenly; to go off; to run away; to die. The allusion in this Briticism is to the bird that *hops the twig* just before the hunter is ready to shoot. The term is most commonly used in Britain today to connote the avoiding of one's creditors. First appearing in the latter half of the 18th century, the expression has also been used to connote the departure at death.

> He kept his bed three days, and hopped the twig on the fourth. (Mary Robinson, *Welsingham*, 1797)

make tracks—To leave rapidly; to hotfoot it; to flee or escape. This expression alludes to the trail or tracks created by the passage of human beings or animals through woods, snow, etc. The phrase has been in widespread use since the early 19th century.

> I'd a made him make tracks, I guess. (Thomas Haliburton, *Clockmaster*, 1835)

pull up stakes—To move or relocate; to leave one's job, home, etc., for another part of the country.

> They just pulled up stakes and left for parts unknown. (*The New Orleans Times-Picayune Magazine*, April 1950)

Stakes are sticks or posts used as markers to delimit the boundaries of one's property. In colonial times, literally pulling up stakes meant that one was giving up one's land in order to move on, just as driving them in meant that one was laying claim to the enclosed land to set up housekeeping.

saddler of Bawtry—A person who leaves his friends at the tavern too early. The suggestion in this expression is that if one leaves his drinking too soon, he will suffer for it. The original saddler of Bawtry, on his way to be hanged, refused to stop at the local pub for the usual free drink regularly offered to those about to be executed. As a result, his reprieve arrived a moment too late: he had already been hanged when the message came.

> He will be hanged for leaving his liquor behind, like the saddler of Bawtry. (Samuel Pegge, *Curialia Miscellanea*, 1818)

shake the dust from [one's] feet—To depart resolutely from an unpleasant or disagreeable place; to leave in anger, exasperation, or contempt.

> I then paid off my lodgings, and "shaking the dust from my feet," bid a long adieu to London. (Frances Burney, *Cecilia*, 1782)

The expression, which implies a certain abruptness, is found in Matthew 10:14 where Jesus is speaking to the disciples before sending them out to preach the Word:

> And whosoever shall not receive you, nor hear your words, when ye depart out of that house or city, shake off the dust of your feet.

shoot the moon—To remove one's household furnishings by night to avoid paying the rent or to avoid one's creditors. Although this British slang expression usually implies a stealthy departure from one's lodgings for nonpayment of the rent, it may also imply a furtive departure for some other clandestine reason. The term has been in use since the early 18th century.

> He having just "shot the moon" . . . I had to follow him to a cockloft in St. Giles's. (Colonel Peter Hawker, *Diary*, 1837)

Related terms, *do a moonlight flit* and *make a moonlight flitting* have the same meaning and are more commonly heard today.

> The whole covey of them, no better than a set of swindlers, . . . made that very night a moonlight flitting. (David M. Moir, *Mansie Wauch*, 1824)

take a powder—To depart hastily; to flee. This expression is usually associated with an underworld or underhanded situation, describing a person or persons who suddenly leave to avoid capture or detection. Apparently of American origin, the phrase has been in use since the early 1900s. Although the exact origin is uncertain, the *Oxford English Dictionary* does list a verb *powder*, labeled "*colloquial and dialectal*," whose meaning is 'to rush out impetuously.' There is also a variant *take a run-out powder*.

take to the tall timber—To depart unexpectedly and with little to-do; to escape. *Tall timber* originally referred to a heavily timbered, uninhabited area in the forest. This colloquial Americanism, often used literally, dates from the early 1800s.

> I fell off *three times*; finally the disgusted critter took to the tall timber, leaving me to hike onward and to get across the frigid stream as best I could. (*Sky Line Trail*, October 18, 1949)

Variants of this expression include *break for tall timber* or *strike for tall timber* or *pull for tall timber*.

DERISION
SEE INSULT

DESERTION
SEE ABANDONMENT

DESIRE

Attic figs—Things coveted but not attainable (used as a warning to one who is thinking unrealistically). Xerxes, king of Persia, boasted after he had defeated the Greeks at Thermopylae (480 B.C.) that he would go to Attica and eat the figs there. His boast proved hubristic, for he was decisively defeated by the Greek forces at Salamis later that year. Ever since, *Attic figs* has been used to denote covetousness or wishful thinking.

big eyes—A great lust or desire for a person or object. This jazz term, in use since the 1950s, may have come from the older, less picturesque to *have eyes for* 'to be attracted to or desirous of,' used as early as 1810 in *The Scottish Chiefs* by Jane Porter. *Big eyes* has a corresponding negative expression, *no eyes*, also in use since 1950s, meaning 'lack of desire, or disinclination.'

forbidden fruit—A tempting but prohibited object or experience; an unauthorized or illegal indulgence, often of a sexual nature. The Biblical origin of this phrase appears in Genesis 3:3:

> But of the fruit of the tree which is in the midst of the garden, God hath said, Ye shall not eat of it, neither shall ye touch it, lest ye die.

The expression has been used figuratively for centuries.

> The stealing and tasting of the forbidden fruit of sovereignty. (James Heath, *Flagellum*, 1663)

give [one's] eyeteeth—To gladly make the greatest sacrifice to obtain a desired end; to yield something precious in exchange for the achievement of one's desire. The eyeteeth, so named because their roots extend to just under the eyes, are the two pointed canines which flank the front teeth of the upper jaw. Since excruciating pain accompanies their extraction, this expression came to imply making a painful sacrifice.

> He'd give his eyeteeth to have written a book half as good. (W. S. Maugham, *Cakes & Ale*, 1930)

give [one's] right arm—To be willing to make a great sacrifice or to endure great pain or inconvenience; to trade something as irreplaceable as part of one's body for an object of desire. In our predominantly righthanded society, to forfeit one's right arm signifies a great loss. This phrase has been popular since the early 1900s. Earlier, in the late 19th century, *willing to give one's ears* was a common expression. It is said to allude to the ancient practice of cutting off ears for various offenses.

> Many a man would give his ears to be allowed to call two such charming young ladies by their Christian names. (William E. Norris, *Thirlby Hall*, 1883)

go through fire and water—To be willing to suffer pain or brave danger in order to obtain the object of one's desire; to undergo great sacrifice or pay any price to achieve a desired end; to prove oneself by the most demanding of tests. The expression is thought to derive from ordeals involving fire and water which were common methods of trial in Anglo-Saxon times. To prove their innocence, accused persons were often forced to carry hot bars of iron or to plunge a hand into boiling water without injury. The phrase is now used exclusively in a figurative sense, as illustrated by the following from Shakespeare's *Merry Wives of Windsor:*

> A woman would run through fire and water for such a kind heart.
> (III,iv)

itching palm—Avarice, greed, cupidity; an abnormal desire for money and material possessions, often implying an openness or susceptibility to bribery. The expression apparently arose from the old superstition that a person whose palm itches is about to receive money. The figurative sense of *itching* 'an uneasy desire or hankering' dates from the first half of the 14th century. Shakespeare used the phrase in *Julius Caesar:*

> Let me tell you, Cassius, you yourself
> Are much condemned to have an itching palm.
> (IV,iii)

make [one's] mouth water—To excite a craving or desire, to cause to anticipate eagerly. This expression has its origin in the stimulation of the salivary glands by the appetizing sight or smell of food. Both literal and figurative uses of the phrase date from the 16th century.

> [She would] bribe him . . . to write down the name of a young Scotch peer . . . that her mouth watered after. (Daniel Defoe, *The History of D. Campbell*, 1720)

my kingdom for a horse!—An expression used when one would gladly trade an obviously valuable possession for one of seemingly lesser worth, usually because the lack of the latter renders the former meaningless or useless. It was the cry of Shakespeare's Richard III at Bosworth Field:

> A horse! A horse! My kingdom for a horse!
> (V,iv)

wait for dead men's shoes—To covetously await one's inheritance; to eagerly anticipate the position or property that another's death will bring. This expression, infrequently used today, derives from the former Jewish custom surrounding the transfer or bequeathing of property, as related in Ruth 4:7. A bargain was formally sealed by removing and handing over one's shoe. Similarly, inheritance due to death was signaled by pulling off the dead man's shoes and giving them to his heir. *Dead men's shoes* was often used alone to indicate the property so bequeathed or so awaited.

yen—A craving or strong desire; a yearning, longing, or hankering. One theory regarding the origin of this expression claims that *yen* is a corruption of the Chinese slang term *yan* 'a craving, as for opium or drink.' Another theory states that *yen* is probably an altered form of *yearn* or *yearning*. The term dates from at least 1908.

> Ever get a yen to "take off" a day or two and see the country? (*Capital-Democrat* [Tishomingo, Oklahoma], June 1948)

DESTITUTION
SEE POVERTY

DESTRUCTION
SEE DOWNFALL

DETERMINATION
SEE PERSEVERANCE

DICTION
SEE LANGUAGE

DIFFERENTIATION
SEE PERCEPTIVENESS

DIFFICULTY
See also IMPEDIMENT

bed of nails—An uncomfortable position; a difficult situation. This expression, alluding to the actual bed of nails which Indian fakirs lie on to demonstrate their faith, originally came into use about 1800, fell into disuse shortly thereafter, but returned to popularity because the media gave such extensive coverage to Ray Gunter's use of the term in 1966 to describe the position of Minister of Labour in the British government.

> I asked whether he thought he had been given a bed of nails in his job. He said, "No, it appeals to me as a challenge." (*The Times*, June 8, 1973)

dogs in dough—A difficult predicament; an ungainly situation; inability to extricate oneself gracefully. This 19th-century expression refers to the stickiness of dough and invokes the image of a dog's inability to disengage himself from a mass of it: if he frees a foot, he must place it back in the dough to lift another foot, *ad infinitum*.

> Like dogs in dough, i.e., unable to make headway. (G.F. Northall, *Folk Phrases*, 1894)

a hair in the butter—An American cowboy expression for a delicate or ticklish situation. The difficulty of picking a single hair out of butter makes this analogy appropriate.

a hard nut to crack—A poser, a puzzler, a stumper; a hard question, problem, or undertaking; a difficult person to deal with, a tough cookie; also *a tough nut to crack*.

> You will find Robert Morris a hard nut to crack. (James Payn, *The Mystery of Mirbridge*, 1888)

hard row to hoe—A difficult or uphill task, a long haul, a hard lot, a tough situation; also *a long row to hoe*. This American expression is an obvious reference to the dispiriting task of hoeing long rows in rocky terrain.

> I never opposed Andrew Jackson for the sake of popularity. I knew it was a hard row to hoe, but I stood up to the rack. (David Crockett, *An Account of Col. Crockett's Tour to the North and down East*, 1835)

have [one's] work cut out—To be facing a difficult task; about to undertake a demanding responsibility of the sort that will test one's abilities and resources to the utmost; to have one's hands full. This common expression is a variation of the earlier *cut out work for*, meaning simply to prepare work for another, may have a sense that its origins in tailoring; it apparently carried no implications of excessiveness in quantity or difficulty. Perhaps it is the nature of superiors to be exceedingly demanding, or at least for underlings to assume so; in any event, when the expression "changed hands," so to speak, it took on these added connotations, along with the frequent implication that the person who "has his work cut out for him" has more than he can capably manage.

hold an eel by the tail—To try to grasp something slippery and elusive; to try to control an unmanageable situation; to encounter or deal with a deceitful, unreliable person. In use since the early 16th century, this expression exemplifies what any angler knows: holding an eel by the tail is a near impossibility; the squirmy, twisting, slippery creature will wrench itself from the grasp of anyone who attempts the feat.

> He may possibly take an eel by the tail in marrying a wife. (Thomas Newte, *A Tour in England and Scotland in 1785*, 1791)

hot corner—Third base in baseball; any difficult position. This term, which by extension has come to specify any situation that is hard to handle, is derived from the game of baseball. Baseball players nicknamed third base the *hot corner* because of the number of "hot" or fast-moving ground balls and line drives which are consistently hit to that spot. The business world, in particular, has picked up the phrase to indicate placement on a difficult job, one that could be too hot to handle.

hot potato—A controversial question; an embarrassing situation. This familiar saying is of obvious origin.

> The Judge had been distressed when Johnny agreed to take the case, was amazed at first at the way he handled it—hot potato that it was. (Carson McCullers, *Clock Without Hands*, 1961)

The term is often used in the expression *drop like a hot potato*, meaning to swiftly rid oneself of any unwanted thing or person.

> They dropped him like a hot potato when they learned that he had accepted a place on the Republican Committee of the State. (B. P. Moore, *Perley's Reminiscences*, 1886)

TOUGH NUT TO CRACK

make heavy weather of—Find more difficult than anticipated; make a relatively easy task more difficult than necessary; create a fuss about a simple job. The allusion in this British expression is to the stupidity or pessimism of some people over simple situations, such as the person who slogs along a muddy road during a heavy rain storm when he could make his way much more easily along the grassy edge of the highway.

Murphy's law—This law states that if anything can possibly go wrong, it will, and at the worst possible moment. The term has been in use since at least the 1950s and was devised to describe the futility that is often characteristic of the human condition. There are many corollaries to the law, such as: if one gets in the shower, the phone will ring; if it's going to rain, it will happen on the weekend; if one is going to get the flu, it will occur during one's vacation. A related British term is *Sod's law*.

spit cotton—To spit with difficulty; to suffer from thirst or embarrassment. This 19th-century Americanism alludes to the white, sticky spittle which forms in the mouth when one is extremely thirsty and one's mouth is unusually dry. Such a phenomenon also often takes place when one is aroused in some way emotionally, as with anger or fear.

> The Kansas City vote frauds... have Attorney General Tom Clark spitting cotton, they believe. (*Chicago Daily News*, June 14, 1947)A related term, *cotton mouth thirst*, is a thirst which causes one to *spit cotton*, in both the figurative senses.

> We were both old hands at the business, had each in our time suffered the cotton mouth thirst. (Stewart E. White, *Arizona Nights*, 1907)

Cotton mouth is also used to refer to a very parched condition of the mouth which frequently occurs the morning after consuming much wine.

sticky wicket—A difficult predicament; a perilous plight; an awkward situation requiring delicate, cool-headed treatment. This expression, primarily a British colloquialism, alludes to the sport of cricket and describes the tacky condition of the playing field near the *wicket* 'goal' after a rainstorm. Because of the sponginess and sluggishness of the ground, the ball does not roll and bounce as predictably as on a dry field, and the player must therefore adapt to the situation by being exceptionally accurate and careful. The phrase is often used in expressions such as *bat on a sticky wicket, be on a sticky wicket*.

ugly customer—A disagreeable person who is likely to cause trouble if interfered with; one who may turn vicious if not dealt with carefully; one who is quarrelsome, contentious; a person with whom one feels ill-at-ease. The term originated in reference to those customers of retail establishments whom salespeople found impossible to satisfy. By extension, the term came into general use for anyone difficult to get along with, especially one who might become verbally or physically abusive. The term has been in use since about 1800.

> You will find him, my young sir, an Ugly Customer. (Charles Dickens, *Martin Chuzzlewit*, 1844)

A related term, *tough customer* implies that one is demanding but not necessarily unpleasant.

venom is in the tail—The difficulty lies in the conclusion; the real trouble comes at the end; the danger arises just when one thinks safety is imminent. The allusion in this phrase is to a confrontation with a scorpion, where the real danger lies in the poisonous sting in its segmented tail. The term is also occasionally used in reference to the spur usually found at the end of each lash on a cat-o-nine-tails.

> The venom of a scorpion is in its tail, that of a fly in its head, that of a serpent in its fangs; but the venom of a wicked man is to be found in all parts of his body. (Anonymous, *Niti Sastras*, 1250)

vicious circle—In logic, the proper definition of a *vicious circle* is a situation where the solution to one problem creates new problems which eventually bring back the original problem in a more difficult form. Consequently, the problem goes full circle. The term is often applied figuratively to situations other than those found in logic.

> Thus the practice proceeds, in a vicious circle of habit, from which the patient is rarely extricated without ... injury to his future health. (Sir Henry Holland, *Medical Notes and Reflexions*, 1839)

A related term is *arguing in a circle*, in which one draws a conclusion, using the conclusion as part of the argument to reach that conclusion.

DILIGENCE
SEE EXERTION

DISADVANTAGE
SEE VULNERABILITY

DISAPPOINTMENT
SEE FAILURE

DISAPPROVAL
SEE CRITICISM; INSULT

DISARRAY
SEE DISORDER

DISCERNMENT
SEE PERCEPTIVENESS

DISCOMFORT
SEE DIFFICULTY; ILL HEALTH

DISDAIN
SEE HAUGHTINESS

DISHONESTY
SEE MENDACITY; UNSCRUPULOUSNESS

DISHONORABLENESS
SEE UNSCRUPULOUSNESS

Disorder

DISORDER
See also CONFUSION

all shook up—Excited; agitated; stimulated; shaken with worry or concern. This American slang expression came into the language about 1955 from the world of rock and roll music. It was given major impetus in 1958 when Elvis Presley recorded a hit song of that name; teenage slang has kept the term current since that time, along with a shorter version *shook up*.

> I lay back on my lumpy mattress in the reformatory so shook up I could not sleep. (*Life*, April 28, 1958)

at sixes and sevens—In a state of disorder and confusion; higgledy-piggledy; unable to agree, at odds. Originally *set on six and seven*, this expression derives from the language of dicing and is said to be a variation of *set on cinque and sice*. This early form of the expression dates from the time of Chaucer when it often applied to the hazardous nature of one's fate in general. By the 18th century, the plural *sixes* and *sevens* was standard; earlier, the expression had undergone other changes: the verb *set* was dropped, *at* replaced *on*, and the applicability of the expression broadened to accommodate any situation or state of affairs. Although the *OED* authenticates the dicing theory as the source of this expression, many stories—some more plausible than others—have been related to explain its origin.

> If I was to go from home ... everything would soon go to sixes and sevens. (Mrs. Elizabeth Blower, *George Bateman,* 1782)

bollixed up—Thrown into disorder or confusion; chaotic, topsyturvy; messed up, bungled, flubbed. *Ballocks* 'testes' dates from 1000 and its variant *bollocks* from 1744. *Bollix* is close in pronunciation and related in meaning to *bollocks* although the former is used as a verb and the latter only as a noun. As a verb, *bollix* is akin to *ball up* 'make a mess, bungle.' The change in meaning from 'testes' to 'confusion, nonsense' is itself confusing and is a relatively recent development (late 19th century). *Bollix* and *bollixed up* date from the early 1900s.

> Watch your script.... You're getting your cues all bollixed up. (J. Weidman, *I Can Get It For You Wholesale,* 1937)

confusion worse confounded—See EXACERBATION.

72

Fred Karno's army—A motley, disorganized group, a disorderly mob. The origin of this phrase can be traced directly to Fred Karno, a music-hall comedian, who incorporated into one of his acts a burlesque army. This army became a symbol of any milling, churning throng of people with little or no apparent purpose. In 1913 Karno brought his army in *A Night in an English Music Hall* to New York City; among his company of players were Charlie Chaplin and Stan Laurel. A related American term is *Coxey's Army*. Coxey led a large group of unemployed workmen to Washington, D.C., in 1894 to appeal to Congress for unemployment relief. The American term is seldom heard today except among the elderly.

Men and generals between them have made up 'Coxey's Army' and a very misty, queer, mixed up lot they are. (*Life*, May 10, 1894)

go haywire—To go out of control, to go awry, to run riot; to go crazy, to go berserk, to go out of one's mind. One source hypothesizes that the phrase derived from the unmanageability of the wire used in binding bales of hay. More reputable sources see its origin in the adjective *haywire* 'poor, rough, inefficient' (from the use of haywire for makeshift or temporary repairs). The phrase dates from at least 1929.

Some of them have gone completely haywire on their retail prices. (*The Ice Cream Trade Journal*, September 1948)

a hell of a way to run a railway—In a state of confusion and disorder; in chaotic disarray; in a disorganized manner; in a jumbled mess. This expression grew in national prominence after it appeared as a cartoon caption in a 1932 edition of *Ballyhoo* magazine. In the cartoon a railroad signalman makes this flippant remark as he looks down from his control tower upon two trains which are about to crash head-on. In modern use the term alludes to a lack of clear-cut leadership, or the chaos created when two strong leaders attempt to take people in opposite directions. An excellent example of the latter use was made during the conflict between General MacArthur and President Truman over the extent of American aggressiveness toward China during the Korean War.

It is, in the idiom of Missouri, a hell of a way to run a railway. (Arthur Schlesinger, Jr. and Richard Rovere, *The General and the President*, 1951)

higgledy-piggledy—In a confused state; topsy-turvy; helter-skelter. This amusing expression may have derived from the disheveled appearance of a pig sty.

In a higgledy-piggledy world like this it is impossible to make very nice distinctions between good luck and good work. (*Daily News*, January 1890)

huggermugger—See SECRECY.

hurly-burly—Tumult; disorder; great noise or commotion. This expression, immortalized by the Weird Sisters in *Macbeth* (I.i),

> When the hurly-burly's done,
> When the battle's lost or won.

is of uncertain origin. It may be a reduplication of the Middle English *hurlen*, 'to be driven with great force,' but the *OED* questions this derivation since the earliest written use of *hurly-burly* yet discovered is 1539, whereas the earliest written use of *hurly* is 1596. At any rate, the term is still in everyday use.

> Nor could such a Deity ever have any quiet enjoyment of himself, being perpetually filled with tumult and *hurly-burly*. (Ralph Cudworth, *The True Intellectual System of the Universe*, 1678)

hurrah's nest—A confused jumble, an unholy mess. The first recorded use of this expression *(hurra's nest)* appears to have been in Samuel Longfellow's biography of his poet-brother (1829). No clear explanation of its origin has been found, though it seems likely the term is related to the matted, tangled branches of the hurrah bush. S. W. Mitchell in an 1889 issue of *Century Magazine* parenthetically defined a *hurrah's nest* as:

> a mass of leaves left by a freshet in the crotch of the divergent branches of a bush.

By that time, however, the expression had already attained its figurative meaning.

> Everything was pitched about in grand confusion. There was a complete hurrah's nest. (R. H. Dana, *Two Years Before the Mast*, 1840)

kettle of fish—A confusing, topsy-turvy state of affairs; a predicament; a contretemps. Literal use of this originally British expression refers to the kettle of fish served at a riverside picnic, and by extension, to the picnic itself.

> It is customary for the gentlemen who live near the Tweed to entertain their neighbours and friends with a Fete Champetre, which they call giving "a kettle of fish." Tents or marquees are pitched...a fire is kindled, and live salmon thrown into boiling kettles. (Thomas Newte, *A Tour in England and Scotland in 1785*, 1791)

Some believe that *kettle* is a corruption of kiddle 'a net placed in a river to catch fish.' However, neither this suggestion nor the many other theories offered to account for the figurative use of *kettle of fish* are plausible.

> Fine doings at my house! A rare kettle of fish I have discovered at last. (Henry Fielding, *The History of Tom Jones*, 1749)

Fine kettle of fish, pretty kettle of fish, nice kettle of fish, and *rare kettle of fish* are frequently heard. Ironic use of the adjectives serves to highlight the implied confusion and disorderliness.

make a hash of—To botch, spoil, or make an unholy mess of. *Hash* is literally a hodgepodge of foods cooked together. By extension, it applies to any incongruous combination of things; and carried one step further, *make a hash of* is to inadvertently create a confused chaotic mess in an attempt to deal with the particulars of a situation or plan.

> Lord Grey has made somewhat of a hash of New Zealand and its constitution. (R. M. Milnes Houghton, *Life, Letters, and Friendships,* 1847)

mare's nest—A state of confusion or disarray; a spurious and illusionary discovery. A mare's nest would indeed be a bogus discovery since horses do not display nesting habits.

> Colonel S.'s discovery is a mere mare's nest. (*The Times,* October 1892)

Perhaps as an allusion to the bewilderment which would accompany the finding of a *mare's nest,* the expression now denotes a jumbled or chaotic state of affairs.

the natives are restless—An expression used to denote an unfriendly or dissatisfied audience or a disgruntled group of workers or students. This phrase is often used to explain one of those mysterious days when, for no apparent reason, an attitude of uneasiness and general unrest seems to pervade a sizeable group of people. The term has been common since about World War II and probably owes its popularity to its frequent use as a stereotyped scene in adventure films depicting the nervousness of, say, an African safari when it encounters a large and suspiciously hostile-looking native tribe. John Crosby, in *The White Telephone* (1974), writes of some lesser Federal agents who are eager to get started on an important case and have been troubling the President's secretary.

> The President picked up the phone. "The natives are getting restless," said Miss Doll.

no-man's-land—An area, literal or figurative, not under man's control; a scene of chaos or disorder; a desolate, hostile, or uninhabitable tract of land.

> Until the Dutchman Yermuyden came to the scene...to control...
> the river Great Ouse...much of the region was a marshy no-man's-land through which...the only means of transport was by boat.
> (*Country Life,* June 1975)

The expression is used in a similar sense to describe a land area sandwiched between two contending armies. Recently, however, *no man's land* acquired the new figurative meaning of a sphere of human undertaking marked by complexity and confusion.

> One question chased another... question that got lost in a no-man's-land of conjecture. (H. Carmichael, *Motive,* 1974)

out of joint—Disordered, confused; out of kilter. In literal use, this phrase describes a dislocated bone. Figuratively, *out of joint* applies to operations, conditions, and formerly, to individuals in relation to their behavior. The phrase has been in print since the early 15th century, and is especially well known from Shakespeare's *Hamlet:*

> The time is out of joint. Oh cursed spite
> That ever I was born to set it right!
> (I,v)

out of kilter—Out of working condition; out of order. This American expression refers to either machinery or the human body. The implication is that some small part is malfunctioning; therefore, the whole apparatus is running unevenly. The British equivalent of *kilter* is *kelter,* a form that predates American usage by at least 150 years. The date of origin is unknown; the *OED* lists the first written use as:

> Their Gunnes . . . they often sell many a score to the English, when they are a little out of frame or kelter. (Roger Williams, *A Key Unto the Language of America,* 1643)

the right hand doesn't know what the left hand is doing—Confusion, disorder, disarray. Now used derogatorily to indicate a lack of coordination, organization, or direction, in its original New Testament context (with hands reversed) the phrase denoted a desirable state. In his Sermon on the Mount, Jesus tells His listeners not to broadcast their good deeds, but to keep them to themselves:

> But when thou doest alms, let not thy left hand know what thy right hand doeth: that thine alms may be in secret. (Matthew 6:2–4)

The current meaning apparently stems from the fact that in different circumstances keeping something to oneself is undesirable, leading to a lack of communication, which in turn brings on chaos, confusion, and disorganization.

run riot—To act in disorderly fashion; to go haywire; to run out of control. This expression arose in England during the Middle Ages to describe the actions of a pack of hunting dogs that had lost the scent of the game, and therefore were running wild. It was a simple step to transfer the actions of unruly dogs to those of a disorderly group of people.

> They ran riot, would not be kept within bounds. (Lord Chesterfield, *Letters,* 1748)

shambles—A scene of slaughter; disorder; confusion; a slave market. Originally a *shamble* was a footstool, but in time the word came to signify the low tables butchers used to display their wares in a public market place. By the 14th century the *shambles* signified the slaughterhouse and market itself. The destruction and disorder so evident in the *shambles* soon led to the figurative use of the expression for any scene of carnage or of disarray.

> I've feared him; since his iron heart endured
> To make of Lyon one vast human shambles.
> (Samuel Coleridge, *Robespierre,* 1794)

During the period in American history preceding the Civil War, the term also signified a slave market.

> An older sister went to the shambles to plead with the wretch...to spare his victims. (Harriet Beecher Stowe, *Uncle Tom's Cabin*, 1852)

Today the word is used almost exclusively to indicate ruination, both physical and mental.

topsy-turvy—Upside-down, helter-skelter, in a state of utter confusion and disarray. The expression appeared in Shakespeare's *I Henry IV*:

> To push against a kingdom, with his help
> We shall o'erturn it topsy-turvy down.
> (IV,i)

Although the expression is of obscure origin, etymologists have conjectured that its original form was *topside, turnaway*, from which evolved *topside-turvy*, and then finally *topsy-turvy*. The modern form, dating from 1528, retains its figurative meaning of dislocation or chaos.

> A world of inconsistencies, where things are all topsy-turvy, so to speak. (Robert M. Ballantyne, *Shifting Winds*, 1866)

DISORIENTATION
SEE CONFUSION

DOMINATION
SEE CONTROL; MANIPULATION

DOWNFALL
See also FAILURE

come a cropper—To fail badly in any undertaking, particularly after its apparent initial success; to encounter a sudden setback after an auspicious beginning. This figurative meaning derives from the literal *come a cropper* 'to fall or be thrown headlong from a horse.' Although the precise origin of the expression is not known, it may be related to the earlier phrase *neck and crop* meaning 'bodily, completely, altogether.' Both literal and figurative uses of the expression date from the second half of the 1800s.

come a purler—To be thrown head foremost from one's horse; to be knocked to the ground face forward; to fail badly, as in business. This colloquial expression, although often applied figuratively to indicate a failure or a fiasco, is more frequently used literally to describe a bad fall.

> All went well till...on a very slippery surface I came an awful 'purler' on my shoulder. (H. G. Ponting, *Great White South*, 1921)

One definition of the word *purl*, 'to turn head over heels,' gave birth to the colloquial term *purler*. Originally denoting a fall forward from a horse, *purler* later came to signify any fall. The term has been in use since the early 1800s.

Custer's last stand—An all-out, noble effort that ends in utter, embarrassing failure. In June of 1876, U.S. General George A. Custer's troops were annihilated by Sioux warriors under Sitting Bull at the Battle of Little Big Horn. Since then, *Custer's last stand* has gained currency as a phrase used in comparisons to emphasize those aspects of a given situation which fit the pattern of an all-out effort negated by total defeat, as established by the historical Custer's last stand.

go to the well once too often—To make use of a trick or device once too often, so that one is finally thwarted; to try to carry on past one's ability to perform; to deplete one finances. This expression, dating from at least the 14th century, is derived from the parable of taking a pitcher to the well so often that eventually it gets dropped and broken. After he was defeated by "Gentleman Jim" Corbett for the heavyweight championship of the world on September 7, 1892, John L. Sullivan remarked:

The old pitcher went to the well once too often.

hoist with [one's] own petard—See REVERSAL.

meet [one's] Waterloo—To suffer a crushing and decisive defeat; to succumb to the pressures of a predicament, tragedy, or other unfavorable situation; to meet one's match; to get one's comeuppance. This expression alludes to the Battle of Waterloo (1815) in which Napoleon was decisively vanquished by the Duke of Wellington.

Every man meets his Waterloo at last. (Wendell Phillipps, in a speech, November 1, 1859)

the slippery slope—The path to hell; the road to destruction, ruin, or oblivion; the downhill route to moral degradation; the skids. The place of punishment or damnation is, in most religions, pictured as being in the underworld, a place to which one must travel downward. Hence, the road to hell is usually pictured as a slope upon which one finds it difficult to regain his balance or grip once he begins the downward trend. Tennyson makes allusion to that fall in his poem, *Vision of Sin* (1842).

At last I heard a voice upon the slope
Cry to the summit, "Is there any hope?"

DRINKING
SEE FOOD AND DRINK

all mops and brooms—Intoxicated; half-drunk. In use since the early 19th century, the phrase is of uncertain origin. One conjecture is that the *mop* of the expression derives from that word's use in some districts of England for the annual fairs at which servants were hired, and at which much drinking was done. Women seeking employment as maids reputedly carried mops and brooms to indicate the type of work sought. Thomas Hardy's use of the expression in *Tess of the D'Urbervilles* (1891) makes its meaning clear:

> There is not much doing now, being New Year's Eve, and folks mops and brooms from what's inside 'em.

barfly—A hanger-on at a bar; an alcoholic or heavy drinker; a barhopper. This U.S. slang phrase was in print as early as 1928.

> Andy Jackson, Kit Carson and General Grant—all good American barflies in their day. (B. de Casseres, *American Mercury*, August 1928)

This early use of *barfly* implies a goodnatured backslapping attitude, without the stigma attached to heavy drinking. Today, calling someone a barfly is an insult; the label is often used judgmentally to describe a woman who flits from one bar to another.

brick in [one's] hat—Intoxicated; drunk; in one's cups. The origin of this American expression is rather obscure. An interesting explanation, attributed to one Timothy W. Robinson of Morrill, Maine, appears in the April 1948 issue of *American Speech*.

> Then they (matches) were made so that one using them had to have a brick to scratch them on, and the saying was that he carried a brick in his hat, so when anyone had been to the store and walked a little crooked, the boys would say 'he had a brick in his hat.'

Whether Mr. Robinson was being whimsical in his explanation cannot be ascertained; in any event, a more plausible explanation attributes the phrase to the loss of equilibrium anyone would experience from carrying the additional weight of a brick on his head.

> Her husband had taken to the tavern, and often came home very late "with a brick in his hat." (Henry W. Longfellow, *Kavanagh*, 1849)

drink like a fish—To drink excessively, particularly alcoholic beverages; to drink hard. The allusion is to the way many fish swim with their mouths open, thus seeming to be drinking continuously. This popular simile, dating from at least 1640, is usually used to describe a drinker with an extraordinary capacity to put away liquor.

drunk as a fiddler—Highly intoxicated, inebriated; three sheets to the wind. In the past, fiddlers received free drinks as payment for their services. Thus, their predictable and notorious overindulging gave rise to this popular expression.

drunk as a lord—Intoxicated, soused, blind or dead drunk, pickled. In the 18th and 19th centuries, not only was gross intoxication prevalent, but men prided themselves on the amount they could consume at one sitting. It was considered a sign of gentility to overindulge. Thus, it was not an uncommon sight to behold dinner guests helplessly sprawled under the table in front of their chairs, having successfully drunk each other "under the table."

drunk as Davy's sow—Extremely drunk or inebriated. According to Grose's *Classical Dictionary of the Vulgar Tongue* (1785), this expression arose from the following circumstances.

> A pub keeper in Hereford, David Lloyd, had a sow with six legs which he kept on public display. One day, after his wife had imbibed a bit too heavily, she retired to the pig sty to sleep it off. To some customers he brought out to see his porcine oddity, Davy exclaimed, "There is a sow for you! Did you ever see the like?" Whereupon one viewer replied, "Well, it's the drunkest sow I ever beheld." From that day Mr. Lloyd's wife was known as Davy's sow.

The expression has been in use since about 1670, sometimes in the form *drunk as David's sow*.

> When he comes home . . . as drunk as David's sow, he does nothing but lie snoring all night long by my side. (Nathan Bailey, tr. *Erasmus Colloquies*, 1725)

feel as if a cat has kittened in [one's] mouth—To have an extremely distasteful sensation in the mouth as a result of drunkenness; the morning-after blues. This expression, one of the more graphic and picturesque, is used to describe the taste in one's mouth that often accompanies a hangover. It is first cited in the 1618 play *Amends for Ladies* by Nathaniel Field, a British playwright.

fishy about the gills—Suffering the after-effects of excessive drinking; hung over. In this expression, *gills* carries its figurative meaning of the skin beneath the jaws and ears, a place where the symptoms of crapulence are often manifested. The phrases *blue around the gills* and *green around the gills* carry similar meanings, often extended to include the deleterious consequences of gross overeating.

full as a tick—Extremely drunk, loaded, smashed; also *full as an egg* or *full as a bull*. A tick is a bloodsucking parasite that attaches itself to the skin of men and certain animals. It buries its head in the flesh and gradually becomes more and more bloated as it fills up with blood. This Australian and New Zealand slang expression dates from the late 19th century.

half-cocked—Partially drunk; tipsy. This American colloquialism, often shortened to merely *cocked*, is of unknown origin, though it may have some relationship to *half-cocked* 'foolish, silly.'

half seas over—Thoroughly drunk, intoxicated; having had a few too many, a mite tipsy. Authorities agree that the term's origin is nautical, but they have widely divergent explanations of its meaning. Those who say the expression means 'half-drunk' move from its early literal meaning of 'halfway across the sea' to the later figurative 'halfway to any destination' or 'halfway between one state and another.' Others see in it the image of a ship nearly on its side, about to founder and sink; hence, they consider the term descriptive of one decidedly unsteady due to drink, lurching and staggering, barely able to maintain his balance and likely to fall at any minute.

have a jag on—To be drunk, to be inebriated or intoxicated, to be loaded. This U.S. slang expression apparently derives from the dialectal and U.S. sense of *jag* 'a load, as of hay or wood, a small cartload.' By extension, *jag* came to mean a "load" of drink, or as much liquor as a person can carry.

> Others with the most picturesque "jags" on, hardly able to keep their feet. (*The Voice* [N.Y.], August 1892)

have a package on—Drunk; loaded; having really tied one on. More common in Britain than in the U.S., this expression may have arisen as a variation of *tie a bag on*.

have the sun in [one's] eyes—To be intoxicated or drunk, to be under the influence; also the slang phrase *to have been in the sun*. The expression may be a euphemistic explanation of the unsteady walk of one who has had a few too many, implying that his stagger is due to sun blindness. Another possibility is that the phrase refers to the red color one's complexion acquires or the bloodshot eyes resulting from too much sun as well as from too much drink. The expression dates from at least 1770.

> Last night he had had "the sun very strong in his eyes." (Charles Dickens, *The Old Curiosity Shop*, 1840)

in bed with [one's] boots on—Drunk, extremely intoxicated; passed out. The reference is, of course, to one so inebriated that he cannot take his boots off before going to bed.

in [one's] cups—Intoxicated, inebriated. This expression has been common since the 18th century. Because of its literary and euphemistic tone, it is now often employed jocularly. Jeremy Bentham used the phrase in an 1828 letter to Sir F. Burdett:

> I hear you are got among the Tories, and that you said once you were one of them: you must have been in your cups.

An early variant, now obsolete, is *cupped*.

> Sunday at Mr. Maior's much cheer and wine,
> Where as the hall did in the parlour dine;
> At night with one that had been shrieve I sup'd,

Well entertain'd I was, and half well cup'd.
(John Taylor, *Works*, approx. 1650)

in the altitudes—Light-headed; giddy; drunk. *In the altitudes*, as opposed to *having both feet planted on the ground*, is one of many similar expressions meaning drunk. Attributed to the British dramatist and poet Ben Jonson, it is clearly analogous to contemporary expressions such as *high*, *spacey*, *flying*, and *in the ozone*.

in the bag—Drunk; often *half in the bag*. This may be a shortened version of the now infrequently heard *tie a bag on*, which may itself be related to *bag* as nautical slang for 'pot of beer.' The precise origin is unknown.

jug-bitten—Intoxicated. This obsolete expression is derived from the figurative sense of the liquid contents of a jug.

> When any of them are wounded, potshot, jug-bitten, or cup shaken, . . . they have lost all reasonable faculties of the mind. (John Taylor, *Works*, 1630)

like an owl in an ivy bush—See VISAGE.

malt above the meal—Under the influence of alcohol; in one's cups; drunk. The reference in this expression is to the use of malt to make alcoholic beverages; therefore, a person who lets the malt take priority over food is losing control. First used in the late 1500s, the term is also used to indicate that one is verging on alcoholism.

> "Come, come, Provost," said the lady, rising, "if the malt gets above the meal with you, it is time for me to take myself away." (Sir Walter Scott, *Redgauntlet*, 1824)

one over the eight—Slightly drunk, tipsy; one alcoholic drink or glass too many. One could infer from this British colloquial expression that a person should be able to drink eight pints or glasses of beer without appearing drunk or out of control. *One over the eight* appeared in print by 1925.

on the sauce—Drinking heavily and frequently, boozing it up, hitting the bottle; alcoholic, addicted to alcoholic beverages; also to *hit the sauce* 'to drink excessively.' *Sauce* has been a slang term for hard liquor since at least the 1940s.

> He was already as a kid (like General Grant as a boy) on the sauce in a charming schoolboy way. (S. Longstreet, *The Real Jazz Old and New*, 1956)

pie-eyed—Drunk, intoxicated, inebriated, loaded.

> He is partial to a "shot of gin," and on occasion will drink till he is "pie-eyed." (*T. P.'s and Cassell's Weekly*, September 1924)

The origin of this term is confusing, since drunkenness tends to cause the eyes to narrow, just the opposite of what *pie-eyed* implies.

put to bed with a shovel—To be extremely drunk, dead drunk; to bury a corpse. The more common, former sense of the phrase refers to an extraordinarily intoxicated person who requires much assistance in getting home to bed. The latter, less figurative meaning, from which the former probably derives, is an obvious allusion to burial of a corpse. The expression is rarely used.

queer in the attic—See ECCENTRICITY.

shoot the cat—See ILL HEALTH.

three sheets in the wind—Very unsteady on one's feet due to excessive indulgence in drink; barely able to stand or walk without weaving and lurching and swaying about. Though *three sheets to the wind* is more commonly heard today, *three sheets in the wind* is the more accurate term. This expression for drunkenness is another creation of some metaphorically minded sailor—*in the wind* being the nautical term describing the lines or 'sheets' when unattached to the clew of the sails, thus allowing them to flap without restraint. Older ships often had three sails, and if the sheets of all three were "in the wind," the ship would lurch about uncontrollably. The currency of *three sheets to the wind* may be due to the erroneous belief that the sheets are the sails, rather than the lines that control them. This expression has been used figuratively to mean drunkenness since the early 19th century.

tie one on—To go on a drunken tear; to get drunk. This very common American slang expression is probably an elliptical variation of *to tie a bag on*, which in turn could have spawned the phrase *in the bag*, all of which have the same meaning. It is uncertain whether they are related to the supposed nautical slang use of *bag* 'pot of beer.'

under the table—Drunk, intoxicated to the point of stupefaction; not only too drunk to stand, but too drunk to maintain a sitting position. The expression derives from the days when excessive consumption of liquor was the mark of a gentleman. In subtle oneupmanship the lords would vie in "drinking each other under the table."

under the weather—See ILL HEALTH.

up to the gills—Drunk, intoxicated; really soused, pickled. When used in reference to human beings, *gills* refers to the flesh under the jaws and ears. So one who has consumed liquor "up to the gills" has imbibed a considerable quantity.

wine of ape—At the point of drunkenness where one becomes surly; extremely intoxicated to the point of being incoherent or obnoxious. According to early Rabbinical literature, once when Noah was planting grape vines, Satan appeared to him and killed a lamb, a lion, an ape, and a pig to teach Noah that there are four stages which a man goes through in his drunkenness: in the first stage, or when he first begins to drink, he is like the lamb; in the second stage, like the lion; in the third stage, like the ape; and in the final or fourth stage, like the sow. The French *Kalendrier et Compost des Bergiers* (1480) also lists four stages, but as: the choleric man has *vin de lyon*, the sanguine *vin de singe*, the phlegmatic *vin de mouton*, and the melancholic *vin de pourceau*. Geoffrey Chaucer, in *The Manciple's Prologue*, the penultimate of *The Canterbury Tales* (1387–1400), has the manciple satirically describe the cook as being so inebriated that he is, neither playful nor jolly, but surly and dull.

I trowe that ye dronken han wyn ape.

DURATION
SEE ENDURANCE; TIME

DURESS
SEE COERCION

ECCENTRICITY
See also FATUOUSNESS

barmy on the crumpet—Eccentric; a bit daft; wacko. This picturesque British expression plays on *barmy* 'balmy, foolish' and *barmy* 'yeasty'—a crumpet being a breadlike muffin, here metaphorically standing for one's head.

bug house—Lunatic asylum; insane; extremely eccentric; crazy. This expression, dating from about 1800, is a slang term for the building or institution that accommodates the mentally deficient. The phrase apparently has its source in a slang expression for the inmates, *bugs*, coined because they seem to move about in a purposeless manner, like small insects.

> Thet thar man yer've jest hired's a lunatic, or was, last I knew. Was in the bughouse a long spell, anyhow. (Bertha Damon, *A Sense of Humus*, 1943)

Shortly after its inception as a noun, the term added the function of an adjective or an adverb, as in, "He is completely bughouse now." A related term *funny house* also denotes a mental institution.

> Who put me in your private funny house? (Raymond Chandler, *Farewell, My Lovely*, 1940)

cockeyed—Confused; eccentric; chaotic; somewhat intoxicated; out of kilter. This term, originally designating a person who is cross-eyed or has a squint, may derive from the actions of a cock, which tilts his head and rolls his eyes as he struts about the farmyard. The term, dating from about 1800, is in current use, usually employed figuratively to signify a state of confusion, misalignment, or inebriation.

> It's all cockeyed that a man who makes his living with a pen would rather wallow in a greasy boat bilge. (F. Tripp, *Associated Press Release*, July 31, 1950).

crackpot—Eccentric; somewhat mad; a harmless fanatic. The allusion here is to the similarity of a crack in a pot, probably earthenware, to a crack in the brainpan. Dating from at least the 16th century, the term has somehow taken on the connotation of fanaticism, of extremism as seen in so-called mad scientists.

> Crackpotism finds it hard to get a foothold in the warm Florida sands. (*Harpers Magazine*, February 1955)

A related term, *crack-brained*, implies a less extreme case of eccentricity.

> The crack-brained bobolink courts his crazy mate,
> Poised on a bulrush tipsy with his weight.
> (Oliver Wendell Holmes, *Spring*, 1852)

Doolally tap—Eccentric or neurotic behavior; temporary dementia. In the 19th century British soldiers who had completed their Indian service were sent to Deolali, a sanatorium in Bombay, to wait a troopship departing for home. They often had to wait for extended periods of time; as a result boredom set in, and they often got into trouble. Some were jailed, some acquired venereal diseases, and others became mentally disturbed. Their peculiar behavior became known as the *Doolally tap*, *tap* being the Hindustani word for fever. Although the Deolali sanatorium was closed shortly after 1900, the expression is used occasionally today to indicate mental disorder.

flake—One who is unconventional or eccentric; an offbeat person; a screwball; a nut. This word is a noun derivative of the adjective *flaky*, a 1950s slang term, of uncertain origin, used to denote unconventionality or eccentricity in a person.

> Republicans refer to him as the granola governor, appealing to flakes or nuts. (*The New York Times*, May 20, 1979)

Both terms received a boost in popularity during the 1960s when sports journalists began using them frequently to refer to wacky baseball players and some of their scatterbrained activities.

have a moonflaw in the brain—To be a lunatic; to behave in a very bizarre or peculiar manner. A *moonflaw* is an abnormality or idiosyncrasy ascribed to lunar influence. This now obsolete expression appeared in Brome's *Queen and Concubine* (1652):

I fear she has a moonflaw in her brains;
She chides and fights that none can look upon her.

have a screw loose—To be eccentric, crotchety, or neurotic; to be irregular or amiss. As early as 1884, the phrase *loose screw* was used figuratively to apply to a flawed condition or state of affairs.

I can see well enough there's a screw loose in your affairs. (Charles Dickens, *The Life and Adventures of Martin Chuzzlewit*, 1884)

A more recent and increasingly common figurative meaning applies *have a screw loose* to states of mind or mental health. This slang meaning is used in regard to whimsical, unusual behavior rather than to disturbed or sick behavior, although the phrase tends to conjure up images of "falling apart" or "breaking down." A British variant is *have a tile loose*.

have bats in [one's] belfry—To be eccentric, bizarre, crazy, daft. The erratic flight of bats in bell towers interferes with the proper ringing and tone of the bells, just as crazy notions darting about one's brain weaken its ability to function. The slang term *batty* is a derivative of this phrase, which appeared as early as 1901 in a novel of G. W. Peck:

They all thought a crazy man with bats in his belfry had got loose. *(Peck's Red-Haired Boy)*

The analogy between sanity and finely tuned bells is an old one; its most famous expression is in Ophelia's description of the "mad" Hamlet:

Now see that noble and most sovereign reason,
Like sweet bells jangled, out of tune and harsh.
(III,i)

midsummer madness—Extreme folly; the height of madness. In 16th-century England midsummer madness was generally believed to be caused by the midsummer moon, the lunar month in which the summer solstice (about June 21) falls. During that period it was supposed that lunacy was prevalent because hot weather made one especially susceptible to lunar influences. In Shakespeare's *Twelfth Night*, Olivia, commenting on Malvolio's strange remarks, says:

Why, this is very midsummer madness. (III,iv)

A related term, to *have but a mile to midsummer*, indicates a touch of lunacy; i.e., one doesn't have far to go to be *round the bend*.

Miss Nancy—A prissy, overprecise man; a man who exhibits effeminate mannerisms and speech; a foppish youth; a homosexual male. This expression, originally conceived in Britain about 1824, is used to designate any male who demonstrates decided feminine characteristics.

I think a dash of femininity in a man is good; but I hate a 'Miss Nancy'. (Mrs. Lynn Linton, *The Speaker*, July 20, 1901)

HAVE A SCREW LOOSE

Although occasionally used to insinuate that a man is homosexual, more common terms for homosexuality are *Nancy boy*; *queer*; *ginger*, from Cockney rhyming slang *ginger beer*, rhyming with *queer*; and *queen*, a shortened form of *Queen of the May*.

> The room beyond my beaverboard wall is occupied by a colored queen who always keeps his door open; well, not always but always when he's plucking his eyebrows. (Edward Albee, *The Zoo Story*, 1959)

off [one's] trolley—Crazy, demented; in a confused or befuddled state of mind; ill-advised; senile. This expression alludes to the once-common spectacle of a motorman's attempts to realign the contact wheel of a trolley car with the overhead wire. Since this contact wheel is also called a "trolley," *off one's trolley* may refer either to the conductor's actions or to the fact that when the wires are "off the trolley," the vehicle no longer receives an electric current and is, therefore, rendered inoperative.

> The medium is clear off her trolley, for my father has been dead [for] three years. (Warren Davenport, *Butte and Montana Beneath the X-Ray*, 1908)

A similar expression is *slip one's trolley* 'to become demented.' In the more widely used variation, *off one's rocker*, *rocker* is most often said to refer to the curved piece of wood on which a cradle or chair rocks. But since both *off one's trolley* and *off one's rocker* became popular about the time streetcars were installed in major American cities, and since *rocker*, like *trolley*, also means the wheel or runner that makes contact with an overhead electricity supply, it is more likely that the *rocker* of the expression carries this latter meaning.

> When asked if he had swallowed the liniment, he said, "Yes, I was off my rocker." (*Daily News*, June 29, 1897)

out in the sun too long—Crazy; daft; in a confused state of mind; eccentric; bizarre. This American expression, dating from the early 1900s, alludes to the effect that the sun can have on the mind if is exposed to its heat for too long. It is usually used in a jocular vein.

queer in the attic—Eccentric or feebleminded; intoxicated. In this expression, attic carries its British slang meaning of 'the mind'; thus, this colloquialism alludes to stupidity, insanity, or drunkenness, all of which may generate bizarre behavior.

round the bend—Insane, crazy. In this British expression, *bend* describes one's mental faculties as being 'out of alignment, bent, or out of kilter.'

> Right round the bend ... I mean ... as mad as a hatter. (John I. M. Stewart, *The Guardian*, 1955)

Related expressions are *go round the bend* and *be driven round the bend*.

EFFORT
SEE EXERTION

ELATION
SEE ENJOYMENT

ENDURANCE
See also PERSEVERANCE

bite the bullet—To suffer pain without expressing fear; to grit one's teeth and do what has to be done. This phrase derives from the supposed practice of giving a wounded soldier a bullet to bite on to channel his reaction to intense pain. This practice preceded the first use of anesthesia (in the U.S.) in 1844. By 1891, the phrase was used figuratively.

> Bite on the bullet, old man, and don't let them think you're afraid.
> (Rudyard Kipling, *The Light that Failed*, 1891)

It is analogous to other phrases describing rituals such as *take a deep breath* and *grit your teeth*, which refer to preparing oneself or pulling oneself together in order to experience or do something unpleasant.

creaking gate hangs long on its hinges—Because a gate creaks, one must not assume it has outlived its usefulness; frail people often outlive presumably healthier people. This expression is most commonly used to assure the elderly or infirm that life can be meaningful in spite of aches and pains. Originating in the 1700s, the term is heard occasionally today.

> Your mother may yet live a score of years. Creaky gates last longest.
> (S. Baring Gould, *Mehalah*, 1880)

A variant, *a creaking cart goes long on its wheels*, carries the same meaning.

keep the pot boiling—Keep things going; maintain everyone's interest in the matter at hand; bring in enough money so as to earn a living. The most common sense for this phrase is 'provide for one's livelihood,' in other words, provide enough fuel to keep activity going. This expression came into use during the early 17th century.

> I think this piece will help to boil my pot. (John Wolcott [Peter Pindar],
> *The Bard Complimenteth Mr. West*, 1790)

Burton Stevenson in *The Home Book of Proverbs, Maxims and Familiar Phrases* (1948) theorizes that Wolcott's quotation may be responsible for the birth of the familiar literary term *potboiler*, 'an inferior piece of writing.'

roll with the punches—To endure with equanimity, not to be thrown by the blows of fate; to be resilient, bending slightly under pressure then bouncing back; to have the balanced perspective that comes of experiencing hardship. This common metaphor obviously owes its origin to pugilism.

stand the gaff—To endure punishment, criticism, or ridicule; to sustain oneself through a period of stress or hardship; to keep one's chin up. In this expression, *gaff* may refer to the steel spurs worn by fighting cocks, or it may derive from a Scottish term for noisy and abusive language.

> Neil has got to stand the gaff for what he's done. (W. M. Raine, *B. O'Connor*, 1910)

take it on the chin—To face adversity courageously; to withstand punishment, to persevere against the odds; to bounce back from hardship with an undefeated attitude. This American slang expression originated in boxing.

> I liked the Williams' because of the way they took life on the chin. (D. Lytton, *Goddam White Man*, 1960)

ENJOYMENT

aim to please—To attempt to furnish pleasure or enjoyment for others; to intend to make things satisfactory for another; to try to satisfy. This phrase is frequently heard in restaurants, motels, and other places of business that furnish service to paying customers. It is sometimes posted as a motto in businesses of lesser quality, "We aim to please," or "Our aim is to please," the expression intended to cover up for a lack of genuine good service. The punsters' version of this expression is sometimes seen as a graffito on the walls of public restrooms: "We aim to please; your aim will help."

get a bang out of—To derive pleasure from, to get a thrill from, to get a charge out of. In this common American expression, *bang* carries its slang meaning of intense exhilaration.

> He seems to be getting a great bang out of the doings. (Damon Runyon, *Guys and Dolls*, 1931)

get a charge out of—To become physically or mentally exhilarated; to enjoy greatly; to get a kick out of. This expression, derived from the physical jolt caused by an electric charge, is commonplace in the United States, but is somewhat less frequently heard in Great Britain.

> It seems to me that people get a bigger charge out of their grandchildren than they did from their own offspring. (*The New York Times Magazine*, May 1963)

get [one's] kicks—To feel a surge of pleasure or enjoyment; to derive excitement from something; to be stimulated. This expression, coined by jazz musicians during the late 1920s, alludes to the stimulating impact caused by a sudden jolt. It was long used in particular reference to the onrush of stimulation felt when certain drugs, such as heroin, take effect.

> Sock cymbal's enough to give me my kicks, man, even on the top of a cigar box with a couple of pencils. (Douglass Wallop, *Night Life*, 1953)

lick [one's] chops—To eagerly anticipate, especially in reference to food; to take great delight or pleasure in, to relish. In this expression, *chops* refers to the mouth or lips. *Lick* refers to the action of the tongue in response to the excessive salivation that often precedes or accompanies the enjoying of food. By extension, one can "lick one's chops" over any pleasurable experience.

life of Riley—A prosperous or luxurious life; the easy life; life high off the hog. Most scholars agree that this expression had its origin in a comic song written by Pat Rooney in the 1880s. Describing what Riley would do if he suddenly came into money, the song comments in the chorus:

Is that Mr. Riley, can anyone tell?
Is that Mr. Riley that owns the hotel?
Well, if that's Mr. Riley they speak of so highly,
Upon my soul, Riley, you're doing quite well.

Some versions of the song spell the name *Reilly*. Another less plausible version of the genesis of the phrase alludes to James Whitcomb Riley, the poet, and his images of barefoot boys and lazy summer days.

He was having a wonderful time. He was living the life of Riley.
(Samuel Hopkins Adams, *The Incredible Era*, 1939)

music to the ears—Pleasing or agreeable news, good tidings, just what one wanted to hear; usually in the phrase *that's music to my ears*. Good news is as pleasant to hear as sweet music.

play for love—To play a game, especially cards, without stakes; to play for fun. This expression is simply a 19th-century term for the modern *play for fun*, i.e., to play the game simply for the enjoyment of it, not to try to win money or prizes.

I play over again for love, as the gamesters phrase it, games for which I
once paid so dear. (Charles Lamb, *New Year's Eve*, 1821)

A more recent slang variant is *play for grins*.

pleasure bent—A propensity for enjoying oneself; a tendency to get a kick out of things; eager to enjoy. This term, in which *bent* means 'inclination toward' or 'leaning in favor of,' is obvious in its connotation. The first written example of the phrase appears in William Cowper's *John Gilpin's Ride* (1782).

O'erjoyed was he to find
That, though on pleasure she was bent,
She had a frugal mind.

In modern slang the term is sometimes heard in reference to bowlegs on a woman, an obviously carnal reference.

stolen sweets—Things obtained by stealth, seeming to taste better; things gained illicitly and having an attractive aura of intrigue about them. The idea of stolen objects being more palatable to the tongue goes back at least to the days of Solomon who said:

> Stolen waters are sweet, and bread eaten in secret is pleasant. (Proverbs 9:17)

Thomas Randolph's drama, *Amyntos* (1638), which was translated from its original Latin by the poet Leigh Hunt, contains the first known use of the term *stolen sweets*.

> Stolen sweets are always sweeter,
> Stolen kisses much completer,
> Stolen looks are nice in chapels,
> Stolen, stolen be your apples.

tickle [one's] fancy—To appeal to someone, to please, to make happy, to delight, to amuse.

> Such . . . was the story that went the round of the newspapers at the time, and highly tickled Scott's fancy. (John G. Lockhart, *Memoirs of the Life of Sir Walter Scott*, 1837)

Tickle in this phrase means 'to excite agreeably' and *fancy* is equivalent to 'imagination.' Figurative use of this popular expression dates from about the late 18th century.

warm the cockles of the heart—To induce sensations of joy, comfort, or love. The cockle, a palatable mollusk, was often compared to the heart by early anatomists because of its shape and valves. Furthermore, the scientific name for cockle is the Greek *cardium* 'heart.' The phrase enjoys frequent use today, usually in reference to the kindling of pleasurable emotions.

> An expedition . . . which would have delighted the very cockles of your heart. (Scott, in Lockhart, *Letters*, 1792)

ENTIRETY
SEE INCLUSIVENESS; TOTALITY

EQUIVALENCE

even steven—Equal; fair; on a basis of share and share alike; without advantage to either side. Although the source of this expression is uncertain, it is often attributed to Jonathan Swift, who wrote, in a *Letter to Stella* (January 20, 1711):

> "Now we are even," quoth Steven, when he gave his wife six blows to one.

At any event, the phrase became popular in both the United States and Britain and is frequently heard in modern conversation in both countries.

> Give me the hundred and fifty, and we'll call it even steven. (Dashiell Hammett, *Blood Money*, 1945)

neck and neck—Even, equal, on a par; abreast, at the same pace. Based on available citations, figurative use of this expression is as old as the literal horseracing one, both dating from the early 19th century. It still finds frequent application.

> Production ran neck and neck in the studios, but the second version... reached the public screen last. (*The Times*, June 1955)

nip and tuck—So close as to be of uncertain outcome; neck and neck, on a par, even; up in the air, questionable. This chiefly U.S. term is of puzzling origin and inconsistent form, appearing in print in the 1800s as *rip and tuck*, *nip and tack*, and *nip and chuck*, before assuming its present *nip and tuck*. Its original restriction to contexts describing close contests, usually athletic, lends credence to the claim that it originated as a wrestling term (Barrère and Leland, *Dictionary of Slang*, 1890). The expression is now employed in much broader contexts, indicative of any kind of uncertainty.

> It is nip and tuck whether such a last great achievement of the bipartisan foreign policy can be ratified before ... the Presidential race. (*The Economist*, May 1948)

pull devil, pull baker—Even; equal; each is as bad as the other. This expression, dating from the early 1700s, refers to the public's opinion of bakers. From the Middle Ages until the 1800s, bakers were considered to be underhanded fellows who overcharged for their bread and thus were prime targets for the devil. One of the old puppet shows presented a figurative tug-of-war between a baker and the devil, who had come for the baker's soul. The term *devil's dozen*, twelve plus one for the devil, establishes the association between devil and baker even more closely. In Rolf Boldrewood's *Robbery under Arms* (1888), Captain Starlight, a bush ranger, i.e., an outlaw operating in Australian bush country, comments:

> It's all fair pulling, "pull devil, pull baker," someone has to get the worst of it. Now it's us [bushrangers], now it's them [police] that gets...rubbed out.

strike a balance—To achieve a position between two extremes; to take an intermediate position; to calculate the difference between two sides of a ledger; to attain mental tranquillity. The allusion in this phrase is to a set of balance scales and the equality of weight on each side. The first reference to the image given in the *OED* is:

> Those rewards and punishments by which ... the balance of good and evil in this life is to be struck. (Bishop John Wilkins, *New World*, 1638)

swings and roundabouts—Six of one and a half dozen of the other; bad luck one day, good luck the next. This Briticism is simply a shortened version of a longer expression, *what one loses on swings, he gains on roundabouts*; in other words, what one loses one way he gains another. The allusion is to common amusements to be found at playgrounds and fairs.

Roundabout is the British term for a merry-go-round, and *swing* is a term common in meaning to both England and the United States.

> In money matters, as in most other things, one is prepared to make up on the swings what one loses on the roundabouts. (F. B. Young, *A Man About the House*, 1942)

A related term derived from the fishing industry is *lose in hake, gain in herring*. Although hake are an edible fish, they attack herring; therefore, herring fishermen attempt to drive hake away from their fisheries.

> What we lose in hake, we shall have in herring. (Richard Carew, *The Survey of Cornwall*, 1602)

ERRONEOUSNESS

all wet—Totally mistaken, in error; perversely wrong. This slang expression dates from the early 1930s and is still in common use.

> Alfalfa Bill Murray may be all wet in his stateline bridge and oil production controversies. (*Kansas City Times*, August 29, 1931)

Although the exact origin of *all wet* is unknown, *wet* as a negative word is familiar in phrases such as *wet blanket* and in the British use of *wet* to mean 'feeble or foolish.'

back the wrong horse—To be mistaken in one's judgment, to support a loser. The expression, originally a reference to betting on a losing horse, is now used popularly to denote the support or backing of any losing person or cause.

bad-ball hitter—A person of questionable judgment, so-called from the baseball term for a batter who swings at pitches well outside the strike zone.

bark up the wrong tree—To pursue a false lead; to be misled or mistaken. This Americanism clearly comes from hunting; specifically, according to some, nocturnal raccoon hunting in which the dogs would often lose track of their quarry.

> I told him...that he reminded me of the meanest thing on God's earth, an old coon dog, barking up the wrong tree. (*Sketches and Eccentricities of Col. David Crockett*, 1833)

full of prunes—Mistaken; absolutely wrong; completely misinformed or totally unknowledgeable about the subject; exaggerated. This phrase is a euphemistic method of telling another that what he says does not seem believeable, that he is *full of crap* or *full of shit*, the reference to prunes being to their laxative effect. Two common variants, *full of beans* (in one sense) and *full of hops*, both make the same inference; these foods cause flatulence or intestinal catharsis.

get the wrong sow by the ear—Make a mistake; seize the wrong individual; give an unsatisfactory explanation. This expression, dating from at least the 16th century, is a rustic metaphor for the jeopardy that one might be placed in from dealing with the wrong individual or becoming involved with the wrong person.

> I knew when he first meddled with your Ladyship, that he had a wrong sow by the ear. (John Taylor, *Wit and Mirth*, 1630)

Common variants of this expression are *get the wrong pig by the ear, get the wrong bull by the tail,* and *get hold of the wrong end of the stick.*

in the wrong box—In the wrong place; in a false position; in error. The origin of this expression is uncertain. One plausible explanation attributes the phrase to Cesare Borgia's placing poisoned comfits in a box to be served to a visiting cardinal. However, Borgia's father was served from the wrong box and died. Another explanation assigns the phrase to Lord Lyttleton who complained that whenever he went to Vauxhall, he was *in the wrong box*, for pleasure seemed to be all about him.

> I very much question whether the Clerkenwell Sessions will not find themselves in the wrong box. (Charles Dickens, *Oliver Twist*, 1838)

make a blot—Commit a fault; make an error; expose a man. The reference in this phrase is to the game of backgammon. Dating from at least the Middle Ages, backgammon has remained a popular game through the years. If one leaves a piece exposed during the course of the game, he is in danger of having the piece taken and returned to the starting point; hence he has *made a blot.*

> He is too great a master of his art, to make a blot which may be so easily hit. (John Dryden, *Aeneld: Dedication*, 1698)

The counterplay in backgammon, *hit a blot*, implies taking advantage of another's error.

> You never used to miss a blot, especially when it stands so fair to be hit. (Henry Porter, *The Two Angry Women of Abingdon*, 1599)

miss the cushion—To make a mistake; to fail in an attempt. It has been hypothesized that *cushion* is another word for 'target' or 'mark'; thus, the expression is thought to derive from the unsuccessful attempt of an archer to hit the mark. Now obsolete, *miss the cushion* dates from the early 16th century.

> Thy wits do err and miss the cushion quite. (Michael Drayton, *Eclogues*, 1593)

off base—Badly mistaken, completely wrong. In baseball, a runner leading too far off the base is likely to be thrown out. This expression is also obsolete slang for 'crazy or demented.'

off the beam—Disoriented; incorrect; confused; daft. The reference is to an airplane pilot that has lost, or failed to find, his radio directional signal. Thus, an airplane that is *off the beam* is wandering about helplessly among the clouds. The term has been extended to the human mental condition. It dates from the 1930s.

out in left field—Wildly mistaken, absolutely wrong; disoriented, confused. This American slang term refers to the left outfield position in baseball, a game in which the infield is the center of activity. Nothing inherent in the game, however, makes the left field position more appropriate than the right for inclusion in the expression. Perhaps the negative associations of *left* (clumsiness, backwardness) account for its use.

overshoot the mark—See EXCESSIVENESS.

pull a boner—To make an obvious, stupid mistake, to blunder; to make an embarrassing, amusing slip of the tongue. This originally U.S. slang expression dating from the turn of the century may have derived from the antics of the two end men, Mr. Bones and Mr. Tambo, of the old minstrel shows. The interlocutor would carry on humorous conversations with the end men who sometimes provoked laughter by "pulling a boner."

> Got his signals mixed and pulled a boner. (*American Magazine*, September 1913)

A common variant is *make a boner*.

> This Government has made about every boner possible. (*Spectator*, October 7, 1960)

take in water—To be flawed or weak; to be invalid or unsound. This obsolete expression, dating from the late 16th century, alludes to a vessel that is not watertight. By extension, it applies to flawed ideas or statements.

> All the rest are easily freed; St. Jerome and St. Ambrose in the opinion of some seem to take in water. (Bishop Joseph Hall, *Episcopacie By Divine Right Asserted*, 1640)

wide of the mark—Inaccurate, erroneous, off base; irrelevant, not pertinent. Dating from the 17th century, this expression most likely derives from the unsuccessful attempt of an archer to hit the "mark" or target. Variants of this expression include *far from the mark* and *short of the mark*.

yellow dog under the wagon—Unreliable; untrustworthy; inconstant; erroneous. The origin of this expression, which is seldom heard today, is uncertain; however, it was in popular use throughout 19th-century America. Perhaps some tinker, or some other itinerant peddler, was accompanied by an unreliable yellow dog that would emerge from beneath the wagon and bite passers-by. At any event, *The Spirit of the Times*, a publication for race horse enthusiasts, uses the term to comment rather caustically on the reliability of another publication in its December 19, 1857 edition.

> For *Potomac's* pedigree, see page 407 of 'Edgar's General Stud Book' which is about as long and reliable as that of 'the big yellow dog under the wagon.'

ESCAPE
SEE DEPARTURE

EVIL
SEE UNSCRUPULOUSNESS

EXACERBATION

add fuel to the fire—To make a bad situation worse; to intensify; to say or do something to increase the anger of a person already incensed. Literally adding fuel to a fire increases the strength with which the flames blaze, just as metaphorically adding "something that serves to feed or inflame passion, excitement, or the like... especially love or rage" (*OED*), intensifies the passion.

add insult to injury—To heap scorn on one already injured. The phrase is from the Aesop fable of a baldheaded man who, having been bitten on his pate by a fly, tries to kill the insect. In doing so, he gives himself a painful blow. The fly jeeringly remarks:

> You wished to kill me for a mere touch. What will you do to yourself, since you have added insult to injury?

confusion worse confounded—Chaos compounded or made greater than before. John Milton uses the expression in *Paradise Lost* (1667):

> With ruin upon ruin, rout on rout,
> Confusion worse confounded.

The unusual syntactical structure of this expression may be clarified by noting that the obsolete or archaic meaning of *confound* was 'to overthrow, to bring to ruin' while the obsolete meaning of *confusion* was 'overthrow, ruin.' Thus, the line *confusion worse confounded* follows the pattern of repetition found in the previous line.

cut off [one's] nose to spite [one's] face—To cause one's own hurt or loss through spiteful action; to cause injury to oneself or one's own interests in pursuing revenge. This proverbial expression first appeared in print in 1785, when it was defined in Francis Grose's *A Classical Dictionary of the Vulgar Tongue*:

> He cut off his nose to be revenged of his face. Said of one who, to be revenged on his neighbour, has materially injured himself.

This saying is believed to have come from the French *se couper le nez pour faire dépit à son visage.*

escape the bear and fall to the lion—To be free of one predicament only to get involved in another more trying, complex, or dangerous one; to go from bad to worse. In use as early as the beginning of the 17th century, this expression suggests that there is danger to be met at every turn.

heap Pelion upon Ossa—To make matters worse, to compound or aggravate things; also, to indulge in fruitless or futile efforts. The allusion is to the Greek myth of the giants who unsuccessfully tried to get to Olympus, home of the gods, by stacking Mount Pelion on Mount Ossa.

Job's comforter—One who either intentionally or unwittingly adds to another's distress while supposedly consoling and comforting him. The allusion is to the Biblical Job's three friends who come to commiserate with him over his misfortunes and who instead of consoling him only aggrieve him more by reproving him for his lack of faith and his resentful attitude. The term has been in use since at least 1738.

> You are a Job's comforter with a vengeance. (Mrs. B. M. Croker, *Proper Pride,* 1885)

out of the frying pan into the fire—From bad to worse, from one disastrous situation to one even worse.

> If they thought they could get away from the State by disestablishment, they would find that they were jumping out of the frying-pan into the fire. (*The Guardian,* October 1890)

Use of the expression dates from the early 16th century.

rub salt in a wound—To maliciously emphasize or reiterate something unfavorable or disagreeable with the express purpose of annoying someone; to continually harp on a person's errors or shortcomings, especially those of which he is acutely conscious. Since salt, when placed on an open wound, causes painful stinging and discomfort, to actually *rub* salt into a wound would be excessively cruel and sadistic. Although recent medical research has shown that salt (such as in seawater) actually helps wounds to heal with minimal scarring, it is safe to assume that a person who figuratively rubs salt in a wound is not motivated by therapeutic concern. A popular and more widely used variation is *rub it in.*

> Ye needn't rub it in any more. (Rudyard Kipling, *Captains Courageous,* 1897)

when push comes to shove—When a situation goes from bad to worse; when worse comes to worst; when the going gets tough. In this expression *shove* refers to an exaggerated—bigger and harder—push. Thus, *when push comes to shove* refers to the point at which subtlety gives way to flagrancy.

WHEN PUSH COMES TO SHOVE

EXACTNESS
SEE PRECISION

EXAGGERATION
SEE MENDACITY

EXCELLING
SEE OUTDOING

EXCESSIVENESS

Excessiveness

baker's dozen—Thirteen; a dozen plus one. Bakers at one time reputedly gave an extra roll for every dozen sold in order to avoid the heavy fines levied against those who short-changed their customers by selling lightweight bread. The phrase appeared in the early 17th century in *Tu Quoque* by John Cooke.

bare as a barn—Barren; in need of interior furnishings and accouterments; extremely stark. This American expression, dating from at least the mid-19th century, reflects the condition of the interior of a barn, especially in late spring and early summer when the winter's hay has been consumed and the animals are all outdoors. The term is usually used in a derogatory manner and implies either lack of taste or penury.

> The most contemptuous word that could be applied to an interior in those days was 'bare'—as bare as a barn. (*House and Garden*, April 1982)

blue blazes—Impulsively; rashly; vehemently; in the extreme. This slang expression refers to the blue flames created by the burning of brimstone; hence, a direct reference to hell and the devil. An old superstition ascribed a blue flame to the presence of the devil. In his *History of the Devil* (1726), Daniel Defoe comments:

> That most wise and solid suggestion that when the candles burn blue the Devil is in the room.

In modern use the term is employed almost exclusively to indicate anything excessive, and is usually preceded by *as* or *like*.

> It was as cold as blue blazes. (Howell Vines, *The Green Thicket World*, 1904)

break a butterfly on a wheel—To employ a degree of force or energy disproportionate to the needs of a situation; to overkill. The wheel was formerly an instrument of torture upon which a criminal was stretched and beaten to death. Considering the fragile nature of a butterfly, the analogy is self-evident. The phrase appears in Alexander Pope's *Epistle to Dr. Arbuthnot:*

> Satire or sense, alas! can Sporus feel?
> Who breaks a butterfly upon the wheel?

100

Carthaginian peace—A peace so harsh that it cripples; a treaty with terms so severe that they destroy the defeated nation. This phrase arises from the destruction that Rome wreaked upon Carthage at the conclusion of the Third Punic War in the 2nd century B.C. M. Porcius Cato, after visiting Carthage and recognizing the threat that state represented to Rome, concluded all of his speeches in the Senate with *Delenda est Carthago*, 'Carthage must be destroyed.' His constant warning influenced all of Rome to such a degree that after Carthage had been overwhelmed, the city was obliterated and the earth within and about it was sowed with salt to assure that nothing would ever rise there again. *Delenda est Carthago* has become a proverbial manner of saying "whatever stands in our path to greatness must be eliminated."

die for want of lobster sauce—To die or suffer greatly on account of some minor disappointment, irritation, or disgrace. This expression is said to have had its origins in a sumptuous banquet given by Louis II de Bourbon (the great Condé) for Louis XIV at Chantilly. Legend has it that when the chef was informed that the lobsters which he had intended to make into a sauce had not been delivered in time for the feast, he was so overcome with humiliation that he committed suicide by running upon his sword.

drug on the market—A commodity which is no longer in demand; anything which is so readily available that it tends to be taken for granted or undervalued; a glut on the market. *Drug* alone was used as early as the 1600s; *in the market* was introduced in the 1700s. The phrase "a drug in the market of literature" appeared in Thomas Walter's *A Choice Dialogue Between John Faustus, A Conjurer, and Jack Tory his Friend* (1720). Today *drug on the market* is more frequently heard. Perhaps this expression derives from the fact that drugs induce a dulling effect similar to that caused by too much of anything—in other words, by any type of overindulgence.

enough [something] to choke Caligula's horse—A lot, a great deal, plenty, more than enough. Caligula, Roman emperor from A.D. 37–41, was thought to be insane because of his extravagant claims, his wholesale murdering and banishment of his subjects, and his wild, foolish spending. It is perhaps in reference to this last quality that the expression *enough [something] to choke Caligula's horse* arose. There is, however, no evidence to substantiate this theory, and no theory at all regarding the rest of the phrase.

gingerbread—Garish or tasteless ornamentation; superfluous embellishments. This term is derived from the ornate decorations a baker uses to adorn a gingerbread house. Figuratively, *gingerbread* describes excessive or tacky furnishings and decorations.

> Some people would have crammed it full of gingerbread upholstery, all gilt and gaudy. (Lisle Carr, *Judith Gwynne*, 1874)

101

go overboard—To go to great extremes; to express either overwhelming opposition to or support for a person or cause. One who shifts all his weight to one side of a small boat may literally go overboard. Likewise, one who radically directs all his energies toward one thing figuratively "goes overboard." This very common phrase as used by Dwight MacDonald is cited in *Webster's Third:*

> ... went overboard for heroes and heroines who don't seem so heroic today.

go through the roof—To go beyond prescribed limits; to climb precipitously and unexpectedly. The figurative use of this expression is usually associated with a sudden burst of prosperous financial activity; however, it is also occasionally associated with an extreme fit of passion, especially anger.

> Those who haven't traveled for a couple of years are going on a binge and the market is going through the roof. (*Time*, July 25, 1983)

had it up to here—Unable to continue because of excessive fatigue; in such a state of exhaustion that one is unable to respond any further; so thoroughly annoyed and disgusted that one has lost all interest. This American expression, dating from about 1940, is usually accompanied by a hand gesture pointing to the neck just below the chin line, or to the top of one's ear, to indicate figuratively to what level one has had it.

make two bites of a cherry—Take two turns to do a job when it might be done in one; to do something piecemeal; to separate something into pieces too small. This expression alludes to taking two bites of a cherry rather than popping the whole piece of fruit into one's mouth; i.e., wasting time and motion. The term dates from at least 1500.

> Take it all, man—take it all—never make two bites of a cherry. (Sir Walter Scott, *The Two Drovers*, 1827)

A variant is *make three bites of a cherry*.

nineteen bites to a bilberry—Make a meal of a mouthful; much ado about nothing; go overboard; overdo. This British expression, which dates from the early 17th century, refers to making a major production of an inconsequential act. A *bilberry* is about one-quarter inch in diameter and to make nineteen bites of such a tiny fruit is, to say the least, excessive. A variant is *nineteen bits to a bilberry*.

out Herod Herod—See OUTDOING.

overshoot the mark—To exceed or go beyond prescribed limits; to be off base, irrelevant, or inappropriate. Literally, a missile or other projectile "overshoots the mark" when it misses its target by going above or beyond it. Figuratively, this expression is said of any attempt or idea which errs on the side of excess. Such use dates from the late 16th century.

The greatest fault of a penetrating wit is not coming short of the mark but overshooting it. (*The English Theophrastus*, 1702)

paint the lily—To adorn or embellish an already beautiful object, thereby destroying its delicate balance and rendering it gaudy and overdone; to detract from the natural, full beauty of an object by trying to add ornamentation where none is required. This expression derives from Lord Salisbury's speech in Shakespeare's *King John*:

Therefore, to be possess'd with double pomp,
To guard a title that was rich before,
To gild refined gold, to paint the lily,
To throw a perfume on the violet,
To smooth the ice, or add another hue
Unto the rainbow, or with taperlight
To seek the beauteous eye of heaven to garnish,
Is wasteful, and ridiculous excess.
(IV,ii)

Gild the lily is actually more familiar to most people, although few are aware that it is a corruption of *gild refined gold* and *paint the lily*.

run into the ground—To overdo, to continue beyond a period of effectiveness to the point of counterproductivity; to beat to death. The expression frequently appears in contexts dealing with argument or with utilization of material objects. One runs a topic into the ground when he undermines a point already effectively made because his persistence and long-windedness antagonize his listeners. Objects are "run into the ground" when a user wrings the last ounce of service from them. In either case, what is "run into the ground" is effectively buried.

sow [one's] wild oats—Indulge in excesses during one's youth; behave in a profligate manner. The origin of this expression is obscure, but it may have reference to the Biblical "Whatsoever a man soweth, that shall he also reap." (Galatians 6:7), with the implicit warning against irresponsible behavior, wild oats being utterly useless.

We meane that wilfull and unruly age, which lacketh rypeness and discretion, and (as wee saye) hath not sowed all theyre wyeld Oates. (*Touchstone of Complexions*, 1576)

tempest in a teapot—A great commotion, disturbance, or hubbub over a relatively insignificant matter; excessive agitation or turmoil caused by something of trifling importance. This expression and variations thereof have been common at least since the time of Cicero (106–43 B.C.), as evidenced in *De Legibus:*

Gratidius raised a tempest in a ladle, as the saying is.

The implication, of course, is that something as small as a teapot (or ladle) is hardly an appropriate place for a *tempest* 'violent or stormy disturbance.'

103

What a ridiculous teapot tempest. (*Peterson Magazine,* January 1896) Common variations are *tempest in a teacup* and *storm in a teacup.*

M. Renan's visit . . . to his birthplace in Brittany has raised a storm in the clerical teacup. (*Pall Mall Gazette,* September 19, 1884)

throw out the baby with the bath water—To reject the essential or valuable along with the unimportant or superfluous. This graphic expression appeared in print by the turn of the century. It is frequently used in reference to proposals calling for significant change, such as political and social reforms or largescale bureaucratic reorganization.

Like all reactionists, he usually empties the baby out with the bath. (George Bernard Shaw, *Pen Portraits and Reviews,* 1909)

towering ambition—Aspiration that extends beyond limits; awesome intent of purpose; overweening resolve to get ahead. When a falcon reaches the highest point of its ascent and proceeds to hover at that point, it is said to *tower,* a meaning derived from a comparison to castle towers, the highest points in the countryside during the Middle Ages. Thus, *towering ambition* alludes to a reaching above normal heights.

Nothing less than the writing of a play can satisfy his towering ambition. (*The English Theophrastus,* 1702)

EXCLAMATIONS
SEE LANGUAGE; RETORTS

EXERTION

against the collar—With difficulty; at a disadvantage; requiring constant exertion. The collar in this phrase alludes to a horsecollar. When pulling a heavy load or going up hill, the horse strains *against the collar,* exerting constant, fatiguing effort.

The high road ascends . . . until it comes in sight of Cumner. Every step against the collar yet so gradual is the ascent . . . (Charles Dickens, *Doctor Marigold,* 1868)

The expression dates from about 1850 and has given rise to two other terms, *collar-work* and *work up to the collar.*

blood, sweat, and tears—Adversity, difficulty; suffering, affliction; strenuous, arduous labor. The now common expression is a truncated version of that used by Winston Churchill in addressing the House of Commons shortly after his election as Prime Minister.

I say to the House, as I said to the Ministers who have joined this Government, I have nothing to offer but blood, toil, tears and sweat. (May 13, 1940)

The phrase gained additional currency when it was adopted as the name of a music group popular in the late 1960s.

buckle down—To adopt a no-nonsense attitude of determination and effort; to set aside frivolous concerns or distractions and concentrate on the task at hand. *Buckle down to* dates from 1865, and appears to be but a variation on the earlier *buckle to* or *buckle oneself to*, both of which probably have their antecedents in the act of buckling on armor to prepare for battle.

elbow grease—Strenuous physical effort or exertion; hard physical work or manual labor; vigorous and energetic application of muscle. This expression dates from at least 1672. A hint of its original meaning is provided by the definition found in *A New Dictionary of the Terms Ancient and Modern of the Canting Crew* (1700): "a derisory term for sweat."

get [one's] teeth into—To work with vigor and determination; to come to grips with a task or problem; also, *sink one's teeth into*. This expression may be derived from the greater effort required to chew food than to sip it. Similarly, one who gets his teeth into something of substance is directing a great deal of physical or mental effort into completing the task.

hewers of wood and drawers of water—Common workmen; drudges; slaves; the lowest type of laborers. This Biblical expression is from Joshua 9:21 and, although its literal meaning suggests those who are either in bondage or are the lowest kind of drudges, its figurative reference is to workers who are the backbone of a house of worship. Its most common use is in the literal sense.

> When Foes are o'er come, we preserve them from slaughter,
> To be Hewers of Wood and Drawers of Water.
> (Jonathan Swift, *A Serious Poem*, 1724)

in there pitching—Putting forth one's best effort; working energetically and diligently; directing one's energy and talent toward a specific goal. It is debatable whether the sense of *pitch*, as used here, is originally from baseball or from the sales pitch of a carnival pitchman, reinforced by the greater frequency of the baseball term.

> Everybody on the system is in there pitching, trying to save a locomotive or piece of locomotive. (*Saturday Evening Post*, June 26, 1943)

knuckle down—To apply oneself earnestly to a task; to attack a chore vigorously.

> *Knuckle down* is a particular phrase used by lads at a play called taw, wherein they frequently say, *knuckle down to your taw*, or *fit your hand exactly in the place where your marble lies*. (Dyche and Pardon, *A New General English Dictionary*, 1740)

105

This expression, dating from at least the 17th century, has become generalized so that now it represents any diligent application to the situation at hand.

pump iron—To lift weights; to work out on a weight machine; to be a weight lifter. This expression gained currency in the 1970s, primarily because of Arnold Schwarzenegger's propaganda campaign to make people more aware of the health-giving qualities of weight lifting. Using magazine articles, books, and films, Schwarzenegger and others popularized *pumping iron* so successfully that today the term has become a part of the common vocabulary.

> When Lisa Lyon, 26, met muscleman-actor Arnold Schwarzenegger two years ago . . . she began to pump iron, and—voilà—today the 5'3" cutie can heft 265 lbs. like straw. (*New York Post*, October 19, 1979)

put in [one's] best licks—In America *lick* has come to mean a burst of energy or effort; a further development has yielded the sense of an opportunity to make an effort, as in team sports like baseball, where *last licks* refers to the chance to win given a team that comes to bat in the second half of the ninth inning. Thus, *one's best licks* refers to the opportunity to make a winning effort. The term has been in use since the 1700s.

> I saw comin' my gray mule, puttin' in her best licks, and a few yards behind her was a grizzly. (T. A. Burke, *Polly Peaseblossom's Wedding*, 1851)

put [one's] shoulder to the wheel—To strive, to exert oneself, to make a determined effort, to work at vigorously. The reference is to the teamster of yesteryear who literally put his shoulder to the wheel of his wagon when it got stuck in a rut or in mud in order to help his horses pull it out.

work up to the collar—To labor diligently; to perform strenuous tasks energetically. A beast of burden is not considered to be working at its utmost capacity unless its collar is straining against its neck. This expression sees little use today.

EXPLOITATION

all is fish that comes to his net—See ABILITY.

double dip—To work at a government job while receiving a government pension; to appropriate money twice from a single operation. This term, derived from the underworld term *dip*, 'to pick pocket,' was originally used to describe a retired military person or civil servant who had procured another government job while drawing a pension from his previous service with the government. Today, it has been extended to include state and municipal employees as well as federal employees. *Double dipping* has come to connote unethical behavior on the part of the *double dippers*, especially among those who are receiving disability pensions while working at another job.

> The critics, including many Congressmen, consider "double-dipping" typical of the ways in which the military pension system has become overly generous and helped to inflate military manpower costs. (*The New York Times*, April 10, 1977)

feather [one's] nest—To look after one's own interests; to accumulate creature comforts, money, or material possessions either through one's own efforts or at the expense of others; to be completely selfish, totally unconcerned with the well-being of others. This expression stems from the fact that many birds, after building a nest, line it with feathers to make it warm and more comfortable. The expression *line one's nest* is a variation.

fish in troubled waters—To take advantage of adversity, stress, or unrest for personal gain; to make the best of a bad situation. Fishermen often experience their greatest success when the water is rough. In its figurative use, the phrase implies that though things may be troubled on the surface, at a deeper level, the situation holds potential for gains.

grist for the mill—Any experience, fact, discovery, or object with potential for one's personal profit; a seemingly worthless item employed to one's personal gain or benefit. Grist is unground grain to be converted to meal or flour by milling. In the figurative expression, *grist* is anything that serves as the raw material which a person's talents or abilities transform into something of value.

make hay while the sun shines—To make the most of an opportunity, to take full advantage of an occasion for profit, to be opportunistic. Hay is made by spreading mown grass in the sun to dry, an impossibility if the sun is not shining both when the grass is cut and when it is set out to dry. A variant of the expression dates from at least 1546. It is often used as an admonition to be provident, as it was by an unknown American author in 1788:

> It is better to make hay while the sun shines *against* a rainy day. (*The Politician Out-witted*)

milk—To extract all potential profit from a person or situation, often with connotations of excessiveness or victimization. Used figuratively as early as the beginning of the 16th century, this term derives from the literal act of extracting milk from an animal by manipulating its udder.

> This their painful purgatory... hath of long time but deceived the people and milked them from their money. (John Frith, *A Disputation of Purgatory*, 1526)

Unlike *bleed*, *milk* is not limited in its figurative use to money-related matters.

> To overplay an audience for applause is called milking the audience. (Hixson and Colodny, *Word Ways*, 1939)

To milk someone usually implies taking unfair advantage, and is often heard in the expression *to milk [someone] for all he is worth*.

pick [someone's] brains—To exploit the ideas of another; extract another's knowledge and use it without his permission; to avail oneself of another's artistic concepts. This colloquialism suggests the gathering of the fruit of another's labor, and the profit to be realized by such an act. The term, first used in the early 19th century, has gained fresh popularity since the 1960s with the increasing practice of *brain drain*, the wooing of outstanding scholars, especially scientists, from other countries.

> If one wanted to know what books to read in any line, one had only to pick his brains. (A. C. Benson, *From a College Window*, 1907)

play the field—To remain open to multiple opportunities by not restricting one's role; to engage in a variety of activities, causes, etc., instead of focusing on just one; to socialize with no one person exclusively.

> Japan Plays the Field. Peace and Trade with Everyone. (*The New Republic*, March 1966)

In baseball, the outfielders have the largest area of ground to cover and therefore the widest range of playing room, a fact which probably gave rise to the expression. In addition, an outfielder often rotates among all three outfield positions. This American phrase has been in use since at least 1936.

robber barons—Business and financial tycoons who were merciless in their despoilment of public lands and in the exploitation of people. In the foreword of Matthew Josephson's book, *The Robber Barons* (1934), the author quotes a description by Sir Francis Bacon that could have been formulated specifically for the *robber barons*.

> There are never wanting some persons of violent and undertaking natures, who, so that they may have power and business, will take it at any cost.

Coined in the late 1800s, this term typified a group of powerful financial magnates, who, unrestrained by government regulations or income tax and unhampered by ethical considerations, amassed huge fortunes and tremendous political power by their rapacious misuse of the land and the people. The modern concept of the term has been modified somewhat to include any landowner or businessman who is guilty of exploitation.

> He was...about the greediest and cruelest robber baron in the West. (D. G. Phillips, *Plum Tree*, 1905)

seize the day—To make the most of the day, to live each day to the fullest, to enjoy the present to the utmost; originally, Latin *carpe diem*. This proverbial expression of Epicurean philosophy was apparently first used by the Roman poet and satirist Horace. Both the original Latin and the later English version remain in common use.

> The reckless life of Algeria ... with ... its gay, careless carpe diem camp-philosophy. (Ouida, *Under Two Flags*, 1867)

strike while the iron is hot—To lose no time in acting when an opportunity presents itself, to seize an opportunity to one's advantage, to act when the time is right. A blacksmith heats the iron he is working on until it is red-hot and most malleable before hammering it into the desired shape. The equivalent French phrase is *il faut battre le fer pendant qu'il est chaud*. A variant of the expression dates from at least 1386.

> It will become us to strike while the iron is hot. (W. Dummer, in *Baxter Manuscripts*, 1725)

take time by the forelock—To act quickly in seizing an opportunity, to take full and prompt advantage of an opportunity for gain or advancement. Phaedrus, a Roman fable writer, describes Father Time (also called Father Opportunity) as an old man, completely bald at the back of his head but with a heavy forelock. Thus, a person who takes time by the forelock does not wait until opportunity passes before taking advantage of what it offers. The expression has been attributed to Psittacus of Mitylene, one of the seven sages of Greece. Variants of the expression date from the late 16th century.

work both sides of the street—To avail oneself of every opportunity to attain a given end; to seek support from opposing camps, to court the favor of rival interests; to walk a tightrope or to play both ends against the middle. The phrase probably derives from salesmen's lingo. Currently it is said of one who compromises principle in an attempt to garner some desideratum, who slants his approach or pitch to align with what his listeners will "buy."

> In a crucial election year ... was shrewdly working both sides of the street. (*Time*, cited in *Webster's Third*)

EXPULSION
SEE REFUSAL

EXTEMPORANEOUSNESS
SEE SPONTANEITY

EXTORTION
SEE COERCION; PAYMENT

EXTRAVAGANCE
SEE EXCESSIVENESS

FACIAL APPEARANCE
SEE VISAGE

Failure

FAILURE
See also DOWNFALL

back to the drawing board—An acknowledgment that an enterprise has failed and that one must begin again from scratch, at the initial planning stages. The drawing board in question is the type used by draftsmen, architects, engineers, etc., for blueprints and such schematic designs. A similar phrase is *back to square one*, by analogy to a games board. Its meaning is the same—"We've got to start all over, from the very beginning."

broken reed—An undependable thing; something not to be trusted; an unreliable person. This expression can be traced directly to the Bible.

> Lo, thou trusteth in the staff of this broken reed, on Egypt; whereon if a man lean, it will go into his hand and pierce it: so is Pharaoh King of Egypt to all that trust him. (Isaiah, 36:6)

The term has retained the same symbolic meaning through the years and remains in everyday use.

> You lean upon a broken reed, if you trust to their compassion. (Tobias Smollett, *The Reprisal*, 1757)

[one's] cake is dough—One's project or undertaking has failed, one's expectations or hopes have come to naught; one never has any luck. A cake which comes out of the oven as dough is clearly a total failure. Shakespeare used this now obsolete proverbial expression in *The Taming of the Shrew* (V,i):

> My cake is dough; but I'll in among the rest,
> Out of hope of all but my share of the feast.

damp squib—An enterprise that was to have been a great success, but fizzled out; a lead balloon; a dud. In this British colloquialism, *squib* is another word for a firecracker. If it is damp, it will not explode as expected. It may fizzle or, in some cases, turn out to be a dud.

dead duck—A person or thing that has become completely worthless or has failed; any person or thing that is doomed to failure; a goner. This American slang expression is actually a shortened version of an old pioneer saw, *never waste powder on a dead duck*. From that advice the term *dead duck* came to represent anything that is done in or played out. The expression remains in common use.

WORK BOTH SIDES OF THE STREET

Any politician that doesn't come out 100 percent against the proposed dams . . . will be a dead duck politically. (*New Mexico Quarterly Review*, Spring 1948)

The British equivalent of the American term is *derby duck*.

down the tube—To be lost, gone, finished; failed in a course in school; down the drain; down the pipe. The expression seems an obvious allusion to water going down a drain, but its recent popularity may be attributed to terms used in the sport of surfing. Surfers try to *shoot the tube*, that is, to ride under the curl on a big breaker as it moves toward shore. Since *shooting the tube* requires an awkward stance on the board, and involves an above average chance for failure, *tube it* has become a surfers' slang term for failing an exam or a course in school.

By extension the term *down the tube* came to mean any irretrievable loss. Related terms are *down the drain* and *down the pipe*.

> After all, the President had twice picked Agnew as his running mate. Said one aide: "Let's face it; if Agnew goes down the tube, that rubs off on the old man, too." (*Time*, October 1, 1973)

A variant, *down the tubes*, has the plural form, probably a superfluous addition.

fall by the wayside—To drop out, either from physical or emotional weakness; to give up; to give out; to collapse from sheer physical exhaustion. The metaphorical implication of this phrase is drawn from a person's actually collapsing by the roadside during the course of a journey. The term is used today to symbolize the dropping out of a project or the giving up of a cause, either by one's own accord or because of circumstances. It is also used in a religious sense to indicate one who has gone over to the ways of sin. The British say *fall by the way*.

> If you fall by the way, don't stay to get up again. (Jonathan Swift, *Polite Conversation*, 1738)

the game is up—It's over; all has ended; the plan has come to naught; all is lost. This phrase usually implies the termination of some long-term scheme which has resulted in failure. In Shakespeare's *Cymbeline*, (III,iii), Belarius, who has kidnapped and raised Cymbeline's two sons as if they were his own, realizes that his masquerade is about to end.

> Myself Belarius, that am Morgan call'd, They take for their natural father. The game is up.

An equivalent term was used as early as 161 B.C. by Terence, the Roman dramatist.

get a duck—To fall on one's face; to fail; to be a flop. This Briticism has its roots in the game of cricket, where *duck egg* is the equivalent of American *goose egg*, i.e., zero. A batsman who fails to score a run in an inning is said to *get a duck* or *be out for a duck*. If he fails to get a run in both innings—

each team has two innings in first class cricket—he is said *bag a brace*, where *brace* is a synonym for *two*. When the batsman makes his first run he is said to *break his duck*, similar to an American baseball hitter *breaking his slump*; both terms are used to indicate that one has made a fresh start, is under way once more.

goose egg—A term used figuratively for lack of success in any endeavor; an instance of not scoring or of missing a point, so-called from the slang term for the numeral "0." As far back as the 14th century, things were compared to goose eggs because of a similarity in shape and size. By the mid-1800s, the term was used in scoring at athletic contests. The British equivalent is *duck egg*.

> At this stage of the game our opponents had fourteen runs—we had five large "goose eggs" as our share. (*Wilkes' Spirit of Times*, July 14, 1866)

Goose egg can also be used as a verb.

> I now had twenty-two consecutive World Series innings in which I goose-egged the National League. (*Saturday Evening Post*, February 28, 1948)

go up in smoke—To come to naught, to be wasted or futile; to be unsuccessful, to fail or flop; also *to end up in smoke* and other variants.

> One might let him scheme and talk, hoping it might all end in smoke. (Jane Welsh Carlyle, *New Letters and Memorials*, 1853)

Use of this expression dates from the 17th century.

lay an egg—To flop or bomb, especially when performing before an audience; to fail miserably. During World War I, *lay an egg* was Air Force terminology for 'drop a bomb,' *egg* probably being associated with *bomb* because of its similar shape. In addition, *egg* or *goose egg* is common slang for 'zero, cipher,' also because of their similar shapes. Thus, to *lay an egg* is 'to bomb' (figuratively, in American English), or to produce a large zero, i.e., nothing in terms of a favorable response from an audience, supervisor, or other persons evaluating a performance. (Note, however, that in British English, *bomb* refers to success; a play that *bombs* or is a *bomb* is a hit.)

> You would just as well come wearing a shell if you ever took a job [singing] in a spot like this, that is how big an egg you would lay. (John O'Hara, *Pal Joey*, 1939)

lead balloon—A failure, fiasco, or flop; an attempt to entertain or communicate that fails to elicit a desirable response. This phrase is relatively new, having appeared in print no earlier that the mid 1900s. *Lead balloon* was originally heard in the verb phrase *to go over like a lead balloon*, an obvious hyperbolic expression for failing miserably. Today the phrase is used alone substantively or adjectivally. Thus, a joke, plan, etc., can be called a "lead balloon."

What the Dickens? was a lead balloon literary quiz wherein the experts showed only how little they knew. (*Sunday Times*, April 19, 1970)

lemon—An object of inferior quality; a dud; something that fails to meet expectations. This expression alludes to the lemons painted on the reels of slot machines or "one-armed bandits." Whenever a lemon appears on one of the reels, regardless of what appears on the other reels, the gambler automatically loses his money. *Lemon* was in popular use by 1905, less than ten years after slot machines were invented. The expression remains almost ubiquitous, particularly in its most common current application, i.e., in reference to automobiles which experience almost constant mechanical difficulties. Today, some states have so-called "lemon laws" to protect consumers from sellers of defective cars.

> Mechanics are less than delighted to see lines of lemons converging on their service departments. (*Saturday Review*, June 17, 1972)

lose [one's] shirt—To be financially devastated. This common expression implies that a shirt is the last of one's possessions to be lost in a financial upheaval.

a miss is as good as a mile—A proverb implying that it does not matter how close one comes to hitting or attaining a goal, a near miss is still a miss, a near success is still a failure, etc. This expression is probably a corruption of an earlier, more explicit adage, "An inch in a miss is as good as an ell." (An ell is a former unit of measurement.) It has also been suggested that the original expression was "Amis is as good as Amile," alluding to two of Charlemagne's soldiers who were both heroes, both martyrs, and both saints—thus, to many people, they were virtually indistinguishable.

> He was very near being a poet—but a miss is as good as a mile, and he always fell short of the mark. (Sir Walter Scott, *Journal*, 1825)

miss the boat—To miss out on something by arriving too late, to lose an opportunity or chance; to fail to understand; also *to miss the bus*. These phrases bring to mind the image of someone arriving at the dock or bus stop just in time to see the boat or bus leaving without him. Although both expressions date from approximately the early part of this century, *to miss the boat* is by far the more common.

> Some firms were missing the boat because their managements were not prepared to be adventurous. (*The Times*, March 1973)

[my] Venus turns out a whelp—See REVERSAL.

put the shutters up—To go bankrupt; to go broke; close one's business at the end of the day. This British expression, dating from the mid 1800s, is usually associated with the permanent closing of an operation, especially a business establishment. The allusion is self-evident.

A few old established houses . . . put up their shutters and confessed themselves beaten. (Sir Arthur Conan Doyle, *Captain Polestar*, 1890)

sad sack—An inept person; a luckless, forlorn person. Perhaps a polite contraction of *sad sack of shit*, this term originated in the early 1930s but achieved its great popularity from George Baker's cartoon creation, *The Sad Sack*. Carried by many armed services publications throughout World War II, the comic strip became so popular that it continued as a regular feature in many of the nation's newspapers. A maladjusted, downtrodden, but well-meaning soldier, Sad Sack manages to find himself in constant trouble. Consequently, the allusive use of the term has come to evoke either sympathy or derogation.

take a bath—To be ruined financially, to lose everything, to be taken to the cleaners; usually used in reference to a specific financial venture. This figurative American slang use of *to take a bath*, meaning 'to be stripped of all one's possessions,' plays on one's physical nakedness when bathing.

washed out—To have met with failure or financial ruin; disqualified from social, athletic, or scholastic pursuits. One theory suggests that this phrase originated as an allusion to the former military custom of whitewashing a target after shooting practice, but the connection is difficult to discern. In modern usage, this expression is often applied in an athletic context to one who, because of injury or inferior ability, can no longer compete. In addition, the expression often implies a total depletion of funds.

> I would sit in with . . . hustlers who really knew how to gamble. I always got washed out. (Louis Armstrong, *Satchmo, My Life in New Orleans*, 1954)

wither on the vine—To fail to mature, develop, or reach fruition; to die aborning; to go unused, to be wasted. The expression describes lost opportunity, unrealized ambitions or talents, unfulfilled plans, etc. It often implies negligence or oversight; if such had been properly tended and nourished, they would have blossomed. An obvious antecedent of the expression appeared in the 17th century:

> Like a neglected rose
> It withers on the stalk with languish't head.
> (John Milton, *Comus*, 1634)

FALLACIOUSNESS
SEE ERRONEOUSNESS

FAMILIARITY
SEE FRIENDSHIP

FATUOUSNESS

See also ECCENTRICITY; IGNORANCE

airy-fairy—Light and delicate; superficial; pretentious. This expression, originally designating someone or something exquisitely dainty, first appeared in Tennyson's poem *Lilian* (1830).

> Airy, fairy Lilian
> Flitting, fairy Lilian
> When I ask her if she love me,
> Claps her tiny hands above me,
> Laughing all she can.

There is some question as to whether Tennyson coined the term or simply "borrowed" it. Whatever the case, the phrase shortly assumed a connotation of pretentiousness or superficiality, as seen in William S. Gilbert's *Only a Dancing Girl* (1869).

> No airy-fairy she,
> As she hangs in arsenic green,
> From a highly impossible tree,
> In a highly impossible scene.

The phrase retains the same pejorative sense today. It is encountered mainly in Britain.

beans are in flower—Temporarily demented; crack-brained; fatuous. Although the origin of this expression is uncertain, it may have derived from our ancestors' belief that the aroma from a flowering bean caused men to feel light-headed. Thus, *beans are in flower* became a catch-phrase to explain away a man's temporary abnormal behavior.

> With the bean-flower's boon,
> And the blackbird's tune,
> And May, and June!
> (Robert Browning, *De Gustibus*, 1855)

cockamamie—Absurd; ludicrous; nearly valueless; trifling; almost worthless; quixotic. Decalcomania, the process of transferring a decal, a design or picture on a specially prepared paper, to another surface, such as porcelain or glass, apparently gave birth to the word *cockamamie*. During the late 1920s, a process was devised to transfer nontoxic decals to the human skin. The application of these decals to various parts of the human anatomy became a fad among the young for a while, and the slang word *cockamamie* was coined in response to the absurdity of the practice; the ultimate origin remains obscure. However, Bob Kane, the creator of Batman, was quoted in the *New York Post* of January 9, 1931:

> When I make a statement on canvas, I'm not just doing cockamamie drawings.

In the vocabulary of today the term has taken on a number of meanings, all commonly connoting some degree of worthlessness or absurdity.

I figure it has to be a lawyer to figure out this whole cockamamie scheme. (Maxwell Nurnberg, *I Always Look Up the Word E-gre-gious*, 1981)

ding-a-ling—A person who repeatedly makes silly mistakes or foolish and inappropriate remarks; one whose behavior is unconventional or eccentric. A *ding-a-ling* is one who behaves as if he hears bells in his head. The implication is that a head full of ringing bells must be devoid of brains and sense. A newer and equivalent American slang term is *dingbat*.

Doctor Doddypoll—A dolt; a simpleton; a nincompoop; a blockhead. The origin of this expression is questionable. The most plausible explanation attributes it to a combining of the words *poll* 'head,' and *doddy*, an old form of the modern word *dotty*, meaning 'slightly demented or feeble-minded.' Occasionally the term is simplified to *doddypoll*.

> What ye brain-sycke fooles, ye hoddy peckes, ye doddye poulles!... are you seduced also? (Hugh Latimer, *Third Sermon before Edward VI*, 1549).

The term originated during the latter half of the 15th century. In 1595 a comedy, *The Wisdom of Doctor Doddypoll*, was staged in London. Although of unknown authorship, the play is often ascribed to George Peele. A related expression of ironic intent, *as wise as Doctor Doddypoll*, means 'not wise at all.'

an elephant in the moon—A spurious discovery; a mare's nest; an illusion. This expression owes its genesis to an actual series of events. In the 17th century a scientist of the Royal Society, Sir Paul Neale, made the startling announcement that he had discovered *an elephant in the moon*. Close observation by one of his fellow scientists proved that a little mouse had somehow got into his telescope. Samuel Butler wrote a poetic satire directed against Neale and his amazing discovery. Butler's satire, *The Elephant in the Moon*, contributed to the popularity of the phrase, which is still in use in reference to chaos as a result of buffoonery.

find a giggles' nest—This British expression, in use since the early 19th century, is said to have originated in Norfolk where it was directed at one who was laughing to excess, at someone who "has the giggles." The term itself suggests an imaginary giggles' nest, a place of plentiful giggles, or perhaps a room full of giggling girls.

full of beans—Uninformed, ignorant, stupid; silly, empty-headed. This use of *full of beans* may have derived from an indirect reference to a bean's small value. Thus, to be "full of beans" is to be full of insignificance and inanity.

go to Battersea, to be cut for the simples—This phrase, an admonishment to one who makes a foolish comment, is often truncated to *go to Battersea* or to *be cut for the simples*. The allusion here is to the *simples*, medicinal herbs which were once grown in great quantities in what is now the Battersea section of London. Apothecaries from London would travel to Battersea to select the choicest herbs. The term, dating from the mid 17th century, is also a pun on the word *simple*; hence, the expression, most often used jocularly or as a snide remark, implies that one is becoming weak in the mind. Variants are to *have their simples cut* and *He must be cut of the simples*. It is rarely encountered outside of England.

> What evils might be averted ... by clearing away bile, evacuating ill humors, and occasionally by cutting for the simples. (Robert Southey, *The Doctor*, 1834)

have windmills in [one's] head—To be full of dreamlike illusions; to live in a fool's paradise. This obsolete expression implies the circulation of fanciful ideas in the vacuity of a daft mind.

> He hath windmills in his head. (John C. Clarke, *Paroemiologia*, 1639)

head of wax—A head consisting of a substance that is easily molded, possessed by someone who is very impressionable, easily deluded. This term designates one who is easily led astray, one who carries the opinions of the last person who spoke to him.

> If your head is wax, don't walk in the sun. (Benjamin Franklin, *Poor Richard's Almanack*, 1749)

The expression has been in use since the early 18th century and is common throughout Europe. The French have a proverb: *If your head is wax, stay away from the fire.*

in the ozone—In a daze, in another world; spacey, spaced-out. The ozone layer or ozonosphere is a region in the upper atmosphere characterized by a high concentration of ozone and a relatively high temperature owing to the assimilation of ultraviolet solar radiation. Hence, *in the ozone* is equivalent to *out in space*. This American slang expression appears to be of very recent coinage.

not have all [one's] buttons—To be whimsical, odd, or crazy; to be out of it or not all there. In the 19th century, this expression was used to describe unintelligent, irrational behavior. It is now considered a slang phrase which emphasizes the eccentric, idiosyncratic aspects of behavior rather than characteristics indicative of stupidity or dullness.

silly as a coot—Simple; stupid; witless; fatuous; inane. This simile, dating from the 17th century, alludes to the rather comic facial features of the coot, as well as to the bird's extravagant behavior at mating time. The males thrash about in the water, uttering weird cries, flapping their wings, thrusting their beaks and slashing their talons at other males. Frequently heard variants are *crazy as a coot* and *stupid as a coot*.

simple Jack—A simpleton; a fool; a person of no consequence. This British expression is a simple transference of the French *Gros-Jean*. The famous French author, Jean de la Fontaine, in his *Fables* (1678) tells of a dairy maid, one Gros-Jean, carrying a full pail of milk on her head. As she is making her way to market, she thinks of all the things she can do with the money she will get for the milk. However, the pail falls from her head before she arrives, and she is *Gros-Jean comme devant* 'Gros-Jean as before,' that is, no better than before. From this French expression comes the English *simple Jack* and the equivalent English proverb *simple Jack as before*.

slaphappy—Severely confused or befuddled; cheerfully irresponsible; giddy; happy or elated, as if dazed. This term alludes to the apparent exhilaration which sometimes accompanies a concussion caused by a series of blows to the head, such as might be inflicted in a boxing match.

A sample [of talk] designed to knock philologists slap-happy. (*Newsweek*, May 23, 1938)

A related expression which, like *slaphappy*, employs an internal rhyme is *punch-drunk*. A variation is *punchy*.

social butterfly—An irresponsible person who flits aimlessly from one social gathering to another. The source of this term is unknown, but the use of butterfly as a metaphor for one who flutters about from one place to another goes back to at least the 16th century. Today's *social butterfly* is often busy climbing the *social ladder* and flits about from ball to banquet, a member of the *social whirl*. The social ladder is, of course, for those trying to make it to the top rungs.

The noble has gone down on the social ladder, and the roturier has gone up. (John Stuart Mill, *Edinburgh Review*, 1840)

The *social whirl* refers to the cycle of activities sponsored each year during the "season," attended by fashionable society.

Tom Noddy—A foolish or half-witted person; a simpleton; a name for a fool, an idiot. This name is probably a derivative of the verb *nod*; however, it may derive from puffins, also known as *noddies* or *Tom Noddies*, rather silly birds that one can walk up to and bash with a stick or club. A third, but rather weak, suggestion is that the term is a nickname for Nicodemus. Dating to the early 19th century, the term was popularized by the Reverend Richard Harris Barham when *My Lord Tomnoddy* appeared as a character in *The Ingoldsby Legends* (1840).

My Lord Tomnoddy got up one day;
It was half after two; he had nothing to do,
So his lordship rang for his cabriolet.

And a few years later in a satirical poem, *My Lord Tomnoddy*, Robert B. Brough wrote of hereditary titles:

My Lord Tomnoddy is thirty-four;
The Earl can last but a few years more.

My Lord in the Peers will take his place:
Her Majesty's councils his words will grace.
Office he'll hold and patronage sway;
Fortunes and lives he will vote away;
And what are his qualifications–ONE!
He the Earl of Fitzdotterel's eldest son.

wimp—A boring, introverted person; a person who is out of touch with current trends, fads, and ideas; a sissy or weakling. This American slang expression, dating from the late 1950s, is of uncertain derivation, but most experts believe it originated with Wimpy, the hamburger-gulping simpleton featured in the *Popeye* comic strip. However, Stanley Meisler, a *Los Angeles Times* correspondent in Toronto, Canada, attributes it to "an onomatopoeic merger of the words *whimper* and *limp*." Whatever the case, the term is popular today, especially among the young.

The sensitive, unathletic kid refused to stifle his artistic instincts. He served as President of the Art Association (Twenty of us little wimps reading *Artform*, says Wheelwright). (William Casselman, *Macleans*, October 9, 1978)

wise men of Gotham—Simpletons; stupid, foolish people; boneheads; dumbbells. Somehow during the Middle Ages the English village of Gotham acquired a reputation of being a village of idiots. The legend was strengthened by a collection of stories published during the reign of Henry VIII. Relating stupid actions on the part of the village people, the collection was entitled *Merry Tales of the Mad Men of Gotham*. One tale tells of a wall the men of Gotham built around a cuckoo so that the village would enjoy the season of spring all year round, for cuckoos stayed in their countryside only during the springtime; however, much to their chagrin the cuckoo flew away. Another tale recounts how King John visited Gotham with the idea of purchasing a castle there, but when he saw the idiotic games that the people played to amuse themselves, he decided to purchase it elsewhere and traveled on. The *wise men of Gotham* are said to have remarked, "More fools pass through Gotham than remain in it." Other cultures have their "Gothams": in Eastern Europe, the town is called *Chelm*.

FAULTFINDING
SEE CRITICISM; REPRIMAND

FAVORITISM
SEE INJUSTICE; PREJUDICE

FAWNING
SEE OBSEQUIOUSNESS

afraid of [one's] own shadow—To be unusually fearful; to be unreasonably frightened or scared; to be exceedingly tense or jumpy. The suggestion here is, of course, that it is a mark of excessiveness to fear something so commonplace as one's own shadow. The expression has been in use since Plato, more than 300 years before Christ.

A considerable part of Concord are in the condition of Virginia today, afraid of their own shadows. (Henry D. Thoreau, *Autumn*, November 30, 1859)

the creeps—A feeling of dread or fear; an unpleasant sensation as if things were creeping over one's body. This colloquialism dates from the early 19th century and alludes to the strange sensation one experiences when confronted with a fearful or eerie situation. The horripilation occasioned at such a moment creates a sensation of things creeping on one's skin.

In the old country mansions where the servants . . . commence . . . to have shivers and creeps. (Edmund Yates, *Broken to Harness,* 1864)

A related colloquialism, *creep*, was coined in the 1930s to signify the type of person who gives one *the creeps*, and is used more loosely to denote any repulsive individual.

goose pimples—A condition of the skin resembling a plucked goose's skin, caused by cold or fear; a rough, pimply condition of the skin caused by erection of the papillae; horripilation. This expression, in use since at least the 1600s, had its inception as a result of the similarity between the flesh of a freshly plucked goose and the rough, prickly condition of the human skin at times of fear or cold. When a goose is plucked, the minute muscles that offer feather control contract, giving the same appearance as the skin of a frightened or cold human being; hence, *goose pimples*, or the variations, *goose flesh* and *goose bumps*.

The way it scraped in this maneuver makes goose pimples on my spine even now. (*The New York Times*, February 2, 1947)

have [one's] heart in [one's] mouth—To be frightened or scared, apprehensive or afraid, anxious or tense. The allusion is to the throbbing feeling one experiences in the upper chest and lower throat in moments of tense excitement.

Having their heart at their very mouth for fear, they did not believe that it was Jesus. (Nicholas Udall, *Erasmus upon the New Testament,* translated 1548)

make the hair stand on end—To terrify, to scare or frighten, to fill with fear. The allusion is to the way an animal's hair, especially that on the back of the neck, involuntarily stiffens and becomes erect in the face of danger and to the prickly sensation of the scalp felt at times of great emotion or excitement.

As for the particulars, I'm sure they'd make your hair stand on end to hear them. (Frances Burney, *Evelina*, 1778)

scare the daylights out of [someone]—To frighten a person intensely; to make one's hair stand on end; to alarm inordinately. Originally, *daylights* was underworld and boxing slang for the eyes, but by extension came to mean one's consciousness or vital organs.

I scared the daylights out of you with the toy gun. (*The New York Times Everyday Dictionary*, 1982)

Variants are *shake the daylights out of someone* and *shoot the daylights out of someone*.

I'll shoot the everlasting daylights out of you! (E. S. Field, *The Sapphire Bracelet*, 1910)

shake in [one's] shoes—To be petrified, terrified, panic-stricken; to be scared out of one's wits. The expression is not limited in application to people.

It had set the whole Liberal party "shaking in its shoes." (*Punch*, March 15, 1873)

Variations are *quake in one's boots* or *shake in one's boots*.

shake like an aspen leaf—To tremble, quake; to shiver, quiver. This simile refers to the aspen tree with its delicate leaves perched atop long flexible stems that flutter even in the slightest breeze. The expression was used as early as 1386 by Chaucer in his *Canterbury Tales.*

FINALITY
SEE TERMINATION

FINANCE
SEE INDEBTEDNESS; MONEY

FLAMBOYANCE
SEE OSTENTATIOUSNESS

FLATTERY
SEE OBSEQUIOUSNESS

FOOD AND DRINK
See also DRUNKENNESS

Adam's Ale—Another name for water, sometimes applied humorously. On occasion the term is applied sardonically by drinking men, as Matthew Prior exhibits in "The Wandering Pilgrim":

A Rechabite poor will must live,
And drink of Adam's ale.

This name is based on the obvious fact that the first man, Adam, had nothing else available to drink.

> Adam's ale, about the only gift that has descended undefiled from the Garden of Eden! (Storrs, *Ale*, 1875)

banyan days—Days when no meat is served; in the British Royal Navy, the two days in each week when no meat was served. In the late 16th century, Europeans exploring the coast of the Gulf of Persia near Bandar Abbas, Iran, discovered a huge tree under which a caste of Hindu tradesmen and moneylenders known as Banians or Banyans had built a small pagoda. These Hindu merchants observed strict religious rites, refusing to eat any type of flesh. Not only did that particular tree (a variety of the fig) become known as a *banyan*, from the name for the traders, but the name was extended to the entire species. Furthermore, the Banyans' refusal to eat meat gave rise to the use of *banyan* as a synonym for 'meatless.' The Australians in the Outback soon named those days when meat was not available as *banyan days*, and the British Royal Navy adopted the term to designate the two days a week when meat was not served to the sailors.

> I was not very much tempted with the appearance of this dish, of which, nevertheless, my messmates ate heartily, advising me to follow their example, as it was banyan day, and we could have no meat till next noon. (Tobias Smollett, *Roderick Random*, 1748)

belly-timber—Food or nourishment; provisions. According to *Brewer's Dictionary of Phrase and Fable*, there is a connection between the French phrase *carrelure de ventre* 'refurnishing or resoling the stomach,' and the origin of *belly-timber*. Apparently Samuel Butler and his contemporaries were the last to use the term seriously.

> ... through deserts vast
> And regions desolate they pass'd
> Where belly-timber above ground
> Or under, was not to be found.
> (Samuel Butler, *Hudibras*, 1663)

cambric tea—This American expression, dating from the early 1800s, denotes a cup of hot water with milk added, usually served to children as a substitute for tea. *Cambric* is a fine, white linen cloth, originally manufactured at Cambray in Flanders (*Kameryk*, in Flemish), and apparently the expression is derived from the similarity of color of the fabric and of the tea.

> She gave me a vast easy chair to sit in ... and offered me tea, cambric tea to be sure, but in a beautiful cup. (*Chicago Union Signal*, January 21, 1888)

eye opener—A drink of whiskey, especially the first one in the morning; a *pick-me-up*. This American slang expression, dating from the early 1800s, originally referred to an alcoholic drink taken upon arising to alleviate the effects of a hangover or to shake off early morning drowsiness.

> Others, who, fuddled last night, are limp in their lazy beds, till soda water lends them its fizzle. Eye-openers these of moderate caliber. (Theodore Winthrop, *John Brent*, 1861)

The term is also used to indicate a person who delivers some startling bit of news or offers some knowledge that leads to sudden enlightenment about a subject, or to the news itself.

> He felt his mission to be that of an agitator, of an eye opener, of a merciless yet undogmatic critic. (*Manchester Guardian*, August 31, 1928)

A related term, *pick-me-up*, is used to indicate a drink taken at any time during the day to give one a quick lift.

fast food—Food, such as pizzas, hamburgers, hot dogs, fried chicken, etc., that is prepared and served with minimal delay. This expression has arisen since World War II from the growing popularity of eating establishments that are designed to get food out to the public quickly and inexpensively. Originating in the United States, these *fast food* chains have expanded throughout the world, making the term common to most English-speaking countries.

> The fast food pollution [in Paris] isn't new, or—hedonist faithful pray—fatal. (Graham Greene, *New York*, July 8, 1974)

firewater—Whiskey; hard liquor. This expression is a literal translation of the Algonquin Indian *scoutiouabou* 'liquor.' The reference, of course, is to the burning sensation caused by the ingestion of strong liquor and, since most liquor at that time was of the clear "moonshine" variety, its waterlike appearance. *Firewater* was commonly used in the pioneer and Wild West days, but is now mainly a humorous colloquialism.

> He informed me that they [the American Indians] called the whiskey fire water. (John Bradbury, *Travels in the Interior of America*, 1917)

a hair of the dog that bit you—A cure identical to the cause of the malady; usually and specifically, another drink of the liquor that made you drunk or sick the previous night or caused your present hangover. The expression derives from the former belief that the only effective antidote for a mad dog's bite was its own hair, a belief based on the homeopathic principle *similia similibus curantur* 'likes are cured by likes.' The expression dates from at least 1546.

hooch—Intoxicating liquor, especially cheap, homemade whiskey; moonshine. This term originally designated an alcoholic whiskey distilled by the Hoochinoo Indians of Alaska. The drink, which was sold illicitly, was known originally by the tribal name, *hoochinoo*, but by the end of the 19th century it had been shortened to *hooch*.

> Among the Indians of the extreme north...there is a liquor made which...is called hoochinoo. The ingredients...are simple and innocent, being only yeast, flour, and either sugar or molasses. (Edward R. Emerson, *Beverages, Past and Present*)

By the Prohibition Era the name *hooch* had come to designate any (then) illegal beverage, and the expression remains in common use.

hush puppy—A deep-fried ball of cornmeal dough, popular in the American South; a cornmeal fritter. The origin of this term is uncertain, but the most popular explanation ascribes it to hunters who would carry these fried cornmeal cakes in their pockets and throw them to their dogs when they wanted them to be quiet. Another version attributes it to the outdoor fish fries of the South which would attract neighborhood dogs. To stop their whining and barking, the cook would fry up some cornmeal dough and throw it to them, crying "Hush, puppies." The expression arose about 1900.

> Fishing parties, dances, hush-puppy suppers, and fish fries left the MGMers almost too pleasantly busy to proceed with their filming. (*New Orleans Time-Picayune Magazine*, May 15, 1949)

L. L. Whisky—A high-quality whiskey. The initials *L. L.* stand for "Lord Lieutenant." Apparently, the Duke of Richmond, Lord Lieutenant from 1807 to 1813, requested that a cask of his favorite whiskey be preserved. The cask was labeled "L. L.," and since then, *L. L. Whisky* has referred to any whiskey of a comparable high quality.

Mary Jane cookies—Cookies containing marijuana; any cookies with drugs as part of the recipe. The origin of Mary Jane cookies is unknown; however, a well-known recipe is that of Alice B. Toklas, the live-in confidante of Gertrude Stein in her Paris salon. The term *Mary Jane* is a literal translation of *marijuana*, derived from two Spanish female names, *Maria* and *Juana*; why the weed received the name is unknown.

Mexican breakfast—This modern expression alludes to smoking a cigarette and drinking a glass of water for one's breakfast, usually because one is hung over, broke, or too tired to eat. Why such a breakfast is to be considered Mexican is unclear. A related term is *secretary's breakfast* which consists of a cup of coffee and a cigarette, a time-saving practice of the modern-day office worker that allows more time for sleep.

Mickey Finn—A drink to which a drug such as a narcotic, barbiturate, or purgative has been added, sometimes as a joke but usually with the intention of rendering an unsuspecting person unconscious or otherwise causing him discomfort; the drug itself; knockout drops, especially chloral hydrate. This eponymous term purportedly refers to a notorious underworld character who lived in Chicago in the 19th century. Although originally a nickname for a horse laxative, *Mickey Finn* has, since the 1930s, been expanded to include a much wider range of drugs used as adulterants. It is commonly shortened to *Mickey* and frequently appears in expressions such as *slip someone a Mickey [Finn]*.

> She had been about to suggest that the butler might slip into Adela's bedtime ovaltine what is known as a knockout drop or Mickey Finn. (P. G. Wodehouse, *Old Reliable*, 1951)

moonshine—Illegally distilled liquor. This expression is derived from the clandestine nighttime manufacture of whiskey, an industry particularly widespread during Prohibition (1920–33). The phrase was figuratively used prior to that era, however, especially in reference to the homemade spirits of the Appalachian backwoods.

> The manufacture of illicit mountain whiskey—"moonshine"—was formerly, as it is now, a considerable source of income. (*Harper's Magazine*, June 1886)

mountain dew—Liquor, particularly scotch whisky, that is illegally distilled; moonshine. This expression is derived from the illicit manufacture of spirits in stills that are concealed in the mountains.

> The distilled spirits industry...wages an expensive propaganda campaign against...mountain dew. (*The Times*, October 1970)

mountain oysters—The testicles of sheep, calves, or hogs when used as food. This expression originated perhaps as an analogy to the shape of oysters.

> I have consumed mountain oysters and prairie dancers that are actually poetic. (E. Paul, *Springtime in Paris*, 1951)

nightcap—A bedtime drink, usually alcoholic, consumed to help one sleep; a final drink of the evening. This expression has two suggested derivations, one of which alludes to the nightcap, a now obsolete article of sleepwear worn on the head. Since for many people two essential activities before retiring were donning a nightcap and downing an alcoholic drink as a soporific, the latter came by association to be also called a *nightcap*. Since the decline in the popularity of nightcaps as headgear, *nightcap* now refers almost exclusively to a drink. A second possibility is that *cap* is used in the sense of 'to complete or finish.' Thus, one caps off an evening's activities with a drink before retiring.

> I neither took, or cared to take, any wine with my dinner, and never wanted any description of "nightcap." (Thomas Trollope, *What I Remember*, 1887)

In recent years, however, *nightcap* has been expanded to include any prebed beverage—alcoholic or nonalcoholic—consumed to aid one's falling asleep.

"Ovaltine"... The world's best "nightcap" to ensure sound, natural sleep. (*Daily Telegraph*, April 9, 1930)

nineteenth hole—A bar or restaurant where players congregate for refreshments and relaxation after playing eighteen holes of golf. This slang expression developed sometime during the early 1900s as a nickname for the country club bar, and, during Prohibition in the United States, for the locker room. Today, at most country clubs, the *nineteenth hole* has become a rather elaborate restaurant and cocktail lounge combination, usually serving food and drink until quite late in the evening.

He dug into his pocket for $10,000 in prize money, played more for the fun of it than in the hope of beating anybody, and helped entertain on the 19th hole. (*Time*, January 19, 1948)

pot likker—Juice of ham or fatback after cooking with turnip or collard greens. This expression from the American South is a phonetic spelling of the words *pot liquor*. Often served with corn pone, *pot likker* was the subject of an ongoing controversy among Southern epicures during 1931. Some maintained the corn pone should be dunked in the broth; others maintained it should be crumbled. In a poll of the general public conducted by an Atlanta newspaper, it was determined that the crumblers were in the majority; however, most politicians were careful to say that they liked it either way.

He always smelled slightly of turnip greens, as Miss Amelia rubbed him... with pot liquor to give him strength. (Carson McCullers, *The Ballad of the Sad Cafe*, 1951)

potluck—See MIXTURE.

punk and plaster—Bread and butter; bread and margarine. Originally coined by American hoboes to describe bread and butter, this term first appeared about 1880. It was extended to signify food in general by the 1910s.

She gives you a slice of sow-belly an' a chunk of dry punk. (Jack London, *The Road*, 1907)

One variant, *punk and plaster John* refers, in hobo lingo, to a vagrant who specializes in begging bread and butter, thereby avoiding work. Such beggars, often also called *chronikers*, work the *punk and plaster route*, Pennsylvania Dutch farm country.

put out the miller's eye—To add too much water to a recipe, especially one thickened with flour; to dilute anything, especially spirits, with an excess of water. One plausible theory for the origin of this phrase points

127

out that *miller's eye* was an expression for lumps of flour not fully mixed into batter or dough. In certain recipes, leaving such lumps is considered desirable, but adding too much liquid to the batter can eliminate them, hence, *putting the miller's eyes out*. Whatever its exact origin, the term has been in use since about 1678.

> If after... putting out the miller's eye by too much water, you add flour to make it stiff. (Esther Copley, *Housekeeper's Guide*, 1834)

The term *drown the miller* has the same sense but alludes to the fact that old-fashioned millers, who frequently employed water-wheels for power, had little need for more water. It has also taken on an additional connotation 'to go bankrupt.'

red-eye—Low-quality liquor; cheap, strong whiskey. This expression is plausibly derived from the alcohol-induced dilatation of blood vessels in the eye. The now infrequently used phrase usually referred to bootlegged whiskey during its Prohibition heyday.

> This fellow paid a thousand dollars for ten cases of red-eye that proved to be nothing but water. (Sinclair Lewis, *Babbitt*, 1922)

rotgut—Low-quality liquor; bootlegged whiskey; red-eye. This expression is derived from the deleterious effects that such intoxicants have on one's insides. The phrase is widely used in Great Britain as well as in the United States.

> It's the real stuff—pure Prohibition rot gut. (H. Allen Smith, *Putty Knife*, 1943)

rubber chicken—This term is the derogatory expression used by politicians, athletes, and other public figures to describe the customary fare served at banquets around the country. For politicians on the campaign trail, evening meals become a series of banquets sponsored by local political committees. This *rubber chicken circuit* is also traveled by many famous athletes during the so-called off season. As the principal speakers at these dinners, they are often subjected to the same fare for weeks at a time and develop what is known as the *rubber chicken syndrome*. *Rubber chicken* and *rubber chicken circuit* have been in use since the 1960s; *rubber chicken syndrome* is a more recent phenomenon.

> This incidence has resulted in the discovery of a mysterious illness that a leading sociologist has termed "The Rubber Chicken Syndrome." (*New Haven Journal-Courier*, February 9, 1982)

sneaky pete—Cheap wine, usually laced with alcohol or with a narcotic. Although this phrase is of unknown origin, it may perhaps refer to the slowly creeping inebriation caused by such spirits. Today, the expression often refers specifically to cheap wine.

> ... A pint of forty-cent wine known under the generic title of "Sneaky Pete." (*Commonwealth*, December 1952)

SOS—Creamed chipped beef on toast; any sloppy, runny meat dish served over toast. A military slang term since the early 1900s, this expression has been adopted into the common vocabulary, probably through the agency of the large number of men who were in military service during World War II and brought the term home with them. Creamed chipped beef (dried beef served in a cream sauce and poured over a piece of toast) was such a common, and apparently detestable, part of the military diet that it became known as *shit on a shingle*, abbreviated to *SOS*.

square meal—A hearty, satisfying, stick-to-the-ribs type of repast. This American expression, in common use since the late 19th century, probably alludes to the sense of *square* 'honest, above-board'; hence, an honest and full meal.

> I want...three square meals a day for which I'm willing to pay. (*Duluth News-Tribune*, January 19, 1947)

three-martini lunch—A lunch with cocktails, purportedly for business purposes and hence used as a tax write-off. According to William Safire in *Safire's Political Dictionary* (1978), Senator George McGovern of South Dakota popularized this term during his 1972 presidential campaign. In his attack on the government's concessions to big business, the senator pointed to expensive entertainment as an example of unnecessary business deductions made at the expense of the taxpayers. Later, the Carter administration also exploited the term in attacking business practices that skirted the tax laws.

> Other reforms that the President proposed would further restrict certain tax shelters for well-off people... and cut in half permitted deductions for business meals—an attack on the by now fabled three-martini lunch. (*Time*, January 30, 1978)

tiger's milk—British slang for gin; also sometimes for whisky or for brandy and water. This term, apparently originally army slang, appeared as an entry in George R. Gleig's *The Subaltern's Log-Book*, published in 1828.

torpedo juice—Homemade alcoholic beverages of the lowest quality. This expression originated during World War II, when soldiers who desperately craved intoxication developed makeshift beverages to substitute for the unavailable quality whiskey. The expression itself arose from the grain alcohol drained from torpedos, although alcohol was also extracted from fuel, hair tonics, and medications. Usually, this alcohol was combined with fruit juice, resulting in a somewhat palatable concoction.

FOOLISHNESS
SEE FATUOUSNESS

FORCE
SEE COERCION

FRANKNESS
SEE CANDIDNESS

FRENZIEDNESS
SEE DISORDER

Friendship

FRIENDSHIP
See also LOVE

bosom buddy—A confidant; an intimate friend. This expression is an armed forces version of the old term *bosom friend*.

> There is nothing better than a bosom friend with whom to confer. (Robert Greene, *Never Too Late*, 1590)

The inference here is that one cherishes in his bosom a person for whom he feels a special friendship, one with whom he can share his innermost secrets. During World War II the term *bosom buddy* became especially popular, apparently because of the common use of *buddy* as the armed services synonym for *pal*. Other common synonyms are *bosom chum* and *old buddy*.

close as the bark to the tree—Intimate, close; interdependent, symbiotically related, mutually sustaining. The phrase is used particularly of the closeness between husbands and wives. Though occasionally used to indicate physical proximity, the expression usually carries implications that such is indicative of a spiritual or psychological intimacy or dependency.

> She would stick as close to Abbot as the bark stuck to the tree. (Cotton Mather, *The Wonders of the Invisible World*, 1692)

The "bark and the tree" as symbolic of "husband and wife" was in print as early as the mid-16th century. The analogy assumes that spouses interrelate in the interdependent, mutually nourishing patterns characteristic of the relationship between a tree and its bark.

eat [someone's] salt—To share someone's food and drink, to partake of someone's hospitality. Among the ancient Greeks to eat another's salt was to create a sacred bond of friendship between host and guest. No one who had eaten another's salt would say anything against him or do him any harm. *Salt*, as it is used in this phrase, symbolizes hospitality, probably because it once was of considerable value. (Cf. the etymology of *salary*.) The first *OED* citation given for this expression is dated 1382.

good ole boy—A friend; a familiar term of address, sometimes used disdainfully. This term, which dates from about 1890, has undergone a new surge of popularity since the advent of CB radios. Originally slang of the southern United States, in recent years the expression has spread throughout North America. A variant is *good buddy*, most commonly used as a form of direct address.

> ... it gives women's rights advocates something to cheer about, and it gives good ole boys something to cry in their beer about. (*New York Daily News*, November 22, 1981)

hobnob—To be chummy, familiar, or intimate with; also, *hob and nob*. This expression originated as *hab-nab* 'have or have not,' 'give or take.' Shakespeare employed this early sense in *Twelfth Night*:

> He is a devil in private brawl .... Hob, nob, is his word, give't or take't. (III,iv)

The 'give or take' sense of this expression was subsequently extended to include the exchange of toasts as a sign of comradeship. Consequently, the phrase evolved its contemporary figurative meaning of being on friendly or familiar terms.

> It cannot be her interest to hob and nob with Lord Fitzwilliam. (Lady Granville, *Letters*, 1828)

the mahogany—The dining room table, as symbolic of sociability, conviviality, friendship, conversation, etc. This popular 19th-century British colloquial term usually appeared in phrases such as *around the mahogany*, *over the mahogany*, or *with one's feet under the mahogany*.

> I had hoped ... to see you three gentlemen ... with your legs under the mahogany in my humble parlour. (Charles Dickens, *Master Humphrey's Clock*, 1840)

Currently *mahogany* is a colloquial term for a bar.

> From the moment Mr. Primrose appeared behind his own mahogany and superseded the barmaid, he dominated everything. (N. Collins, *Trinity Town*, 1936)

on a good footing with [someone]—Have a friendly understanding with another; to be in a position to ask another for favors; to be in good standing. This expression has been attributed to a borrowing of the French, *Être sur un grand pied dans le monde*, which translates freely as 'to have a large foot in society.' However, a more credible explanation attributes it to a friendship or understanding as resting on a solid foundation, i.e., *on a good footing*.

The phrase has been in figurative use since the mid 18th century.

rub shoulders—To mingle or socialize; to hobnob. This expression is derived from the bumping and grazing of bodies against each other at social gatherings. The phrase quite often describes the mingling of persons of diverse background and social status at cocktail parties, political gatherings, and the like.

stand sam—Pay for the drinks; pay the reckoning. This expression, of uncertain origin, has been explained as an allusion to the *U.S.* on the knapsacks of American soldiers, as if a reminder to imbibing troops that *Uncle Sam* is *standing* for the drinks. A more likely explanation lies in an early, now obsolete, definition of *sam*, 'to bring together in friendship.' One who bought a round of drinks was attempting to bring all the patrons together in conviviality.

> I must insist upon standing Sam upon the present occasion. (William Ainsworth, *Rookwood*, 1834)

A related term, *Nunky pays for all* probably has some basis in fact in the explanation above, *Nunky*, a playful variant of *uncle*, being a frequent reference to *Uncle Sam*.

thick as thieves—Intimate, familiar, friendly; close, tight. This expression is thought to derive from the notion that thieves must often cooperate closely to accomplish their aims. The *OED* dates the expression from the early 1800s. The English expression may well owe its existence to the French proverb *ils s'entendent comme larrons en foire* 'as thick as thieves at a fair,' where *thick* means 'crowded, densely arranged.' When *at a fair was dropped* from the expression, the figurative jump to *thick* 'close, intimate' occurred; Theodore Hook used the truncated form in *The Parson's Daughter* (1833):

> She and my wife are as thick as thieves, as the proverb goes.

Pickpockets, cutpurses, and their kind frequented fairs and other large gatherings where the prospects of gain and escape were both high.

FURTIVENESS
SEE SECRECY

FURY
SEE ANGER; VEXATION

FUTILITY

bark at the moon—To labor or protest in vain; to choose an ineffectual means to achieve a desired end, or to attempt the impossible, thereby making any effort futile by definition; also often *bay at the moon*. The phrase refers to the common practice of dogs to bay at the moon, as if to frighten or provoke it. Connotations of the foolishness of barking at the moon, based on the disparity between the earthly dog and the mystical moon, are carried over into the figurative usage, as if to imply that barking at the moon is like beating one's head against the wall.

beat [one's] head against the wall—To attempt an impossible task to one's own detriment; to vainly oppose an unyielding force; also *to hit one's head* *against the wall, knock one's head against the wall,* or *bang one's head against the wall,* often *a stone wall.* The allusion is to the futility and frustration occasioning such an action and the resulting harm.

beat the air—To strike out at nothing, to labor or talk idly or to no purpose; to shadowbox. The phrase may well derive directly from the last definition, as suggested by its use in the King James Version of the New Testament:

> I therefore so run, not as uncertainly; so fight I, not as one that beateth the air. (I Corinthians 9:26)

the blind leading the blind—Ignorance on the part of both leaders and followers; lack of guidance and direction resulting in certain failure; futility. The phrase is of Biblical origin. Speaking of the Pharisees, Jesus says:

> They be blind leaders of the blind. And if the blind lead the blind, both shall fall into the ditch. (Matthew 15:14)

The expression is also the title of a famous painting by Pieter Breughel the Elder (1568).

bore four holes in the blue—This expression, used to describe a useless mission or purposeless flight, had its inception during World War II. The allusion is to the four engines of a large aircraft accomplishing nothing better than "boring four holes in the sky."

> My navigator got lost, and there we were boring four holes in the blue. (*American Speech,* October 1956)

cast stones against the wind—To labor in vain; to work without accomplishing anything.

> I see I swim against the stream, I kick against a goad, I cast a stone against the wind. (Grange, *Golden Aphrodite,* 1577)

cry for the moon—To desire the unattainable or the impossible, to want what is wholly beyond one's reach; also *to ask for the moon* or *wish for the moon.* Although some sources conjecture that this expression comes from children crying for the moon to play with, that theory seems a bit forced. The moon has long typified a place impossible to reach or object impossible to obtain, and was so used by Shakespeare in *Henry VI, Part II* (1593):

> And dogged York, that reaches at the moon,
> Whose overweening arm I have plucked back.
> (III,i)

A similar French expression is *vouloir prendre la lune avec les dents* 'to want to take the moon between one's teeth.'

flog a dead horse—To attempt to rekindle interest in a wornout topic, flagging discussion, doomed or defeated legislation, or other matter; to engage in futile activity. The figurative use of this expression is closely related to the literal, i.e., it is useless to attempt to revive or stimulate something that is dead.

> In parliament he again pressed the necessity of reducing expenditure. Friends warned him that he was flogging a dead horse. (John Morley, *The Life of Richard Cobden,* 1881)

A variation is *beat a dead horse* or *whip a dead horse.*

hog shearing—An action which results in a great cry and little wool; something involving much labor and small reward, many words and little sense. The original proverb from the Middle Ages *great cry and little wool as the devil said when he sheared the hogs* alludes to the medieval mystery play, *David and Abigail.* Nabal, Abigail's first husband, is presented as shearing his sheep; the devil is seen beside him, imitating him, but shearing a hog which is making great squealing noises.

> Thou wilt at best but suck a bull,
> Or shear swine, all cry and no wool.
> (Samuel Butler, *Hudibras,* 1663)

Kafkaesque—Resembling the world created in the writings of Franz Kafka, where man is overwhelmed by bureaucratic red tape or vanquished by an overpowering faceless authority; nightmarish; weird; frightening. This eponym was derived from the name of the eminent Czech novelist of the early 1900s. In Kafka's novels, *The Trial, The Castle,* and *Amerika,* as well as in the majority of his many short stories, man finds himself in a hopeless situation confronting the edicts of an authority which he cannot contact, or is faced with bureaucratic regulations which he can not fathom.

> Thanks to M. Blanchot there is now a "Kafkaesque" stereotype of the fantastic, just as there is a stereotype of haunted castles and stuffed monsters. (Jean-Paul Sartre, "Aminadab," *Literary Essays,* 1957)

kick against the pricks—See REBELLIOUSNESS.

make bricks without straw—To try to accomplish a task without the proper materials or essential ingredients. The current sense of this expression is traced to a misinterpretation of the Biblical story (Exodus 5:6–19) from which it comes. The Israelites were not ordered to make bricks without straw at all, as is popularly believed. Rather, they were told that straw for the sun-dried mud-and-straw bricks they were required to make would no longer be provided for them, and that they would have to go out and gather it themselves. Making bricks without straw would be an impossible task since straw was the essential element in holding the sun-dried mud bricks together. Use of the expression dates from the mid 17th century.

> It is often good for us to have to make bricks without straw. (Sir Leslie Stephen, *Hours in a Library,* 1874)

many words will not fill a bushel—Words without actions are worthless; words don't fill one's stomach; promises don't feed the poor. This 17th-century expression indicates the practical need for solid foodstuffs, not mere words, to fill a bushel basket; hence, substance is necessary in any undertaking.

> For the more compliment, the less sincerity. Many words will not fill a bushel. (John Bunyan, *Christ, a Complete Saviour*, 1692)

milk the ram—To engage in an activity destined to fail, to try in vain to do something which cannot be done; also *to milk the bull*. A ram is a male sheep and a bull is a male bovine. The old proverb "Whilst the one milks the ram, the other holds under the sieve" probably spawned this phrase; it appeared in *Several Tracts* by John Hales in 1656.

a nod is as good as a wink to a blind horse—An obsolete proverb of obvious, explicit literal meaning. Figuratively, this expression implies that regardless of how obvious a hint or suggestion may seem, it is useless if the person to whom it is directed cannot be aware of it. Thus, subtlety and tact can, at times, be inappropriate, particularly when dealing with a person known for his obtuseness. It is likely that this adage had been current for several centuries before its earliest literary usage in 1794 by William Godwin in *The Adventures of Caleb Williams*.

oppose Preston and his mastiffs—To be reckless or brash; to engage an overpowering force. This British term can be traced directly to one Christopher Preston, an entrepreneur of the late 17th century. Establishing a bear garden at Hockley-in-the-Hole, a place of questionable reputation, Preston used a small pack of mastiffs to protect himself and his place of business. It soon became apparent to the customers that it was futile to oppose Preston's orders because of his dogs. However, the dogs did him no good in the end, for he was mauled to death by one of his bears in 1700.

> ... I'd as good oppose Myself to Preston and his mastiffs loose. (John Oldham, *Satire of Juvenal*, 1683)

plow the sands—To engage in fruitless or futile labor, to waste one's time trying to do an impossible or endless task.

> All our time, all our labour, and all our assiduity is as certain to be thrown away as if you were to plough the sands of the seashore, the moment that the Bill reaches the Upper Chamber. (Herbert Henry Asquith, *Speech at Birmingham*, 1894)

In *Richard II* (II,ii) Shakespeare used a similar expression with the same meaning:

> Alas, poor Duke! The task he undertakes
> Is numbering sands and drinking oceans dry.

put a rope to the eye of a needle—To attempt the impossible. The metaphor is obvious.

roast snow in a furnace—To pursue ludicrous or meaningless activities; to engage in futile, pointless tasks. The figurative implications of this expression are obvious.

shoe the goose—To engage in aimless, trivial, unnecessary, or futile activities; to do busy work; to waste time. As this expression implies, putting shoes on a goose is as ludicrous and pointless as it is futile.

> Yet I can do something else than shoe the goose for my living. (Nicholas Breton, *Grinello's Fort*, 1604)

sleeveless errand—Any aimless or futile activity; an endeavor that is sure to be unprofitable or unsuccessful. In this expression, *sleeveless* is probably derived from *sleave* 'knotted threads' such as on the ends of woven fabrics, implying that the task or errand has loose ends which are not tied together in any significant or worthwhile manner. Most popular in the 16th and 17th centuries, *sleeveless errand* commonly referred to a false mission or other bogus activity which would keep a person occupied, and therefore out of the way, for a period of time. Variations such as *sleeveless words*, *sleeveless reason*, etc., have appeared in works by Chaucer, Shakespeare, Milton, and others.

> He was employ'd by Pope Alexander the third upon a sleeveless errand to convert the Sultan of Iconium. (Myles Davies, *Athenae Britannicae*, 1716)

square the circle—To engage in a futile endeavor; to undertake an impossible task. Early mathematicians struggled to find a circle and a square with equal areas. This is an impossibility since a principal factor in the area formula for a circle is π (3.1416 ...), an irrational number, whereas the factors in the area formula for a square are always rational numbers. The expression can now be applied to the attempting of any impossibility.

> You may as soon square the circle, as reduce the several Branches ... under one single Head. (Thomas Brown, *Fresny's Amusements*, 1704)

throw straws against the wind—To vainly resist the inevitable, to sweep back the Atlantic with a broom. A similar expression appeared in John Taylor's *Shilling* (1622):

> Like throwing feathers 'gainst the wind.

Both straw and feathers are very light and no match for the force of the wind.

wash a brick—To work in vain, to engage in utterly useless or futile labor, to plow the sands.

I wish I could make him feel as he ought, but one may as well wash a brick. (Warner in John Heneage Jesse's *George Selwyn and his Comtemporaries*, 1779)

Rarely heard today, this self-evident expression is the English equivalent of the old Latin proverb *laterem lavare*.

wild-goose chase—An impractical and ill-advised search for something nonexistent or unobtainable; a foolish and useless quest; a futile or hopeless enterprise. Originally, a wild-goose chase was a horse race where the second and all succeeding horses had to follow the leader at definite intervals, thus resembling wild geese in flight. Since the second horse was not allowed to overtake the first, it would become exhausted in its futile chase. It has alternately been suggested that *wild-goose chase* may refer to the difficulty of capturing a wild goose, implying that even if caught, the prize is of little value.

"I see you have found nothing," exclaimed Lady Gethin .... "It was a wild goose chase," he replied with a weary look. (Mrs. Alexander, *At Bay*, 1885)

GIBBERISH
SEE LANGUAGE; NONSENSE

GOOD LUCK
SEE SUPERSTITION

GRAFT
SEE PAYMENT

GREED
SEE DESIRE

GRIEVING

come home by Weeping Cross—To suffer disappointment or failure; to mourn, to lament; to be penitent and remorseful. The origin of this now rarely heard expression is obscure. There are several place names of this designation in England, but the common explanation that they were the site of penitential devotions is without substance. Use of the expression may have given rise to the explanation, rather than vice versa; for example, the following passage from Lyly's *Euphues* (1580):

The time will come when coming home by weeping cross, thou shalt confess.

cry [one's] eyes out—To sob long and bitterly; to weep excessively or immoderately; to exceed the limits of reasonable grief. The first written record of the idea behind this term is to be found in Cervantes' *Don Quixote* (1604). Don Quixote demands that Sancho, before conveying a letter to

Quixote's Dulcinea, witness some of the Don's acts of penance. To which Sancho replies:

> Good sir, as you love me, don't let me stay to see you naked; 'twill grieve me so to the heart, that I shall cry my eyes out.

in sackcloth and ashes—In a state of remorse and penitence; contrite, repentant; in mourning, sorrowful. This expression alludes to the ancient Hebrew custom of wearing sackcloth, a coarse fabric of camel's or goat's hair, and ashes (usually sprinkled on the head) to humble oneself as a sign of sorrow or penitence. Among the Biblical references to this custom is that in the Book of Daniel (9:3):

> Then I turned my face to the Lord, God, seeking him by prayer and supplications with fasting and sackcloth and ashes.

The expression has been used metaphorically for centuries.

> He knew that for all that had befallen she was mourning in mental sackcloth and ashes. (Hugh Conway, *A Family Affair*, 1805)

A common variation is *wearing sackcloth and ashes*.

Jamie Duff—A professional mourner; one who enjoys attending funerals. This Scottish nickname for a mourner at a funeral is derived from an actual person named Jamie Duff, who, it is said, frequently attended funerals because he took pleasure in riding in the mourning coach. The term has been in use since the middle of the 19th century.

wear the willow—To mourn the death of a mate; to suffer from unrequited love. The willow, especially the weeping willow, has long been a symbol of sorrow or grief. Psalm 137:1–2 is said to explain why the branches of the willow tree droop:

> By the rivers of Babylon, there we sat down, yea, we wept, when we remembered Zion. We hanged our harps upon the willows in the midst thereof.

Wear the willow appeared in print by the 16th century but is rarely, if ever, heard today.

> There's . . . Marie . . . wearing the willow because . . . Engemann is away courting Madam Carouge. (Katharine S. Macquoid, *At the Red Glove*, 1885)

HARASSMENT
SEE VEXATION

HAUGHTINESS

arrive in an armchair—To be indifferent about one's tardiness; to be arrogantly unmoved. This expression, popular in the 1920s, indicates that although one is late for an appointment or a meeting, he is obviously

WILD GOOSE CHASE

unconcerned about those people who have been kept waiting. The armchair, like the old sedan chairs of Indian rajahs, connotes an insouciant, unconcerned attitude on the part of the tardy person.

Attic figs—See DESIRE.

be all things to all men—

> To the weak became I as weak, that I might gain the weak: I am made all things to all men, that I might by all means save some. (I Corinthians 9:22)

As originally used by St. Paul, this expression indicated his willingness to change his personality to fit those with whom he was dealing, so that he might convert them to Christianity. However, probably because of its boastful implication, the phrase has come to connote vanity, haughtiness, conceit.

> If they, directed by Paul's holy pen,
> Become discreetly all things to all men,
> That all men may become all things to them,
> Envy may hate, but Justice can't condemn.
> (Charles Churchill, *The Prophecy of Famine*, 1763)

bridle—To tuck in the chin and throw the head back as in vanity or scorn; to put on an air of disdain or offense; sometimes *bridle up* or *bridle back*. The allusion is to the upward movement of a horse's head when the reins are abruptly pulled. In use since 1480, the term appeared in Henry Fielding's *Amelia* (1751):

> "Is she," said my aunt, bridling herself, "fit to decide between us?"

high-hat—To act in an aloof, snobbish, or condescending manner.

> Denver's dignity was mistaken by some for "high-hatting." (Noël Coward, *Australia Revisited*, 1941)

This expression, alluding to the tall headgear formerly worn by the wealthy, usually refers to a manner of behavior, although it is also often used in reference to a pompous or pretentious person.

high in the instep—Haughty; conceited; overly proud. The origin of this expression can probably be ascribed to the belief that the nobility had more delicate features than the peasantry. A noble man or woman supposedly had a higher arch and a higher instep than the peasants whose feet were said to be flat because of their cheap footwear and their constant, heavy toil. To the common people the phrase, in use since about 1540, came to signify the haughtiness associated with the upper classes.

> Too high in the instep . . . to bow to beg a kindness. (Thomas Fuller, *The Church-History of Britain*, 1655)

hoity-toity—Haughty or superior in manner; putting on airs. Although the exact origin of this expression is unknown, many scholars believe its source lies in the obsolete verb, *hoit*, which meant to 'act like a hoyden, romp riotously.' Others believe that *hoity* is a corruption of *haughty* with the reduplicative, *toity*, added for assonance and rhyme. Whatever the case, the term has been employed for more than 300 years. John Keats used it in his poem, *Caps and Bells*, (1820):

It bodes ill to his Majesty—refer
To the second chapter of my fortieth book,
And see what hoity-toity airs she took.

Jack-in-office—A conceited official; one who uses his office for his own gain; a petty official who is fond of power; an upstart; an insolent person in a position of authority. This term had its origins in the 17th century and, although often used in a general sense to indicate insolence, it is most often used to indicate pettiness on the part of one in a position of authority.

A type of Jack-in-office insolence and absurdity . . . a beadle. (Charles Dickens, *Little Dorrit*, 1857)

look down [one's] nose—To regard in a condescending manner; to view with disdain or disgust. A person who literally looks down his nose bears a countenance of disapproval or arrogance. The expression carries a strong suggestion of snobbery or haughtiness.

It is getting more difficult for a lawyer to look down his nose at the courtroom, with consequent impairment of the prestige of the courts. (*Baltimore Sun*, October 1932)

Norman blood—Aristocratic birth; blue blood; the highest social level; snobbishness. The allusion in this phrase is to William the Conqueror and his Norman host that overran the English at the Battle of Hastings in 1066. They immediately set themselves up as the aristocratic class and suborned the native English to lesser status; hence, the tone of disdain often associated with the term.

Kind hearts are more than coronets,
And simple faith than Norman blood.
(Alfred Tennyson, *Lady Clare Vere de Vere*, 1832)

on [one's] high horse—With one's nose in the air; pretentious, arrogant, affected; also *to ride the high horse* or *mount the high horse, to get down off one's high horse*, and other variants. In royal pageants of former times persons of high rank rode on tall horses, literally above the common people. Use of the expression dates from the late 18th century.

Only his mother felt that Mayo was not a rude boy, but his father frequently asked Mayo to get down off his high horse and act like everybody else. (William Saroyan, *Assyrian & Other Stories*, 1950)

on the high ropes—To be excited; to be disdainful; to be arrogant. This expression refers to a tightrope walker who, performing high above, looks down at the audience. Dating from the late 17th century, the phrase suggests a figurative looking down upon someone, as in disdain.

> Nora was rather on the high ropes, just then, and would not notice him. (Mrs. Henry Wood, *Trevlyn Hold*, 1864)

smart Alec(k)—A cocky, conceited person; an obnoxious, pompous know-it-all; a haughty, self- important fool. Although the origin of this American colloquialism is obscure, it was first recorded in a Carson City, Nevada, newspaper in 1862. If the term is derived, and it probably is, from the name of an actual Alec, the apparent possessor of certain undesirable qualities, history does not record his identity.

> In "A Word in Your Ear", the fourth collection of his columns from *The Times* [London], Mr. Howard comes across less like a smart aleck than like a learned uncle. (Calvin Trillin, *The New York Times Book Review*, January 8, 1984)

An adjective form, *smart alecky*, has achieved almost the same level of popularity as the noun form.

> Few grown-ups enjoy an encounter with a smart- alecky child. (*Denison [Texas] Herald*, July 2, 1948)

stuffed shirt—Self-important or ostentatious person who is actually insignificant; a pompous, haughty, grandiose person. The source of this expression apparently lies in the 19th-century practice of retailers' stuffing shirts with tissue paper for advertising display, mannequins being a later development. Appearing genuine on the outside, these stuffed shirts were really devoid of substance.

> I have been accused of many things in my time, but never of being a stuffed shirt. (John Dickson Carr, *Death Turns the Tables*, 1941)

toffee-nosed—Stuck-up, with one's nose in the air, conceited, pretentious, stuffy. Although the origin of this British slang term is not certain, it comes from *toff*, British slang for a pretentious swell.

HEALTH
SEE ILL HEALTH

HELP
SEE ASSISTANCE

HINDRANCE
SEE IMPEDIMENT

HOPELESSNESS
SEE FUTILITY

HORROR
SEE FEAR

HYPOCRISY
SEE PRETENSE

IDLENESS
SEE INDOLENCE

IGNORANCE
See also FATUOUSNESS

as a hog does side saddle—This American cowboy expression is used of a person who has little understanding of a situation:

> He knows as much about it as a hog does a side saddle. (*American Speech*, December 1927)

or who has little, if any use, for something:

> He has no more use for it than a hog does a side saddle. (*American Speech*, December 1945)

The term had its inception in the late 19th century.

blockhead—A dimwit, a numskull. The term comes from the dummy head used by wigmakers and hatters.

cork-brained—Light-headed; giddy. This phrase plays with the analogy between cork cells, which are dead, airfilled cells, and one's brain. *Cork-brained* appeared in print as early as 1630.

dumb Dora—Any stupid woman; any dull-witted or ignorant female; a giddy girl. In common use from the early 1900s, this expression achieved its greatest popularity during the era of the flappers, the 1920s. The origin of the word is obscure, with conjectures ranging from it being an allusion to David Copperfield's child wife to the suggestion that it refers to Great Britain's Defense of the Realm Act, or *DORA*, an unpopular emergency act of World War I which many people thought ill-conceived. In any event, the expression is seldom heard today.

dunce—A dull-witted, stupid person; a dolt, blockhead, or ignoramus. This term makes use of the name of a scholastic theologian of the late 13th century, John Duns Scotus. Originally the term referred to a caviling sophist, derived from the fact that Scotus's doctrines were criticized as a conglomeration of hairsplitting distinctions. Such a person would be full of useless information and perhaps even opposed to progress and learning, as Scotus was regarded.

> A dunce, void of learning but full of books. (Thomas Fuller, *The Holy and Profane State*, 1642)

Dunce also referred to one who is uneducated or incapable of learning.

> But now in our age it is grown to be a common proverb in derision, to call such a person as is senseless or without learning a Duns, which is

143

as much as a fool. (Raphael Holinshed, *The First Volume of the Chronicles of England, Scotland, and Ireland,* 1577–87)

Today *dunce* has lost its connotations of overrefinement and pedantry; it means simply 'stupid, doltish, ignorant.'

dunderhead—A thickheaded, stupid person; a numskull, blockhead, or dullard. The origin of this term is obscure, but it has been speculated that *dunder* is a corruption of the Spanish *redundar* 'to overflow' and is the name given to the lees or dregs of cane juice used in the fermentation of rum. Thus, a "dunderhead" is a head full of dregs, overflowing with this worthless substance. This term has been in use since the early 17th century.

hick—A greenhorn from the country; lowbrow; ignoramus. This expression is rooted in a peculiarity of speech among the rural population of 16th-century England. A common method of forming nicknames among these people was to substitute *h* sounds for initial *r* sounds, as Hob for Rob, Hodge for Rog, and Hick for Rick. Reflecting this rural practice, the word *hick* came to signify any rustic, and eventually came to connote a bumpkin, especially one who falls prey to city slickers.

> One boob may die, but deathless is
> The royal race of hicks—
> When Ahab went to Ascalon
> They sold him gilded bricks.
> (Don Marquis, *Boob Ballad,* 1922)

A related term, *hick town,* describes any small, rural village, usually isolated from the main stream of progress.

Know-Nothing—The name of a political faction; an ignoramus; an anti-intellectual; an agnostic. In 1852 a political group known as the American party set as the principal plank in their platform the elimination of immigrant influence on the American political scene by the adoption of strong naturalization laws and the election of only native-born Americans to office. The name, suggested by the stock answer, "I know nothing," to any questions put to party members about the group's activities, was allegedly coined by E. Z. C. Judson, a leading member of the party. Metaphorical extensions grow out of the original, political sense.

> I am not a Know-Nothing . . . . How could I be? How can anyone who abhors the oppression of Negroes be in favor of degrading classes of white people. (Abraham Lincoln, *Letter to Joshua F. Speed,* August 24, 1855)

not know A from a windmill—To be extremely ignorant or stupid. This expression is said to have been originally suggested by the similarity between the shape of a capital A and that of a windmill. This theory is further reinforced by the now rare or obsolete definition of windmill found in the *OED:* "a figure of a windmill; a sign or character resembling this, as a cross or asterisk." In popular usage until the late 19th century, the phrase appeared as early as 1402 in the Rolls of Parliament.

not know [one's] ass [or *Brit. arse] from [one's] elbow*—Not know the first thing about something, not know what's what, completely ignorant or naïve.

> I wish I'd had a crowd like that for my first crew. We none of us knew arse from elbow when they pushed me off. (N. Shute, *Pastoral,* 1944)

not know B from a battledore—To be illiterate, ignorant, or obtuse. *Battledore* is an obsolete word for a hornbook used as a child's primer. Not to know the letter from the book signified utter ignorance.

> He knew not a B from a battledore nor ever a letter of the book. (John Foxe, *Acts and Monuments of These Latter and Perilous Days,* 1553–87)

Many alliterative variations of the phrase exist, substituting *broomstick, bull's foot,* or *buffalo's foot* for *battledore.*

not know from Adam—Be completely unacquainted with a person; in the dark as to someone's identity; unable to recognize a particular person. Although the source of this expression is uncertain, it seemingly arose from an ancient argument over whether Adam and Eve possessed navels. Many famous paintings depict them with navels, however, it has been argued that they had none, for they were never *in utero.* This anatomical detail was alluded to in 1944, when a number of contributors created *Profile by Gaslight,* a life of Sherlock Holmes. Among the contributions, a Dr. Logan Glendenning set forth a case in which Holmes, after his death, was called upon in heaven to locate Adam and Eve, who had been missing for a great period of time. Holmes located both of them quite readily, for he alone among all the searchers knew the others from Adam—only Adam and Eve were without navels.

> "Who's that fellow?" . . . "Don't know him from Adam." (G. J. Whyte-Melville, *Market Harbor,* 1861)

The French say *Je ne le connais ni d'Eve ni d'Adam,* 'I don't know him either from Eve or from Adam.'

not know from Adam's off ox—Not have the slightest idea who someone is; in the dark as to someone's identity. The off ox is the one farthest from the driver; therefore, the one with whom he is the least familiar. Furthermore, since the driver can't see the terrain as well where the off ox is walking, the off ox has developed a reputation for being clumsy; hence, a stupid or clumsy person is often referred to as an *off ox.* Beyond that, the off ox is less readily manageable, and, as a result, has also come to connote a stubborn, unmanageable person.

> Ez to the answerin' o' questions, I'm an off ox at bein' druv. (James Russell Lowell, *Biglow Papers,* 1848)

Seemingly, the expression *not know from Adam's off ox* came about through a combination of factors. The well-known phrase, *not know from Adam*, somehow was combined with the words suggesting the unfamiliarity of the driver with the off ox, creating the longer phrase.

> People he didn't know from Adam's off ox were bowing to him. (Clive F. Adams, *And Sudden Death*, 1940)

not know if [one] is coming or going—See CONFUSION.

not know shit from shinola—To be totally stupid or ignorant. *Shinola* is the brand name of a shoe polish. The expression is entirely alliterative, and no intentional disparagement of the product is intended. Because of its vulgar origin and implications, the phrase is somewhat limited in written usage.

not know which end is up—Not know what's going on; ignorant, stupid; totally confused or mixed up.

out to lunch—Stupid, daft, or flaky; socially incompetent. This expression relates physical absence to mental vacuity. The common phrase often describes a person whose social ineptness or exceedingly poor judgment is owing to a severe lack of common sense.

> A girl who would be attracted to Bud's mean streak and bad temper must be a little out to lunch. (*Toronto Daily Star*, June 1966)

ILL HEALTH

charley horse—Muscular cramp or stiffness in an arm or, usually, leg. Reliable sources say the origin of this term is unknown. Nevertheless, a story is told of a limping horse named Charley who used to draw a roller in the White Sox baseball park in Chicago. Thus, the (apocryphal) origin of the term is based on the resemblance between the posture of an athlete suffering from a leg cramp and a limping horse.

> Toward the close of the season Mac was affected with a "Charleyhorse" and that ended his ballplaying for 1888. (*Cincinnati Comm. Gazette*, March 17, 1889)

Current today, this North American slang phrase has been popular since the 1880s.

climb up May Hill—To survive the winter and spring months after suffering a long period of ill health. This British expression alludes to the old belief that surviving through the month of May indicates a passing beyond crisis for the sick and indigent. William Hone in his *Every-day Book* (1825) explains:

The month of May is called a trying month to persons long ailing with critical complaints. It is common to say, "Ah, he'll never get up May-hill!" or "If he can climb over May-hill he'll do."
The term has been in use since about 1660.

collywobbles—Dyspepsia accompanied by a rumbling in the intestines; an intestinal disturbance with moderate diarrhea; general indisposition. The *OED* attributes this term to a fantastic formation of *colic*, a stomach upset, and *wobble*, a quaking or trembling. The term has been in use since about 1820.

> He laughingly excused himself on the ground that his songs were calculated to give a white man collywobbles. (Frank T. Bullen, *Sack of Shakings*, 1901).

[one's] days are numbered—Dying, almost dead; with little time remaining, nearing the end. This expression is usually used to describe someone who is critically ill and has but a short time to live; so short, in fact, that one could count the days remaining. The phrase is also frequently used to describe the imminent end of anything, particularly one's employment.

feed the fishes—To be seasick. Herbert Meade used this humorous metaphor in *A Ride through the disturbed districts of New Zealand* (1870):

> His first act was to appease the fishes... by feeding them most liberally.

a frog in [one's] throat—Temporary hoarseness or thickness in the voice; an irritation in the throat. This colloquial expression dates from at least 1909 and is an obvious allusion to the hoarse, throaty croaking of frogs.

have been to Barking Creek—Said of one troubled by a bad cough, laryngitis, or bronchitis. This British expression from the early 19th century is an obvious pun on the barking sound that emanates from the throat of one who is suffering from a serious chest or throat infection. A related term, which is also a pun on coughing, is a *representative for Berkshire*, pronounced "barkshuh," or a *candidate for Berkshire*.

have one foot in the grave—Near death, at death's door, dying. This common expression often refers to one afflicted by a lingering, terminal illness.

> He has twenty thousand a year... And one foot in the grave. (J. Payn, *Luck Dorrells*, 1886)

Hippocratic countenance—The look of one who is dying; the emaciated aspect of one who has suffered a long illness. This expression had its inception in the accurate description which Hippocrates, the ancient Greek physician, gave of the shrunken and livid aspect of the human features immediately preceding death, or when in a state of exhaustion so severe that death appears to be imminent. The term has been in use in English since at least the 17th century.

> . . . with a sharp pinched-up nose, hippocratic countenance. (Hanly, *Philosophical Transactions of the Royal Society*, 1770)

A related term, *Hippocratic face*, has the same meaning.

> Succeeded by . . . Lethargy, a dismal Hippocratic face, staring eyes. (Spregnell, *Philosophical Transactions of the Royal Society*, 1713)

Another related term, *Austerlitz look*, may be only a nonce word; however, it was used to describe the look of complete discouragement and total exhaustion in British Prime Minister William Pitt's face after he received news of the French victory over the Austrians and Russians at Austerlitz in 1805.

in the straw—In labor or giving birth; in childbed; pregnant. This expression probably refers to the ancient custom of placing straw on the doorstep of a house to muffle the footsteps of visitors so as not to disturb a woman in parturition. One source, however, suggests that *in the straw* may allude to the straw-filled mattresses once common among the poor.

> In the phrase of ladies in the straw, "as well as can be expected." (Thomas DeQuincey, *Confessions of an English Opium-Eater*, 1822)

A related expression said of a woman who has just given birth is *out of the straw*.

Montezuma's revenge—Diarrhea, particularly when it afflicts foreigners in Mexico. This expression is named for the last Aztec emperor, Montezuma, who lost his empire in 1520 through the trickery of the Spanish conquistadors. American and European tourists in Mexico are still plagued by this condition, perhaps as a reaction to spicy Mexican food or from dysentery generated by impure water. This expression and some humorous variations appeared in *Western Folklore XXI* (1962):

> The North American in Mexico has coined a number of names for the inevitable dysentery and diarrhea: "Mexican two-step," "Mexican foxtrot," "Mexican toothache," and, less directly if more colorfully, "Montezuma's revenge," the "Curse of Montezuma," and the "Aztec hop."

In keeping with the tradition of *Montezuma's revenge*, various euphemisms for diarrhea have been coined by persons who travel to Egypt, India, Burma, and Japan, as delineated in this citation from an April 1969, *Daily Telegraph*:

> Prevent gippy tummy. Also known as Delhi belly, Rangoon runs, Tokyo trots, Montezuma's revenge.

off [one's] feed—To be ill; to suffer from loss of appetite; to be depressed or disconsolate. This expression, originally a reference to an ailing horse, usually describes a person whose physical or emotional state effects a repulsion to food.

on [one's] last legs—Moribund; in a state of exhaustion or near-collapse; about to break down or fail. In this expression, *legs* is usually used figuratively to describe that part of a person, machine, project, or other item which allows it to move forward or continue. *Last legs* implies that the person or object is tired and will be unable to function at all within a short time.

on the blink—Unwell, in ill health, out of condition; in disrepair, not in working order, *on the fritz*. This common slang expression is of unknown origin. Two possible but highly conjectural theories relate it to the dialectal meaning of *blink* 'milk gone slightly sour,' and to the U.S. fishermen's use of the term for mackerel too young to be marketable.

the runs—Diarrhea. This slang expression is derived not only from the fluid consistency and movement of the feces, but also from the celerity and frequency with which one so afflicted reaches a bathroom. The phrase is commonplace in both the United States and Great Britain. A similar term is *the trots*.

a shadow of [one's] former self—See PHYSICAL APPEARANCE.

shoot [one's] cookies—To vomit. This expression and innumerable variations euphemistically describe the regurgitation of recently eaten food.

> If I'm any judge of color, you're goin' to shoot your cookies. (Raymond Chandler, *Finger Man*, 1934)

Among the more popular variants are *toss one's cookies, shoot one's breakfast* or *shoot one's lunch* or *shoot one's dinner* or *shoot one's supper, return one's breakfast* or *return one's lunch*, etc., *lose one's breakfast* or *lose one's lunch*, etc., *blow lunch, spiff one's biscuits*, etc.

shoot the cat—To vomit, especially as a result of excessive alcoholic indulgence. This British colloquialism alludes to a cat's purported tendency to vomit frequently.

> I'm cursedly inclined to shoot the cat. (Frederick Marryat, *The King's Own*, 1830)

Variations include *cat, jerk the cat, whip the cat*, and *sick as a cat*.

under the weather—Not feeling well, ill; intoxicated; hung over. This expression is derived from the common but unproven belief that atmospheric conditions and health are directly correlated. The phrase usually suggests the affliction of minor ailments.

> They have been very well as a general thing, although now and then they might have been under the weather for a day or two. (Frank R. Stockton, *Borrowed Month*, 1887)

The expression is often extended to include drunkenness and its after-effects.

ILL TEMPER
SEE ANGER

ILLNESS
SEE ILL HEALTH

IMMEDIACY
SEE INSTANTANEOUSNESS

IMMODERATION
SEE EXCESSIVENESS

IMPATIENCE

champ at the bit—To show impatience; to wait restlessly or anxiously to begin. This expression, in figurative use since 1645, refers to the way a horse, eager to be off, chews on the bit in his mouth and stamps the ground with his hooves. Similar phrases with the same meaning are *to bite the bridle*, used figuratively since 1514, and *to strain at the leash*.

cool [one's] heels—To impatiently await the promised and supposedly imminent arrival of one or more persons, especially when the arrival has been intentionally and rudely delayed. Dating from the early 1600s, this expression is an allusion to the fact that one's feet, hot from walking, are cooled by waiting in a stationary position.

> Well, if we're not ready, they'll have to wait—won't do them any harm to cool their heels a bit. (John Galsworthy, *Strife*, 1909)

money burns a hole in [one's] pocket—This expression, used only in reference to money, indicates that the owner is so impatient to spend what he has accumulated that the money actually feels hot; he must take it out and spend it quickly before it falls through the hole it is creating, and lost. The origin of the phrase, in use since the early 1500s, is obscure.

> A man who has more money about him than he requires . . . is tempted to spend it . . . . It is apt to "burn a hole in his pocket." (Samuel Smiles, *Thrift*, 1875)

Another form of the phrase, *money burns a hole in [one's] purse*, although somewhat dated, is still heard occasionally.

need it yesterday—Need it immediately if not sooner; want it now, without any delay. This modern business expression is spoken as a goad to prompt action. It is usually uttered by customers or bosses who seem to expect something to be done as soon as the words leave their mouths.

sit upon hot cockles—To be very impatient or restive; to be on pins and needles. "Hot Cockles" is the name of an ancient children's game in which a blindfolded child tried to guess who had just struck him on the buttocks. Since *sit upon* can mean 'to await' or 'to be seated upon,' to *sit upon hot cockles* probably alludes either to one's fidgety anticipation of the blow, or to the squirming discomfort of one who sits down after having been struck by an enthusiastic player.

> He laughs and kicks like Chrysippus when he saw an ass eat figs; and sits upon hot cockles till it be blazed abroad. (Thomas Walkington, *The Optick Glasse of Humors*, 1607)

soft fire makes sweet malt—A proverbial expression meaning that reckless hurriedness often spoils an undertaking or project.

> Soft fire, They say, does make sweet Malt, Good Squire. (Samuel Butler, *Hudibras*, 1663)

Malt is burnt and its sweetness lost by too intense a fire. This expression, synonymous with the common phrase *haste makes waste*, is now rarely heard.

Sooner—One who acts prematurely to gain an unfair advantage; one who settles on government land before it is legally open to claiming rights; a citizen of the state of Oklahoma. In the late 1800s the United States government proclaimed that federal territory in parts of Oklahoma would be thrown open to claim by those who were willing to settle permanently. A few tried to enter covertly and set up their claims on the choice pieces of land by moving in "sooner" than the officially proclaimed date, April 22, 1889.

> Then there were the "Sooners," who sneaked in too soon . . . . Most of these would-be settlers lost their claims but gave Oklahoma its nickname, the "Sooner State." (*Story of the Great American West*, 1977)

The term has stuck both as a nickname for Oklahomans and as a figurative expression for one who acts hastily or prematurely.

tirl at the pin—To rattle the door latch to gain admittance; to demonstrate impatience; to try to hurry someone. The reference in this phrase, in use as early as 1500, is to *pin*, i.e., the latch of a door which is lifted to gain entrance. When the pin is in a locked position, one *tirls* or rattles the latch to gain the occupants' attention; thus, the variant *tirl at the latch*.

> She tirled fretfully at the pin, the servant maid opened, and we went within. (Samuel Crockett, *The Men of the Moss-Hags*, 1895)

The expression is also used figuratively to refer to someone acting impatiently.

a watched pot never boils—Wishing will not make it so; anxiety never hastens matters. This proverbial expression, usually said to one who is exhibiting impatience, has become so trite that it has lost much of its impact.

> A watched pot never boils, they say—only this one finally did. (Clare Boothe, *Europe in the Spring*, 1940)

Ogden Nash parodied the term in the title of one of his poems, "A Watched Example Never Boils" (1936).

IMPEDIMENT
See also DIFFICULTY

bamboo curtain—An invisible barrier of secrecy and censorship separating Communist China from the remainder of the world.

> The Communist bosses of Peiping dropped a bamboo curtain cutting off Peiping from the world. (*Time*, March 14, 1949)

After Mao Tse-Tung had successfully completed his revolution against the Republic of China and had achieved control of the entire country, he cut off all contact with the Western world, thus creating the so-called *bamboo curtain*, a term probably coined on analogy with *iron curtain*, used of Eastern Europe.

bottleneck—A narrow passage; an impasse; congestion or constriction; a traffic jam. The reference is to the thin, narrow neck of a bottle, which is necessarily constrictive. By extension, the word is used for any point at which passage or flow becomes impeded because the volume of a larger area must move into a smaller. The equivalent French term is *embouteillage*. The word appeared in print by 1907 in the *Westminster Gazette*.

break the egg in [someone's] pocket—To spoil somebody's plan; to create an obstacle in someone's path. This expression, dating from the early 18th century, is obvious in its implication: a broken egg in one's pocket would undoubtedly prove disconcerting enough to slow him down.

> This very circumstance . . . broke the egg . . . in the pocket of the Whigs. (Roger North, *Examen*, 1734)

choke-pear—Something difficult or impossible to "swallow"; something "hard to take"; a difficulty. The figurative sense of this term is an extension of its literal meaning, i.e., a variety of pear with a harsh, bitter taste. Samuel Collins used the expression in *Epphata to F.T.* (1617):

> S. Austens testimony . . . is a chokepear that you cannot swallow.

The term has been used literally since 1530 and figuratively since 1573.

cooling card—Anything that diminishes or lessens a person's ardor or enthusiasm; a damper. According to the *OED*, *cooling card* is apparently a term of some unknown game and is used figuratively or punningly with the meaning above. This expression, now obsolete, dates from 1577. In

Henry Dircks' *Life*, the Marquis of Worcester is quoted as using it thus in 1664:

> It would ... prove a cooling card to many, whose zeal otherwise would transport them.

cramp [someone's] style—To inhibit another's freedom of expression or action; to make someone feel ill-at-ease and self-conscious; to have a dampening effect on another's spirits. The person who cramps another's style usually does so by his mere presence or the attitudes he embodies, rather than by explicit word or overt action. Impersonal forces such as rules or procedures also can cramp a person's style.

derby dog—Something that gets in the way; an interruption that is sure to occur; a hindrance; an obstruction. On Derby Day at Epsom Downs, as soon as the race course is cleared, it seems inevitable that a stray dog wanders out on the course, thus stalling the beginning of the race. The reliability of such an action has brought about the figurative implication of this term, which has been in use since the 1870s.

fly in the ointment—A triviality which ruins an otherwise enjoyable occasion; a negative element or consideration. The Biblical origin of this expression appears in Ecclesiastes (10:1):

> Dead flies cause the ointment of the apothecary to send forth a stinking savour.

In modern usage, the phrase also implies minor inconvenience or untimeliness:

> The present situation is not without its 'fly in the ointment' for those motorists who have patriotically lent the assistance of their cars to the military authorities. (*Scotsman*, September 1914)

iron curtain—A term used to describe the dividing line between Communist Eastern Europe and the democracies of western Europe. Originally attributed to Winston Churchill from his speech at Westminster College, Fulton, Missouri in 1946, the term became the center of a controversy when Sir Vincent Trowbridge, in a letter to *Notes and Queries*, January 1948, revealed that he had used the expression in a *Sunday Empire News* article in October 1945. However, John Lukacs resolved the dispute in his *Great Powers and Eastern Europe* (1953). He revealed that the German Propaganda Minister Joseph Goebbels had made use of the term in an editorial in *Das Reich*, February 23, 1945.

> An iron curtain [*eisenen Vorhang*] would at once descend on this territory, which including the Soviet Union, would be of tremendous dimension.

The original use of the expression was literal and can be traced to the late 18th century when an actual iron curtain was installed in some theaters in

Europe, to be lowered across the stage to protect the audience in case of fire.

pratfall—A fall on one's buttocks; a humiliating blunder; a danger that lies in one's path. This expression is derived from show business lingo. In both the burlesque show and the circus, the *pratfall*, a sudden and unepected loss of one's balance and footing, is a common device used by slapstick comedians and clowns to get laughs. By extension the term has developed the figurative connotation of a trap one must avoid or an obstacle that may trip one up.

> On the principles and pratfalls of the rhyming racket .... (Billy Rose, syndicated newspaper column, January 9, 1950)

skeleton at the feast—A source of gloom or sadness at an otherwise festive occasion; a wet blanket, a party pooper; something that acts as a reminder that life holds sorrow as well as joy. According to the *Moralia*, a collection of essays by Plutarch (A.D. circa 46–120), the Egyptians always placed a skeleton at their banquet tables to remind the revelers of their mortality.

> The skeleton of ennui sat at these dreary feasts; and it was not even crowned with roses. (George Lawrence, *Guy Livingstone*, 1857)

It was also common practice for many monastic orders to place a skull or death's head on the refectory table to remind those present of their mortality.

there's the rub—Said of an impediment, hindrance, or stumbling-block, especially one of an abstract nature; the crux of a problem. In this expression, *rub* alludes to the rubbing of a spoon inside a mixing bowl, an occurrence which interferes with smooth stirring. Although *rub* in this sense had been in use for some time before Shakespeare, he popularized the phrase by incorporating it into Hamlet's famous soliloquy:

> To be, or not to be: that is the question ...
> To sleep: perchance to dream: ay, there's the rub. (III,i)

A variation is *here lies the rub*.

wet blanket—A discouraging or dampening influence on others' enjoyment of a party or similar pleasurable occasion; a person who is habitually grouchy or depressed; a killjoy, party pooper, spoilsport. Literally, a wet blanket is one that has been soaked in water and is used to smother or quench a fire. The figurative implications are obvious.

> Sometimes he called her a wet blanket, when she thus dampened his ardor. (Margaret Oliphant, *Annals of a Publishing House*, 1897)

IMPROPRIETY
SEE UNSCRUPULOUSNESS

INABILITY
SEE FAILURE

INACCURACY
SEE ERRONEOUSNESS

INACTIVITY
SEE INDOLENCE

INANITY
SEE FATUOUSNESS

INCLUSIVENESS
See also TOTALITY

across-the-board—General; all-inclusive and comprehensive; treating all groups or all members of a group equally and without exception. The term refers to the board used to display the betting odds and totals at race tracks. An across-the-board bet is a combination wager in which the same amount of money is bet on a single horse to win, place, or show, thereby ensuring a winning ticket if the horse places at all. The original sporting use of the term dates from about 1935; the more general usage dates from about 1950.

all along the line—At every point; in every particular or detail; entirely, completely. Common variants include *all down the line* and *right down the line*. What the original line was, if indeed one did exist, is uncertain. The expression does, however, seem to presuppose some sort of actual line, be it a line of soldiers going into battle, a geographical line of some kind, or any of the other sundry types of lines that exist. Charles Haddon Spurgeon used the phrase in *The Treasury of David* (1877).

all around the Wrekin—To all one's friends everywhere; to all mankind. This old toast dates from at least the 17th century. Using the Wrekin, a mountain in the Shropshire Hills south of Shrewsbury, England, as a center, the speaker expands his toast to encompass all mankind. Apparently the toast is particularly popular during the Christmas holidays.

> For Christmas Eve rejoicing, put a large clog of wood on the fire, a Yule Clog, and feast and toast all friends 'round the Wrekin. (*Gentleman's Magazine*, 1784)

The dedication of George Farquhar's *The Recruiting Officer* (1706) reads: to all friends round the Wrekin.

all the king's horses (and all the king's men)— Everybody who can be of assistance; every single person; everybody involved in the situation; everything. This expression, adopted from the child's nursery rhyme, *Humpty-Dumpty*, connotes a multitude of people attempting to solve a

155

problem, sometimes implying that there are so many that they get in each other's way.

And if all the king's horses and all the king's men can't make a couple get along on the screen? (*TV Guide*, March 24, 1984)

all the world and his wife—Everybody, especially everybody of important social position; everyone without exception; all men and women; the whole shooting match. This hyperbole, in use since at least the early 18th century, is usually employed to signify a large gathering of people, usually of both sexes.

How he welcomes at once all the world and his wife,
And how civil to folk he ne'er saw in his life.
(Christopher Anstey, *The New Bath Guide*, 1766)

Related terms which are also used to indicate that everybody was present are *everybody and his brother* and *every mother's son*.

The Romans...slew them, every mother's son. (Roger Ascham, *Toxophilus*, 1545)

alpha and omega—Everything; from beginning to end; the whole works; the whole nine yards. *Alpha* and *omega* are the first and last letters, respectively, of the Greek alphabet, hence the signification of all-inclusiveness. Strangely enough, during the Middle Ages the last letter was sometimes listed as *tau*. Consequently, in Middle English literature one often encounters *alpha to tau* rather than *alpha to omega*.

The siege of Dresden is the alpha to whatever omegas there may be. (Thomas Carlyle, *Frederick the Great*, 1865)

bag and baggage—With all one's personal belongings; completely, totally. This phrase was military in origin and applied to the possessions of an army as a whole (baggage), and of each individual soldier (bag). The original expression *to march out [with] bag and baggage* was used in a positive sense to mean to make an honorable retreat, to depart without having suffered any loss of property. The equivalent French expression was *vie et bagues sauves*. The term is now used disparagingly, however, to underscore the absolute nature of one's departure; it implies quite the opposite of an honorable retreat. Used in the original military sense in 1525 by John Bourchier Berners in his translation of Froissart's *Chronicles*, the phrase did not appear in its more contemporary sense until the early 17th century in Thomas Middleton's *The Witch*.

count noses—To take note of the number in attendance; to count the number present, especially those of one persuasion in a vote. This phrase dates back to the 9th century, when, it is said, the Danish conquerors of Ireland took the census by a nose count, and then used that census for the collection of taxes, with those who neglected or refused to pay actually having their noses slit. It is believed that the two expressions *pay through* *the nose* and *bleed one for his money* also originated from this practice. The term is frequently used today to indicate a count of those voting on one side of an issue.

> Some modern zealots appear to have no better knowledge of truth, nor better manner of judging it, than by counting noses. (Anthony Ashley Cooper, *Characteristics of Men, Manners, Opinions, Times,* 1711)

A variant is *telling noses.*

every man Jack—Every single person without exception. The precise origin of this phrase is unknown. A plausible but not entirely convincing theory traces the source of *every man Jack* to the early form *everych one* 'every one,' which in the 16th and 17th centuries was often written as *every chone.* By corruption, *every chone* became *every John,* and since *Jack* is the familiar form of *John,* the phrase was corrupted once again giving rise to the current form *every man Jack.* Thackeray used the phrase in *Vanity Fair.*

> Sir Pitt had numbered every "Man Jack" of them.

Thackeray's use of quotation marks and capitalization of *man* casts doubt on the theory of the origin of *every man Jack* presented above.

everything but the kitchen sink—Everything imaginable, everything under the sun; also *everything but the kitchen stove.* Both expressions date from the first half of this century, although *everything but the kitchen stove* predated *everything but the kitchen sink* by about twenty years according to the *OED* citations. In his *Dictionary of Forces' Slang* (1948) Partridge says that *kitchen sink* was "used only in the phrase indicating intense bombardment—'They chucked everything they'd got at us, except, or including the kitchen sink.'" In other words, every possible kind of missile, including kitchen sinks.

everything that opens and shuts—All-inclusive; everything imaginable; *the whole kit and caboodle.* This Briticism, the equivalent of the American *everything but the kitchen sink,* implies that not only are the necessities there, but also the luxurious extras, too. It can apply to a new house with all the necessary appliances, a new car with every imaginable accessory, or a poker hand with four aces. The expression has been in use since World War II.

from A to Izzard—From A to Z; from beginning to end; from first to last; completely; entirely; the whole ball of wax. This British colloquialism, in use by the early 1700s, employs an old word for the letter Z. Although the word *izzard* for the letter *z* has itself become obsolete, replaced by *zee* in America and *zed* in England, it continues to be heard in this phrase.

> They want everything checked from A to Izzard. (H. S. Keeler, *The Man with the Wooden Spectacles,* 1941)

from China to Peru—All over the world; from Dan to Beersheba; from one end of the world to the other. This term, dating from the 17th century, is a figurative expression to designate something, usually spiritual, occasionally material, that is world-wide in its scope.

> Let observation with extensive view
> Survey mankind from China to Peru.
> (Samuel Johnson, *The Vanity of Human Wishes*, 1748)

The phrase is in use today, usually in reference to the popularity or unpopularity of a political or social issue.

from Dan to Beersheba—From one outermost extreme or limit to the other; everywhere. This expression is based on a Biblical reference:

> Then all the children of Israel went out, and the congregation was gathered together as one man, from Dan to Beersheba. (Judges 20:1)

Judges 19 and 20 discusses the reasons that all of the Israelite nations gathered to attack the Benjamites. Dan was the northernmost city in Israel, Beersheba the southernmost. Thus, from Dan to Beersheba implied the entire kingdom. In more contemporary usage, this expression is often employed by political writers to describe the extent of a person or issue's popularity.

from Land's End to John o' Groat's [House]—From one end of Great Britain to the other; all the way; thoroughly; from alpha to omega; from one extreme to the other. This term, dating from the early 19th century, designates all of Britain by naming those landmarks found in the most southwestern and most northeastern corners of the island, respectively. *John o' Groat's* refers to a house, still standing, located in the northeastern corner of Scotland. It is named for a Dutch immigrant, Jan Groot, who built the house along with his brothers. *Land's End* is the southwestern tip of England that juts out into the Atlantic.

> If you laid it down in sovereigns . . . it would have reached from the Land's End to John o Groat's. (James Payn, *The Burnt Million*, 1890)

from soda to hock—From beginning to end; from A to Z; from first to last; from soup to nuts; from alpha to omega. This Americanism is derived from the game of faro, where the first card, displayed face-up in the dealing box before any bets are made, is called *soda*; and the last card, which may not be used, is known as *hock*, for it is said to be *in hock*. The expression had its origin in the western United States in the late 1800s.

> Young Bines played the deal from soda card to hock. (Harry L. Wilson, *The Spenders*, 1902)

from soup to nuts—From A to Z, from first to last; absolutely everything, as in the phrase *everything from soup to nuts*. This American slang expression alludes to an elaborate multicourse meal in which soup is served as the first course and nuts as the last.

Today's drugstores may have everything from soup to nuts, but they can't boast fascinating remedies like Gambler's Luck, Virgin's Milk,...or Come-Follow-Me-Boy. (*New Orleans Times-Picayune Magazine*, April 1950)

from stem to stern—Completely; entirely; from one end to the other. On ships the stem is the vertical bow member of the vessel, and the stern is the rear. The phrase maintains common figurative use.

I had him stripped and washed from stem to stern in a tub of warm soapsuds. (Elizabeth Drinker, *Journal*, 1794)

kith and kin—All one's relatives and friends; all one's fellow countrymen. This expression, dating from the days of the Anglo-Saxons, continues in everyday use. The Old English *cyth* meaning relationship and *cynn* meaning family were combined into one phrase to create an all-inclusive term. Originally, the term encompassed all one's countrymen, friends, neighbors, and relatives, but during the 15th century its significance was limited to one's relatives and close friends.

One would be in less danger
From the wiles of the stranger,
If one's kin and kith
Were more fun to be with.
(Ogden Nash, *Family Court*, 1931)

ragtag and bobtail—See STATUS.

right and left—From all directions at once, everywhere you look, on all sides; every time, repeatedly. This phrase implying inclusiveness or ubiquity dates from the beginning of the 14th century. *Webster's Third* cites both current usages:

...troops looting right and left (A. N. Dragnich)

[S]ocial events...have been rained out right and left. (*Springfield Daily News*)

run the gamut—To include the full range of possibilities; to extend over a broad spectrum; to embrace extremes and all intermediate degrees of intensity. The gamut is the whole series of notes recognized by musicians. The term was used figuratively by the 18th century; Hogarth referred to "the painter's gamut."

The stocks were running...up and down the gamut from $1 to $700 a share. (*Harper's Magazine*, 1883)

The vitriolic wit of Dorothy Parker once described an actress's performance as "running the gamut of emotion from A to B."

Tom, Dick, and Harry—Men, or people in general; everyone, everyone and his uncle. The phrase, usually preceded by *every*, has been popular in

America since 1815, when it appeared in *The Farmer's Almanack*. Tom, Dick, and Harry are all very common men's first names and so are used in this expression to represent average, run-of-the-mill people. Although first used only in reference to men, the phrase is currently applied to everyone, male or female.

Uncle Tom Cobleigh and all—And all the crew; and everybody else who should be there. This expression usually appears at the end of a partial list of names to avoid naming each individual and to indicate that everybody who should be was there. The phrase was derived from the lyrics of an old ballad, *Widdicombe Fair*. There is an old tale in Devon that at one time seven members of the village borrowed Tom Pearce's grey mare to ride to the Fair. The ballad goes on:

> When the wind whistles cold on the moor of a night,
> All along, down along, out along lee,
> Tom Pearce's old mare doth appear gashly white,
> Wi' Bill Brewer, Jan Stewer, Peter Gurney,
> Peter Davy, Dan'l Whidden, Harry Hawk,
> Old Uncle Tom Cobleigh and all,
> Old Uncle Tom Cobleigh and all.

The expression is still in use but is heard less frequently today.

the whole kit and caboodle—The whole lot, the whole bunch; the entire outfit; also *the whole kit and boodle, the whole kit and biling, the whole kit, the whole boodle, the whole caboodle*. The word *caboodle* or *boodle* in this expression is probably a corruption of the Dutch *boedel* 'property, possessions, household goods.' The phrase has been in use since 1861.

the whole shooting match—Everyone and everything, the whole shebang; the entire matter or affair, the whole deal, the whole ball of wax.

> You are not the whole shooting match, but a good share of it.
> (*Springfield* [Mass.] *Weekly Republican*, March 1906)

A literal shooting match is a contest or competition in marksmanship, but how it gave rise to this popular American slang expression is unclear.

whole shtick—The entire enterprise; all one's talents and attributes. This Yiddicism, which has gained considerable popularity in theatrical circles, especially since World War II, has, in recent years, become widely used as a slang term by the general population.

> The whole shtick is that the taped remarks of a number of political figures are tacked onto questions dreamed up by writers. (*Playboy*, February 1966)

The German word *Stück* for 'play, piece, bit' was the origin of the Yiddish term, which was adopted by theatrical people because it provided them with a single word with which to indicate an act or turn, a talent or ability that elicits a response or appeals to another, an essential in theater parlance.

INDEBTEDNESS
See also POVERTY; VULNERABILITY

gone to my uncle's—Gone to the pawnbrokers; in hock; pawned. Although this term was used in its present sense as early as 1607 by John Dekker, it didn't attain popular use until the mid 18th century. In some unknown manner the word *uncle* became synonymous with the word *pawnbroker*. William R. and Florence K. Simpson in *Hockshop*, (1954) offer the following plausible explanation:

These Simpson nephews . . . were responsible for the word 'uncle' becoming a slang synonym of pawnbroker. When offered unfamiliar collateral . . . they would tell the customer, "I'll have to ask my uncle."

The term has retained its figurative meaning over the years and may be heard in similar context in *call one uncle*, meaning 'to swindle or cheat.' The reference here is to the underhand methods of some pawnbrokers.

hung on the nail—Pawned. The allusion is to the old practice of pawnbrokers' tagging each article with a number, giving the customer a duplicate tag, and hanging the article on a nail. Shelves have replaced the nails, but the expression is still heard as a synonym for anything in pawn.

in Queer Street—In difficulty; short of money; in poor circumstances. This Briticism, of uncertain origin, has been in use since the early 19th century. Alluding to an imaginary street, its origin may lie in the word *query*, for a business man recording his debts might enter such a remark in his books after a delinquent debtor's name. Whatever the case, the term invariably connotes serious financial difficulty today.

The more it looks like Queer Street, the less I ask. (Robert Louis Stevenson, *Dr. Jekyl and Mr. Hyde*, 1886)

in the hole—In debt; in financial difficulties. The story behind this U. S. slang expression has to do with proprietors in gambling houses taking an amount of money out of the pots as a percentage due the "house." When money must be paid up, one "goes to the hole" with a check. The "hole" is a slot cut in the middle of the poker table leading to a locked compartment below. All the checks "in the hole" become the property of the keeper of the place. The gamblers' losses were the keeper's gain. *In the hole* has been popular since the 1890s, although *put [someone] in the hole* 'to swindle or defraud' dates from the early 1800s.

How in the world did you manage to get in the hole for a sum like that? (P. G. Wodehouse, *Uncle Fred in Springtime*, 1939)

Indebtedness

in the ketchup—Operating at a deficit; in debt; failing to show a profit. *Ketchup* is a more graphic term than *red* but the meaning of *in the ketchup* is synonymous with *in the red*. The former, a slang expression of U.S. origin, dates from the mid-1900s.

> Ridgway...has wound up in the ketchup trying to operate a gym. (Dan Parker, *Daily Mirror,* September 11, 1949)

in the red—Operating at a deficit; in debt. This 20th-century colloquial Americanism is so called from the bookkeeping practice of entering debits in red ink. The opposite *out of the red* 'out of debt' (or *in the black*) is also current.

> Rigid enforcement of economies in running expenses will lift the club's balance sheet out of the red where it now is. (*Mazama,* June 1, 1948)

lose [one's] shirt—See FAILURE.

on the rocks—Ruined, especially financially; hence, bankrupt, destitute. The concept, but no record of the actual phrase, dates from the days when a merchant's wealth depended on the safety of ships at sea. Shipwreck—or going on the rocks—meant financial disaster. In Shakespeare's *Merchant of Venice*, Salarino asks Antonio:

> Should I...not bethink me straight of dangerous rocks,
> Which touching but my gentle vessel's side
> Would scatter all her spices on the stream,
> Enrobe the roaring waters with my silks—
> And, in a word, but even now worth this,
> And now worth nothing?
> (I,i)

take a bath—See FAILURE.

washed out—See FAILURE.

INDECISION
SEE VACILLATION

INDECISIVENESS
SEE VACILLATION

INDEPENDENCE
SEE SELF-RELIANCE

INDIGENCE
SEE POVERTY

bed of roses—A situation or state of ease, comfort, or pleasure; the lap of luxury. This phrase and its variants *bed of down* or *bed of flowers* were used as early as the first half of the 17th century by Shakespeare and Herrick, among others. The rose is a symbol of perfection and completeness, giving it more weight than *down* or *flowers*, which may account for why *bed of roses* is the preferred form today. The expression is often used in the negative, as *no bed of roses*, to emphasize the disparity between what is and what could be.

dolce far niente—Delightful idleness, carefree indolence; relaxation, peacefulness, tranquillity. Attesting to the great appeal of such a lifestyle is the fact that equivalent phrases have appeared in different languages dating back to the Roman writer Pliny. English use of the Italian *dolce far niente* 'sweet doing nothing' dates from at least the turn of the 19th century.

> It is there... that the dolce far niente of a summer evening is most heavenly. (Henry Wadsworth Longfellow, *Life*, 1830)

lazy as Lawrence—Extremely sluggish; indolent; lethargic. In the 3rd century when St. Lawrence was being put to death by roasting upon a grill, he asked his captors to turn his body so the other side would be done equally. The torturers somehow misinterpreted this act of Christian courage as an act of laziness and reported it as such; hence *lazy as Lawrence*.

> He was found early and late at his work, established a new character and ... lost the name of 'Lazy Lawrence.' (Maria Edgeworth, *The Parent's Assistant*, 1796)

A variant is *lazy as Lawrence's dog*. Somehow the laziness was transferred to Lawrence's dog; perhaps, simply from Lawrence himself, but more likely from another expression *lazy as Ludlam's dog*. The allusion in this term is to a sorceress, Ludlam, who had a dog that was so lazy that when people approached the cave in which they lived, the dog had great difficulty rousing itself to bark.

> English rustics talk of a man 'as lazy as Ludlam's dog' that leaned his head against the wall to bark. (J. L. Kipling, *Beast and Man*, 1891)

Another variant, *Lawrence bids him high wages*, meaning that a person is lethargic or listless, is apparently a reference to St. Lawrence's Day, August 10, falling during the heat of summer.

> When a person in hot weather seems lazy, it is a common saying that Lawrence bids him high wages. (*Gentleman's Magazine*, 1784)

lotus-eater—An idle dreamer, one who lives a life of indolence and ease. The Lotus-eaters, or Lotophagi, are a mythical people found in Homer's *Odyssey*. Odysseus discovers them in a state of dreamy forgetfulness and contentment induced by their consumption of the legendary lotus fruit.

Having lost all desire to return to their homelands, they want only to remain in Lotus-land living a life of idle luxury. Use of the term dates from the first half of the 19th century.

> A summer like that of 1893 may be all very well for the lotus-eater, but is a calamity to people who have to get their living out of English land. (*The Times*, December 1893)

Paul's man—A shirker; a loafer; one who idles away his time; a braggart; a boaster. During the late 1500s and early 1600s it became a common practice for idlers of all types to spend their time walking the center aisle of Old St. Paul's in London, where they enjoyed bragging of their past exploits. Among these *Paul's walkers*, as they were also called, were many retired soldiers who would sit and recount for hours their adventures in the military to any passer-by who would listen. In Ben Jonson's *Every Man in his Humour* (1616), one of the major characters, Captain Bobadil, a man who takes a back seat to none when it comes to bragging about his military exploits, is referred to as a *Paul's man*.

> Who goes to Westminster for a wife, to Paul's for a man, and to Smithfield for a horse, may meet with a whore, a knave, and a jade. (James Howell, *Proverbs*, 1659)

sit like a bump on a log—Stupidly dumb; to sit in vacuous silence; remain lethargically inarticulate. The first recorded use of this term is to be found in Kate Douglas Wiggin's *The Birds' Christmas Carol* (1887).

> Ye ain't goin' to set there like a bump on a log 'thout sayin' a word ter pay for yer vittles, air ye?

The origin of the expression is uncertain; however, it probably arises from the similarity between the incommunicativeness of a bump on a log and an oafish mute.

woolgathering—Daydreaming, idle imagining or fantasizing; absentmindedness, preoccupation, abstraction; often *to go woolgathering*.

> Ha' you summoned your wits from woolgathering? (Thomas Middleton, *The Family of Love*, 1607)

Although the practice of woolgathering (wandering about the countryside collecting tufts of sheep's wool caught on bushes) is virtually obsolete, the figurative term is still current.

INDUSTRIOUSNESS
SEE EXERTION

INEBRIATION
SEE DRUNKENNESS

INEFFECTUALITY
SEE FUTILITY

INFLUENCE
SEE MANIPULATION

INFREQUENCY
SEE TIME

INITIATION
See also STARTING

baptism of fire—An extremely trying initial experience; a first encounter which tests one to the utmost. The phrase applies literally to the first time a soldier faces battle fire, but even that usage was originally figurative. The expression has its origin in the early Christian belief that an as yet unbaptized believer who suffered martyrdom by fire was thereby baptized, i.e., received into the community of the faithful and consequently saved. A synonymous term for other kinds of martyrdom is *baptism of blood*. Conventional baptism is called *baptism of water*.

break the ice—To initiate a conversation or make a friendly overture; to overcome existing obstacles, prepare the way; begin, dive in, get started; broach a new subject. In the late 16th century, *break the ice* meant literally to facilitate a ship's passage by breaking the ice. Soon after, it was used figuratively in regard to any efforts made to begin a new project or to upset the status quo of a stalemate, deadlock, impasse or such. In modern figurative use, *break the ice* is heard mostly in the context of interpersonal relationships. Any attempt to cut through another person's reserve is considered "breaking the ice."

> I availed myself of a pause in the conversation to break the ice in relation to the topic which lay nearest my heart. (Henry Rogers, *The Eclipse of Faith*, 1853)

get [one's] feet wet—To get a start in or begin something new; to get one's first taste of, to get the feel of. The allusion is to the way a bather tests the water by putting his toes or feet in before committing himself to total immersion.

get the ball rolling—To initiate or begin; to assume active leadership of a project, event, or other matter; to set an activity in motion. This expression probably originated in the ancient British game of *bandy*, a hockeylike sport in which players kept a ball in constant motion as they attempted to score points by getting it in the goal of the opponent. A variation is *start the ball rolling*.

A related expression, *keep the ball rolling*, is probably also derived from bandy. It means to continue or to spark renewed interest and enthusiasm in an activity or project already underway. One source credits the popularity of this expression to the 1840 presidential campaign of William Henry

165

Harrison whose followers wrote political slogans on a huge paper ball and then pushed it from city to city shouting, "Keep the ball rolling."

get under way—To get started, begin moving. This is borrowed from an old nautical idiom *under way* 'in forward motion.'

ring up the curtain on—To begin or initiate a project, plan, or activity; to start the ball rolling. Originally limited to use in the theater, this expression referred to raising the curtain on cue (usually the ringing of a bell) to mark the start of a performance. Though still used in this theatrical context, *ring up the curtain on* is often applied figuratively to describe the inauguration of a project or other endeavor.

> Before the curtain was rung up on the great spectacular drama of Vaal Krantz...(M. H. Grant, *Words by an Eyewitness; The Struggle in Natal,* 1901)

A variation is the shortened *ring up.*

> Look sharp below there, gents,... they're agoing to ring-up. (Charles Dickens, *Sketches by Boz,* 1837)

See also **ring down the curtain on**, TERMINATION.

INJUSTICE
See also PREJUDICE

get away with murder—Do something unconventional or illegal and not be punished; violate the rules of decency. This expression, dating from about 1910, is heard primarily in social situations. If one flaunts social custom and the impropriety is overlooked, he is said to *get away with murder.*

Montgomery's division, all on one side—A one-sided distribution of the gains; a concern only for one's own profit; victimization of others engaged in a mutual project. This expression originated in the time of free companies, bands of discharged soldiers who plagued France during the mid 1300s sacking and looting the countryside for their own gain. This phrase, a translation of an old French apothegm, refers to a certain man named Montgomery who, as leader of a medieval free company, became notorious for keeping the spoils of plunder for himself.

We wuz robbed—Describing a situation felt to be completely unjust or absolutely wrong; the officials cheated. Mike Jacobs, the manager of Max Schmeling, shouted this remark into the microphone on a nationwide broadcast, immediately after Jack Sharkey had been awarded the heavyweight boxing title by decision on the night of June 21, 1932. Since that fateful evening, it has become a jocular cry used by those questioning a decision in any field of endeavor.

INQUISITIVENESS
SEE CURIOSITY

INSANITY
SEE ECCENTRICITY; IRRATIONALITY

INSIGNIFICANCE

anise and cumin—Insignificant matters, petty concerns. The term is usually found within a context implying that one ought to be about more important work or focus his attention on larger concerns. The origin of the phrase lies in Jesus' reproach to the Scribes and Pharisees:

> Ye pay tithe of mint and anise and cummin, and have omitted the weightier matters of the law, judgment, mercy, and faith; these ought ye to have done, and not to leave the other undone. (Matthew 23:23)

Anise and cumin are aromatic herbs often used in both cookery and medicine.

beautiful downtown Burbank—This American expression was born in 1968 on the popular TV show *Laugh-In*. Gary Owens, the announcer, used the phrase with ironic intent as part of his introductory spiel:

> ... coming to you from beautiful downtown Burbank.

(The show originated from studios in Burbank, California, a suburb of Los Angeles.) The phrase gained immediate recognition through its national exposure each week on prime-time television, and it came to represent any architecturally poor and culturally deprived community in the United States.

cat's cradle—A children's game; a complicated or fanciful idea with little or no meaning; a worthless accomplishment. The origin of this term, which dates to at least the early 18th century, is uncertain. The game is played by looping a piece of string through the fingers, and, by passing the string from player to player, intricate and symmetrical designs are formed. It is suggested that the name came from the first pattern in the game which resembles a *cratch*, an obsolete word meaning 'hayrack,' and from the final pattern which resembles a cradle; hence, the original form of the term *cratch-cradle*, which in later years was corrupted to its present form *cat's cradle*. The *OED*, besides listing the noun form of *cratch*, also lists an obsolete verb form which meant to snatch or grab, thus lending more credence to this concept of the expression's origin. A less plausible supposition is that the term derived from a kitten playing with a ball of yarn. Whatever the case, the expression is still in common use, both literally and figuratively.

> One of those cat's-cradle reasoners who never see a decided advantage in anything but indecision. (*Edinburgh Review*, 1824)

167

cheap-Jack—Any insignificant or inconsequential person, especially one who travels about selling cheap goods; a small time hawker. This expression makes use of the ubiquitous English *Jack,* a common appellation assigned to an unknown person. Coined sometime in the mid 1800s, the term originally was applied only to itinerant small-time salesmen who went about the countryside offering cheap wares at cheap prices; hence, the epithet for anyone of small consequence.

> Making a sort of political Cheap Jack of himself. (George Eliot, *Middlemarch,* 1872)

A common variant is *cheap-John.*

> Another chapter, gents, in the hist'ry of that air crazy institution, to wit an' namely, Uncle Sam's Cheap John Congress. (Stuart Henry, *Conquering Our Great American Plains,* 1930)

chronicle small beer—To register insignificant events; to write down matters of little or no importance. Since the 16th century *small beer* has been synonymous with weak beer, hence, figuratively, something trifling or of little consequence.

> She had found that most worried men felt better if she chronicled small beer. (H. C. Bailey, *The Apprehensive Dog,* 1942).

come from Wigan—To be completely provincial; to behave like a rustic. In use since at least 1890, this Briticism is of uncertain origin. Somehow Wigan, a small manufacturing community northeast of Liverpool, has come to be a national symbol of provincialism, one of those dull, out-of-the-way towns that has lost contact with the outside world—counterpart to the mythical *Podunk, U.S.A.* A common music hall gag, *that went better in Wigan,* frequently fired at the audience when a joke flopped, probably helped create Wigan's unhappy image.

dog's body—A menial; an errand boy; any insignificant, unskilled drudge; a junior naval officer, especially a midshipman. Originally a sailor's slang expression for dried peas boiled in a cloth, this Briticism has been in use since the mid 19th century. For some unknown reason it also came to mean a junior naval officer, and by extension any undistinguished underling.

> A midshipman is known in the service as a 'snottie' . . . if he is a junior midshipman he is also a dog's body. I defy anyone to be accurate and sentimental about a snottie who is a dog's body. (*Daily Express,* April 3, 1928)

A related term is *gofer,* any flunky whose main function is to go for this and to go for that.

down in the boondocks—In a remote rural area; away from civilization; in isolated terrain. This American slang expression originated among armed forces personnel stationed in the Philippine Islands and achieved great popularity during World War II. Although other branches of the armed forces make use of the term, it seems to be especially popular among the Marine Corps.

> Today, Marines use boondock clothes and boondock shoes for hikes and maneuvers. (Harvey L. Miller, *Wood Study*, October 1950)

The word *boondock* is most likely a corruption of the Tagalog *bundok*, meaning mountain. A related term *boondockers* refers to a heavy hiking shoe, especially used in troublesome terrain.

a drop in the bucket—An absurdly small quantity in relation to the whole; a contribution so negligible or insignificant that it makes no appreciable difference; also *a drop in the ocean*. The expression appears in the following passage from the King James version of the Bible:

> Behold, the nations are as a drop of a bucket, and are counted as the small dust of the balance. (Isaiah 40:15)

A drop in the ocean was apparently coined by analogy. It dates from the early 1700s.

fly in amber—An unimportant person or incident remembered only through association with a person or matter of significance. The origin of this phrase is credited to certain extinct pine trees that produced a resin called amber which, while flowing down the trees, trapped and preserved small insects, thus fossilizing organisms of virtually no scientific interest.

> Full-fledged specimens of your order, preserved for all time in the imperishable amber of his genius. (C. Cowden Clarke, *Shakespeare-characters*, 1863)

forgotten man—The decent, hardworking, everyday citizen; the average American working man. This term was coined in 1883 by William G. Sumner, a professor at Yale University, who characterized as the *forgotten man* that industrious, ordinary sort of man who supports his family, pays his taxes, but never seems to profit in the larger scheme of things. Franklin Delano Roosevelt revived its popularity during the 1932 presidential campaign but with a slightly different connotation; he made the *forgotten man* more of an *underprivileged man*.

> These unhappy times call . . . for plans that put their faith once more in the forgotten man at the bottom of the pyramid. (Radio Address, April 7, 1932)

hill of beans—Of little value, insignificant; trifling. This expression alludes to the once small value of beans. A bean has been used symbolically since at least the 13th century to designate a thing of small value, whether material or spiritual, and carries the same connotation today.

> Captain Willard didn't know beans about fighting Apaches. (*Range Riders Western*, May 1948)

A *hill of beans* is almost always used in a negative or derogatory sense; the most common forms are *not worth a hill of beans, doesn't amount to a hill of beans,* and *does not know beans about,* as in the citation above.

That oath he took here don't amount to a hill of beans. (*Chicago Tribune*, January 23, 1947)

Jack-a-Dandy—An insignificant person; a contemptuous name for a fop or a dandy; a loafer; a sponge. Although conjectures are rife, the origin of this term is uncertain. The *OED* records its first appearance in English as 1632 and further states that the term is probably the root for *dandy*, which didn't make its appearance in the language until the late 18th century.

Tom did not understand French but ... despised it as a jack-a-dandy acquirement. (Samuel Lover, *Handy Andy*, 1842)

Variants are *Jack-o-Dandy* and *jack-a-dandyism*.

Meriden audience—This expression is a theatrical term for a specific audience, one man and one boy. The term refers to an evening in the autumn of 1888 in Meriden, Connecticut. One of Countess Helena Modjeska's traveling troupes, led by the destined-to-be-famous Julia Marlowe, opened in Meriden that autumn evening to an audience of two people, a man and a boy. Dr. Davis, the mayor and a local surgeon, wrote a letter of glowing praise about Miss Marlowe's performance to a local newspaper. Apparently he was the man; who the boy was has never been discovered.

Mickey Mouse—Cheap or inferior; small, insignificant, worthless; petty, trivial; simple, easy, childish. The allusion is to the cartoon character created by Walt Disney in 1928. Because this character is internationally famous, *Mickey Mouse* has been applied figuratively in innumerable and widely varied contexts. The connotation of cheapness and inferiority probably originated in the mid 1930s when the Ingersoll Watch Company marketed a popular wristwatch, with Mickey Mouse on its face and his arms serving as pointers or hands, which sold for $2. The watch was not made well enough to last long, hence the allusion to flimsiness and poor quality.

One reason for the AFL's reputation as a Mickey Mouse league is that it gave new life to NFL rejects. (J. Mosedale, *Football*, 1972)

At Michigan State [University] ... a "Mickey Mouse course" means a "snap course." (Maurice Crane, "Vox Box," in *American Speech*, October 1958)

mom and pop—Relating to a small business establishment, frequently a retail store, usually run by a husband and wife or by a family. The allusion in this phrase is to a small business establishment that can't afford to employ any help outside the family. Conceived about 1962, the term has, in recent years, come to mean any small, low-overhead business.

What started as a "Mom and Pop" television shop, with two reporters and six line producers, has grown into a factory employing more than 70 people, including 21 producers and 16 film editors. (*The New York Times Magazine*, May 6, 1979)

no great shakes—Unimportant or unimpressive; not exceptional or extraordinary; common, dull, boring. There are several suggested derivations of this expression: a low roll on a shake of the dice, a negative appraisal of someone's character made on the basis of a weak handshake, or a negligible yield resulting from shaking a barren walnut tree. Alternate meanings of *shake* are also cited: 'reputation,' 'a shingle from the roof of a shanty,' or 'plant stubble left after harvesting.' One source alludes to the Arabic *shakhs* 'man.' At any rate, *no great shakes* has long implied that a person or thing is common, unimportant, or of no particular merit or ability.

> [He] said that a piece of sculpture there was "nullae magnae quessationes" ['of no great shakes'] and the others laughed heartily. (Lord Henry Broughton, *Recollections*, 1816)

not worth an iota—Insignificant; worthless; hardly worth mentioning; of little, if any, use. *Iota*, a letter of the Greek alphabet composed of a small, single stroke, came to represent anything insignificant or trifling, as Edmund Burke demonstrated in his *Correspondence* (1771):

> They never depart an iota from the authentic formulas of tyrrany and usurpation.

The expression, *not worth an iota*, came into use during the 17th century in Britain; *not worth a jot* followed hard upon, for, since the letters *i* and *j* were originally interchangeable, *iota* and *jot* referred to the same thing. A related expression from the Italian is *not worth an h*, for in the Italian language the letter *h* is seldom used, and when it does appear, it has no spoken value, i.e., it is always silent.

one-horse town—An extremely small, insignificant town. A farmer whose plow was pulled by one horse instead of two was considered small-time and of limited resources. Similarly, a one-horse town refers to a small, often rural community which could presumably survive with only one horse. The phrase maintains common usage in the United States despite the fact that horses are no longer the principal means of transportation.

> In this "one-horse" town, . . . as our New Orleans neighbors designate it. (*Knickerbocker Magazine*, 1855)

oyster part—One line to speak in a theatrical production; insignificant; unimportant. This theatrical slang term for a one-line part in a play apparently is derived from the uncommunicativeness of an oyster. Like a clam, an oyster is a symbol of one who is tight-lipped or close-mouthed. The term has been in theatrical jargon since the 1920s.

peanut gallery—A source of unimportant or insignificant criticism; in a theater, the section of seats farthest removed from the stage. In many theaters, peanuts and popcorn were sold only to the people in the least expensive seats, usually those in the rear of the balcony, hence the nickname *peanut gallery*. Since these seats are traditionally bought by those of meager means and, by stereotypic implication, those with a minimal appreciation of the arts, comments or criticisms from people in the *peanut gallery* carried little, if any, weight, thus the expression's more figurative meaning.

pebble on the beach—An insignificant or unimportant person, especially one who was once prominent; a face in the crowd, a fish in the sea. This expression is one of many that minimize the importance of someone by virtue of the fact that he is just one of a multitude. It usually follows phrases such as "There's more than one ..." and "You aren't the only ...," and is most commonly used in situations involving a jilted sweetheart.

penny-ante—Insignificant or unimportant; strictly small-time; involving a trifling or paltry amount of money. Originally, *penny ante* was a poker game in which the ante or minimum wager was one penny. Though this literal meaning persists, the term is used figuratively as well.

> Compared to the man Bilbo, 63-year-old John Rankin is strictly penny ante and colorless. (*Negro Digest*, August 1946)

play footsie—To fool with idly; to treat with little concern; to indicate a casual interest. The allusion in this phrase is to the surreptitious passing of foot signals underneath a table, either while participating in a game of cards or as a message sending device used by clandestine lovers, especially while in the presence of their spouses. Modern use has broadened its application to characterize any act of a frivolous nature.

> "But eventually we have to make a decision," he said. "The last impression we want to give is that we're playing footsie with the thing." (*The* [*New London, Conn.*] *Day* January 5, 1984)

Podunk—Any hick town; the boondocks, the sticks; the middle of nowhere. This name, of Indian origin, may refer either to the Podunk near Hartford, Connecticut, or to that near Worcester, Massachusetts. But how either gained the notoriety necessary to make it representative of all such insignificant, out-of-the-way towns is unknown.

> He might just as well have been John Smith of Podunk Centre. (*Harper's Weekly*, September 1901)

shoot deer in the balcony—This colorful image refers to a theater so devoid of paying customers that the actors feel as if they are playing to open spaces. Derived from the old show business expression "Business was so bad you could shoot deer in the balcony," the phrase became standard theatrical jargon for a sparse or empty house. Raquel Welch in an article in *Family Weekly*, November 7, 1982, used *shoot moose in the theater*, a somewhat corrupted version of the traditional phrase.

> I figured if the critics hated me, even if you could shoot moose in the theatre, they couldn't close me because it was only two weeks.

small potatoes—An inconsequential, trivial person; an irrelevant or unimportant concept or notion; a small amount of money. This familiar saying is evidently derived from the short-lived satiation of one who has eaten a small potato. Although the expression retains its human application, *small potatoes* more often describes an insignificant amount of money, especially when such a pittance is compared with one's projected future earnings or with a much greater cash sum.

> The $7 billion was of course pretty "small potatoes" compared to the vast inflationary borrowings of the federal government. (*Proceedings of the Academy of Political Science*, May 1948)

tank town—A small town located on a railroad; a one-horse town; a hick town. This American colloquialism, in common use since the late 1800s, designates a tiny town with a railroad water tank, but too small for a station. It is a representative term for scores of such towns throughout the United States and symbolizes a slow-paced type of life with little interest in the progress of the world.

> Out they went for sixteen weeks in the theatres, opera houses, and musty lodge halls of the tank towns. (*Saturday Evening Post*, April 9, 1949)

A few of the many variants for this term are: *jerkwater town, one-horse town, hick town,* and *cowtown.*

three blue beans in a blue bladder—Empty words; many words with little matter; a meaningless torrent of words. This British expression has its roots in the Middle Ages when a common practice among peasants was to create a baby's rattle by putting beans in a bladder. The resulting rattling noise, loud but meaningless, characterized an idea that was soon transferred to the noise emanating from some people's mouths.

> Putting all his words together,
> 'Tis three blue beans in one blue bladder.
> (Matthew Prior, *Alma*, 1718)

INSOLVENCY
SEE INDEBTEDNESS

Instantaneousness

before you can say "Jack Robinson"—Instantly, immediately. There are two common but equally unsubstantiated theories as to the origin of this phrase. One holds that a rather mercurial gentleman of that name was in the habit of paying such brief visits to neighbors that he was gone almost as soon as he had been announced. The other sees the source in these lines from an unnamed play:

A warke it ys as easie to be done
As tys to saye, Jacke! robys on.

In popular use during the 18th century, the expression appeared in Fanny Burney's *Evelina* in 1778.

before you can say "knife"—Very quickly or suddenly; before you can turn around. This colloquial British expression is equivalent to *before you can say "Jack Robinson."* Mrs. Louisa Parr used it in *Adam and Eve* (1880).

curry a short horse—This phrase, frequently heard in the passive, a *short horse is soon curried*, and in use since the Middle Ages, is simply a figurative way of saying that a little chore is soon completed, that a little business is soon transacted.

A short tale is soon told—and a short horse soon curried. (Sir Walter Scott, *The Abbott*, 1820)

in a jiffy—In a trice, in a minute, right away. Although the exact origin of this expression is unknown, it is thought by some to be the modern spelling of the earlier *gliff* 'a glimpse, a glance,' and by extension 'a short space of time, a moment.' The phrase dates from the late 18th century.

They have wonderful plans for doing everything in a jiffy. (Charles Haddon Spurgeon, *John Ploughman's Pictures*, 1880)

in a pig's whisper—In a short time; soon. A pig's whisper was originally a short grunt, one so brief that it sounded almost like a whisper.

You'll find yourself in bed, in something less than a pig's whisper. (Charles Dickens, *Pickwick Papers*, 1837)

in the twinkling of a bed staff—Immediately, instantly; in two shakes of a lamb's tail; right away. One explanation of the source of this expression attributes it to a playful tilt in the late 13th century between Sir John Chichester, armed with a sword, and one of his servants, armed with a bed staff, in which the servant was accidentally killed. Another interpretation attributes it to the action of a maid beating the bedding with a bed staff. The *OED* offers the most plausible explanation. Bed staffs, an aid for making beds that had been built into recesses, were readily available sturdy household items; consequently, they were readily accessible as weapons in an emergency. A later variation is *in the twinkling of a bed post*. The common, related phrase, *in the twinkling of an eye* first appears in the Book of Corinthians:

We shall not all sleep, but we shall all be changed,
In a moment, in the twinkling of an eye, at the last trump: for the
trumpet shall sound, and the dead shall be raised incorruptible, and
we shall be changed. (15:51–52)

in two shakes of a lamb's tail—Immediately, right away; instantly. *The Ingoldsby Legends* (1840). Anyone familiar with sheep knows the quivering suddenness with which those animals twitch their tails.

one fell swoop—All at once; with a single blow or stroke. The *swoop* of the phrase may carry its obsolete meaning of 'blow,' or refer to the sudden descent of a bird of prey; *fell* carries its meanings of 'fierce, savage, destructive.' Macduff uses the phrase in Shakespeare's *Macbeth* when he learns that his wife, children, and servants have all been killed. In doing so, he plays on its associations with birds of prey:

All my pretty ones?
Did you say all? Oh Hellkite! All?
What, all my pretty chickens, and their dam
At one fell swoop?
(IV,iii)

Contemporary usage does not restrict the phrase to serious contexts of fatal destruction; in fact, the expression is so often used lightly that it has generated the common spoonerism *one swell foop*.

on the double—Instantly, without delay; quickly, at a swift pace. This expression originated as military jargon for double-time marching. The term's current civilian use is commonplace in the United States.

They came with me on the double. (James M. Cain, *The Postman Always Rings Twice*, 1934)

p. d. q.—Immediately, at once. This widely used abbreviation of "pretty damn quick" was coined in 1867 by Don Maginnis, a Boston comedian.

He changed her mind for her p. d. q. (John O'Hara, *The Horse Knows the Way*, 1964)

right off the bat—Immediately; at once; instantaneously. This very common expression is of obvious baseball origin.

You can tell right off the bat that they're wicked, because they keep eating grapes indolently. (*The New Yorker*, May 1955)

The less frequently heard synonymous *right off the reel* may derive from the specific sports use of *reel* in fishing, though many of the more general uses of *reel* could account equally well for its origin.

sudden death—Extra playing time added at the end of a regulation game that ends in a tie, in which the first team to score, or the first team to score a set number of points, becomes the victor; any undetermined situation that is settled suddenly and conclusively. The precise origin of this expression is obscure, but it is believed to have its source in the game of basketball. To eliminate tie games, which are always a source of dissatisfaction to the fans, overtime periods were devised, in which teams played a certain number of minutes to determine a victor, with as many overtimes played as were necessary to determine a winner. The sudden death overtime was later created to determine a winner in a reasonable amount of time, avoiding the problem of successive overtime periods that would physically exhaust the players. Several sports picked up the practice, notably ice hockey, soccer, and, recently, professional football. In golf, *sudden death* (extra) holes are played by those who have finished a tournament with a tie score, play continuing until one winner has been decided. In tennis, the *sudden death* is called a *tiebreaker*, the winner being the player who first wins five out of nine points, or seven out of twelve with a margin of two. In recent years the term has come into vogue in the business world, where it is used to indicate the rapid, and sometimes unexpected, resolution of a pending deal.

INSULT

Anne's fan—The gesture of placing the tip of the thumb to the end of the nose and spreading wide the fingers, an indication of disdain. This expression, dating from the early 18th century, signifies a universal gesture of contempt meaning 'kiss the cheeks of my posterior.' The gesture can be made more forceful by wiggling the fingers or by adding the other hand with the fingers similarly outspread. The term was derived from the fact that the English Queen Anne (1665–1714) was wont to conceal part of her face with her outspread fan. Variants are *Queen Anne's fan* and *Spanish fan*. Related verb forms describing the gesture are *pull bacon* and *cock a snook*. See also **cock a snook,** below.

barrack—To boo or hiss; to voice loudly one's disapproval of a player, performer, or team at a public event. This British term is thought by some to be a back formation of the cockney word *barrakin* 'senseless talk,' although the *OED* claims an Australian origin. The word appeared in use in the late 19th century. The term *to barrack for* has the opposite meaning: 'to cheer for, or support vocally.'

bite [one's] thumb at—To insult or show contempt for someone. The gesture, as defined by the 17th-century English lexicographer Randle Cotgrave, meant "to threaten or defy by putting the thumb nail into the mouth, and with a jerk [from the upper teeth] make it to knack [click or snap]." A famous use of the phrase is from Shakespeare:

> I will bite my thumb at them; which is a disgrace to them, if they bear it. (*Romeo and Juliet*, I,i)

CAT CALL

catcall—A harsh, whistling sound, something like the cry of a cat, used by theater and other audiences to express their disapproval, displeasure, or impatience; the whistlelike instrument used to make this sound. This term dates from the mid 1600s.

cock a snook—A British slang expression for the gesture of putting one's thumb on one's nose and extending the fingers, equivalent to *thumb one's nose*. The origin of *snook* is obscure, and based on citations from as early as 1879, it can refer to other derisive gestures as well. An earlier form of this phrase is *to take a sight*.

> "To take a sight at a person" a vulgar action employed by street boys to denote incredulity, or contempt for authority, by placing the thumb against the nose and closing all the fingers except the little one, which is agitated in token of derision. (John C. Hotten, *A Dictionary of Modern Slang, Cant, and Vulgar Words*, 1860)

A current variant of *snook* is *snoot*, a slang term for the nose.

fork the fingers—To use one's digits in a disdainful motion toward another person, in an apparent imitation of the appearance of two horns. The gesture symbolizes a curse invoking the devil, like, "May the Devil take you!"

> His wife... Behind him forks her fingers. (Sir John Mennes and J. Smith, *Witts Recreations*, 1640)

See also make horns at, below.

give the bird—To hiss or boo; to dismiss or fire; to receive unsupportive, hostile feedback. The original phrase was *give the goose*, a theater slang expression dating from the beginning of the 19th century. *Goose* or *bird* refer to the hissing sound made by an audience mimicking the similar sound made by a goose. It expresses disapproval, hostility, or rejection, and was directed at a performer or the play. Today it is a popular sound effect used by crowds at sporting events, although *give the bird* is also heard in other unrelated contexts. For example, an employer who dismisses an employee is said to *give the bird*, akin to *give the sack*. And in interpersonal relationships, *the bird* is analogous to *the brushoff* or *the gate*.

> She gave him the bird—finally and for good. So he came to Spain to forget his broken heart. (P. Kemp, *Mine Were of Trouble*, 1957)

Another familiar meaning of *give the bird* is to make the obscene and offensive gesture of extending the middle finger.

give the fig—To insult; also *the fig of Spain* and the now obsolete *to give the fico*. The fig or Italian *fico* is a contemptuous gesture which involves putting the thumb between the first two fingers or in the mouth. English versions of both expressions date from the late 16th century. The equivalent French and Spanish phrases are *faire la figue* and *dar la higa* respectively.

give [someone] the finger—To extend the middle finger, outward and upward, as an obscene gesture meaning 'fuck you,' or 'up your ass,' made maliciously, derisively, or jocularly. This term refers to a gesture that was originally used only as an extreme insult but has in recent years come to indicate simple distaste or disagreement. Figuratively, the expression has come to be used when one's attempts to achieve something have been thwarted or frustrated by another.

> Let me show you how to give that guy the finger . . . she was giving me the polite finger. (Budd Schulberg, *What Makes Sammy Run*, 1941)

give the raspberry—To show ridicule or disapproval by making a vulgar noise; to respond in a scornful, acrimonious manner. *Raspberry*, a slang term dating from the turn of the century, refers to any expression of disapproval or scorn.

> The humorist answered them by a gesture known in polite circles as a "raspberry." (T. Burke, *Nights in Town*, 1915)

> Convict son totters up the steps of the old home and punches the bell. What awaits him beyond? Forgiveness? Or the raspberry? (P. G. Wodehouse, *Damsel in Distress*, 1920)

However, the most common raspberry is the sound effect known also as the *Bronx cheer*, made by sticking out the tongue through closed lips and blowing. *Razz*, short for *raspberry*, is a slang verb meaning 'to ridicule or deride,' akin in use to *jeer*.

go to Putney—Go to the devil; go to the deuce; get out of here. Among a number of common Cockney street sayings originating from music hall songs of the early 1800s, this expression was first conceived as *go to Putney on a pig*. The phrase is seldom heard today.

> Now in the year 1845, telling a man to go to Putney was the same as telling a man to go to the deuce. (Charles Kingsley, *The Water-Babies*, 1863)

left-handed compliment—An insincere compliment; an insult that masquerades as praise. *Left-handed* denotes underhandedness, insincerity, derogation; hence, a *left-handed compliment* implies no compliment at all, but rather an incivility; for example, "Mary celebrated her 40th birthday yesterday." "Oh, really! She doesn't look a day over 39." One explanation of how *left-handed* came to imply something undesirable is the practice of ancient Greek seers who, during an augury, faced north with the east, the lucky side to their right, and west, the unlucky side to their left. From this practice the left came to imply misfortune. Another explanation attributes it to the *left-handed marriages* or *morganatic marriages* of Germany. In such marriages, a noble married a commoner, but as a symbol that neither she nor their common progeny might inherit his titles and properties, the noble offered his left hand to the bride during the ceremony. The most credible

179

explanation attributes the undesirableness of being left-handed to a prehistoric attitude that viewed anything different with great suspicion and often assigned irrational qualities to any unusual trait. Whatever the case, *left-handed* connotes insincerity, and a *left-handed compliment* is undesirable.

make horns at—To insult by making the offensive gesture of extending the fist with the forefinger and pinkie extended and the middle fingers doubled in. This now obsolete derisive expression implies that the person being insulted is a cuckold.

> He would have laine withe the Countess of Nottinghame, making horns in derision at her husband the Lord High Admiral. (Sir E. Peyton, *The Divine Catastrophe of the ... House of Stuarts*, 1652)

See also fork the fingers, above.

Parthian shot—The last word; any barbed, parting remark; a parting shot. The Parthians, a tribe from what is now northeast Iran, developed the ability to fire their arrows backward over their shoulders as they retreated or feigned retreat. Consequently, the term connotes any aggressive action or remark made upon departure.

> Casting back Parthian glances of scornful hostility. (Lisle Carr, *Judith Gwynne*, 1874)

Related terms are *Parthian glance*, *Parthian shaft*, and *Parthian fight*. *Parting shot* is a corruption of *Parthian shot* and carries the same meaning.

a plague on both your houses—An imprecation invoked upon two parties, each at odds with the other; often a denunciation of both of America's two leading political parties. Shakespeare coined this expression in *Romeo and Juliet* (III,i):

> I am hurt.
> A plague o' both your houses! I am sped.
> Is he gone, and hath nothing?

a slap in the face—A stinging insult; a harsh or sarcastic rejection, rebuke, or censure. This expression alludes to a literal blow to the face, a universal sign of rejection or disapproval. The implication is that a verbal blow, particularly an unexpected one, can be just as painful and devastating as a physical one.

> [He] could not help feeling severely the very vigorous slap on the face which had been administered to him. (Thomas Trollope, *La Beata*, 1861)

thumb [one's] nose—Literally, to put one's thumb to one's nose and extend the fingers, a gesture expressive of scorn, derision or contempt. This U.S. phrase came into use concurrently with *give the raspberry* in the early

1900s and is popular today. The gesture is considered offensive, but not as vulgar as the gesture known as *the bird*.

> He thumbed his nose with both thumbs at once and told me to climb the Tour d'Eiffel and stay there. (B. Hall, *One Man's War*, 1916)

In Britain the expression is *cock a snook* (see above).

INTENSIFICATION
SEE EXACERBATION

INTOXICATION
SEE DRUNKENNESS

INTRODUCTION
SEE INITIATION

INTRUSIVENESS
SEE CURIOSITY

IRRATIONALITY

beside [oneself]—In an intensely emotional state; unable to control or contain one's feelings; highly excited. Though one may be beside oneself with feelings ranging from pleasure to rage, the essence of the state is irrationality—being out of one's wits. The phrase is akin to the French *hors de soi*, and both relate to the concepts of being possessed or transported. Caxton used the expression in the late 15th century.

coop-happy—Insane from confinement; stir-crazy; punch-drunk from being cooped up. *Coop* 'a confined area,' is also a slang term for jail. *Happy* is used euphemistically in this phrase to mean dull-witted or "feeling no pain," whence the term.

crazy as a bedbug—Completely insane; absolutely irrational; stark, raving mad; off one's trolley. The image conveyed by this early American expression suggests one who has become completely psychotic, but why the simile with *bedbug* is uncertain. Perhaps because (with transferred use), their victims twitch and jump about madly when bitten.

> On the subject of the relations of organized capital and organized labor it [*The New York Sun*] is as crazy as a bedbug. (*Buffalo Commercial*, August 2, 1904)

crazy as a loon—Insane; demented; irrational; erratic; stark, raving mad. One of the cries of the loon, an aquatic bird of North America, is a rather dismal cry which resembles the laughter of a demoniac; hence, the inception of this phrase to indicate one who has lost his wits. Of American origin, the expression has been in use since about 1840.

Insult

Irrationality

181

The next morning Costler was as crazy as a loon....the mountain fever had attacked him. (Charles D. Ferguson, *Experiences of a Forty-Niner*, 1888)

The term *loony* does not have its origin in *loon*, as some people believe, but rather is a slang term derived from *lunatic*.

flip [one's] lid—To react wildly or enthusiastically; to be delighted or outraged; to be knocked off one's feet or bowled over with shock; to lose one's head. This relatively new slang phrase of American origin plays with the idea that a "lid" serves to prevent something from escaping—in this case one's common sense and control. Thus, to "flip one's lid" is to lose self-control, leaving one unbalanced or crazed.

> Present war emergencies plus strain and stress seem to have been too much for local governmental officials. I fear they have flipped their lids. (Letter to the editor, Ithaca, N.Y., *Journal*, January 30, 1951)

Currently, *flip* is heard more frequently than the longer *flip one's lid*.

> Our food and service are great. Our decor's delightful. Your club treasurer will flip over our low rates. (*Boston Globe*, May 18, 1967)

Another variant, *flip out*, implies a more serious degree of losing control, as from drugs, a nervous breakdown, etc. It is analogous to *freak out* and *go off the deep end* in flavor and usage.

freak out—To withdraw from reality; to become irrational; to abandon normal conventions and values; to suffer a bad experience as a result of taking drugs; a bad trip. This expression, popularized during the 1960s, originally denoted one who suffered from mental aberrations, especially resulting from a bad reaction to drugs. From the drug sub-culture, the expression was soon adopted into the common vocabulary to indicate anyone who acted in an irrational manner.

> One of the men happened upon the shrine in the isolated town of Hawley...sometime before the New Year's Eve fire, freaked out at the sight of the Oriental architecture and planned the fire with the other two men. (AP Release, January 5, 1984)

go bananas—To go wild with excitement or rage, to act in an irrational or uncontrollable manner. The phrase supposedly comes from the chattering antics of a hungry monkey at the sight of a banana. It is nearly always used hyperbolically to indicate reason temporarily overcome by emotion; rarely would it be used to describe true mental derangement or disturbance.

go haywire—See DISORDER.

go off the deep end—To overreact, to get inappropriately angry or excited; to go overboard, to overdo it; to go in over one's head; to freak out. The "deep end" refers to the end of a swimming pool at which the water is deepest. Floundering unprepared and confused in the "deep end," one is apt to behave wildly and without a sense of propriety or concern for appearances. Dating from the early 1900s, this expression most often describes emotional outbursts, including occasionally those severe enough to be classified as mental breakdown.

go round the bend—To go crazy; to go out of one's mind; to lose control. This 19th-century expression suggests that one's mind has taken a turn away from normalcy. During World War II the phrase and a transitive form, *drive round the bend*, became especially popular. Both expressions are heard frequently today, chiefly in Britain.

lose [one's] head—To lose one's equilibrium or presence of mind; to be out of control, off balance, or beside oneself. The head is associated with reason, sense, and rationality. Thus, to "lose one's head" is to become irrational and out of control. Its figurative use dates from the 1840s.

> It has now and then an odd Gallicism—such as "she lost her head," meaning she grew crazy. (Edgar Allan Poe, *Marginalia*, 1849)

The phrase is often used to explain behavior (such as a temper tantrum or show of affection) that would otherwise be considered out of character or inappropriate.

lose [one's] marbles—To go crazy; to act or speak in an irrational manner. Since the early 1900s, *marbles* has been equated with common sense and mental faculties. Therefore, to lose one's marbles is to lose one's wits, especially when there has been a sudden behavioral change which manifests itself in eccentric or irrational acts or babblings.

> You lost your goddam' marbles? You gone completely crazy, you nutty slob? (J. Wainwright, *Take-Over Men*, 1969)

A related expression is *have some marbles missing*.

mad as a hatter—Crazy, insane, demented; stark raving mad; violently angry, livid, venomous. It is probable that this expression is a corruption of *mad as an atter*, in which *atter* is an Anglo-Saxon variation of *adder* 'viper,' a poisonous snake. Thus, the original expression implied that a person was venomous, ready to strike with malicious intent. One source suggests that *mad as a hatter* may allude to the insanity and loss of muscular control caused by prolonged exposure to mercurous nitrate, a chemical once commonly used in the manufacture of felt hats. At any rate, in current usage, *mad as a hatter* refers to lunacy more often than to anger.

> In that direction... lives a Hatter; and in that direction... lives a March hare... They're both mad. (Lewis Carroll, *Alice's Adventures in Wonderland*, 1865)

mad as a March hare—Agitated, excited, worked up; frenzied, wild, erratic; rash; insane, crazy. This expression probably alludes to the behavior of hares during mating season when they thump the ground with their hind legs, and jump up and down, twisting their bodies in midair. Several sources suggest that the original expression may have been *mad as a marsh hare*, implying that due to lack of protective shrubbery in marshes, these hares act more wildly than others.

> As mad not as a March hare, but as a mad dog. (Sir Thomas More, *The Supplycacyon of Soulys*, 1529)

This expression was undoubtedly the inspiration for the March hare in Lewis Carroll's *Alice's Adventures in Wonderland* (1865). A common variation is *wild as a March hare*. The related term *harebrained* describes a person who is reckless or eccentric, or a plan, scheme, project, or other matter that is of dubious merit.

> Whilst they, out of harebrained lunacy, desire battle. (John Stephans, *Satyrical Essays, Characters, and Others*, 1615)

stir-crazy—To behave neurotically as a result of long-term imprisonment; to be climbing the walls; to act dull-witted or punch-drunk from confinement. *Stir* is a slang term for jail or prison. Although originating as underworld lingo, *stir* is now fairly common, especially in the phrase *stir-crazy* which is no longer limited in use to prison-related neurosis. Rather, any lack of activity or temporary isolation can make one stir-crazy. The term is rarely if ever used literally almost always hyperbolically.

tarred with the troppo brush—Insane, especially from prolonged tropical duty; extremely agitated from overexposure to tropical conditions. This Australian slang expression is derived from a shortening of *tropical*, adding the ubiquitous Australian *o*, and *tarring*, defiling the body and brain with the noxious horrors of the tropics.

> "Speak for yourself, Captain," said another voice. "We are not all tarred with the troppo brush. You can call yourself barmy if you like, but there's nothing wrong with me." (Colleen McCullough, *An Indecent Obsession*, 1981)

IRREVERSIBILITY
SEE IRREVOCABILITY

IRREVOCABILITY

cry over spilt milk—To regret or bemoan what cannot be undone or changed, to lament or grieve over past actions or events. This proverbial expression, in common use in both America and Britain, was apparently first used by the Canadian humorist Thomas C. Haliburton in *The Clockmaker; or the Sayings and Doings of Samuel Slick of Slickville* (1835), in which a friend of the hero says,

> "What's done, Sam, can't be helped, there is no use in cryin' over spilt milk."

the die is cast—A statement meaning that a decisive and irrevocable step has been taken, that the course has been decided once and for all and that there will be no going back. The original Latin *alea jacta est* would have more meaning for modern ears if rendered in the plural—'the dice have been thrown.' The phrase is attributed to Julius Caesar at the time of his famous crossing of the Rubicon. Although the *OED* dates this specific expression from 1634, Shakespeare's *Richard III* contains a similar concept:

I have set my life upon a cast,
And I will stand the hazard of the die.
(V,iv)

the fat's in the fire—What's done is done, and the negative consequences must be paid; usually used in reference to an irrevocable, potentially explosive situation; also *all the fat is in the fire*. The allusion is probably to the way fat spits when burning. This expression, in use since 1644, appeared in an article by William Dean Howells in the February 1894, issue of *Harper's Magazine*:

The die is cast, the jig is up, the fat's in the fire, the milk's spilt.

let the dead bury the dead—Let bygones be bygones; don't dwell on past differences and grievances. The implication in this expression is that one should not be tied down by things in the past, but should begin anew and look toward favorable prospects in the future.

Jesus said unto him, Follow me; and let the dead bury their dead. (Matthew 8:22)

point of no return—A situation or predicament from which there is no turning back; a crucial position or moment in an argument, project, or other matter which requires total commitment of one's resources. This expression was first used by aircraft pilots and navigators to describe that point in a flight when the plane does not have enough fuel to return to its home base, and so must continue on to its destination.

that's water over the dam—A proverbial phrase expressing the sentiment that what's past is past and nothing can be done about it; also *that's water under the bridge*.

IRRITATION
SEE ANGER; VEXATION

LAMENTATION
SEE GRIEVING

LANGUAGE
See also PROFANITY

bombast—Pretentious speech; high-flown or inflated language. It is but a short step from the now obsolete literal meaning of *bombast* 'cotton-wool padding or stuffing for garments' to its current figurative sense of verbal padding or turgid language. Shakespeare used the word figuratively as early as 1588:

> We have received your letters full of love,
> Your favors, the ambassadors of love,
> And in our maiden council rated them
> At courtship, pleasant jest and courtesy,
> As bombast and as lining to the time.
> (*Love's Labour's Lost*, V,ii)

bumf—Official documents collectively; piles of paper, specifically, paper containing jargon and bureaucratese; thus, such language itself: gobbledegook, governmentese, Whitehallese, Washingtonese. This contemptuous British expression comes from *bumf*, a portmanteau contraction for *bum fodder* 'toilet paper.' It has been used figuratively since the 1930s.

> I shall get a daily pile of bumf from the Ministry of Mines. (Evelyn Waugh, *Scoop*, 1938)

buzz word—An important-sounding word often employed by members of a profession or by politicians to impress laymen; a catch word in current popular use. This term was originally coined in the world of technology to describe those words that specialists used to impress the general public, or, as was frequently the case, to complicate an issue to such a degree as to befuddle the general public. In recent years the expression has taken on the more benign meaning, referring to any popular use of a specialized term.

> The buzz words these days are "commitment," "intimacy," and "working at relationships." (*Time*, April 9, 1984)

civic illiteracy—The lack of understanding of technical issues. This expression was coined to explain the average citizen's growing confusion about the jargon employed by technological experts to befog issues. Such *civic illiteracy* causes citizens to make uninformed decisions, to depend upon so-called experts with blind faith. The expression first came into use in the late 1970s.

> Bafflement over technical jargon used in the MX missile debate and the 1979 Three Mile Island nuclear power crisis were cited as examples of civic illiteracy. (*The Hartford Courant*, November 26, 1981)

claptrap—Bombast, high-sounding but empty language. The word derives from the literal *claptrap*, defined in one of Nathan Bailey's dictionaries (1727–31) as "a trap to catch a clap by way of applause from the spectators at a play." The kind of high-flown and grandiose language actors would use in order to win applause from an audience gave the word its current meaning.

dirty word—A word which because of its associations is highly controversial, a red-flag word; a word which elicits responses of suspicion, paranoia, dissension, etc.; a sensitive topic, a sore spot. *Dirty word* originally referred only to a blatantly obscene or taboo word. Currently it is also used to describe a superficially inoffensive word which is treated as if it were offensive because of its unpleasant or controversial associations. Depending on the context, such a word can be considered unpopular and taboo one day and "safe" the next.

ghost word—A word that never actually existed; a word created by a typographical error. This expression alludes to an accidental word form that was never in established usage. For example, *Webster's Third* cites: *phantomnation* a ghost word combining the words *phantom* and *nation* and erroneously defined as though a formation with the suffix *-ation*.

According to *Harper Dictionary of Contemporary Usage*, another ghost word, *Dord* after a series of printing convolutions and editorial errors, appeared in *Webster's Second* listed as a noun, and was allowed to stand, even after discovery by the editorial staff. *Harper's* further reports that the word was allowed to remain through a number of printings out of the editors' curiosity about reader reaction.

gobbledegook, gobbledygook—Circumlocutory and pretentious speech or writing; official or professional jargon, bureaucratese, officialese. The term's coinage has been attributed to Maury Maverick.

The Veterans Administration translated its bureaucratic gobbledygook. (*Time*, July 1947)

inkhorn term—An obscure, pedantic word borrowed from another language, especially Latin or Greek; a learned or literary term; affectedly erudite language. An inkhorn is a small, portable container formerly used to hold writing ink and originally made of horn. It symbolizes pedantry and affected erudition in this expression as well as in the phrase *to smell of the inkhorn* 'to be pedantic.' The expression, now archaic, dates from at least 1543.

Irrevocable, irradiation, depopulation and such like, . . . which . . . were long time despised for inkhorn terms. (George Puttenham, *The Art of English Poesy*, 1589)

jawbreaker—A word difficult to pronounce; a polysyllabic word. This self-evident expression appeared in print as early as the 19th century.

You will find no "jawbreakers" in Sackville. (George E. Saintsbury, *A History of Elizabethan Literature*, 1887)

malapropism—The ridiculous misuse of similar sounding words, sometimes through ignorance, but often with punning or humorous intent. This eponymous term alludes to Mrs. Malaprop, a pleasant though pompously ignorant character in Richard B. Sheridan's comedic play, *The Rivals* (1775). Mrs. Malaprop, whose name is derived from the French *mal à propos* 'inappropriate,' continually confuses and misapplies words and phrases, e.g., "As headstrong as an allegory on the banks of the Nile." (III,iii)

> Lamaitre has reproached Shakespeare for his love of malapropisms. (*Harper's Magazine*, April 1890)

A person known for using malapropisms is often called a *Mrs. Malaprop.*

pidgin English—A jargon used to bridge the gap between certain exotic languages, especially Chinese, and English; a simplified mixture of Chinese and English used for communication between people of those cultures, especially in business. English traders, when they first started trafficking along the Chinese coast in the 17th century, needed to create a simple form of communication between two entirely different tongues; hence, *pidgin English.* In *pidgin English* many short words take the place of a longer, more difficult word not known by the natives. The term, which was later shortened to *pidgin*, probably developed from the Chinese mispronunciation *bidgin* for 'business,' hence, *this is not my pidgin* means 'this is not my business, this is not my affair.'

> I include pidgin-English . . . even though I am referred to in that splendid language as 'Fella belong Mrs. Queen.' (Duke of Edinburgh, *Speech* [to English-Speaking Union Conference at Ottawa], October 29, 1958)

A related term, *bêche-de-mer* or *Beach-la-Mar*, designates a kind of pidgin, now called Neo- Melanesian, that developed about the same time between European traders and the people of the South Pacific islands.

portmanteau word—A word formed by the blending of two other words. *Portmanteau* is a British term for a suitcase which opens up into two parts. The concept of a *portmanteau word* was coined by Lewis Carroll in *Through the Looking Glass* (1872):

> Well, 'slithy' means "lithe and slimy" . . . You see it's like a portmanteau— There are two meanings packed into one.

Carroll's use of *portmanteau* has been extended to include the amalgamation of one or more qualities into a single idea or notion. This usage is illustrated by D. G. Hoffman, as cited in *Webster's Third:*

> Its central character is a portmanteau figure whose traits are derived from several mythical heroes.

red-flag term—A word whose associations trigger an automatic response of anger, belligerence, defensiveness, etc.; an inflammatory catchphrase. A red flag has long been the symbol of revolutionary insurgents. *To wave the* red flag is to incite to violence. In addition, it is conventionally believed that a bull becomes enraged and aroused to attack by the waving of a red cape. All these uses are interrelated and serve as possible antecedents of *red-flag* used adjectivally to describe incendiary language.

rigmarole—A long-winded, disconnected account; a rambling, unending yarn; a series of incoherent statements. This term is a corruption of *Ragman Roll*, a document presented to King Edward I by Balliol, the king of Scotland, in 1296. Edward, who had gone to Scotland to receive homage, was presented with a signed and sealed scroll from which was appended such a large number of seals that it was nicknamed the *Ragman Roll*. Sometime thereafter the monotonous intoning of any endless list came to be called a *rigmarole*. The original roll may still be seen in the Records Office in London.

> His speech was a fine sample, on the whole,
> Of rhetoric, which the learn'd call rigmarole.
> (Lord Byron, *Don Juan*, 1818)

sling the bat—To be able to speak the colloquial language of a foreign country. This 19th-century Briticism is derived from the Hindi word *bat* 'speech or language,' and was brought back to England by the men who had served in India. Applied originally only to the tongues of India, the term came to include all foreign languages. A common variant is *spin the bat*.

> Native words picked up by the soldier in India who had learned to sling the bat. (*Atheneum*, July 18, 1919)

weasel words—Words that seem to promise much but actually guarantee nothing; words that destroy the force of another word or expression; equivocating words that weaken a statement. This expression appeared in "The Stained Glass Political Platform," an article by Stewart Chapman in the June 1900 issue of *Century Magazine*.

> "The public should be protected —" "Duly protected," said George. "That's always a good weasel word."

The term is derived from the practice of weasels, who suck the substance from eggs while leaving the shell intact. President Theodore Roosevelt offered an explanation in a speech he delivered in 1916.

> One of our defects as a nation is a tendency to use what have been called weasel words. When a weasel sucks eggs, the meat is sucked out of the egg. If you use a weasel word after another word, there is nothing left of the other.

LAZINESS
SEE INDOLENCE

LEAVE-TAKING
SEE DEPARTURE

LICENTIOUSNESS
SEE PROMISCUOUSNESS

LOCOMOTION
SEE VEHICLES

LONGING
SEE DESIRE

LOOKS
SEE PHYSICAL APPEARANCE

LOOSENESS
SEE PROMISCUOUSNESS

Love

LOVE
See also FRIENDSHIP

carry a torch for—To suffer from unrequited love; to love one who doesn't reciprocate; to carry the memory of a rejected love; to crusade for a cause. Originally, this expression alluded to carrying a torch in a parade while one was marching for a cause. In time, it came to symbolize any person, sometimes called a *torch-bearer*, who crusaded wholeheartedly to win others to what he considered the "right" way of thinking, and, finally, in the early 1920s came to indicate anyone who crusaded to regain a lost love or to win the love of one who did not reciprocate.

> He fell in love with a beautiful girl, only to find that she was carrying the torch for W. C. Fields. (*Philadelphia Bulletin*, September 6, 1949)

A related term, *torch song*, denotes a sentimental song of unrequited love, usually sung by a *torch singer*.

> If love is returned the popular song is a simple ballad; if it is unrequited, the song is a torch song. (*Haskins News Service*, August 12, 1952)

heartthrob—A lover, paramour, or sweetheart; a romantic idol. This common expression describes the exhilarating cardiac pulsations that supposedly accompany every thought, sight, or touch of one's true love. *Heartthrob* may also refer to a celebrity of whom one is enamored.

> Rudolph Valentino was the great heartthrob of the silent screen in the nineteen-twenties. (*The Listener*, June 1966)

hold [one's] heart in [one's] hand—To offer one's love to another; to make an open display of one's love. In Shakespeare's *The Tempest* (III,i), Ferdinand offers his hand to Miranda, to which she responds in kind:

> And mine, with my heart in it.

Christopher Marlowe, a contemporary of Shakespeare's, also used this expression.

With this hand I give to you my heart. (*Dido*, III,iv)

look babies in the eyes—To gaze lovingly into another's eyes; to look at closely and amorously. Two unrelated theories have been advanced as to the origin of this expression. One states that the reference is to Cupid, the Roman god of love, commonly pictured as a winged, naked baby boy with a bow and arrows. The other maintains that the phrase originated from the miniature reflection of a person staring closely in the pupils of another's eyes. In use as early as 1593, the term, now obsolete, was used to describe the amorous gaze of lovers:

She clung about his neck, gave him ten kisses.
Toyed with his locks, looked babies in his eyes.
(Thomas Heywood, *Love's Mistress*, 1633)

love-tooth in the head—A propensity to love. This obsolete expression implies a constant craving for romance.

I am now old, but I have in my head a love-tooth. (John Lyly, *Euphues and His England*, 1580)

rob the cradle—To date, marry, or become romantically involved with a significantly younger person. This self-explanatory expression, often substituted by the equally common term *cradlesnatch*, usually carries an implication of disapproval.

I don't usually cradlesnatch. But there was something about you that made me think you were older. (J. Aiken, *Ribs of Death*, 1967)

take a shine to—To take a liking or fancy to, to be fond of, to have a crush on. This colloquialism of American origin dates from the mid 19th century. Perhaps *shine* refers to the "bright and glowing" look often attributed to love.

I wonst had an old flame I took sumthin of a shine to. (*Davy Crockett's Almanac*, 1840)

tender trap—Love; marriage; emotional involvement with one of the opposite sex. This post- World War II colloquialism, implying that love is really a trap which one falls into, gained popularity as a result of the 1954 Broadway comedy production, *The Tender Trap*, written by Max Shulman and Robert Paul Smith. In 1955 the play was adapted as a film starring Debbie Reynolds and Frank Sinatra, whose recording of the title song became a smash hit, further promoting popular usage of the phrase.

wear [one's] heart on [one's] sleeve—To make no attempt to hide one's lovesickness; to plainly show that one is suffering from unrequited love; to publicly expose one's feelings or personal wishes. This expression is said to come from the practice of a knight wearing his lady's favor pinned to his sleeve when going into combat. In Shakespeare's *Othello* (I,i), the duplicitous Iago says:

> For when my outward action doth demonstrate
> The native act and figure of my heart
> In compliment extern, 'tis not long after
> But I will wear my heart upon my sleeve
> For daws to peck at.

LUNACY
SEE IRRATIONALITY

LUST
SEE DESIRE; PROMISCUOUSNESS

LYING
SEE MENDACITY

MANIPULATION
See also CONTROL

backstairs influence—Indirect control, as of an advisor; power to affect the opinions of one in charge. *Backstairs* refers to the private stairways of palaces, those used by unofficial visitors who had true access to or intimate acquaintance with the inner circles of government. Connotations of deceit and underhandedness were natural extensions of the "indirect" aspect of the backstairs. Examples of this usage are cited as early as the beginning of the 17th century. Today *backstairs influence* has come to mean the indirect influence or sway that certain individuals or groups are able to exert over persons in power.

brainwashing—A method of changing an individual's attitudes or allegiances through the use of drugs, torture, or psychological techniques; any form of indoctrination. Alluding to the literal erasing of what is in or on one's mind, *brainwashing* used to be associated exclusively with the conversion tactics used by totalitarian states on political dissidents. This use of the word gained currency in the early 20th century.

> Ai Tze-chi was Red China's chief indoctrinator or, as he was generally called, Brainwasher No. 1. (*Time*, May 26, 1952)

Today application of the phrase has been extended to include less objectionable but more subtle sources of control such as television and advertising.

clockwork orange—Something mechanical that appears organic; a human automaton. This paradoxical expression, derived from the Cockney *queer as a clockwork orange*, alludes to a human being who has been so transformed by scientific conditioning that his response, even if it involves moral choice,

BRAIN WASHING

has become automatic. The term came into popular use shortly after 1962, when Anthony Burgess's novel, *A Clockwork Orange* was published; it was also made into a popular film. Set in the future, the story tells of Alex, a violent, teen-age gang leader, who, primarily through aversion therapy, is transformed into a conforming member of proper society, a thorough-going automaton in a human body.

Bandura feels the behavior-modification process is misunderstood by the public. "They see salivating dogs, shocks, clockwork oranges. They misunderstood the process," he says. (*Science News*, March 16, 1974)

in [someone's] pocket—To be under another's influence or control; to be at the disposal or mercy of someone else. Dating from the turn of the 19th century, this expression evokes an image of one person being held in the pocket of another, much larger person, and thus conveys feelings of manipulation, insignificance, and helplessness.

Lord Gower...seemed charmed with her, sat in her pocket all the evening, both in a titter. (Countess Harriet Granville, *Letters*, 1812)

Although usually used in this interpersonal sense, *in [someone's] pocket* is applied to the control of inanimate objects as well.

He was sitting with the family seat in his pocket. (William Makepeace Thackeray, *The English Humorists*, 1851)

nose of wax—A malleable or accommodating nature; a flexible or yielding attitude. This expression is clearly derived from the pliability of a waxen nose. Originally, the phrase alluded to the Holy Scriptures which, in 16th-century England, were subjected to multitudinous and often conflicting interpretations. The expression was later extended to include other controversial philosophies and laws that were subject to numerous explications.

Oral Tradition, that nose of wax, which you may turn and set, which way you like. (Anthony Horneck, *The Crucified Jesus*, 1686)

Although the expression's initial figurative meaning has been virtually obsolete since the 16th and 17th centuries, *nose of wax* is still occasionally used in describing a wishy-washy or easily manipulated person.

He was a nose of wax with this woman. (Benjamin Disraeli, *Endymion*, 1880)

play both ends against the middle—To play two opposing forces off against each other to one's own advantage. According to several sources, "both ends against the middle" is a technique used to rig a deck of cards in dealing a game of faro; a dealer who used such a deck was said to be "playing both ends against the middle." His maneuvers ensured that competing players lost and that he (or the house) won.

play fast and loose—To connive and finagle ingeniously but inconsiderately to gain one's end; to say one thing and do another; to manipulate principles, facts, rules, etc., irresponsibly to one's advantage. "Fast and Loose," also called "Pricking the Belt," was a cheating game from the 16th century practised by gypsies at fairs. The game required an individual to wager whether a belt was fast or loose. However, the belt would be doubled and coiled in such a way that its appearance prompted erroneous guesses and consequent losses. Shakespeare referred to the trick in *Antony and Cleopatra*:

Like a right gypsy hath at fast and loose
Beguiled me to the very heart of loss.
(IV,xii)

And in *King John*, Shakespeare uses *play fast and loose* figuratively as it is also currently heard:

Play fast and loose with faith? So jest with heaven, ...
(III,i)

pull [someone's] chestnuts out of the fire—To be forced to save someone else's skin by risking one's own; to extricate another from difficulty by solving his problem; to be made a cat's paw of. This expression derives from the fable of the monkey and the cat.

pull strings—To influence or manipulate persons or things secretly to one's own advantage; used especially in reference to political maneuvering; also *to pull wires*.

Lord Durham appears to be pulling at 3 wires at the same time—not that the 3 papers—the Times, Examiner and Spectator are his puppets, but they speak his opinions. (Samuel Rogers, *Letters to Lord Holland*, 1834)

The allusion is to a puppeteer who, from behind the scenes, controls the movements of the puppets on stage by pulling on the strings or wires attached to them. Although both expressions date from the 19th century, *to pull wires* apparently predated *to pull strings*. The latter, however, is more commonly used today.

twist [someone] around [one's] little finger—To have complete control over, to have limitless influence upon, to have at one's beck and call; also *wind [someone] around [one's] little finger* or *turn [someone] around [one's] little finger* or *have [someone] around one's little finger*. *Twist* connotes the extreme malleability of the subject; *little finger*, the idea that the slightest movement or merest whim will suffice to manipulate him. The expression is often used of a woman's power over a man.

Margaret...had already turned that functionary round her finger. (John Lothrop Motley, *Rise of the Dutch Republic*, 1855)

under [someone's] thumb—Under the influence, power, or control of; subordinate, subservient, or subject to. This expression alludes to controlling someone in the same way one can control a horse by pressing his thumb on the reins where they pass over the index finger.

> She is obliged to be silent. I have her under my thumb. (Samuel Richardson, *The History of Sir Charles Grandison*, 1754)

work the oracle—To wheel and deal, to scheme to one's own advantage, especially for money-raising purposes; to engage in artful behind-the-scenes manipulation of those in a position to grant favors. This British expression uses *oracle* as the means or medium through which desired information or goods are obtained.

> With . . . big local loan-mongers to work the oracle and swim with them. (John Newman, *Scamping Tricks*, 1891)

the world's [one's] oyster—Great pleasure and profit are there for the taking with little or no effort. The allusion in this phrase is to a prize pearl in an oyster which only needs to be opened in order for someone to claim the treasure. This expression, like so many others, came from the pen of William Shakespeare. When Falstaff refuses to lend money to him, Pistol replies:

> Why, then the world's mine oyster,
> Which I with sword will open.
> (*The Merry Wives of Windsor*, II, ii)

MASTERY
SEE CONTROL

MATURITY
SEE AGE

MEANINGLESSNESS
SEE NONSENSE

MEDDLESOMENESS
SEE CURIOSITY

MENDACITY

Baron Münchhausen—A teller of tall tales; one who embellishes and exaggerates to the point of falsehood; a creator of whoppers; a liar. Baron von Münchhausen (1720–97), a German who served in the Russian army, gained renown as a teller of adventurous war stories. These were collected by Rudolph Erich Raspe and published in 1785 as *Baron Münchhausen's Narrative of His Marvelous Travels and Campaigns in Russia*. His name has since become synonymous with tall tales and untruths, whether their intent be to entertain or to deceive.

Cock Lane ghost story—A horror story without truth; a fictitious account of ghostly activities. In 1762 William Parsons reported hearing strange knocking in his residence at 33 Cock Lane, Smithfield, England. Attributed to the ghost of one Fanny Kent, an alleged murder victim, the strange noises were later discovered to be made by Parson's daughter rapping on a board in her bed. The story spread rapidly throughout England and many people, including some royal parties, visited the scene. When the hoax was discovered, Parsons was indicted and punished by being pilloried. The expression arose shortly after the discovery of the fraud.

cry wolf—To give a false alarm; to use a trick or other deceitful stratagem to provoke a desired response. This well-known expression alludes to the equally well-known fable about a shepherd lad who often cried "wolf" to get the attention of his neighbors. When they finally grew wise to his trick, a real wolf appeared and the boy cried "wolf," to no avail—no one heeded his call. *OED* citations date the phrase from the late 17th century.

> She begins to suspect she is "not so young as she used to be"; that after crying "Wolf" ever since the respectable maturity of seventeen—
> ... the grim wolf, old age, is actually showing his teeth in the distance. (Mrs. Dinah M. Craik, *A Woman's Thoughts About Women*, 1858)

Equivalent expressions and fables appear in many nations throughout the world.

dress the house—Seat the customers so as to give the appearance of a full theater. This expression derives from theater parlance and refers to a technique whereby the manager of a theater, by the astute assigning of seats, creates the illusion of a full house. A related term, *paper the house*, alludes to another such practice. The manager hands out a good many free passes, *paper* in theatrical jargon, to give the illusion of a sellout performance.

from the teeth outward—To say but not mean; to speak insincerely. This archaic phrase implies that vocal protestations of friendship, trust, etc., are often of questionable value after their utterance.

> Many of them like us but from the teeth outward. (John Udall, *Diotrephes*, 1588)

lie for the whetstone—To be a great liar; to exaggerate outrageously; to present a fanciful prevarication. This expression, dating from the Middle Ages, had its inception in the old custom of placing a whetstone about the neck of a liar. This custom probably arose from the lie-matches once staged at the Whitsuntide celebration, when a contest was held to determine which entrant could tell the largest lie. The winner was rewarded by having a whetstone hung about his neck with which he could sharpen his wit for the next contest.

This is a lie well worthy of a whetstone. (*Harleian Miscellany*, 1625) Related terms are *give the whetstone*, implying to another person that the speaker has just told a "whopper" and *get the whetstone*, implying to the speaker that he himself has just told a "whopper."

lie through [one's] teeth—To purposely tell flagrant and obvious falsehoods; to speak maliciously and untruthfully; to prevaricate with blatant disregard for the truth. The use of *teeth* in this expression serves to underscore the severity of the lie or lies. Variations include *lie in one's teeth*, *lie in one's throat*, and *lie in one's beard*.

lie with a latchet—A great falsehood; a thorough- going lie; a flagrant and obvious falsehood. Although the origin of this expression is somewhat shrouded, it was probably derived about 1600 from an older phrase, *go above* (or *beyond*) *one's latchet*. A *latchet* is a strap or thong used to fasten a shoe, and to *go beyond one's latchet* was to meddle in affairs not of one's concern; hence, to *lie with a latchet* came to mean to go beyond others in the extent of one's lying, to tell a falsehood with only the flimsiest of evidence to back it up, to lie on a shoestring, so to speak. Thomas Fuller demonstrates the term with a bit of doggerel in his *Gnomologia* (1732):

That's a lie with a latchet.

All the Dogs in the Town cannot match it.

out of whole cloth—False, fictitious, fabricated, made-up; also *cut out of whole cloth*.

Absolutely untruthful telegrams were manufactured out of "whole cloth." (*The Fortnightly Review*, July 1897)

The origin of this expression is rather puzzling in that literal whole cloth (i.e., a piece of cloth of the full size as manufactured, as opposed to a piece cut off or out of it for a garment) seems to lend itself to positive figurative senses rather than negative ones. It has been conjectured that the change in meaning came about because of widespread cheating on the part of tailors who claimed to be using whole cloth but who actually used pieced goods, or cloth stretched to appear to be of full width. Thus, ironic use of the phrase may have given rise to the reversal in meaning. On the other hand, it may come from the sense of 'having been made from scratch,' that is, 'entirely made up' or 'fabricated.' The expression dates from the late 16th century.

snow job—An attempt to deceive or persuade, usually by means of insincere, exaggerated, or false claims; a line, particularly one used to impress a member of the opposite sex or a business associate; excessive flattery; a coverup. Snow, especially in large amounts, tends to obscure one's vision and mask the true nature or appearance of objects on which it falls; thus, the expression's figurative implications.

trump up—To devise in an unscrupulous way; to fabricate; to make up something, as a lie or an alibi; to create through one's ingenuity. The key word in this expression, *trump*, derived during the 14th century from the French *tromper* 'to deceive or beguile,' still carries the denigratory connotation usually associated with the word.

He had to flee ignominiously with a trumped up explanation, for how could he confess the simple truth. (Conrad Aiken, *Ushant*, 1952)

a white lie—A harmless or innocent fib; a minor falsehood that is pardonable because it is motivated by politeness, friendship, or other praiseworthy concern. This expression draws on the symbolism often associated with the color "white" (purity, harmlessness, freedom from malice). An interesting definition of *white lie* was offered in a 1741 issue of *Gentleman's Magazine*:

A certain lady of the highest quality ... makes a judicious distinction between a white lie and a black lie.

A white lie is that which is not intended to injure anybody in his fortune, interest, or reputation but only to gratify a garrulous disposition and the itch of amusing people by telling them wonderful stories.

William Paley, on the other hand, presents a different view:

White lies always introduce others of a darker complexion. (*The Principles of Moral and Political Philosophy*, 1785)

window dressing—Misrepresentation or deceptive presentation of facts, particularly those relating to financial matters, to give a false or exaggerated impression of success or prosperity. Literally, window dressing is a technique of attractively displaying goods in a store window. The expression is figuratively applied to any specious display, but is used most often in contexts implying financial juggling which borders on the illegal, usually obeying the letter, though certainly not the spirit, of the law.

The promise of high duties against other countries deceives nobody: it is only political window-dressing. (*Westminster Gazette*, March 9, 1909)

MISCELLANEOUSNESS
SEE MIXTURE

MISTAKENNESS
SEE ERRONEOUSNESS

MIXTURE

cabbages and kings—Anything and everything; odds and ends; assorted and diverse topics, items, etc. The expression comes from Lewis Carroll's *Through the Looking-Glass* (1871):

"The time has come," the Walrus said,
"To talk of many things:
Of shoes—and ships—and sealing-wax—
Of cabbages—and kings—
And why the sea is boiling hot—
And whether pigs have wings."

chip basket—A hodgepodge; an olio; a medley; a conglomeration. This American expression was apparently derived from the variegated appearance of different shapes and colors created by a basket of wood fragments. In use since the 1800s, the term is seldom heard today.

> She throws you into her chip basket of beaux and goes on dancing and flirting as before. (Harriet Beecher Stowe, *Dred*, 1856)

hodgepodge—A heterogeneous mixture, a jumble, a farrago, a gallimaufry, a potpourri. This term is a corruption of the earlier *hotchpotch*, which in turn is a corruption of *hotchpot*, from the French *hochepot* (*hocher* 'to shake, to shake together' + *pot* 'pot'), a cookery term for a dish containing a mixture of many ingredients, especially a mutton and vegetable stew. *Hodgepodge* itself was used figuratively as early as the 15th century.

> They have made our English tongue a gallimaufry or hodgepodge of all other speeches. (E. K., *Epistle Dedicatory and Glosses to Spenser's Shepherds Calendar*, 1579)

mishmash—A jumble, hodgepodge, or potpourri; a confused mess. *Mash* alone means 'confused mixture,' suggesting that *mishmash* may have originated as alliterative wordplay. It has also been suggested that *mishmash* comes from the Danish *mischmasch*. Still current, the term and its variants *mishmosh* and *mishmush* have been in print since the 16th century.

> The original *Panorama* had consisted of a mishmash of disconnected and frequently frivolous items. (*The Listener*, October 30, 1975)

olla podrida—An olio; a mixture of meat and vegetable scraps; any heterogeneous mixture; a miscellany. This expression is a borrowing from the Spanish, and although it translates as putrid pot, it signifies an edible *pot au feu*, a mixture of leftover vegetables, meat, and spices all cooked together. The term, originally used in English in the 16th century, took on a connotation of a mélange of miscellaneous pieces in art, literature, music about the mid 17th century.

> My little Gallimaufry, my little Oleopodrido of Arts and Arms. (Abraham Cowley, *Cutter of Coleman-street*, 1663)

potluck—Leftovers, odds and ends; potpourri, hodgepodge; an entity of uncertain composition. This expression is derived from, and still most commonly refers to, leftover food that has been placed in a pot, usually over a period of several days, and then served as a meal at a later date. The rationale for *luck* is that one takes his chances, that is, does not know what food to expect, when he is invited to partake of a potluck dinner. By extension, *potluck* can refer to any conglomeration from which a person makes a blind or indiscriminate selection.

> [He] took the same kind of pot-luck company in those days when he was not so shy of London. (Madame D'Arblay, *The Early Diary of Frances Burney*, 1775)

threads and thrums—Odds and ends, scraps, fragments; a hodgepodge, a mishmash. Thrums are the unwoven portions of warp yarn which remain attached to the loom when the web is cut off, useless fragments of knotted threads.

> The confused and ravelled mass of threads and thrums, ycleped Memoires. (Thomas Carlyle, "Diderot," *Miscellaneous Essays*, 1833)

See also **thread and thrum**, TOTALITY.

MONEY
See also PAYMENT

Abe's cabe—A five-dollar bill; a fin; a fiver. This American slang expression, originating in the 1930s, was born in the world of jazz. Adopted by the rock and rollers about 1955, the term continued in common use in the world of subculture. *Cabbage*, a common slang expression for money, has been shortened to *cabe*, and combined with an allusion to the picture of *Abe*, Abraham Lincoln, on a five-dollar bill, to form this rather unusual slang expression. The term is seldom heard outside the realm of jazz.

almighty dollar—Money as an object of worship; money conceived of as a source of power; commercial idolatry. Washington Irving apparently coined this term in 1836 in an essay, "The Creole Village," which appeared in an 1837 Christmas annual, *The Magnolia*, and in a collection of his essays.

> The almighty dollar, that great object of universal devotion throughout our land, seems to have no genuine devotees in these peculiar villages. (Irving, *Woolfert's Roost*, "The Creole Village," 1855)

Probably patterned after Ben Jonson's *almighty gold* (1616), the phrase describes some men's belief that the power of money can achieve anything.

axle grease—Australian slang for money, which greases the wheels of life, so to speak, helping things to run along more smoothly.

boodle—A street term for money; ill-gotten gains; bribery. This American slang expression, apparently derived from the Dutch *boedel* 'property,' probably gained popularity when the New York newspapers of 1884 used the term in reference to the New York Board of Aldermen who were charged with taking bribes for granting a franchise for a street railroad on Broadway. Today the term is in general use as the money one receives as the recipient of a bribe. A variant form of the word is part of the expression *the whole kit and caboodle*.

chicken feed—Small change; a paltry or inconsequential amount of money. This American slang expression, which dates from 1836, is an allusion to the scraps and seeds fed to chickens.

cry all the way to the bank—Although the source of this phrase is unknown, it is generally attributed to the famous pianist Liberace, who popularized the expression in the 1950s.

> He likes to say that he and his brother George cry all the way to the bank and to dedicate his theme song, *I Don't Care*, to his critics. (*Current Biography: Liberace*, November 1954)

It is usually heard today as an ironic justification for engaging in an activity that, despite adverse criticism, is nonetheless financially rewarding.

fast buck—Money acquired quickly and effortlessly, usually through illegal or unscrupulous methods. In this expression, *buck* carries the American slang meaning of dollar, making the origin of the term self-evident.

> Trying to hustle me a fast buck. (A. Kober, *The New Yorker*, January 1949)

filthy lucre—Money; money or other material goods acquired through unethical or dishonorable means, dirty money. This expression was first used in an epistle by St. Paul:

> For there are many unruly and vain talkers and deceivers...who subvert whole houses, teaching things which they ought not, for filthy lucre's sake. (Titus 1:10–11)

golden handshake—Originating in Great Britain, this expression refers to a generous gift of money presented to a departing officer or an outstanding employee at retirement. The term has been in use since about 1950. See also SECRECY.

harp shilling—An Irish coin worth twelve pence in Ireland but only ninepence in England; something not worth its face value.

> The said Harp shillings should have...the name and value only of twelve pence Irish... being in true value no more than nine pence English. (Rogers Ruding, *Annals of the coinage of Britain and its Dependencies: A Proclamation of 1606*, 1817)

The so-called *harp shillings* received their name not only from the fact that they were issued in Ireland but also because the image of a harp was stamped on the coin. Because of the lesser value of the coin, the term soon came to connote cheapness or tawdriness.

a king's ransom—A very large sum of money. This expression, perhaps familiarized by the hefty sum demanded for the release of the kidnapped King Richard the Lion-Hearted, maintains frequent usage.

> I couldn't look upon the babby's face for a king's ransom. (Mrs. Anna Hall, *Sketches of Irish Characters*, 1829)

loaves and fishes—Monetary fringe benefits to be derived from public or ecclesiastical office; the personal profit one stands to gain from an office or public enterprise. This use of *loaves and fishes* derives from John 6:26:

> Jesus answered them and said, Verily, verily, I say unto you, Ye seek me, not because ye saw the miracles, but because ye did eat of the loaves, and were filled.

Today the phrase is also sometimes heard in referring to any unanticipated, miraculous proliferation or abundance. This emphasis on abundance rather than personal gain derives from the actual description of the miracle of the loaves and fishes (John 6:11–13).

mad money—Money for frivolous purchases or little luxuries; money for a bit of riotous living-it-up. Originally mad money was that carried by a woman in the event her escort made advances prompting her to leave him in the lurch and finance her own return home. It subsequently came to be applied to money used for any emergency, but at some point took the grand leap from necessity to luxury. Perhaps today it might qualify as what economists call *discretionary income.*

make [one's] pile—To accumulate a fortune; to become wealthy; to make enough money to retire. This expression derives its meaning from the piling up of any substance. In modern idiom, however, it has been restricted to the amassing of money. The idea of piles of money has been expressed since the Middle Ages, but the elliptical sense of this term, as an implication of accumulated wealth, didn't come about until the early 1700s.

> Capitalists who had made their pile were consumed by a desire to walk over their own broad acres. (Augustus Jessopp, *Arcady for Better or Worse*, 1887)

Midas touch—An uncanny ability to make money; entrepreneurial expertise. Midas, legendary king of Phrygia, was divinely granted the power to transform anything he touched to gold. The gods relieved Midas of his power when the king realized that everything he touched, including food and his daughter, changed to gold. Still in general use, this expression often describes the moneymaking abilities of an entrepreneur.

> Picasso, with his Midas touch, has at first try made the lino-cut a more dignified medium. (*The Times*, July 1960)

money burns a hole in [one's] pocket—See IMPATIENCE.

money doesn't grow on trees—This truism, dating from the 19th century, is most frequently directed toward children by their parents. The phrase, of course, is supposed to make the hearer aware that there is no unending source of supply for money, that it all must be earned by hard work. An exasperated tone usually accompanies the phrase.

monkey's allowance—A trifling amount of money; a pittance; a paltry sum. This expression is derived from the saying, "He gets a monkey's allowance—more kicks than halfpence." At one time, trained monkeys performed tricks and then collected money from passers-by. If the monkey performed poorly, its owner often kicked or otherwise punished the animal. Thus, the monkey's allowance was frequently more abuse than money. By extension, a person who receives a "monkey's allowance" is one who works diligently but receives little, if any, payment for his labor. A related expression is *monkey's money* 'something of no value.'

nest egg—Money saved, particularly a reserve fund for use in emergencies or retirement; a bank account or other form of investment which regularly increases in value by virtue of interest accrued or additional deposits made. Originally, a nest egg was a natural or artificial egg which was placed in a hen's nest to induce her to lay eggs of her own. Though the term retains this connotation, it has been extended to imply that once a person has saved a certain amount of money, he is likely to save more.

> A nice little nest egg of five hundred pounds in the bank. (John Ruskin, *Fors Clavigera,* 1876)

nimble ninepence—A pliable silver coin worth nine pence; an Irish shilling; a love token. A silver ninepence was in circulation in Britain until 1696, when all were recalled by the government. These *nimble ninepence,* made of pliable, or nimble, silver, were often used as love tokens. The popularity of the term was given a boost in the mid 1800s by the business proverb *a nimble ninepence is better than a slow shilling,* meaning that it is a better business practice to move articles that cost ninepence than to stagnate with articles that cost a shilling (12 pence).

pin money—A small amount of money set aside for nonessential or frivolous expenditures; an allowance given to a woman by her husband. When common or straight pins were invented in the 13th century, they were expensive and relatively scarce, being sold on only one or two days a year. For this reason, many women were given a regular allowance called pin money which was to be saved until the pins were once again available for purchase. In the 14th and 15th centuries, it was not uncommon for a man to bequeath to his wife a certain amount of money to be used for buying pins. Eventually, as pins became cheaper and more plentiful, the pin money was used for trifling personal expenses, but the expression persisted.

If he gives me two hundred a year to buy pins, what do you think he'll give me to buy fine petticoats? (Sir John Vanbrugh, *The Relapse*, 1696)

pretty penny—A relatively large sum of money; an exceptionally large sum of money. The origin of this phrase is uncertain, but it is often attributed to the special gold pennies, worth 20 silver pennies, that Henry III had coined in 1257. Since they were more valuable, and more noticeable, than the silver pennies, they became known as *pretty pennies*.

The captain might still make a pretty penny. (Bret Harte, *Maruja*, 1885)

raise [one's] screw—To get an increase in wages; to improve one's salary; to gain a better way of life. A practice of some employers in the past was to hand out wages screwed up in a piece of paper, and from that practice the British slang term *screw*, for wages, was born.

It was in payment of my screw—my salary. (Hunter and Whyte, *My Ducats and My Daughter*, 1884)

The more money the paper contained, the higher it had to be twisted or *screwed*; hence, when one *raised his screw*, he received more money.

ready rhino—Ready cash; money. This British slang expression, which never caught on in the United States, has been in use since the late 1600s. Although the origin of the term is obscure, a most credible explanation attributes it to the value of the horn of the rhinoceros. In the Far East, especially in Malaya, it was—and in some areas, is still—believed that the powdered horn of the rhinoceros is a powerful aphrodisiac; it therefore commands a high price. Hence, to have a rhino was like having cash in one's hand. Related terms that developed from the slang expression are *rhino fat* and *rhinocerical*, both meaning 'rich' or 'having plenty of money.'

Cash, cash, cash, that's what we're looking for,
There's nothing like the good old rhino.
(M. H. Rosenfeld, *There's Nothing Like It*, 1887)

root of all evil—The original Biblical quotation as it appeared in I Timothy, 6:10 is:

The love of money is the root of all evil.

However, later misuse of the expression shortened it to *money is the root of all evil*, a phrase which misrepresents the original's intention. Both Mark Twain and George Bernard Shaw are credited with a more jocular, but perhaps more believable version:

The lack of money is the root of all evil.

rubber check—A bad check; a check not covered by sufficient funds. A check issued for an amount greater than the account balance is said to bounce, because it is returned to its payee.

She had bought the car and paid for it with a rubber check. (*This Week Magazine*, September 1949)

a shot in the locker—A reserve, usually financial; a last resource or chance. *Locker* is a nautical term for the compartment on board a vessel in which are stored ammunition, clothes, etc. *Shot in the locker* is literally stored ammunition; figuratively, it refers to a stash of money.

> As long as there's a shot in the locker, she shall want for nothing. (William Makepeace Thackeray, *Vanity Fair*, 1848)

This expression is often heard in the negative *not a shot in the locker*, meaning no money or means of survival.

slush fund—Money procured from the sale of grease or garbage on a naval vessel and used to buy small luxuries for the crew; money set aside for corrupt or unethical ends; money raised by a group, such as office personnel, for gifts, parties, or other special occasions. The origin of this term lies in the word *slush*, meaning the fat or grease accumulated on shipboard during a voyage. The excess slush, which had amassed from the boiling of meat, was sold in port and put into a fund to buy small luxuries for the crew. Eventually this expression, which had its origin in the 18th century, found its way into 20th-century American political slang, where the fund was used to bribe those who were willing to corrupt themselves for luxuries they otherwise couldn't afford. In later years the phrase was added to office jargon to designate a fund for entertainment or other special uses.

> They gave liberally to a slush fund which he collected periodically and distributed where it would do the most good. (Asbury, *Sucker's Progress*, 1938)

small potatoes—See INSIGNIFICANCE.

sugar and honey—Rhyming slang for *money*. This expression dates from the mid 19th century. *Sugar* alone is a popular slang term for money, in Britain as well as in the United States, where most people are unaware that the term is a truncated version of a rhyming slang expression.

that ain't hay—That's a great deal of money; an expression referring to a great deal of anything, material or spiritual, most often money. In this expression, *hay* is used to symbolize something of little or no value. The phrase is always used to contrast hay to something, usually to money, as in "He brings home $250,000 a year and that ain't hay." Of unknown origin, the phrase was originally used only in reference to a sum of money, but later its application broadened to other objects of value, especially of spiritual value. In *Strong Cigars and Lovely Women* (1951), John Lardner makes such use in reference to Lou Ambers, the lightweight boxing champion from 1936–1938 and 1939–1940.

> If Louie Ambers
> Should come our way,
> He brings the title,

And that ain't hay.

worship the golden calf—To abandon one's convictions for the sake of money; to humble oneself before riches; to worship wealth. The expression is an allusion to the Biblical tale found in Exodus: 32. When Moses was called up to Mount Sinai to receive instructions from God, the people who waited for his return eventually grew restless and lost faith. Finally, they called upon Aaron to create an idol which they might worship. Aaron collected all their gold, melted it, and fashioned an idol in the form of a golden calf to which the people made sacrifices. Hence, to *worship the golden calf* is to throw aside one's deepest convictions and pay homage to the false god, gold.

MOURNING
SEE GRIEVING

MUTUALITY
SEE RECIPROCITY

NAKEDNESS
SEE PHYSICAL APPEARANCE

NEGLECT
SEE ABANDONMENT

NEWNESS
SEE AGE

NONSENSE

applesauce—Nonsense, balderdash, bunk; lies and exaggeration; flattery and sweet talk. The first of these meanings is now most common, and the last, least in use. According to a 1929 article in *Century Magazine*, however, the term originally meant "a camouflage of flattery" and derived from the common practice of boarding houses to serve an abundance of applesauce to divert awareness from the paucity of more nourishing fare. It seems equally plausible, though, that its origin might lie in the association of applesauce with excessive sweetness, mushiness, pulpiness, and insubstantiality.

balderdash—Nonsense; a meaningless jumble of words. Used throughout most of the 17th century to mean a hodgepodge of liquors, this word began to be used in its current sense in the latter part of the same century.

banana oil—Bunk, hokum, hogwash, nonsense. This American slang term for insincere talk derives from the literal banana oil, a synthetic compound used as a paint solvent and in artificial fruit flavors, itself so called because its odor resembles that of bananas. Its figurative use combines its characteristics of excessive sweetness and unctuousness.

bunkum—Empty or insincere talk, especially that of a politician aiming to satisfy local constituents; humbug; nonsense; also *buncombe* or the shortened slang form *bunk;* sometimes in the phrase *talk to Buncombe* or *talk for Buncombe*, or *speak for Buncombe* or *speak to Buncombe*. The term comes from a speech made by Felix Walker, who served in Congress from 1817 to 1823. It was so long and dull that many members left. The exodus of his fellow Congressmen did not bother Mr. Walker in the least since he was, in his own words, bound "to make a speech for Buncombe," a North Carolina county in his district. *Bunk*, the abbreviated slang version of *bunkum*, did not appear until 1900, although *bunkum* itself dates from much earlier:

> "Talking to Bunkum!" This is an old and common saying at Washington, when a member of congress is making one of those humdrum and unlistened to "long talks" which have lately become so fashionable. (*Niles' Register*, 1828)

cock and bull story—A preposterous, improbable story presented as the truth; tall tale, canard, or incredible yarn; stuff and nonsense. Few sources acknowledge that the exact origin of this phrase is unknown. Most say it derives from old fables in which cocks, bulls, and other animals are represented as conversational creatures. In one of the Boyle Lectures in 1692 Richard Bentley says:

> ...cocks and bulls might discourse, and hinds and panthers hold conferences about religion.

Matthew Prior's *Riddle on Beauty* clearly shows the nonsensical flavor of "cock and bull":

> Of cocks and bulls, and flutes and fiddles,
> Of idle tales and foolish riddles.

The phrase is current today, as are the truncated slang forms—*cock* in Britain and *bull* in the United States—which mean 'nonsense.'

fiddlesticks—Nonsense, hogwash, balderdash. This word is virtually synonymous with *fiddle-de-dee* and *fiddle-faddle*. Literally, a fiddlestick is the bow used to play a fiddle. Figuratively, it is often used as an interjectional reply to a totally absurd statement.

> Do you suppose men so easily damage their natures? Fiddlestick! (William Makepeace Thackeray, *Miss Tickletoby's Lecture*, 1842)

go to Bath—The inference in this expression is that the person addressed has spoken nonsense or balderdash, and should *go to Bath* to gain the benefit of the mineral waters to cure his mental disorder. The waters of Bath were believed, especially during the 18th century, to cure physical and mental disorders; hence, lunatics were often sent there to benefit from

COCK AND BULL STORY

the water's curative powers. The term has been in use since the 17th century.

moonshine—Nonsense, hogwash; foolish notions or conceptions. Moonshine is the light which, although appearing to be generated by the moon, is actually sunlight reflected off the lunar surface; hence, the expression's figurative connotation of illusion or fallacy.

> Coleridge's entire statement upon that subject is perfect moonshine. (Thomas DeQuincey, *Confessions of an English Opium-Eater*, 1856)

See also **moonshine**, FOOD AND DRINK.

tommyrot—Nonsense, poppycock, balderdash. This expression combines *tommy* 'simpleton, fool,' with *rot* 'worthless matter' to form a word denoting foolish utterances.

> My fellow newcomers... thought nothing of calling some of our instructor's best information "Tommy Rot!" (Mary Kingsley, *West African Studies*, 1899)

NOURISHMENT
SEE FOOD AND DRINK

NUISANCE
SEE VEXATION

OBJECTION
SEE CRITICISM

OBSCENITY
SEE PROFANITY

OBSEQUIOUSNESS

affable as a wet dog—Overly-gracious; servile; subservient. The origin of this 19th-century expression is obvious to any dog owner. It seems that any dog which has just emerged from the water has an overwhelming desire to endear itself to its master or to any other nearby person, often shaking itself vigorously to get rid of excess water on its coat, wetting anyone nearby.

apple-polisher—A sycophant or toady; an ingratiating flatterer. This informal U.S. term stems from the schoolboy practice of bringing an apple to the teacher, supposedly to compensate for ill-prepared lessons. It has been in common student use since 1925 and has given us the now equally common verb phrases *apple-polish* and *polish up the apple* or *shine up the apple*, both meaning to curry favor with one's superiors.

ass kisser—A fawning flatterer, especially one who is two-faced—submissively deferential to superiors in their presence but boldly badmouthing them in their absence. The once taboo, self-explanatory term has gained general currency in spoken usage. It has yet to become an acceptable word in the written language, however. It is sometimes abbreviated to *A.K.*

bootlick—A self-explanatory but stronger term for an apple-polisher or toady. The phrase *to lick* [*someone's*] *boots* or *shoes* has the same connotation of abject servility and devotion.

brownie points—Credit earned by servility, or by performing beyond expectations to ingratiate oneself with one's superiors. This expression alludes to the points accumulated for particular accomplishments by Brownies, junior members of the Girl Scout organization. The term, in popular use since about 1940, has been reinforced by *brown nose*, a common slang expression for a bootlicker.

brown-nose—A fawning flatterer, an obsequious sycophant. The term is more strongly derogatory than *apple-polisher*, and was once considered vulgar owing to its derivation from the image of the ass kisser. Frequent use has rendered the term innocuous, though still insulting. Its corresponding verb form means to curry favor.

curry favor—To seek to ingratiate oneself with one's superiors by flattery or servile demeanor. The original term *to curry Favel*, in use until the early 17th century, derived from a 14th-century French satirical romance in which the cunning, duplicitous centaur Fauvel granted favors to those who curried, or rubbed down, his coat. The natural English transition to *favor* appeared as early as 1510, and after a century of coexistence, totally replaced the earlier *favel*.

dance attendance on—To be totally servile to another; to wait upon obsequiously. This expression originated from an ancient tradition that required a bride to dance with all the guests at her wedding. The phrase, found in literature dating from the 1500s, appears in its figurative sense in Shakespeare's *Henry VIII* (1613):
A man of his place, and so near our favour,
To dance attendance on our lordship's pleasure.
(V,ii)

lickspittle—The most servile of sycophants, the basest of groveling, parasitic toadies. An early use underscores the self-evident origin of the term:
Gib, Lick her spittle
From the ground.
(Sir William Davenant, *Albovine*, 1629)

make fair weather—To conciliate or flatter by behaving in an overly friendly manner; to ingratiate oneself with a superior by representing things in a falsely optimistic light. Shakespeare used this expression in *Henry VI, Part II*; however, it goes back even earlier to the turn of the 15th century.

> But I must make fair weather yet awhile,
> Till Henry be more weak, and I more strong.
> (V,i)

Stepin Fetchit—An obsequious, shuffling black servant; a servile, Uncle Tom type of black person. This eponym is derived from the famous vaudeville and film actor, Lincoln Theodore Monroe Andrew Perry, who adopted the stage name, *Stepin Fetchit*, from the name of a racehorse on which he had won some money. Appearing in many Hollywood productions of the 1930s and 1940s, Perry was typecast as the eye-rolling, shucking and jiving, fawning black servant who "yassuh"-ed and "no-ma'am"-ed his way through life. During the Black movement of the 1950s, *Stepin Fetchit* came to represent a stereotype, the black man who demonstrated servility before whites; the term retains that negative connotation today.

> The driver, from a small town outside Houston, though white, seemed to have taken a course at the Stepin Fetchit school of etiquette. No matter what I said or asked, his answer was the same, "Yassuh." (*Maclean's*, March 1974)

Tantony pig—Anyone who follows another in a servile manner; anyone who follows another closely. This term, dating from the late 16th century, was originally applied to the smallest pig in a litter which, according to legend, would follow its owner wherever he went. *Tantony* is a contraction of *St. Anthony*, the patron saint of swineherds.

> Lead on, little Tony, I'll follow thee, my Anthony, my Tantony, sirrah, thou shalt be my Tantony, and I'll be thy pig. (William Congreve, *The Way of the World*, 1700)

toad-eater—A servile and obsequious attendant or follower; one who will go to any lengths to comply with a superior's wishes; a toady (whence the term) or sycophant. According to the *OED*, the original toad-eaters were charlatans' assistants who ate, or pretended to eat, poisonous toads, thus providing their mountebank masters with the opportunity to display their curative powers by expelling the deadly toxin.

tuft-hunter—A self-seeking flatterer, particularly of the prestigious and powerful; one who attempts to enhance his own status by consorting with those of higher station. Formerly, titled undergraduates at Oxford and Cambridge were, in university parlance, called *tufts*, after the tuft or gold tassel worn on their mortarboards as an indication of their rank. Those of lesser standing who sought their attentions and company thus came to be known as *tuft-hunters*.

ward heeler—A minor political hanger-on who undertakes party chores, often of an underhanded nature. This American slang expression, in use since the late 1800s, usually connotes dishonesty. A ward is a division of a city made for the convenience of political organization; the *heeler* is usually a servile underling who runs about the ward delivering messages and performing other services. Like a dog, he heels at his master's command. Some heelers, however, may rise to positions of power.

> The local man, often called a heeler, has his body of adherents. (A.B. Hart, *Actual Government*, 1903)

OBSOLESCENCE
SEE AGE

OBSTACLE
SEE IMPEDIMENT

OLD AGE
SEE AGE

OLDNESS
SEE AGE

OPENNESS
SEE CANDIDNESS

OPPORTUNENESS
See also TIME

field day—A favorable time for accomplishment; a time rich with opportunity for enjoyment, profit, or success. This expression originally referred to a day scheduled for military maneuvers and war games. It still carries the literal meaning of a school day set aside for various outdoor activities and amusements, such as sports, games, or dances. The phrase was used figuratively by Aldous Huxley in his *Letters* (1953):

> Industrial agriculture is having a field day in the million acres of barren plain now irrigated.

the goose hangs high—Things are looking good, everything is rosy, the future looks promising. No satisfactory explanation has yet been offered to account for the origin of this expression. The theory that the phrase was originally *the goose honks high*, based on the unsubstantiated notion that geese fly higher on clear days than on cloudy ones, must be discounted for lack of evidence. This expression, which dates from at least 1863, was used to describe fine weather conditions before it was applied to the state of affairs in general.

> If you believe there is a plethora of money, if you believe everything is lovely and the goose hangs high, go down to the soup houses in the city of New York. (*Congressional Record*, February 1894)

pudding-time—A favorable or opportune time; not too late; often in the phrase *to come in pudding-time*. This expression, now obsolete, literally meant in time for dinner since pudding was at one time served at the start of this meal. Later, when pudding was served as a dessert, it aptly came to mean a particularly opportune moment, as one had arrived for the sweet. The term dates from 1546.

strike while the iron is hot—See EXPLOITATION.

Tom Tiddler's ground—Any place where it is easy to pick up money or other considerations. This expression is derived from a children's game originating in the 1800s. In the game one player represents Tom Tiddler and protects an area marked off by lines on the ground. The other players run onto *Tom Tiddler's ground* and cry, "Here we are picking up gold and silver on Tom Tiddler's ground." When another player is caught, he becomes Tom Tiddler. The term has come to symbolize any area where one can make easy money or receive information or favors that will lead to success.

> I would rather regard literature as a kind of Tom Tiddler's ground, where there is gold as well as silver to be picked up. (Arthur C. Benson, *From a College Window*, 1907)

OSTENTATIOUSNESS

Bartholomew doll—A gaudily dressed woman; a flashy or overdressed female; a prostitute. This term is derived from the similarity between the original *Bartholomew dolls*, flashy, bespangled handmade dolls offered for sale at Bartholomew Fair, and the tawdry, overdressed women to be found at the Fair. From 1133 the Fair was held annually in the priory of St. Bartholomew in West Smithfield, London. As the years progressed the Fair became more and more boisterous and unruly, until finally in 1840 it was moved to Islington, where, 15 years later, it was closed for good.

cut a swath—To show off or attract attention to oneself; to make a pretentious display; to cut a dash. This expression, which dates from 1843, is a figurative extension of *swath* 'the strip or belt cut by the sweep of a scythe.'

drugstore cowboy—This expression describes the young men who loiter at drugstores, dairy bars, and candy stores, showing off and trying to impress the girls. The exact origin of the term is uncertain; however, it clearly alludes to the masculine image of the American cowboy which many try to emulate. Originating in the 1930s, the expression is still in popular use.

> ... bell-bottom trousers so much in vogue with the drugstore cowboys of today. (Alan Hynd, *We Are the Public Enemies*, 1949)

A related variant, *urban cowboy*, became popular with the release of a movie by that name in 1980.

English—Any extra something that gives flourish or pizzazz to an otherwise ordinary movement or gesture; side spin on a ball. The following explanation of the origin of this American term appeared in the *Sunday Times* [London] in April 1959:

> The story goes that an enterprising gentleman from these shores travelled to the United States during the latter part of the last century and impressed the Americans with a demonstration of the effect of "side" on pool or billiard balls. His name was English.

This expression, which dates from 1869, is most often used in reference to billiard or tennis balls, though it is sometimes used in other contexts.

fine feathers make fine birds—This saying suggests prententiousness, overconcern with one's appearance, or overdressing to impress. The expression, in varying forms, dates back to the 1500s. From the outset its connotation was primarily sarcastic.

> It may rightly be said of these costly clad carcasses, that the feathers are more worth than the bird. (Stefano Guazzo, *Civil Conversation*, 1574)

Based on Aesop's fable of the jay and the peacock, the phrase apparently was put into its present form by Bernard Mandeville in *The Fable of the Bees* (1714). In modern use the term is applied only derisively.

> Fine feathers make fine birds, but they don't make lady-birds. (J.C. Bridge, *Cheshire Proverbs*, 1917)

flat hat—To fly dangerously low in an airplane; to hedgehop; to buzz; to show off; to make an ostentatious display. This expression derives from an incident alleged to have happened in the 1920s when the hat upon a man's head was crushed by a low flying plane. It is more likely that it is a colorful coinage not owing to any real incident. A variant *flat hatter* signifies a pilot who flies in such a manner.

flourish of trumpets—An unnecessarily flamboyant introduction; a pretentious display. This expression is derived from the musical fanfare associated with the arrival of royalty or other distinguished, high-ranking officials. The expression is used figuratively to describe an inappropriate show of pomposity.

foofaraw—Ostentation; gaudy wearing apparel; cheap and showy; a braggart; a windbag; a blowhard. This colloquial expression is a derivation of the French *fanfaron,* 'fanfare.' Corrupted in spelling and meaning, the word has taken on a connotation of anything or anyone that is showy or gaudy, or one who draws attention to himself by causing an unnecessary disturbance. First used in the 1600s, the term has many variants, among which are *fofaraw,* a simple variation in spelling; *fanfaron,* retaining its original French meaning but in addition signifying a braggart; *fanfaronade,* 'boisterous language'; and *fanfarrado,* a nonce word.

> She had no business acting so foofaraw for she was just a yaller gal. (Leland Baldwin, *The Keelboat Age on Western Waters,* 1941)

froufrou—Elaborate ornamentation; unnecessary decoration; affected elegance; fanciness. Originally used to describe the rustling sound of women's petticoats and dresses, this term, by transference, came to describe any type of elaborate decoration on a woman's dress. In time it was extended to any kind of decoration, especially to overly ornate or trivial adornment. Today the term is used almost exclusively to indicate frilly fashions in women's wear.

> Is that what you want in a girl—chi-chi, frou-frou, fancy clothes, permanent waves? (Max Shulman, *Dobie Gillis,* 1951)

A related term, *chi-chi,* suggests a less startling bit of embellishment than *froufrou.*

> Another bit of chi-chi that has come to our notice lately is Eleanor Roosevelt's letterhead. (*The New Yorker,* December 1, 1951)

fuss and feathers—Pretentious, ostentatious display; exaggerated concern and preoccupation with one's appearance. *Fuss and feathers* is reputed to have been the nickname given to U.S. General Winfield Scott by those who thought him finicky, vain, and self-important. According to the *OED,* this expression appeared in print by 1866, the year of Scott's death.

grandstand—Done to impress onlookers; done merely for effect or attention, used especially of an athletic feat.

> It's little things of this sort which makes the 'grandstand player.' They make impossible catches, and when they get the ball they roll all over the field. (M. J. Kelly, *Play Ball,* 1888)

This common expression is sometimes extended to *grandstand play,* an athletic maneuver done to draw applause from the spectators, and *grandstand finish,* a thrilling, neck-and-neck finale to a sporting event.

ham—A performer who overacts and exaggerates to show off on stage; an inexperienced, inferior actor; frequently extended to any person who enjoys being the focus of others' attention and behaves in such a way as to attract it; an exhibitionist or showoff. There are several different but related theories as to the origin of this phrase. One of the best known states that, for economic reasons, poorly paid performers used cheap ham fat instead of the more costly cold cream to remove their makeup, thus giving rise to the term *ham*. Similarly, the *OED* theorizes that *ham* is short for *hamfatter* 'an ineffective, low-grade actor or performer.' A related synonymous term is *hamfat man*, also the title of a popular minstrel song. All of these terms are U.S. slang and date from the 1880s.

hot-dog—To show off, especially by performing flashy, difficult, intricate maneuvers in sports; to grandstand, to play to the crowd; also *to hot-dog it*. The verb *to hot-dog* is a back formation from the surfing slang terms *hotdogging* 'riding a hot dog surfboard' and *hotdogger* 'a surfer who rides a hot dog board.' A *hot-dog* surfboard is relatively small and probably got its name from its cigarlike shape, similar to that of a hot dog. Although the verb *to hot-dog* dates only from the 1960s, the noun *hot dog* 'hot shot, showoff' dates from the early part of this century. This figurative sense of the noun probably derived from the exclamation *hot dog!* 'great, terrific,' used originally in reference to the food.

> Looking good on a little wave is hard. If you can hot dog on two foot waves you are "king." (*Pix* [Australia], September 1963)

play to the gallery—To overact or overplay to get a rise out of the less refined and educated members of a group; to appeal to the vulgar tastes of the common man; to seek recognition by showy, overdramatized antics. This expression dates from the 17th century when the *gallery* referred to the less expensive seats in the theater where the *gallery gods* (See STATUS) congregated to watch a play.

> His dispatches were, indeed, too long and too swelling in phrase; for herein he was always "playing to the galleries." (*Standard*, October 23, 1872)

Today *gallery* refers to any uncultured group of undiscerning judgment. An analogous expression deriving from baseball is *play to the grandstand*.

posh—Sumptuously opulent; luxurious. Although the origin of this term is in dispute, many people still adhere to the expression's purported acronymous derivation from 'port out, starboard home,' a reference to the shady, more comfortable north side of a ship traveling between England and India. The phrase, originally a British saying, is now commonplace on both sides of the Atlantic.

> I'd like to have . . . a very cozy car, small but frightfully posh. (John B. Priestley, *The Good Companions*, 1929)

Saint Audrey's lace—Cheap lace sold at the annual fair of Saint Audrey, from which the word *tawdry* was derived. When Ethelreda, a daughter of a 6th-century king of Northumbria, was a child, she enjoyed wearing pretty necklaces. Hundreds of years later, after Ethelreda had been canonized as Saint Audrey and had become the patron saint of Ely, the townspeople sold necklaces at their annual fair. These Saint Audrey's laces, as they were called, soon gave way to a cheap and showy lace that became known throughout Britain for its gaudiness. About 1700 the word *tawdry* appeared, a corruption of *Saint Audrey*, to describe these necklaces, and to this day denotes anything cheap or gaudy.

shoot [one's] cuffs—To show off; to flaunt or strut one's stuff; to grandstand; to put on the dog. In the Middle Ages, affectedly ostentatious noblemen often wore shirts with large, flamboyant lace cuffs which protruded from the sleeves of their equally ornate coats. Since the display of this type of cuff was clearly intended to impress, these quasi-aristocrats were derisively said to be "shooting their cuffs." With the decline in the popularity of such garish forms of dress, the expression became figurative and still enjoys occasional contemporary use. A variation is *shoot one's linen*.

tinhorn gambler—Pretentious bettor who wagers only small amounts; small-time gambler who pretends to be big-time. Two plausible explanations exist for the genesis of this American slang expression, coined early in the 19th century. One involves the use of a gaming device, called a *tinhorn*, which gambling house operators of the American Old West employed for those wishing to wager on a small scale. The second and more plausible explanation compares the fine appearance but poor quality of an actual tin horn with the fine appearance but poor financial condition of some gamblers.

zoot suiter—A person of brash tastes; one who dresses in loud clothing; one who thinks he's with it. The suggestion in this term is the flamboyance demonstrated by one who will wear garish clothing. The *zoot suit*, developed in the late 1930s, consists of high-waisted, striped or multi-colored trousers, called *peg trousers*, full in the legs but tight at the ankles, a drape-shape jacket with excessively padded shoulders and very wide lapels, a wide, flowing tie, a broad-brimmed hat, and a knee length key or watch chain. Although this faddish style died out shortly during World War II, because of the shortage of materials, the term *zoot suiter* has remained in occasional use to designate certain ostentatious types of people.

I thought you'd begin to like me again if I changed into a zoot suiter. (*Miss America*, June 1948)

OUTDOING

beat all hollow—To surpass completely or thoroughly; to outdo; to excel. The exact origin of this phrase is unknown. *Hollow* is the key word, meaning 'thoroughly, outandout,' and *all hollow* is an American colloquial variant. Various forms of the phrase (*have it hollow* or *carry it hollow*) were used as early as the middle of the 17th century. Today the most frequently heard form is the full phrase *beat all hollow*, which appeared as early as 1785 in the *Winslow Papers:*

> Miss Miller ... is allowed by your connoiseurs in beauty to beat Miss Polly Prince all hollow.

beat Banagher—To outdo, excel, or surpass in absurdity, incredibility, or preposterousness. This Irish expression has been said to derive both from an actual town of that name, and from a hypothetical storyteller of that name, but no authenticating anecdote or evidence for either theory has been proffered.

beat the Dutch—To astonish or surprise owing to excess of any sort; to outdo or surpass. The expression is an Americanism dating from the days of the early Dutch settlers. Some say it owes its origin to their reputation as merchants and traders offering the best bargains and fairest prices. Others see it as an outgrowth of the English-Dutch hostility in the New World. Either theory may be correct, since the phrase is used either positively or negatively.

knock [one's] socks off—Beat soundly; overwhelm; astound; astonish; overcome with amazement. This Americanism, dating from the 1840s, is used figuratively in two different ways. It is used to express a thorough and decisive beating, a beating so thorough that one's socks are literally torn from one's feet, probably a variation of the older term, *knock someone's block off*. It is also used to express astonishment.

> Dressing sexy is great, but it's undressing sexy that really knocks your socks off. (*Playboy*, December 1973)

knock the spots out of—To surpass or excel by an exceeding degree; to prove superior in a given skill or talent. This phrase, common in the United States in the 19th century, is said to derive from the former practice of developing one's proficiency in the use of firearms by aiming at the spots on playing cards which had been nailed to a tree. A marksman able to hit any given spot from a regulation distance could "knock the spots out of" another or another's performance. In describing the Duke "learning" Hamlet's soliloquy to the King, Huck Finn says:

> All through his speech, he howled, and spread around, and swelled up his chest, and just knocked the spots out of any acting ever *I* see before. (Mark Twain, *The Adventures of Huckleberry Finn*, 1885)

out-Herod Herod—To outdo in excessiveness or extravagance; to be more outrageous than the most outrageous. The expression first appeared in Shakespeare's *Hamlet:*

> I would have such a fellow whipped for o'erdoing Termagant—it out-Herods Herod. Pray you, avoid it. (III,ii)

In these lines Hamlet is admonishing the players to perform with restraint, warning that a bombastic style of acting is not to his taste. In medieval mystery plays Herod was conventionally presented as a roaring tyrant, much given to ranting and raving and extravagant gesture. Use of the expression *out-Herod Herod* dates from the early 19th century. While it still most often describes blustering behavior or speech, it is by no means limited to such contexts. A person may "out-Herod Herod" by going beyond any other in any particular.

> As for manner, he [Alexander Smith] does sometimes, in imitating his models, out-Herod Herod. (Charles Kingsley, *Miscellanies*, 1853)

Out-Herod often occurs alone, with the character and characteristic in question completed by context; e.g., "He out-Herods Muhammad Ali in fancy talk and footwork."

run rings around—To be unquestionably superior; to easily surpass another's performance; to defeat handily. No satisfactory explanation of this very common phrase has been found. One source conjectures it stems from races in which one contestant could literally run around his opponent and still come out the victor. Another says the phrase derives from Australian sheepshearing contests, but fails to provide a clear explanation of the relationship; however, the earliest known citation is from Australia, lending this latter theory a degree of credibility.

> Considine could run rings around the lot of them. (*Melbourne Argus*, October 1891)

steal the show—To be the outstanding or most spectacular person or item in a group, especially unexpectedly; to usurp or get the credit for. This expression is rooted in the theater and refers to an actor or actress whose performance is so impressive and striking that it is the most memorable element in a stage production. Although still used in theater, *steal the show* is applied figuratively in varied contexts to describe a person or thing whose extraordinary qualities totally overshadow those of other members of a group. One who or that which "steals the show" is often called a *showstealer*.

take the cake—To be conspicuously good or bad; to be so extraordinary or preposterous as to surprise or stun into momentary incredulity; to excel or surpass. Cakes were often prizes in competitions of different sorts in many cultures, but most theorists agree that this phrase comes from the Black American dance competition called the cakewalk, in which couples would promenade around a large cake, and the one judged most graceful would get the cake as a prize. Though originally used in this sense of "win the prize" or "bear away the bell," the expression is now almost always heard used ironically. *Take the cake* more often means to be the worst than to be the best.

KNOCK THE SPOTS OUT OF

Pack up and pull out, eh? You take the cake. (Theodore Dreiser, *Sister Carrie,* 1900)

upstage—To outdo or surpass; to be a standout; to steal public attention and acclaim from another; to ignore or snub, especially condescendingly. In theater, upstage is the back half of the stage. To upstage an actor, then, is to stand toward the rear of the stage foreing the other actor has to turn his back to the audience so that its attention is effectively diverted from one actor and focused on the one who is doing the upstaging. By extension, *upstage* is applied in many nontheatrical contexts where one person overshadows or otherwise diminishes the importance of another.

Nada Nice has upstaged the Kid . . . at your order. (Harry Witwer, *The Leather Pushers,* 1921)

As an adjective, *upstage* means condescending, aloof, haughty, stuckup.

Although Costello . . . had definite ideas . . . in connection with his art, as he took pictures seriously, he was never the least bit "upstage" with us youngsters. (*Sunday Express,* May 10, 1927)

OVERSHADOWING
SEE OUTDOING

OVERWORK
SEE EXERTION

PARITY
SEE EQUIVALENCE

PAYMENT
See also MONEY; REWARD

cash on the barrelhead—Immediate payment; money on the spot. This Americanism probably gained currency during the days when many perishable items were kept in barrels to retain freshness. To purchase something, one had to put *cash on the barrelhead.* Today the phrase is used to indicate that no credit is extended.

No more divorces in Holt County until there is cash on the "barrelhead," is the edict. (*Kansas City Times,* April 7, 1932)

County Clare payment—No payment at all; a thank-you rather than payment. This 19th-century British expression probably alludes to the indigence of the Irish farmer and his inability to pay for even the smallest of services.

Only a thank-you job; a County Clare Payment, "God spare you the health." (Lady Gregory, *New Comedies,* 1913)

foot the bill—To pay or settle an account; to assume responsibility for expenses incurred by others. This expression stems from the custom of signing one's name at the bottom, or foot of a bill, as a promise of payment. Over the years, this phrase has come to describe someone who pays an entire bill himself, rather than allow or force it to be divided among the parties involved.

> The annual bill we foot is, after all, small compared with that of France. (*Leeds Mercury*, July 18, 1891)

fork over—To pay up immediately; to hand over; to pay out. This expression, in common use since about 1840, alludes to the similarity between the fingers of the human hand and the tines of a fork; hence, *fork over* is simply another way to say *hand over*.

> He accordingly forked over the castings, 600 in number. (*Spirit of the Times*, September 21, 1844)

Variants are *fork out* and *fork up*.

the ghost walks—Salaries will be paid; there is money in the treasury; it's payday. This expression, inspired by Shakespeare's *Hamlet*, has two possible explanations, one of which cites Horatio's asking the ghost (of Hamlet's father) if it walks because:

> ...thou hast uphoarded in thy life
> Extorted treasure in the womb of earth.
> (I,i)

A more plausible, and certainly more colorful, theory tells of a 19th-century British theater company that threatened to strike because their salaries had not been paid for several weeks. The ghost was played by the leader of the company, a highly acclaimed actor. During a performance, the ghost, in answer to Hamlet's exclamation, "Perchance 'twill walk again," shouted from the wings, "No, I'm damned if the ghost walks any more until our salaries are paid!" Their salaries were paid and the performance continued. From then on, the actors met every payday to determine whether the ghost would walk, i.e., whether they would be paid. This expression gave rise to *ghost*, theatrical slang for a paymaster or treasurer of a theater or theater company.

go on tick—To buy an item on credit; to be indebted for what one purchases; also, *get on tick*. In this expression, *tick* is a shortening of *ticket*, where *ticket* carries its obsolete meaning of a written note acknowledging debt. Although the phrase never attained great popularity in the United States, it has been a commonplace expression in Great Britain for centuries.

> A poor wretch that goes on tick for the paper he writes his lampoons on. (William Wycherley, *Love in a Wood*, 1672)

the never-never plan—Installment buying, buying on credit; the layaway plan. This British colloquialism for their own *hire-purchase* is usually abbreviated to the slang *never-never*. It appeared in print as early as the 1920s, and continues in common usage.

> They've still not paid off their mortgage, you know, and I wouldn't mind betting that Rover of theirs is on the never-never. (J. Wilson, *Truth or Dare*, 1973)

nickel and dime to death—To drain a person of his money bit by bit; to eat away at one's monetary resources a little at a time; to exhaust one's finances by an accumulation of small expenses. This U.S. colloquial expression has become common in recent years, probably because of continued inflation and "built-in obsolescence." It might appear in a context such as: "It's not the initial outlay or major maintenance that makes automobile ownership expensive, but they nickel and dime you to death with piddling repairs that result from shoddy workmanship."

no tickee, no washee—Pidgin English for no ticket, no laundry; no goods or services without a receipt or payment; no credit. Arthur Taylor in *The Proverb* (1931) explains:

> No tickee, no washee, i.e., "without the essential prerequisite, a desired object cannot be obtained," with its evident allusion to the Chinese laundryman, bespeaks for itself a recent origin.

The expression dates from the late 19th century and has most commonly been applied, seriously or jocularly, to a situation where credit or the return of goods is denied if certain conditions are not met. A variant is *no tickee, no shirtee*. A related term, *no money, no Swiss*, indicates no assistance as well as no credit. The term originated from the willingness of Swiss soldiers to serve as mercenaries for the crowned heads of Europe; they continue to serve as armed guards for the Pope today.

> After long observation I find it to hold truer *no money, no mistress* than *no money, no Swiss*. (Thomas Brown, *Works*, 1704)

on the cuff—On credit; on a special payment plan; on tick. Although the origin of this expression is obscure, a plausible derivation is that, at one time, storekeepers and bartenders kept track of debts by making marks on their shirt cuffs, which, till the 1920s, were available in Celluloid and, like collars, were not sewn to the shirt. Written on in pencil, they could easily be wiped clean. The phrase is used frequently today.

> Money was not important at all. All business was transacted on the cuff. (B. Macdonald, *Egg and I*, 1945)

on the nail—On the spot, at once, immediately, right away or now; used in reference to money payments. Although the origin of this expression is obscure, it may be related to the French phrase *sur l'ongle* 'exactly, precisely' (literally, 'on the (finger)nail'). The expression appeared in Maria Edgeworth's *Popular Tales* in 1804:

> The bonnet's all I want, which I'll pay for on the nail.

No longer in common use, this phrase dates from the late 16th century.

on the nod—On credit, on the cuff, with no money down. This expression, in use since the late 19th century, is said to have come from the practice of bidders at auctions, who signify their acceptance of a stated price with a nod of the head, on the understanding that the formalities of paying would be taken care of later. In any case, this gesture has long been used to show assent or agreement when entering into a bargain.

> Drunks with determined minds to get bacon, bread, cheese, on the nod. (*The Bulletin* [Sydney], July 1934)

pay as you go—This term, although it was in use as early as 1855, did not achieve popularity until the federal government's introduction of periodical income tax withholding during World War II. Beardsley Ruml, treasurer of Macy's and a director of the New York Federal Reserve Bank, presented the program, his own brainchild, to the Senate Finance Committee in 1942. Originally rejected by the Committee because of the Treasury Department's opposition, the plan was finally implemented in 1943 after President Franklin D. Roosevelt announced his approval. Advertising agencies soon picked up the phrase and popularized it through the media.

> Now, thanks to the pay-as-you-go policy, there are many who find they owe the government nothing. (*Saturday Evening Post*, March 5, 1949)

In Great Britain a similar program was initiated under the acronym *P. A. Y. E.* 'pay as you earn.'

pay [someone] peanuts—To pay someone extremely low wages; to earn an insignificant profit. Peanuts are so cheap and plentiful that they have for many years symbolized anything trifling and unimportant. In this American slang term, dating from the late 1800s, they characterize a sum of money so trivial that it is almost not worth mentioning.

> They got you working for peanuts. (Budd Schulberg, *What Makes Sammy Run*, 1941)

The British equivalent, *pay someone in washers*, is, like the American term, almost always uttered contemptuously.

pay [one's] scot—To make payment; to pay one's share, especially for entertainment; to settle one's tavern score. From the 1200s until about 1400 *scot* meant 'contribution,' a direct carryover from the Old English *sceot*; but about 1400 the term took on the meaning of a tax, an assessment according to one's ability to pay, especially in the phrase, *scot and lot*. Consequently, the two phrases are often confused as to meaning. To *pay scot and lot* connotes to pay in full, to settle with once and for all; to *pay one's scot* connotes a contribution toward the ethical, rather than the practical, modes of life.

No system of clientship suits them; but everyman must pay his scot. (Ralph W. Emerson, *Conduct of Life: Wealth*, 1860)

shell out—To hand over money; to pay up. This figurative expression probably derives from the similarity between shelling vegetables, such as peas from the pod, and shelling money out of one's pocket or purse. The *OED* lists the word's earliest use as 1801.

If you are one of the taxpayers who are paying by installments, get ready to shell out again. (A.P. Release, October 12, 1949)

PERCEPTIVENESS

feel a draft—To sense negative feelings of others toward oneself; to perceive subtle manifestations of hostility, often racial. This phrase, obviously based on the dual dimensions of physical and emotional coldness, originated in the jazz world.

The black audience would send a draft toward the Negro leader who hired a white man instead of a black man of comparable talent and stylistic inclination. (*Downbeat*, May 16, 1968)

The British use the expression *feel the draught* to describe a sense of inconvenience or discomfort, often in relation to one's financial situation.

With only so much national advertising to go round...the oldest commercial stations are feeling the draught as well. (*Listener*, June 1966)

have [someone's] number—To know a person's real motives or intentions; to be a perceptive and astute judge of character; to size another up. The practice of assigning numbers to identify people is the probable source of this expression. Although one's *number* is a superficial designation, the expression connotes a deeper, more profound understanding of a person. *Have [someone's] number* dates from the mid 19th century and is current today.

Do you remember the day before when he made that crack at you in front of Miss Crozier? I had his number right then. (R. D. Paine, *Comr. Rolling Ocean*, 1921)

I wasn't born yesterday—Said by one who asserts that he is not a fool, not easily taken in; said by a person who wants to inform another that he is aware of the other's attempt at manipulation. The implication is, of course, that one is not naive or easily misled owing to inexperience. The expression has been in use since the early 19th century.

The widow read the letter and tossed it into the fire with a "Pish! I was not born yesterday, as the saying is." (Frederick Marryat, *Snarleyvow*, 1837)

know a hawk from a handsaw—To be capable of differentiating between two things; to be wise, not easily fooled or duped. *Handsaw* is a corruption of *heronshaw* 'a young heron.' Thus, to differentiate between two similar things implies a more refined intelligence than is suggested by the expression in its present form. Shakespeare used this expression in *Hamlet:*

> I am but mad north-northwest. When the wind is southerly, I know a hawk from a handsaw. (II,ii)

It has also been conjectured that *hawk* refers not to the bird of prey but to a tool like a pickax. In that case, both *hawk* and *handsaw* would denote instruments.

know chalk from cheese—To be able to differentiate between two things that are superficially alike but essentially dissimilar; to be discerning, to have a keen mind; to know the real thing from a counterfeit. As early as the 14th century, these two words were set apart as opposites.

> Lo, how they feignen chalk for cheese. (John Gower, *Confessio Amantis,* 1393)

The implication is that cheese is superior to or finer than chalk. Thus, to be as *different as chalk and cheese* is to be as different as black and white, or day and night, even though chalk and cheese are similar in appearance.

look beneath the surface—To go beyond appearances to try to perceive the true nature of something; not to be fooled by superficial glitter or plainness. This proverbial saying is attributed to the Roman Emperor, philosopher, and writer Marcus Aurelius (121–180):

> Look beneath the surface; let not the several quality of a thing nor its worth escape thee. *(Meditations)*

look through a millstone—To be discerning and sharpsighted; to exercise keen powers of perception. A millstone is a large, opaque stone used in grinding grains. Therefore the physically impossible challenge to see through a millstone can be met only figuratively by one of extraordinarily keen perception. The expression appeared in print by the mid-16th century.

> Your eyes are so sharp, that you cannot only look through a Millstone, but clean through the mind. (John Lyly, *Euphues and his England,* 1680)

read between the lines—To understand the implications of another's words or actions; to see beyond the explicit and be sensitive to the implications of subtleties and nuances; to get the underlying message, whether intended or not, regardless of the words that couch it or the actions that convey it. The phrase was once literal; methods of cryptogrammic communication included the use of invisible ink for writing between the lines or the practice of relating the secret message in alternate lines. Thus, *reading between the lines* was crucial to receiving the message sent. Today the expression often refers to an ability to sense an author's tone or a person's ulterior motives.

> People who have not the shrewdness to read a little between the lines ... are grievously misled. (*The Manchester Examiner*, January 1886)

read [someone] like a book—To perceive another's motives; to understand the subtleties of another's actions; to know a person thoroughly. This expression, dating from the early 19th century, refers to a person's ability to discern another's character, simply by observing him and talking to him, as easily as one can read a book.

> That lady, who read him like a book, preserved an appearance of complete unconsciousness. (George Whyte-Melville, *Uncle John*, 1874)

see through [someone]—To perceive or understand another person's motives or intentions; to judge another with precision. The quality expressed in this phrase most frequently connotes negativism, i.e., the understanding of ulterior motives or sly intentions. The implication is that the person the speaker *sees through* is not acting charitably but selfishly and surreptitiously. The expression has been in use since the early 16th century.

> He is a mere piece of glass, I see through him. (Ben Jonson, *Cynthia's Revels*, 1599)

Related terms, meaning 'astute' or 'sagacious' and dating from about the same time, are *see through a millstone* and *see far in(to) a millstone*.

> She thought she had seen far in a millstone when she got a husband. John Heywood, *Proverbs*, 1546.

Another related term, which appeared somewhat later but is still heard today, is *see through a brick wall*.

> He could see through a brick wall as well as most men. (Henry Kingsley, *Ravenshoe*, 1861)

PERPLEXITY
SEE CONFUSION

PERSEVERANCE
See also ENDURANCE

bloody but unbowed—Beaten but not subdued; defeated but unyielding; proud in adversity. This expression can be traced directly to William E. Henley, who penned the term while a patient in a tuberculosis hospital:

> In the fell clutch of circumstance
> I have not winced nor cried aloud.
> Under the bludgeonings of chance
> My head is bloody, but unbowed.
> (*Invictus*, 1888)

Originally intended in a serious vein, the phrase has become so overworked that today it is generally employed in a jocular sense.

come hell or high water—Come what may, no matter what; also *in spite of hell or high water*. P. I. Wellman in *Trampling Herd* (1939) claims the following as the origin of the expression:

> "In spite of hell and high water" ... is a legacy of the cattle trail when the cowboys drove their hornspiked masses of longhorns through high water at every river and continuous hell between.

Whether originally a cowboy expression or not, *hell* and *high water* symbolize any difficulties or obstacles to be overcome. The expression has been in use since at least 1915.

diehard—A hardcore supporter; one who struggles and resists to the bitter end, particularly against change or innovation; literally one who dies hard. This expression reputedly had its origin in the Battle of Albuera (1811) where the 57th Regiment of Foot of the British Army fought desperately to maintain a strategic position. In the midst of the fighting, Colonel Inglis is said to have urged his men on by shouting "Die hard! 57th, die hard!" The last-ditch courage and stamina with which the 57th fought that day earned them the nickname the *Diehards,* by which their regiment is known to this day. Use of this term dates from at least 1844.

do a Nelson—To withstand great danger; to be undaunted by adversity; to maintain one's courage and resolve; to stand firm. This expression became popular in England during World War II, and, strangely enough, refers to the statue of Lord Nelson which stands in Trafalgar Square rather than to the naval hero himself. The term became almost a catch phrase among the Civil Defense people who served during the 'great blitz' of 1940–42. Laurie Atkinson summed up their attitude in a speech on July 1, 1948:

> Knowing that whatever may befall, as upon Nelson on his column in Trafalgar Square, one will, like him, "be there" tomorrow.

dog in a doublet—A bold, determined man. This phrase alludes to the practice in northern Europe during the Middle Ages of protecting boarhounds with a leather jacket buttoned about their bodies. These dogs presented such a resolute appearance in these doublets that they came to symbolize a determined man. They are pictured in many of Peter Paul Rubens' paintings. A variant of this expression is *as proud as a dog in a doublet.*

> Boswell: I think it is a new thought in a new attitude.
> Johnson: It is the old dog in the new doublet. (James Boswell, *Life of Johnson*, 1778)

A related expression, *a dog in one's doublet,* is used to signify a false friend.

229

don't give up the ship—Keep fighting or trying, hang in there. Although this expression was not new at the time of the Battle of Lake Erie (September 10, 1813) when Commodore Perry adopted it as his battle cry, it was he who popularized the words and made them memorable. The expression has extended beyond its naval origins and application and is now currently used to give encouragement to people in all walks of life.

hang in there—Don't give up; stick to it; persevere; refuse to give in. This exclamation, used as a phrase of encouragement, is usually addressed to one who is struggling to continue under difficult or adverse circumstances. Although the phrase's origin is unknown, it may come from the world of boxing, where a fighter, who is tiring near the end of the bout is often told to *hang in there*, literally meaning that he should go into clinches and hand on his opponent to save his energy. The term soon became a part of the general sports vocabulary and rather quickly after that found its way into everyday use as a general term of encouragement to a friend who is suffering from depression or seems about to surrender in the midst of a difficult endeavor.

The way those tough Bronx mothers wouldn't have quit. The way my mother would have hung in there. (*Playboy,* October 1973)

hang tough—To persevere; to remain firm in one's resolve; to refuse to give up. This American slang expression dates from about 1970 and probably owes its genesis to the expressions *hang loose* and *hang in there*.

Chretien decided to hang tough rather than give in to opposition demands for sweeping cuts in personal income taxes. (Ian Urquhart, *Maclean's*, November 27, 1978)

happy warrior—One who is undaunted or undiscouraged by adversity, a diehard; often used of a politician who is a perennial candidate for nomination or election to high office. The nickname *Happy Warrior* was first applied to Alfred E. Smith, Democratic candidate in the presidential election of 1928.

He [Alfred E. Smith] is the "Happy Warrior" of the political battlefield. (Franklin Delano Roosevelt, *The New York Times,* June 1924)

The term was later applied to Hubert Humphrey, Democratic candidate for President in 1968 and many times a candidate for the Democratic presidential nomination. The term was first used in the conventional sense of an excellent soldier, a fighter—a meaning which is reflected in its figurative application to political warriors.

have scissors to grind—To have ends to attain or ambitions to achieve; to have labor to do or a purpose to serve. Not to be confused with the more common *have an ax to grind*, which connotes selfishness, this term deals with one's aspirations and duties in life, and most commonly connotes "We

HANG IN THERE

all have problems in life, and I must get on with solving mine; I don't have time for yours."

hold [one's] ground—To firmly maintain or defend one's position; to resist the pressure to compromise one's ideals. Although this expression can refer to maintaining ground literally, as in a battle, it is more frequently heard in regard to defending a philosophical stance. The two levels of usage are related, however, because even in war there is a philosophical basis for defending one's *ground*, meaning 'territory, land,' etc. This expression and its variants *keep* or *stand one's ground* appeared in print by the 17th century.

It is not easy to see how it [Individuality] can stand its ground. (John Stuart Mill, *On Liberty*, 1859)

keep a stiff upper lip—To keep one's courage when confronted with adversity, to remain resolute in the face of great difficulties, not to lose heart. The allusion is to the quivering of the upper lip when a person is trying to maintain control and keep from crying in the face of danger or great emotional stress.

"What's the use o' boohooin'? . . .
Keep a stiff upper lip; no bones broke—don't I know?" (John Neal, *The Down Easters*, 1833)

The expression dates from the early part of the 19th century.

keep [one's] chin up—To maintain one's courage and resolve, to keep one's spirits up, to keep one's head held high. This American expression has been in use since at least 1938.

Keep your chin up honey. (I. Baird, *Waste Heritage*, 1939)

keep [one's] nose to the grindstone—To persist in an unpleasant task; to labor continuously, especially at hard, monotonous work; to labor unceasingly; to drudge. The allusion is perhaps to laborers hovering over grindstones or whetstones to sharpen tools made dull from constant use. The expression and variants, which date from at least 1532, originally meant to oppress someone else by exaction of labor.

keep [one's] pecker up—To *keep one's chin up*, to hold one's head high, to keep one's spirits or courage up. In this British slang expression *pecker* means 'spirits, courage.' It probably derives from the term *pecker* for a bird's beak or bill. Cockfighting is sometimes cited as the source of the phrase, since a gamecock's pecker or beak sinks when he is tired and near defeat. Thus, the expression literally means to keep up one's beak (British slang for *nose*). This of course cannot be done without keeping the head and chin up as well. The expression, which dates from at least 1853, is avoided in the United States, where *pecker* has an altogether different and vulgar slang meaning.

nail [one's] colors to the mast—To fight or hold out until the bitter end; to refuse to compromise, concede, or surrender; to persist or remain steadfast, especially in the face of seemingly overwhelming opposition. It has long been nautical custom for a ship to signify its nationality or allegiance by flying that country's colors (i.e., flag) from its tallest mast. In battle, a captain could signal his surrender or defeat by lowering the flag. If the colors were nailed to the mast, however, they could not be lowered, implying that surrender was not possible.

> If they catch you at disadvantage, the mines for your life is the word, ... and so we fight them with our colours nailed to the mast. (Sir Walter Scott, *The Pirate*, 1821)

praise the Lord, and pass the ammunition—Keep up the struggle, don't give up. This expression, although rarely used today, was the title of a popular song during World War II. It has been attributed to Chaplain Howell Forgy, who was on board the cruiser *New Orleans* in Pearl Harbor at the time of the Japanese attack in 1941. During the assault the chaplain helped fuel a counterattack by carrying ammunition to the ship's guns. He is purported to have said the now famous words "Praise the Lord, boys—and pass the ammunition."

the show must go on—One must persevere; one must be undaunted by adversity; the public must be served. Contrary to popular belief, this expression had its origin in the circus, not in the theater. In case of an emergency, such as a fire, the band was to continue playing, the troupers to continue performing, with the hope that the audience, thus distracted, would not panic. Today, the term is common in theater usage with the sense that in spite of injury or illness a performer should not disappoint the audience nor fail his fellow troupers.

> The hotel business is like the theatre. No matter what happens, the show must go on. (R. Holden, *Speak of the Devil*, 1941)

stick to [one's] guns—To stand firm; to persist in one's point of view, argument, or beliefs; not to yield or give in; to hold one's ground.

> An animated colloquy ensued. Manvers stuck to his guns. (Mrs. Alexander, *Brown, V.C.*, 1899)

Of military origin, this phrase was originally *to stand to one's gun(s)*, meaning literally to stand by one's gun, to keep fighting no matter what.

PERSISTENCE
SEE PERSEVERANCE

PERSONAGES
SEE STATUS

Perseverance

PHYSICAL APPEARANCE
See also VISAGE

bag of bones—A very thin person; someone who has become extremely emaciated. This bit of hyperbole, dating from the early 19th century, implies that a person or animal has lost all its fat and muscle so that nothing remains but skin and bones. It is usually used in a jocular context.

Get down stairs, little bag o' bones. (Charles Dickens, *Oliver Twist*, 1838)

bald as a coot—To be so bald as to resemble a coot. The coot has a straight and slightly conical bill whose base extends onto the forehead forming a broad white plate. Anyone whose pate resembles a coot's forehead is said to be *bald as a coot*. This phrase was used as early as 1430, as cited in the *OED*.

bandy-legged—Bowlegged; having legs curved laterally, especially with the convex side outward. This expression is probably derived from the old Irish game called *bandy*, a game similar to modern ice hockey or field hockey, where the player used a stick with a curve at the end to impel a hard wooden ball. Since the stick itself was called a *bandy*, the transference of the word to a person with legs of similar shape was an easy step. The expression has been in use since the early 17th century.

Nor makes a scruple to expose your bandy legs, or crooked nose. (Jonathan Swift, *Works*, 1755)

beauty is only skin deep—Strength of character is more important than pleasing outward appearance. This proverbial expression, in use since the early 1600s, has in recent years been subjected to some humorous variations. Saki (H. H. Munro) in *Reginald's Choir Treat* (1904) added a wry twist:

I always say beauty is only sin deep.

And Redd Foxx on his television show came to the defense of the saying.

Beauty is only skin deep, but ugly goes right to the bone.

black as isel—Dark as soot; black as cinders. This expression, found only in dialectal use today, dates from the Dark Ages. The *OED* dates the earliest written example found at approximately 1000. The word *isel*, derived from the Anglo-Saxon *ysel*, designates particles of soot or burned out embers.

Killmoulis . . . often torments the goodman sorely by throwing isels or ashes out when sheelin or shelled oats are spread out to dry. *(The Reader*, December 15, 1866)

A variant is *black as itchul*.

black as the devil's nutting-bag—This expression dates from at least the mid 1600s and is a direct allusion to an old superstition.

The devil as some people say,
A-nutting goes Holy Rood day.

(*Poor Robin's Almanack*, 1693)

Historically the young people of England have gone nutting together on Holy Rood Day, September 14th. Whether the warning was sincere and it was actually believed the young people might meet the devil and be swept into the darkness of his nutting-bag, or whether it was a method of frightening the young, thereby lessening the possibility of sexual temptation, is not certain. Whatever the case, the expression is seldom, if ever, heard today.

blush like a black dog—Not to blush; to have a brazen mien; to be shameless. The allusion in this expression, coined in the late 16th century, is probably to the devil, who supposedly assumes the form of a black dog on occasions.

> A black saint can no more blush than a black dog. (Thomas Adams, *Sermons*, 1629)

A variant of later inception is *blush like a blue dog*, in which *blue* is used in a sense suggestive of immorality.

> You'll make Mrs. Betty blush. Blush! ay, blush like a blue dog! (Jonathan Swift, *Polite Conversation*, 1738)

bottlearse—A person broad in the beam; thicker in one end than the other. This expression, dating from the latter half of the 18th century, refers to hand-cast letters in the printing trade. These letters, thicker at one end, were known as *bottlearse letters*. The transference to humans with the same physical appearance took place shortly thereafter.

> Bottlearsed, type thicker at one end than the other—a result of wear and tear. (John Farmer and William Henley, *Slang and its Analogues*, 1890)

A common variant is *bottleass*.

cauliflower ear—This expression refers to a deformed, puffy ear, usually the result of a boxing or wrestling injury. The inordinate growth of reparative tissue actually gives the ear the appearance of a cauliflower. The term, in use since the early 1900s, is an acceptable medical designation.

> Cauliflower ears attest to his earlier ring career about the time of Jeffries and Britton. (*Chicago Sun*, December 26, 1947)

deadpan—An expressionless or blank face, a poker face; to show no emotion; to display a completely expressionless face. This American slang term, which is frequently used to characterize a comic ploy, has been in use since about 1830. *Pan* in this phrase refers to the face, probably not, as some sources say, because it is broad, shallow, and often open, but more likely from the use of pans in lieu of mirrors. Since, other than water, pans were often the only mirror-like objects that early pioneers had, it is at least conceivable that the use of *pan* for *face* came from them, and that *dead pan* is a surviving illustration of this usage with the addition of the adjective *dead* in one of its usual senses.

It's enough to make even deadpan Gromyko laugh. (*New York Daily News*, September 12, 1951)

flat as a pancake—Flat; having a surface that is free from projections or indentations. Though usually used literally, this expression is sometimes employed in its figurative sense to describe something that is flatter than it should be or flatter than one would expect. In his play, *The Roaring Girl* (1611), Thomas Middleton used the expression to describe a woman with small breasts.

freckled as a turkey's egg—This expression describes one whose face or body is liberally sprinkled with freckles. The turkey, a fowl of relatively recent domestication, lays an egg with protective coloration, buff and spotted. The phrase, of American origin, dates from the early 1800s.

Fu Manchu mustache—A long, thin mustache that hangs down from the sides of the mouth. This expression alludes to a malevolent Chinese physician found in the novels (1932–1948) of Sax Rohmer, a British mystery writer. Doctor Fu Manchu, a sort of Oriental underworld leader, presented a sinister image to the world with his drooping mustache and long fingernails. The expression has been in use since the late 1930s.

Roman is a boat bum, at 32, he wears shoulder length hair, Fu Manchu mustache, and glasses thick enough to burn holes in the mainsail. (Peter Wood, *The New York Times Magazine*, September 5, 1976)

handsome is that handsome does—A saying implying that skillfulness of execution is what counts, not merely one's appearance or one's promises. This popular proverb contends that a man's worth is measured by the quality and quantity of work he produces, not by his being agreeable to the eye or dignified of mien. The first recorded use of this term found in the *OED* is:

She would answer, "they are as heaven made them—handsome enough, if they be good enough; for handsome is that handsome does."

A common variant is *handsome is as handsome does.* However, other forms of the term preceded its use by many years. In the *Wife of Bath's Tale*, Chaucer wrote:

That he is gentil that doth gentil dedis ...

and in 1580, the proverb appeared in *Sunday Examples* as:

Goodly is he that goodly dooth.

homely as a mud fence—Extremely plain or crude in appearance. This American expression, dating from the 1830s, alludes to the crude fences made of earth built by the pioneers in the prairie states. Since lumber and rocks of suitable size were in short supply, the building of such rather formless mud fences was a practical solution for enclosing farm animals or marking property lines.

> He didn't care whether she was as beautiful as Lana Turner or as homely as a mud fence. (*Chicago Tribune*, May 29, 1948)

A variant of this term is *homely as a hedge fence*; sometimes the form is *ugly as a mud fence*.

hunker down—To squat close to the ground with the weight resting on the calves of the legs. This phrase, in use since at least the 18th century, may be derived from the Dutch *huken*, meaning 'to squat or to sit upon one's hams'; the etymology is uncertain. Although people don't *hunker down* so much today, the term conjures up a picture of rustic conviviality, of farmers with time on their hands engaged in conversation before a general store.

> Tir'd wi' the steep an' something dizzy, I hunker'd down. (David Davidson, *Thoughts on the Seasons*, 1789)

A related term, *on one's hunkers*, means to be in a squatting position.

in the buff—Nude; naked; in one's birthday suit; ready for action. In this expression, which first appeared about the 15th century, the key word is *buff*, a type of leather made from the hide of a buffalo, elk, or, most commonly, ox. Treated with oil, the hide assumes a color similar to that of human skin, a tannish-white.

> Stripping ourselves to the buff, we hung up our steaming clothes. (Clarence King, *Mountaineering in the Sierra Nevada*, 1872)

Today the phrase, and a variant, *stripped to the buff*, have the additional meaning of one 'thoroughly prepared for action,' with allusion to the boxing ring or gymnasium. Theodore Roosevelt, running on the Progressive Party ticket, proclaimed in a 1912 interview:

> My hat's in the ring. The fight is on and I'm stripped to the buff.

A related term, *in one's birthday suit*, dates to the late 18th century and is a jocular allusion to the nudity of birth.

in the pudding club—Pregnant; great with child. The original English pudding was a mixture of ground meat, oatmeal, seasoning, and, if desired, a few vegetables, packed into the stomach or entrails of an animal, usually a sheep or pig, and boiled separately or roasted within the animal. The parallel here is, of course, to the similarity in appearance between an animal stuffed with a pudding and a pregnant woman. Related terms are *join the pudding club*, 'to become pregnant'; *be put in the pudding club*, 'to make pregnant'; *preggers*, and *preggy*, both slang terms for 'pregnant.' All these terms are of British origin.

> There was your bag, simply preggy with bank notes, lying there on the writing table. (Ngaio Marsh, *Death in a White Tie*, 1938)

In Australia the slang term for 'pregnant' is *prego*.

naked ape—A man; the human animal. Although man has been called a *naked ape* for many decades, especially since Charles Darwin's *The Origin of the Species* (1859) was published, the use of the term became even more popular when Desmond Morris's *The Naked Ape* appeared in 1967.

There are one hundred and ninety-three living species of monkeys and apes. One hundred and ninety-two of them are covered with hair. The exception is a naked ape self-named *Homo sapiens*.

Newgate knocker—A lock of hair twisted into a hard curl and worn back from the temple toward the ear. This expression originated with a practice of the criminals in Newgate prison. They twisted their hair *knocker* style, so named because in appearance it resembled a door knocker. The term came into use in the late 1700s. The *OED* lists as the first written use:

As for the hair they say it ought to be long in front and done in figure six curls or twisted back to the ear Newgate knocker style. (Henry Mayhew, *London Labour and the London Poor*, 1851)

A number of related terms developed from this practice. *Black as the knockers of Newgate* alludes to the lot of the Newgate inmates, *hard as the knockers of Newgate* refers to the degree of intensity of the braiding, and *Newgate fringe* designates the fringe or beard under the chin located where the hangman's rope will adjoin. A *Newgate frill* is another name for *Newgate fringe*.

pilgarlic—A bald-headed man; an unfortunate, pitiable wretch. Originally *peeled garlic*, the term was applied to one whose hair loss was due to disease (venereal by implication) and whose naked scalp supposedly resembled the flaky, shiny bulb of that plant. Eventually *pilgarlic* came to be applied to persons deserving of contempt or censure, probably because of the reputed source of the affliction. It was often used in a quasi-affectionate way, however; frequently for oneself, as in the following passage from Rabelais's *Pantagruel* (1532):

Never a bit could poor pilgarlic sleep one wink, for the everlasting jingle of bells.

a shadow of [one's] former self—Said of one who has become extremely feeble or emaciated. This expression uses *shadow* in the sense of something that resembles the original but lacks substance, thus implying that a person has been reduced to a mere shadow, either through the ravages of disease, aging, stress, etc., or by choice. The expression is sometimes shortened to *shadow of oneself*.

He appeared to wither into the shadow of himself. (Sir Walter Scott, *Guy Mannering; or The Astrologer*, 1815)

A shadow of one's former self is sometimes used complimentarily in good-natured reference to a formerly corpulent person who has lost weight as a result of dieting.

starkers—Nude; in the altogether; also, *starko*. This British colloquialism, a variation of *stark naked* (itself a corruption of *start naked*), has been in use since about 1910.

> The salesgirl had taken away all her clothes and hidden them. It was only the threat of running starkers into the street that brought them back. (Brigid Keenan, in *The Sunday Times* [London], September 1964)

ugly duckling—See REVERSAL.

widow's peak—See VISAGE.

PHYSICAL STATURE
SEE PHYSICAL APPEARANCE

PLEASURE
SEE ENJOYMENT

PLENTY
SEE ABUNDANCE

PLOY
See also TRICKERY

ace up [one's] sleeve—A surprise; something of special effectiveness that is held in reserve or hidden from others; a trump card; sometimes *card up one's sleeve*. Very similar to an *ace in the hole*, this expression comes from the cardsharper's stratagem of hiding needed cards (e.g., aces) in his sleeve until the most advantageous moment to play them. By extension, it has come to mean any secret asset or ploy.

bag of tricks—All of one's resources; the means to an end. This phrase derives from La Fontaine's fable of the fox and the cat.

> But fox, in arts of siege well versed,
> Ransacked his bag of tricks accursed.
> (Elizur Wright, trans., *La Fontaine's Fables*, 1841)

Bag of tricks can refer to one's survival techniques in general, or to a specific design one might have up one's sleeve.

> Men were all alike. A woman didn't have to carry a very big bag of tricks to achieve her purpose. (L. C. Douglas, *White Banners*, 1936)

bottom of the bag—The last resort or expedient in one's bag of tricks; a trump card held in reserve; an ace up one's sleeve. Thomas Burton used the phrase in his *Diary* in 1659:

> If this be done, which is in the bottom of the bag, and must be done, we shall...be able to buoy up our reputation.

have [something] up [one's] sleeve—To have a secret scheme or trick in mind, to have a surprise planned. The allusion is probably to the way magicians use their sleeves as convenient hiding places for the articles employed in executing their feats of magic.

ladies of Barking Creek—This expression refers to women who refuse to engage in sexual intercourse, feigning their menstrual cycle as an excuse. The term is derived from the opening line of a well-known limerick from about 1910.

patch the lion's skin with the fox's tail—To employ craft when force will not work. This saying has been ascribed to Lysander, the famous Spartan commander, who, when told that he should not wage war by deceit, was said to reply, "Where the lion's skin will not reach, it must be patched out with the fox's." The expression has been employed in English since the Middle Ages, but is seldom heard today.

> The Duke of Savoy...though he be valiant enough, yet he knows how to patch the lion's skin with a fox's tail. (James Howell, *Letters*, November 30, 1621)

red herring—A diversionary tactic or misleading clue, a subject intended to divert attention from the real issue; a false trail; from the phrase *draw a red herring across the trail*. In the 17th century, dog trainers followed this practice to sharpen the scent discrimination of hunting hounds. Smoked herring drawn across the trail of a fox is said to destroy or markedly affect the original scent. Figurative use of the term outside the complete phrase dates at least from the late 19th century.

> The talk of revolutionary dangers is a mere red herring. (*Liverpool Daily Post*, July 11, 1884)

roorback—A falsehood published and circulated for political effect. This expression originated in 1844 during the successful campaign of James K. Polk to become the 11th President of the United States. In order to frustrate Polk's chances of election, a group of opponents circulated a falsehood damaging to his reputation. The falsehood involved a fictitious traveler named Roorback who supposedly had written a book of travels in 1836 entitled *Tour through the Western and Southern States*. In this nonexistent book, he had supposedly revealed an incident disparaging to Polk's character. The entire deception was ultimately revealed, but the term has remained in use since that time as a synonym for political duplicity.

> He saw the headlines in the other papers calling it a roorback and him a fool. (Samuel Blythe, *The Fakers*, 1913)

sit up with a sick friend—An expression intended as an excuse to step out on one's spouse or fiance(e) for a night with a member of the opposite sex; an excuse used to get away from one's mate for a night. This American and

British colloquial phrase has become so trite that today it is almost always heard as a jocular expression to taunt one who did not make it home on a certain night, whatever the reason. It has been in use since at least the mid 1800s.

springes to catch woodcocks—Snares for the unsuspecting; traps for the unwary. This expression appears in Shakespeare's *Hamlet* (I,iii), when Polonius warns Ophelia that Hamlet's protestations of affection are but the wily words of a youthful lover, meant to ensnare his naive victim: "springes to catch woodcocks," he calls them. The phrase usually refers to a deceitful ploy.

> Alas, poor woodcock, dost thou go a birding? Thou hast even set a springe to catch thy own neck. (John Dryden, *Wild Gallant*, 1663)

stalking horse—Anything used to conceal a design or scheme, a pretext; a person who serves as a means of allaying suspicion or obscuring an ongoing activity; the agency through which an underhanded objective is attained. The expression appeared in Shakespeare's *As You Like It:*

> He uses his folly like a stalking horse, and under the presentation of that he shoots his wit. (V,iv)

In bygone days, hunters hid themselves behind a horse as they stalked to within shooting range of the game. The expression early carried its still current figurative sense of the intended concealment of plans, projects, or intentions.

> Do you think her fit for nothing but to be a Stalking Horse to stand before you, while you aim at my wife? (William Congreve, *Double Dealer*, 1694)

The expression has evolved the extended political meaning of a person whose candidacy is intended to conceal the true candidacy of another, or whose place on the ballot is meant to split the opposition.

stone soup—A wily stratagem; a deceptive procedure; a trumped-up operation. This expression is derived from a tale which was a favorite in Europe during the 16th and 17th centuries. A beggar, sometimes identified in the story as St. Bernard, stopped at a lord's estate and asked for food, but the servants said they had none. The man asked if he might boil some water to make soup with a stone. Piqued with curiosity, the servants provided him with water and a pan. After the water boiled, the beggar put in the stone and asked for salt and pepper; he then inquired if they had any old scraps of meat or vegetables lying about; they provided some, and when the ingredients were cooked, the servants tasted the *stone soup* and wondered at its savoriness. This guileful concoction is also known as *St. Bernard's soup*. The term is seldom, if ever, heard today, but for many years it served as a metaphor for any act of subterfuge. James Kelly alludes to the idea in *Scottish Proverbs* (1721):

> Boil stones in butter and you may sup the broth.

throw a curve or a curve ball—To employ clever and often deceptive artifice in verbal dealings with another; to trick or surprise so as to entrap; to accomplish one's ends by indirection. The expression derives from baseball; a curve ball is a pitched ball which is thrown with extra rotation, causing it to curve or dip more than a batter might expect. Metaphorically, the expression refers to something that acts in an unusual or unexpected manner, especially a verbal ploy.

throw a tub to the whale—To create a diversion, or to mislead or bamboozle, in order to avoid an awkward, embarrassing, or dangerous situation.

> It has been common to throw out something to divert and amuse the people, such as a plot, a conspiracy, or an enquiry about nothing, . . . which method of proceeding, by a very apt metaphor, is call'd throwing out the tub. (Charles Molloy, *Select Letters taken from Fog's Weekly Journal*, 1728)

Jonathan Swift explains the origin of this expression in the preface to *A Tale of a Tub*:

> Seamen have a custom when they meet a whale, to fling him out an empty tub, . . . to divert him from laying violent hands upon the ship.

Tale of a tub meaning 'an apocryphal story' dates from the 1500s. However, Swift's use of *throw a tub to the whale* in 1704 is the earliest cited use of the expression in the *OED*.

Trojan horse—A snare or trap, a treacherous device or ploy, particularly one appearing as an attractive lure. The allusion is to the tale recounted in Homer's *Odyssey*. The Greeks, pretending to abandon their siege of Troy, left at its gates a gigantic wooden horse, within which were concealed several Greek soldiers. Interpreting the horse as a gift or peace-offering, the Trojans brought it into the city, whereupon those within stole out during the night to admit the entire Greek force and thus conquer the city. See also **beware of Greeks bearing gifts**, PRETENSE.

trump card—An ace in the hole; a decisive, winning argument, ploy, piece of evidence, etc.; a clincher.

> Justice . . . is the trump card of the western world. (*The Times Literary Supplement* as quoted in *Webster's Third*)

A *trump card* is literally any card of a suit which outranks all cards of the other three suits in a card game. *Trump* in this term is a corruption of the now obsolete *triumph* 'a trump card.'

POLITENESS
SEE DEFERENCE

POMPOSITY
SEE HAUGHTINESS; OSTENTATIOUSNESS

POSTPONEMENT
SEE TEMPORIZING

POTENTIAL
SEE ABILITY

POVERTY
See also INDEBTEDNESS

bag lady—This American slang term, in popular use since the 1970s, is used to describe those women who roam city streets, carrying shopping bags in which they keep all their worldly possessions, and picking through trash containers to find items that might be useful to them in their vagabond style of life. Homeless, these women sleep in doorways, subway stations, or any other convenient place that affords them protection from the elements. They are seldom, if ever, beggars, and have become a symbol of independence. The expression is a shortened version of *shopping bag lady.*

> I did a bag lady number on one of the platforms here in the bus station last year, and I almost got arrested. They thought I was the real thing. (*The New Yorker*, October 17, 1977)

beggar's bush—Beggary, financial ruin, bankruptcy; often in the phrases *go by beggar's bush* or *go home by beggar's bush.* The allusion is to a certain tree on the left side of the London road from Huntingdon to Caxton, where beggars once frequently gathered. This British expression, rarely heard today, dates from the late 16th century.

> We are almost at Beggars-bush, and we cannot tell how to help our selves. (Andrew Yarranton, *England's Improvement by Sea and Land,* 1677)

bindle stiff—A vagabond who carries his few personal belongings with him. This hobo slang expression, originating in the early 1900s, denotes a hobo or tramp who carries his bedroll with him as he moves from place to place. *Bindle* is simply a variant of *bundle,* and *stiff* in this phrase is hobo jargon for 'man'. In the 1920s H L. Mencken popularized the writings of an ex-boxer and vagabond named Jim Tully. Tully, a bona fide resident of the hobo jungles, the makeshift refuges of these drifters, explains:

> I was a *bindle stiff.* That's the class that will do some work once in a while. The *grifters* are the desperate characters; the *hobos* are the philosophers.

clay eater—One who is poverty-stricken or abjectly poor; a poor white from the southern United States. This expression, dating from the early 19th century, originally designated certain poor folk who actually ate a sort of clay found in some sections of the American south. However, the term soon came to connote reproach or scorn and became a synonym for poor white trash.

> He was a little, dried-up, withered atomy,—a jaundiced "sand-lapper" or "clay-eater" from the Wassamasaw country. (W. G. Simms, *The Kinsmen*, 1841)

Related terms, *sand-hiller* and *sand-lapper*, derive from the condition of the land from which these people tried to scratch out a living.

down-at-the-heel—Poor, destitute; of slovenly or shabby appearance; also, *out-at-the-heel*. The latter usually refers to holes in one's stockings; the former, to the run-down condition of one's shoes.

> Thus the unhappy notary ran gradually down at the heel. (Henry Wadsworth Longfellow, *Outre-Mer*, 1835)
>
> Some rich snudges . . . go with their hose out at heels. (Thomas Wilson, *The Art of Rhetoric*, 1553)

drown the miller—See **put out the miller's eye**, FOOD AND DRINK.

guttersnipe—A person, male or female, who gathers a living from the gutter; a beggar who picks up junk and trash from the streets; a bag lady; a street Arab. The snipe, a bird native to swamps and marshes, picks a living from the mud along the edge of pools and streams. This expression probably arises from the similarity of impoverished people trying to pick a living from the gutters of city streets. Today the term is used disparagingly.

> Unfurl yourselves under my banner, noble savages, illustrious guttersnipes. (Mark Twain, *Sketches New and Old: Niagara*, 1869)

hard up—In financial straits, short of cash, out-of-pocket. Originally nautical, this expression was usually used in the imperative, directing that the helm or tiller be pushed as far windward as it would go in order to turn the ship's bow away from the wind. Since this maneuver was usually necessitated by a storm or other potentially disastrous situation, the phrase took on the general sense of difficulty or straits. The nonnautical use of this expression dates from the early 19th century.

> You don't feel nearly so hard up with elevenpence in your pocket as you do with a shilling. (Jerome K. Jerome, *The Idle Thoughts of an Idle Fellow*, 1886)

high road to Needham—On the way to financial ruin; in need; poverty-stricken; going broke. This expression, dating from the mid 16th century, is simply a pun on *need*. Although some sources attribute the reference in the phrase to the village of Needham in Suffolk, it is most likely that no such reference is intended as the village and its people have never demonstrated any particularly outstanding symptoms of need.

> They are already a long way on the road to Needham. (Charles H. Spurgeon, *John Ploughman's Talk*, 1869)

Hooverville—A jerry-built camp, usually located on the outskirts of a town, built by the jobless to house themselves and sometimes their families. Although *Hoovervilles* were found throughout the United States during the depression of the 1930s, they were especially plentiful in California, where the influx of the Okies created a massive poverty problem. These settlements were often nothing more than a ramshackle combination of packing crates, tin sheets, and the like knocked together to provide makeshift dwellings. They were named for Herbert Hoover, who, as President at the beginning of the depression, was blamed by some for the severe economic decline.

> The early 1930s . . . Hunger marches and Hooverville stories took up a lot of space in our press. (King Vidor, *A Tree Is a Tree*, 1953)

in Carey Street—Penniless, flat broke, destitute. This British colloquial expression takes its name from Carey Street in London, the former location of the Bankruptcy Court. It has been in use since 1922.

in low water—Financially hard up, strapped, broke, impoverished. Although the exact origin of this expression is unknown, it may be related to the precarious condition of a ship finding itself in low water or about to go on the rocks. This expression dates from the latter half of the 18th century.

> Law-breakers . . . who, having been "put away," and done their time, found themselves in low water upon their return to the outer world. (*Chambers's Journal of Popular Literature*, February 1885)

See also **on the rocks**, INDEBTEDNESS.

on [one's] beam-ends—In financial difficulties, in imminent danger of bankruptcy. The reference is to a vessel on her beam-ends, that is, on her side such that the beams—the transverse timbers supporting the deck—are practically touching the water. Obviously, any vessel in such a state is in immediate danger of overturning. The phrase has been used figuratively since the early 19th century.

on [one's] uppers—Impoverished, down-and-out; shabby-looking, down-at-the-heel. This phrase, of U.S. origin, appeared in *The Century Dictionary* (1891). The *uppers* are the upper leathers of shoes or boots; a person *on his uppers* has worn through both sole and welt. Footgear as indicative of financial status is also found in the term *well-heeled* (though this is probably of unrelated origin), and in the above-noted *down-at-the-heel*.

> The rumor whirled about the Street that Greener was in difficulties. Financial ghouls . . . said . . . "Greene is on his uppers." (*Munsey's Magazine*, 1901)

out at elbows—Shabbily dressed; down-and-out, poverty-stricken; in financial difficulties. A coat worn through at the elbows has long been a symbol of poverty. The expression appeared in print by the time of Shakespeare.

> He was himself just now so terribly out at elbows, that he could not command a hundred pounds. (Mrs. Mary M. Sherwood, *The Lady of the Manor*, 1847)

poor as a churchmouse—Extremely poor; impoverished, insolvent; poor but proud. This expression, popular since the 17th century, is probably derived from a tale which recounts the plight of a mouse that attempted to find food in a church. Since most churches, including that of the story, do not have kitchens, the proud mouse found it difficult to survive since its pickings were slim at best.

> The owner, 'tis said, was once poor as a churchmouse. (*Political Ballads*, 1731)

poor as Job—Poverty-stricken, indigent, destitute. The allusion is to the extreme poverty which befell the central character in the Book of Job. In spite of a series of devastating calamities, Job remained steadfast in his faith and trust in God, and has long been the personification of both poverty and patience.

> I am as poor as Job, my lord, but not so patient. (Shakespeare, *Henry IV, Part II*, I,ii)

A related expression, *poor as Job's turkey*, is credited to Thomas C. Haliburton (1796–1865), a Canadian judge and humorist. Haliburton, using the pseudonym Sam Slick, described Job's turkey as so poor that it had only one feather, and so weak that it had to lean against a fence in order to gobble. Job, of course, never had a turkey—poor or otherwise—as the bird is a native of North America. A variation is *poor as Job's cat*.

ragamuffin—A ragged, dirty boy or man; an unkempt guttersnipe; a dishonorable tatterdemalion. The term *ragamuffin* is derived from the name of a demon, *Ragamoffyn*, who appears in Langland's *Piers Plowman*, (1360–1399). The term came to mean any dirty, disreputable man, but by the 1800s it had become fairly well limited to a descriptive term for street urchins. Charles Dickens made use of it in the latter sense in *Barnaby Rudge* (1840):

> A set of ragamuffins comes a-shouting after us, 'Gordon for ever.'

tobacco road—A poverty stricken area; an impoverished section of a community marked by shabbiness, general slovenliness, and little, if any, moral restraint. This phrase gained popularity in the United States in the early 1930s with the appearance of Erskine Caldwell's novel, *Tobacco Road* (1932), depicting a squalid region of rural Georgia; the long-running Broadway stage production (3,182 performances) based on it followed in 1933.

PRECISION

bang on—Exactly on; directly on; precisely as planned; apt or appropriate. This British slang phrase often appears as *bang on target*, popularized by bomber lingo during World War I.

> It [a play] has enough quality and sense of the theatre to suggest that before long he will land one bang on the target. (*Oxford Magazine*, February 27, 1958)

By extension, the phrase also describes anything which is just right, apt, or appropriate.

> As a realistic tale of low life in London, it is bang on. (*Spectator*, February 14, 1958)

Spot on is British slang phrase which is used interchangeably with *bang on*.

dot [one's] *i* **s and cross [one's]** *t* **s**—To be precise or meticulous down to the last or smallest detail; to particularize in detail so as to leave no room for doubt or uncertainty; to cite chapter and verse. This expression is said to have sprung from the possibility of confusing *is* with *ts* if they are carelessly written without the respective dot and cross. The phrase has been in use since the 1800s.

hit the nail on the head—To do or say the most fitting thing; to cut through extraneous details and come right to the point; to make a clear, pithy statement. This expression has been in print since the 16th century. Hitting a nail properly—that is, squarely on the head—is likened to communicating effectively, or to the point. On the other hand, a bad hit which bends the nail is like rambling which fails to get to the crux of a matter.

> At least they ignorantly hit the nail on the head, saying that the Devil was in him. (*Fryke's Voyage*, 1700)

Occam's razor—The maxim that unnecessary facts or assumptions used to explain a subject must be eliminated. William of Occam, the 14th-century English scholastic philosopher known as "the Invincible Doctor," believed that general ideas have no objective reality outside the mind (nominalism). *Razor* in this expression is a metaphorical term for the precise, dissecting, incisive methods which characterize Occam's intellectual approach.

on the button—Exactly, precisely; punctually, promptly; on the dot; often *right on the button*. This expression derives from the boxing slang use of *button* to mean the point of the chin. Literally then, *on the button* indicates a perfectly aimed punch to the chin or jaw area intended to knock a fighter out or at least seriously impair his ability to retaliate.

on the money—At precisely the right time or place, right on target; often *right on the money*. This American slang expression appears to refer to money placed as a bet against a certain, previously stated outcome.

on the nose—Precisely; right on target; on time. *On the nose* is old radio parlance describing the producer's gesture of putting his finger on his nose to signify that the program was running according to schedule. The phrase is now used especially in regard to time but can describe anything which is accurate, precise, or apt. *On the button* is akin to *on the nose* in meaning and usage, and both are American equivalents of the British phrases *bang on* and *spot on*.

to a T—Exactly; precisely; perfectly.
> All these old-fashioned goings on would suit you to a T. (Harriet Beecher Stowe, *Dred*, 1856)

The *OED* dismisses as untenable the popular belief that this expression is an allusion to the T square, a draftsman's T-shaped ruler for the accurate drawing of right angles, parallel lines, etc. It conjectures instead that it was the initial of a word, perhaps *tittle* 'dot, jot,' since this was in use nearly a century before *to a T* in exactly the same constructions. Use of the expression dates from at least the late 17th century.

PREDICAMENT
SEE DANGER; DIFFICULTY; IMPEDIMENT; INDEBTEDNESS;
VULNERABILITY

PREJUDICE
See also INJUSTICE

a jaundiced eye—A prejudiced perspective or point of view; a skeptical, critical attitude; distorted vision that perceives everything as faulty, inferior, or undesirable. The disease of jaundice gives a yellowish cast to the whites of the eyes. This phrase is based on the assumption that everything appears "yellow"—i.e., negative, distorted—to such eyes.
> All seems infected that the infected spy,
> As all looks yellow to the jaundiced eye.
> (Alexander Pope, *An Essay on Criticism*, 1709)

look through blue glasses—To see things in a preconceived, usually distorted light; to be biased, to be unable to see things for what they are. This expression plays on the negative connotations often carried by the color blue. The image of spectacles gives tangible form to the nonmaterial prejudice which colors one's perceptions.

nothing like leather—An expression mocking one who has a chauvinistic attitude toward his own craft or field. Attributed to an Aesop fable, *nothing* *like leather* was popularized by the following anonymous verse which explains its origin.

Prejudice

> A town feared a siege, and held consultation
> Which was the best method of fortification;
> A grave, skilful mason said in his opinion
> Nothing but stone could secure the dominion.
> A carpenter said, "Though that was well spoke,
> It was better by far to defend it with oak."
> A currier, wiser than both these together,
> Said, "Try what you please, there's nothing like leather."

PREPARATION
SEE STARTING

PRETENSE

Pretense

Abraham man—During the days of the Tudor and Stuart kings of England, those inmates of Bedlam who were not considered dangerously insane were kept in a special ward, called the *Abraham ward*. Dressed in costumes which identified them as *Toms o' Bedlam* 'authorized beggars from the asylum,' these inmates made their way about the streets of London requesting alms from passers-by in order to supplement their meager rations.

> ... my cue is villainous melancholy, with a sigh like Tom o' Bedlam.
> (Shakespeare, *King Lear*, I,ii)

Soon, a group of impostor-lunatics began to appear upon the streets of London, fattening their own purses by posing as *Toms o' Bedlam*. These impostors became known as *Abraham men*, apparently derived from the name of the ward, and from this term arose the expressions, *Abraham-sham* and *sham Abraham*, both meaning to feign illness to avoid work.

ass in a lion's skin—A pretender; a fool posing as a sage. The allusion is to the fable of an ass that donned a lion's skin in an attempt to masquerade as the noble beast, but betrayed itself by its braying.

beware of Greeks bearing gifts—Distrust the kindnesses of known enemies; suspect an ulterior motive when adversaries act as benefactors. This warning to look for guile lest one be made the victim of treachery is a variation on the words of Laocoön in Book II of Virgil's *Aeneid:*

> Whatever it is, I fear Greeks even when they bring gifts.

The lines were spoken in reference to the so-called Trojan horse, left outside the gates of Troy supposedly as a gift or peace-offering from the Greeks, with whom Troy was at war. Laocoön's advice went unheeded, however, and the horse was brought inside the city gates; the Greeks hidden therein thus successfully sacked Troy and razed it to the ground.

borrowed plumes—An ostentatious display; pretense to what one is not; making an ass of oneself. The allusion here is to Aesop's fable of the jay and the peacock. The jay arrayed itself in peacock feathers and went swaggering about, only to become the object of derision of the other birds.

> In the process of his examination, he is stripped of his borrowed plumes. (*Medical and Physical Journal*, 1802)

four-flusher—A bluffer; a pretender; a deadbeat, particularly one who pretends to have money but sponges or borrows from others. This expression derives from the card game of poker in which a flush is a hand (set of five cards) with all cards of the same suit. A *four-flush* is a hand with four cards of one suit and one card of another suit—worthless in poker. A good bluffer, particularly one who is pokerfaced, upon finding himself with a four-flush, might bet in such a way as to make the other players think he is holding a five-card flush—almost a certain winner. Since this kind of bluffing requires heavy betting and involves a substantial risk, many a four-flusher has overextended himself and been unable to cover his losses. Thus, the expression was extended from its poker reference to its current, more general application.

> So, perhaps, was a four-flushing holdup man named Gunplay Maxwell. (Wallace Stegner, *Mormon Country*, 1942)

fox's sleep—Pretended indifference to what is going on; noticing or observing a person, situation, or event without seeming to do so. This expression refers to the belief that foxes sleep with one eye open. Although this is not true in the literal sense, foxes and many other animals seem to remain on a "standby alert" when they sleep, ready for action and totally awake on a moment's notice. A related expression is *sleep with one eye open*.

humbug—A hoax; a fraud; a perpetrator of a hoax. This slang word of obscure origin came into use about the middle of the 18th century. The word made its first appearance, according to the *OED*, in the January 1751 edition of *Student*. The use of the term by Scrooge in Charles Dickens' *A Christmas Carol* brought the word into such popular usage that it became acceptable in standard English.

> I had no idea in those days of the enormous and unquestionably helpful part that humbug plays in the social life of great peoples dwelling in a state of democratic freedom. (Winston Churchill, *My Early Life*, 1930)

iron hand in a velvet glove—Tyranny, harshness, or inflexibility hidden under a soft, gentle exterior. At least one source has attributed this expression, in use since about 1850, to Napoleon. One of the several variations of the expression appeared in *The Victorian Hansard* (January 1876):

They [the Government] have dealt with the Opposition with a velvet glove; but the iron hand is beneath, and they shall feel it.

look as if butter wouldn't melt in [one's] mouth—Used contemptuously to describe a person of deceptively modest appearance, a goody-goody. The implication is always that the person's true nature is something quite different from what it seems. Hugh Latimer uses the expression, which dates from the early 1500s, in his *Seven Sermons Made Upon The Lord's Prayer* (1552):

These fellows . . . can speak so finely, that a man would think butter should scant melt in their mouths.

method in [one's] madness—A reason, plan, or orderliness that is obscured by a person's apparent or feigned insanity or stupidity. This expression developed from a line in Shakespeare's *Hamlet*:

Though this be madness, yet there is method in 't. (II,ii)

It has enjoyed widespread popular usage since the 17th century.

He may be mad, but there's method in his madness. There nearly always is method in madness. It's what drives men mad being methodical. (G. K. Chesterton, *The Man Who Knew Too Much*, 1922)

mutton dressed as lamb—An elderly woman dressed in youthful fashion. This expression, still in popular use, is a variant of an earlier phrase, *an old ewe dressed lamb-fashion*

Here antique maids of sixty three
Drest out lamb-fashion, you might see.
(*Gentleman's Magazine*, 1777)

The reference in both phrases is to the practice of those few butchers who try to pass mutton as lamb.

pass the bottle of smoke—To countenance a white lie; to sanction a falsehood. The allusion in this expression is to smoke as a means of covering or camouflaging. *Smoke* as a synonym for 'dishonesty' has been in use since at least the 1600s, when to *sell smoke* was to defraud or to cheat.

I abandoned their conversation, because I found they were but sellers of smoke. (*Sorel's Comical History of Francion*, 1655)

This expression seemingly gave birth in the 1800s to *pass the bottle of smoke*, 'obscure the facts through pretense'.

. . . to keep up the pretense as a labour and study and patience . . . and all the rest of it—in short, to pass the bottle of smoke according to rule. (Charles Dickens, *Little Dorrit*, 1857)

play possum—To deceive or dissemble; to sham illness or death. This expression alludes to the opossum's defense mechanism of feigning death to ward off predators. In contemporary usage, the common phrase often suggests the feigning of ignorance.

By last week, in the Senate investigation of Washington five-percenters, it became plain that John had been playing possum the whole time. (*Time*, September 1949)

Potemkin village—A false front; a sham; something created so as to deceive or to mislead. This term can be traced directly to Prince Gregory Potemkin, a Russian army officer, political personage, and favorite of Catherine the Great. The Prince is said to have had false cottage fronts and pleasant rural scenes built along the roadway before taking the Empress on a tour of the countryside, thus shielding from her view the poverty that gripped the nation.

quacksalver—A quack; one who pretends to have medical skills; a medical charlatan; a phony. *Quacksalver* is the original name given to itinerant peddlers who set up at country fairs and "quacked" the praises of their salves and medicines. The term came into being in the 16th century and was especially popular during the 17th century, but gave way to the more popular shortened version *quack*.

He's such a quack I'll bet he's web-footed. (A. M. Stern, *The Case of the Absent-Minded Professor*, 1943)

Today *quack* is not restricted to the practice of medicine but has been extended to include anyone who professes skill in any field of which he knows little.

Quaker guns—Empty threats; harmless barbs; all bark and no bite. This expression comes from the former use of counterfeit guns, simulated to bluff the enemy into thinking that a ship or fort was well-fortified. Such were described as *Quaker* owing to that sect's doctrine of nonviolence. This U.S. expression is rarely heard today.

"He's like a Quaker gun," said Haxall—"piles of appearance, but no damage done." (Ella L. Dorsey, *Midshipman Bob*, 1888)

ringer—A person or thing entered in a contest under false pretenses; a person or thing bearing an uncanny resemblance to another. The expression's first sense usually implies the misrepresentation of the contender's identity or potential. Although this American term finds its principal use in the horseracing world, it may be applied to human competitors as well.

As a ringer in the Sadie Hawkins race, she was last heard of pursuing a panicstricken Dogpatcher. (*Newsweek*, November 1947)

The phrase's meaning of two nearly identical persons or things, most often expressed as *dead ringer*, is quite common in the United States.

I saw once...an outlaw... who was a dead ringer for him. (O. Henry, *Options*, 1909)

sail under false colors—To pretend or appear to be what one is not; to put up a false front or façade; to act or speak hypocritically. In the days when buccaneers plundered on the open seas, it was common practice for a pirate ship to hoist the colors (flag) of a potential victim's ally in order to sneak up on the ship without arousing suspicion. At the last moment, the pirates would lower the false colors, "show their true colors," the Jolly Roger, and attack. This expression and its variations are now used figuratively.

Our female candidate ... will no longer hang out false colors. (Sir Richard Steele, *The Spectator*, 1711)

string [someone] along—To manipulate another, psychologically, financially, or romantically; to deceive or mislead; to cheat or beguile. The reference in this phrase is to keeping another dangling on the end of a string while one makes up his mind. Dating to about 1810, the expression was originally used in business dealings to indicate that one was manipulating another's finances. Currently, the phrase is often heard in a romantic context.

I'm afraid that he's just stringing me along, trying to encourage me. (Percy Marks, *The Plastic Age*, 1924)

Suffolk milk—Skim milk; pretension; something which puts on the dog. Robert Bloomfield records in *Suffolk Garland* (1818):

Suffolk milk. Three times skimm'd sky-blue.

In Suffolk a cheese was developed from skim milk which when compared to the richer cheeses of England left much to be desired. The term has come to connote imposture. A related term is *skim milk masquerading as cream*.

What a lamentable example you are of skim milk masquerading as cream. (R. A. J. Walling, *The Spider and the Fly*, 1940)

wolf in sheep's clothing—One who hides his true evil intentions or character behind a façade of friendship; a hypocrite or deceiver. This expression derives from an Aesop fable in which a wolf, wrapped in the fleece of a sheep, enters the fold and proceeds to devour the unsuspecting lambs. *A wolf in a lamb's skin*, in use as early as 1460, seems to be an older variation of the current phrase, which did not appear until 1591. A well-known Biblical passage has served to increase the phrase's familiarity:

Beware of false prophets, who come to you in sheep's clothing, but inwardly are ravening wolves. (Matthew 7:15)

PRETENTIOUSNESS
SEE OSTENTATIOUSNESS

PRIDE
SEE HAUGHTINESS

PRIGGISHNESS
SEE PRUDISHNESS

PRIZE
SEE REWARD

PROCRASTINATION
SEE TEMPORIZING

Profanity

PROFANITY
See also LANGUAGE

air [one's] lungs—To curse or swear. American cowboy slang.

billingsgate—Vulgar or obscene language. The reference is to the coarse language commonly heard at Billingsgate, a London fishmarket. The term was in use as early as the 17th century.

blankety-blank—A euphemism for profane or four-letter words. This expression, in use since at least 1854, derived from the practice of leaving dashes or blank spaces to represent unprintable, vulgar words, as h—— for *hell* or d—— for *damned*. M. Diver used the phrase in *The Great Amulet* (1908):

> Colonel Stanham Buckley . . . inquired picturesquely of a passing official when the blank this blankety blank train was supposed to start.

dickens—A euphemistic word for the devil or Satan, common in such exclamations as *why the dickens* and *what the dickens*. The derivation of this slang term is not known although it has been in use since the time of Shakespeare. *Dickens* is also used in mild imprecations such as *the dickens take you, raise the dickens*, and *go to the dickens*. *Play the dickens* means to be mischievous, or to instigate or stir up trouble and confusion.

dip into the blue—To tell an off-color story; to speak of the erotic or obscene. *Blue* 'lewd, obscene, indelicate, offensive' has been in use since at least as early as the mid 19th century. *Dip into the blue* is a picturesque but rarely heard euphemism.

locker-room talk—Vulgar ribaldry; obscene, scurrilous, or vile language; also, *bathroom talk*. This expression derives from the lewd conversations that males purportedly indulge in when in the confines of a locker room or bathroom.

pardon my French—Please overlook my profane language; excuse my use of taboo words. This expression, dating from the early 20th century, probably originated with British soldiers returning from the the front in France during and immediately after World War I. The phrase is most

WOLF IN SHEEP'S CLOTHING

commonly used immediately preceding or immediately following a burst of blasphemy or obscenity, as a sort of mild excuse.

> Does she cut ball? — if you will pardon my French. (John Mortimer, *The Collaborators*, 1973)

swear like a trooper—To use extremely profane language. This simile, dating from the late 18th century, derives from the language reputedly used by British soldiers. It has become almost a cliché that the language of men in exclusively male company, e.g., soldiers and athletes, is riddled with profanities.

> Women *got drunk* and *swore* like troopers. (William Cobbett, *A Year's Residence in the United States of America*, 1819)

Today the expression *like a trooper* is often used with other verbs to indicate forcefulness, intensity, enthusiasm, etc. One can *sing like a trooper, dance like a trooper, play like a trooper*, and so on.

talk the bark off a tree—To express oneself in strong, usually profane, language. This informal Americanism dates from the 19th century.

> The tracker will be led, perhaps, for mile after mile through just the sort of cover that tempts one to halt and "talk the bark off a tree" now and then. (*Outing*, November 1891)

PROLIFERATION
SEE ABUNDANCE

PROMISCUOUSNESS

alley cat—A sexually promiscuous person; a prostitute, especially one who walks the streets at night. This American slang expression, its figurative use dating from the early 20th century, originally denoted a homeless or stray cat that roamed about the back streets and alleys of a city in search of food. By extension, it came to designate a prostitute or a street walker furtively seeking customers. In time the term came to indicate any sexually promiscuous person.

> I'm not trying to whitewash the alley cats among the weekend war brides. (*Chicago Daily News*, August 2, 1945)

A verb form, *alley-catting around*, was coined in the late 1930s, perhaps by Kaufman and Hart, who used the term in *The Man Who Came to Dinner* (1939). A related term, *painted cat*, was especially popular in the early American West as a designation for a frontier harlot.

Athanasian wench—A loose woman, one of easy virtue, ready to grant sexual favors to any man who desires them. This somewhat irreverent slang phrase has its origin in the opening words of the Athanasian creed—*quicumque vult* 'whoever desires.' The creed, a Christian profession of faith dating from the 5th century, emphasized the doctrines of the Trinity and the Incarnation to combat the Arian heresy which denied the divinity of Jesus Christ.

bank-walker—Exhibitionist; flasher. This American dialect expression (Appalachian region) for a male who enjoys displaying his physical endowments comes from the supposed practice of such a youth to strut about the riverbank unclothed, while his companions quickly hid their nakedness by plunging into the old swimming hole with all deliberate speed.

blue gown—A harlot, prostitute. This British expression came from the blue garb formerly worn by women in houses of correction. In the United States, however, it has no such meaning. Though nonexistent as a discrete term, the phrase would be associated by most people with the all-time popular song "Alice Blue Gown," from the 1919 hit musical *Irene*. As such it would carry connotations of gentility and demureness rather than of brazenness and promiscuousness.

Don Juan—A rake; a libertine; an aristocratic profligate; an intemperate philanderer; a lecher. The legend goes that Don Juan Tenorio was the son of a leading family of Seville who seduced his commander's daughter and killed the commander. Later, when a statue of the commander was placed in a Franciscan convent, Don Juan mockingly invited it to attend a feast. The story has it that the statue agreed and after the evening ceremonies delivered Don Juan to Hell. Don Juan's reputation as a seducer of women is explained by his valet in the Mozart opera *Don Giovanni* (1787), when he says that the Don has in Italy 700 mistresses, in Germany 800, in Turkey and France 91, and in Spain 1003. The prototype of Don Juan was created and his story was first dramatized in *El Burlador de Sevila* by Gabriel Tellez (1571–1641), writing under the name Tirso de Molina. The story was retold by a number of well-known writers and composers, among them Molière, Mozart, Shadwell, Byron, Browning, and Shaw.

> If Don Juans and Don Juanesses only obeyed their desires, they'd have very few affairs. They have to tickle themselves up imaginatively before they can start being casually promiscuous. (Aldous Huxley, *Point Counter Point*, 1928)

gay Lothario—A libertine; a seducer of women; a rake. In *The Fair Penitent* (1703) Nicholas Rowe created the character Lothario, a debauchee who attempted to seduce any woman he met.

> Is this that Haughty, Gallant, Gay Lothario?

The term has become a synonym for any breezy, young womanizer and remains in common use. Related terms, all based on the names of famous male lovers, are *Don Juan*, *Casanova*, and *Romeo*.

One realizes with horror, that the race of men is almost extinct in Europe: only Christ-like heroes and woman-worshipping Don Juans, and rabid equality-mongrels. (D.H. Lawrence, *Sea and Sardinia*, 1921)

group grope—An assemblage of people engaging in sex play; an orgy, bacchanalia, or love-in. This American expression is also applied to the mental or physical probing that transpires during encounter sessions, with the implication that all are floundering about, the blind leading the blind.

high-kilted—Obscene, risqué; or indecent in one's manner of dress; literally wearing one's kilt or petticoat too short or tucked up. This British and Scottish expression dates from the early 17th century.

To dazzle the world with her precious limb,
—Nay, to go a little high-kilted.
(Thomas Hood, *Kilmansegg*, 1840)

laced mutton—A prostitute, strumpet, trollop; a loose or promiscuous woman. The derivation of this expression is uncertain, but there is general agreement that *mutton* 'prostitute' refers to the sheep, an occasional victim of bestiality by shepherds. *Laced* may refer to the elaborately tied bodices worn by ladies of the evening from the 17th through the 19th centuries. One source suggests that the reference may be to *lacing* 'flogging,' a common punishment for harlots at that time. The most plausible explanation is that *laced* is a corruption of *lost*, and that the original expression was a variation or perhaps even a deliberate pun on *lost sheep*. This concept received the punning treatment of William Shakespeare:

Ay, sir: I a lost mutton, gave your letter to her, a laced mutton; and she, a laced mutton, gave me, a lost mutton, nothing for my labor.
(*Two Gentlemen From Verona*, I,i)

Lolita—A girl in pubescence considered sexually desirable; a nymphet. This expression was derived from Vladimir Nabokov's novel *Lolita* (1955), the story of a man in later middle age, Professor Humbert, who becomes involved in a torrid love affair with a twelve-year-old girl. Stanley Kubrick made the novel into a film in 1962. *Lolita* is rapidly becoming the vernacular term for a sexually precocious teenage girl.

make time with—To date a girl or woman for the sole purpose of having sexual relations; to indulge in such endeavors with another's sweetheart or wife. Literally, *make time* means to move swiftly so as to recover lost time. Figuratively, one trying to *make time with* another is attempting a quick seduction with little or no intention of forming a lasting relationship.

At another table, two young men were trying to make time with some Mexican girls. (William Burroughs, *Junkie*, 1953)

masher—A playboy or womanizer; a man who attempts to seduce any woman he meets. This expression, derived from *mash* 'flirtation,' originally referred to certain 19th-century Englishmen who feigned wealth and sophistication while pursuing female companionship at the fashionable society establishments.

> The once brilliant masher of the music hall. (Walter Besant, *Bells of St. Paul's,* 1889)

In modern usage, however, this term is used to describe any male flirt or libertine.

one-night stand—A single sexual encounter; a casual, one-time sex partner. This American slang term comes from the expression's theatrical use to denote either the town in which a touring company gives only one performance, or the single performance itself.

painted cat—A prostitute, harlot, strumpet, daughter of joy. This expression combines *painted* and *cat,* terms both associated with prostitutes: *painted woman, cathouse.* Its usage was limited to American cowboys in the Old West.

quench [one's] thirst at any dirty puddle—To be promiscuous; to obtain partners for sexual activity indiscriminately. This self-explanatory expression is infrequently heard today.

> I had before quenched my thirst at any dirty puddle [of women]. (Davis, *Travels,* 1803)

rag on every bush—This expression is used to describe a young man who pays marked attention to more than one lady at a time. The situation is similar to a sailor who supposedly has a *girl in every port.* The expression, in use since the early 1800s, probably derives from the old practice of hanging rags on bushes as targets, thus creating several possibilities at which one might shoot. When a young man finally decided upon one girl, she was said to *take the rag off the bush.* This term is also heard as an expression of a young lady's beauty:

> That gal certainly takes the rag off the bush. (William Harben, *Westerfelt,* 1901)

It is sometimes used as a jocular method of expressing astonishment.

> One of my neighbors greeted his first airplane with: "Gawd damn! Don't that take the rag off'n the bush?" (*American Speech,* October 1929)

roué—A libertine or playboy; one who leads a life of frivolty and self-indulgence; one who follows the primrose path. This expression was first used figuratively in the early 18th century for the decedant cronies of the Duke of Orleans. *Roué* 'wheel' refers to the punishment for wrongdoers of that time; thus, the term implies that the Duke and his coharts deserved such a penalty.

I knew him for a young roué of a vicomte—a brainless and vicious youth. (Charlotte Brontë, *Jane Eyre*, 1847)

shack up—To cohabit or live together (usually in reference to an unmarried couple); to have a relatively permanent sexual relationship; to have sexual intercourse. During World War II, this expression was a popular means of describing the living arrangements of a soldier who, with a local woman, rented and intermittently lived in an apartment or inexpensive house or *shack* located near the base where he was stationed. Since the 1950s, the expression's major application has shifted somewhat from the idea of actually setting up housekeeping to its more contemporary implications of promiscuous, and oftentimes indiscriminate sexual behavior.

If you drink and shack up with strangers you get old at thirty. (Tennessee Williams, *Orpheus Descending*, 1957)

sow [one's] wild oats—See EXCESSIVENESS.

PROPITIOUSNESS
SEE OPPORTUNENESS

PROPRIETY
SEE PRUDISHNESS

PROSPEROUSNESS
SEE ABUNDANCE; SUCCESS

PROTEST
SEE REBELLIOUSNESS

PROVOCATION
SEE VEXATION

PRUDISHNESS

banned in Boston—This expression originated during the 1920s when the Watch and Ward Society of Boston under the leadership of Anthony Comstock became overly enthusiastic in its censorship of books. The term came to be a jocular synonym for *naughty*, and to have a book banned in Boston became the actual goal of some publishers, for such censorship usually assured increased sales throughout the rest of the country. Comstock's name has been immortalized in the term *comstockery*, meaning prudishness or overzealous censorship, on moral grounds, of books, films, etc.

blue laws—Those statutes that seek to regulate personal morals and individual freedom of choice; laws written to regulate activities on Sunday, especially those activities dealing with business and entertainment. In the

17th century the settlement of New Haven in the colony of Connecticut passed a series of statutes designed to regulate the behavior of its residents on Sundays; these were said to have been published on blue paper. The Reverend Samuel A. Peters in his *General History of Connecticut* (1781) lists these original blue laws. One such law reads:

> No one shall run on the Sabbath day, or walk in his garden, or elsewhere, except reverently to and from meeting.

Although Connecticut became known as "The Blue Law State," such statutes were also adopted by the other colonies. Many blue laws survived into the 20th century, and, in spite of the fact that many have been eliminated in recent years, some still exist and are, on occasion, enforced, especially Sunday closing laws in several states.

> Simple hearts...play their own game in innocent defiance of the Blue-laws of the world. (Ralph Waldo Emerson, *Essays*, 1876)

bluenose—An ultraconservative in matters of morality; a puritan, prude, or prig.

> That this picture may aggravate blue nose censors is not beyond the bounds of possibility. (*Variety*, April 3, 1929)

As early as 1809 Washington Irving used the adjective form *blue-nosed*. The form in the above citation and the noun *bluenose* appeared later. The color blue has long been associated with conservatism and strictness, though for what reason is not clear. In the mid-19th century, conservative students at Yale and Dartmouth were called *blues*.

> I wouldn't carry a novel into chapel to read,...because some of the blues might see you. (*Yale Literary Magazine*, 1850)

The usage may derive from Connecticut's "blue laws"—stringent restrictions on moral conduct with harsh penalties for their infraction—which obtained in the 17th and 18th centuries. They were presumably so called because originally printed on blue paper.

cold as a cucumber—Completely lacking in sexual desire; continent; chaste. This phrase, which predates the more common *cool as a cucumber* by about 200 years, was current in the early 16th century. The expression was originally used to denote a complete lack of sexual drive. Sir Thomas Elyot in *The Castle of Health* (1541) reveals that the eating of cucumbers produces a "cold and thick humor" which "will abate lust."

> I do remember it to my grief;
> Young maids were cold as cucumbers,
> And much of that complexion.
> (Beaumont and Fletcher, *Cupid's Revenge*, 1615)

By the early 18th century, *cold* had been modified to *cool*, with the phrase then indicating that one was feeling composed and collected; the sexual connotation almost completely disappeared.

Thucydides...is as cool as a cucumber upon every act of atrocity. (Thomas De Quincey, *Greek Literature*, 1838)

Goody Two Shoes—A goody-goody, a nice nelly; an appellation for a person of self-righteous, sentimental, or affected goodness; also *Miss Goody Two Shoes*. The original Little Goody Two Shoes was the principal character in a British nursery rhyme thought to have been written by Oliver Goldsmith and published by Newbery in 1765. According to the story, Little Goody Two Shoes owned only one shoe and was so delighted at receiving a second that she went around showing both to everyone, exclaiming "Two shoes!" Although it is not clear why the nursery rhyme character Little Goody Two Shoes came to symbolize self-righteous, excessive, and affected goodness, the term appeared in the writing of the 19th-century author Anthony Trollope in just such a context:

Pray don't go on in that Goody Two-shoes sort of way.

little old lady from Dubuque—Harold Ross, long the editor-in-chief of *The New Yorker*, created the *little old lady from Dubuque* in the 1930s. She serves as the provincial grandmotherly type with whom caution must be exercised in all moral considerations. Her English counterpart is *Aunt Edna*, the brainchild of Terence Rattigan, the dramatist, who comments on her eternal moral presence in the preface to his *Collected Plays*, Volume II:

Aunt Edna is universal, and to those who may feel that all the problems of the modern theatre might be solved by her liquidation, let me add...she is also immortal.

Mrs. Grundy—The personification of conventional opinion in issues of established social propriety; a prudish, straight-laced person who becomes outraged at the slightest breach of decorum or etiquette. In Thomas Morton's *Speed the Plough* (1798), Mrs. Grundy was the unseen character whose opinions in matters of social propriety were of constant concern to her neighbors:

If shame should come to the poor child—I say Jummas, what would Mrs. Grundy say then.

The expression is still used figuratively as the embodiment of public opinion.

And many are afraid of God—and more of Mrs. Grundy. (Frederick Locker, *London Lyrics*, 1857)

nice Nelly—A prudish person of either sex; one who prefers civility to competence. This term can be traced directly to Franklin P. Adams, who created a number of representative characters in his column, *The Conning Tower*. Nice Nelly, one of these characters, represented prudishness and refinement to the point of absurdity.

I've got to use *heck* for *hell* because practically all my editors are...being more rabidly nice Nelly than usual. (George Dixon, *New York Daily Mirror*, July 8, 1952)

Nice Nellyism is used to mean prudishness or excessive modesty.

wowser—A contemptuous term for a puritanical-type person; a kill-joy; a narrow-minded zealot; a teetotaler. This expression, originally Australian slang, has spread to most of the English-speaking world to indicate a moralistic bigot who openly disapproves of other people's minor vices. The origin of the word, in use since the late 19th century in Australia, is obscure. In recent years the term has been used almost exclusively to signify a teetotaler.

> Men of letters, who would swoon at the sight of a split infinitive, such wowsers they are in regard to pure English, will in conversation address you as 'Old thing.'...(*New Statesman*, February 4, 1928)

QUICKNESS
SEE INSTANTANEOUSNESS

RACISM
SEE PREJUDICE

RANK
SEE INSTANTANEOUSNESS

REBELLIOUSNESS

beat generation—That group of people, who, during the late 1940s and early 1950s, rejected the values and conventions of modern society; beatniks. The social rebels of the post-World-War-II decade, often called *beatniks*, expressed themselves through unconventional dress and behavior, which was characteristic of their general dissatisfaction with a materialistic civilization.

> The *Beat Generation* is really a private vision. The originals...dreamed of a generation of crazy illuminated hipsters suddenly rising and roaming America...(E. Burdick, *The Reporter*, April 3, 1958)

The coinage of this term is usually ascribed to the novelist and poet Jack Kerouac, who along with poets Allen Ginsberg and Lawrence Ferlinghetti, is generally regarded as the spiritual leader of the group. Ferlinghetti, especially, increased the popularity of the term by establishing the City Lights Press in San Francisco, where he published much of the work of the *Beat* writers. The movement grew in popularity, spreading to Britain and the rest of Europe, but it dwindled to practically nothing during the early 1960s. Some elements of it revived in altered form in the *hippy movement* of the late 1960s.

263

brush fire—The implication in this term is that a *brush fire* may become a full-blown forest fire at any moment. In its figurative sense it suggests the eruption of any small-scale problem into major proportions. The term has been in use since about World War II.

> The family outcast is stirring up a brush fire of liberal resentment against the Truman administration. (*Chicago Daily News*, May 15, 1947)

Since the mid 1950s the expression appears most frequently in *brush-fire war*, a term used to designate a small scale rebellion that has drawn the political attention and sometimes the military intervention of the superpowers. Occasionally, brush-fire wars expand into major military conflicts, as in Vietnam in the 1960s.

come-outer—One who comes out or withdraws from an established organization, especially from a religious body; a radical reformer; a religious dissenter. In the early 1800s, a mystical religious group, believing that organized Christianity was unnecessary because the only source of divine truth was that which God revealed directly to one in his heart, was founded on Cape Cod. Since these *come-outers* were so decisive in their views of the church, the term soon came to be applied to any religious rebel and eventually to any reformer who left any kind of an organization on principle.

> I am a Christian man of the sect called come-outers, and have had experience. (Thomas C. Haliburton, *Nature and Human Nature*, 1855)

fly in the face of—To defy recklessly or challenge; to act in bold opposition to. A bird or insect that flies in the face of a predator is acting against its instincts and thus courting trouble. The phrase is often used figuratively to describe political or social opposition:

> He had to fly in the face of adverse decisions. (*Nations*, December 1891)

Extensions of the expression include *to fly in the face of danger* and *to fly in the face of providence*, both of which carry a sense of reckless or impetuous disregard for safety.

kick against the pricks—To protest in vain, to resist ineffectually a superior force or authority, especially to one's own detriment. This expression appears several times in the Bible. In Acts 9:5 Jesus answers Saul's question "Who art thou, Lord?" by answering:

> I am Jesus whom thou persecutest: it is hard for thee to kick against the pricks.

Prick in this case literally refers to a sharp, pointed goad for oxen and figuratively to the voice of authority. To literally kick against the pricks then is a thoroughly futile act.

For the past ten years he has known what it is to "kick against the pricks" of legitimate Church authority. (Marie Corelli, *God's Good Man*, 1904)

kick over the traces—To rebel, to resist or rise up against the accepted order, to throw off or defy conventional restraints. A harnessed horse literally kicks over the traces when it gets a leg outside the straps (traces) connecting its harness to a carriage or wagon.

> The effervescence of genius which drives men to kick over the traces of respectability. (Sir Leslie Stephen, *Hours in a Library*, 1876)

left-wing—Espousing radical or progressive political, social, or economic ideologies; favoring extensive political, social, or economic reform; socialistic; Communistic. This expression arose as the result of the French National Assembly of 1789 in which conservatives were seated in the right side, or wing, of the hall, moderates in the middle, and radical democrats and extremists in the left wing. This seating arrangement persists in several contemporary legislatures including the British Commonwealth Assemblies where politicians with radical or socialistic views usually sit to the left of the presiding officer. After World War II, and especially during the McCarthy era, *left-wing* usually implied that one was a Communist or a Communist sympathizer.

> The left-wing challenge over Europe is expected to unseat at least one member of the Labour Party National Executive Committee. (*Times*, September 5, 1972)

People or groups of people with left-wing philosophies are frequently called *left wing*, *left-wingers*, or *the Left*. The radical political activists in the United States in the late 1960s and early 1970s were often called *the New Left* in an attempt to dissociate them and their activities from intimations of Communist influence or complicity.

take the bit between [one's] teeth—To cast off external controls and take charge of one's own life; to rebel against unfair restraints or impositions. The *bit* in this expression refers to the mouthpiece of a bridle, attached to the reins used to control a horse. When a horse takes the bit between his teeth, the pain in his mouth is relieved and he becomes more manageable. This expression, dating from the early 17th century, often implies willful defiance. A variant is *take the bit in one's teeth*.

work-to-rule—A form of trade union slowdown carried out by applying a strictly literal interpretation of rules and regulations; to observe letter for letter the technicalities laid down by the union rule book in order to force concessions from management. This expression, coined in Great Britain about 1962, is used in reference to a sort of job action involving a deliberate slowing of productivity short of an actual work stoppage, frequently the final procedure taken before a strike. The term is used as a verb phrase or, hyphenated, as a noun.

> Hospital consultants began a work-to-rule on 2 January, in protest against the new contract they had been offered. (H. V. Hodson, "United Kingdom," *The Annual Register of World Events in 1975*, 1976)

young Turk—An insurgent; one who advocates reform in a staid, conservative organization; a rebel; a political radical or liberal. In 1891, a group of reformists established the Young Turks, a political party dedicated to realigning the priorities of the Turkish Empire and instituting European ideologies and customs in governmental procedures. After inciting a revolt in 1908 in which the Sultan was deposed, the Young Turks remained a viable political force until the end of World War I. By extension, *young Turk* has assumed figurative implications as evidenced in this quote from John Gunther (1901–70), cited in *Webster's Third:*

> The young Turks . . . [are] opposed to the ossified conservatism of the older, so-called statesmen.

RECANTATION
SEE DENIAL; REVERSAL; VACILLATION

RECIPROCITY

ka me, ka thee—Do a good deed for another and the favor will be returned. This expression appeared in print as early as the mid-16th century. The exact origin is unknown and many variants were used interchangeably with *ka*, such as *kaw, kae, k, kay,* and *kob. Scratch my back, I'll scratch yours* is a current analogous expression which like the proverbial *Do unto others as you would have them do unto you* implies reciprocity of service, flattery, or favors.

> Ka me, ka thee, one good turn asketh another. (John Heywood, *Works,* 1562)

logrolling—The trading of votes or favors, especially among legislators, for mutual political gain; the policy of "you scratch my back and I'll scratch yours." In pioneer days a logrolling was a gathering at which neighbors helped each other roll and pile their logs to a particular spot for burning or other means of disposal. It was similar in nature to barn raisings and husking bees. Literal logrolling also played an important part in lumber camps where members of different camps often joined forces in rolling their logs to the water's edge to catch the flood downstream. This U.S. term apparently came from the proverbial expression "you roll my log and I'll roll yours." Political use of the term dates from the early 19th century.

> Territorial supreme courts have long since become known as a kind of log-rolling machine, in which the judges enter in the business of "you

tickle me and I will tickle you." (*Weekly New Mexican Review*, July 1885)

one hand washes the other—A proverbial expression originally denoting mutual cooperation in its positive sense only, but now carrying the negative connotations of backscratching, cronyism, and logrolling. It appeared as early as the 1500s in the former sense, but within a few centuries began to take on the latter dubious coloration.

> Persons in business...who make, as the saying is, "one hand wash the other." (*Diary of Philip Hone*, 1836)

REFUSAL
See also DENIAL

no dice—No; no way; nothing doing; absolutely not; a negative response or result. Although many tales surround the derivation of this expression, it is likely that, since *dice* often implies luck, *no dice* simply implies no luck.

> I was around at her bank this morning trying to find out what her balance was, but no dice. Fanny won't part. (P. G. Wodehouse, *Barmy in Wonderland*, 1952)

no soap—No; usually said in refusal or rejection. The origin of this expression is unknown, but it may have been originally used to refuse a bribe, since a slang meaning of *soap* is 'bribe money.'

> If you don't know, just say, "No soap." (Marks, *Plastic Age*, 1924)

party pooper—One who refuses to join in the party mood; a wet blanket; a killjoy. *Pooper* in this phrase is an offshoot of the slang expression *to poop out*, 'to run out of steam.' Of course, one who lacks the vitality to participate in the party atmosphere soon casts a pall over the proceedings, and his presence seems to dampen the joyful mood. The term has been in use since about 1945.

> No one can call Mr. Bulganin and Mr. Krushchev party poopers... the Russian leaders demonstrated their suavity and cleverness at the party. (Earl Wilson, in syndicated column, July 5, 1956)

The expression is also used to refer to one who leaves a party well before other guests.

thumbs down—Disapproval, disapprobation, rejection. This expression refers to making a fist and extending the thumb downward, a gesture which, in the days of gladiatorial combats in ancient Rome, indicated that the spectators thought a defeated gladiator had fought poorly and, as a result, should be slain by the victor. The expression is commonly used figuratively as evidenced in a quote from bacteriologist Paul de Kruif (1890–1971), cited in *Webster's Third*:

The government thumbs-down on penicillin for [treating] endocarditis was published.

See also **thumbs up**, APPROVAL.

turn a deaf ear—To turn away from; to refuse to listen to another; to reject another's proposition. The reference is to a refusal to listen to another person's plea by turning off one's sense of hearing, whether literally or figuratively, thereby rejecting him. The term has been common since the early 17th century.

Turn a deaf ear to him, and do not go along with him. (Bishop Simon Patrick, *The Parable of the Pilgrim*, 1663)

wash [one's] hands of—To renounce responsibility for; to disclaim interest in, or further connection with; to have nothing to do with. The allusion in this expression is to Pontius Pilate's denial of the responsibility of Jesus' crucifixion.

When Pilate saw that he could prevail nothing, but that rather a tumult was made, he took water, and washed his hands before the multitude, saying, I am innocent of the blood of this just person: see ye to it. (Matthew 27:24)

People, however, did not accept Pilate's casual dismissal of his guilt, and since that time the phrase has had a hint of deviousness about it. Lady Macbeth represents another who tries unsuccessfully to wash her hands of her guilt when she tries to disburden her conscience of the "damned spot."

He had entirely washed his hands of the difficulty, and it had become ours. (Charles Dickens, *Bleak House*, 1853)

whistle for it—A refusal to do or give something to someone; a rejection; a denial. The reference here is to the old practice of sailors' *whistling for the wind* when their ship was becalmed. A superstition among these seagoing men was that the wind could be influenced to blow if one whistled for it. Somehow the term became corrupted to imply that one would be denied his fancies.

She rode off, telling him he might whistle for his money. (Lady Bloomfield, *Reminiscences*, 1882)

A variant, *go whistle*, is usually heard as a sarcastic refusal of a request.

REJECTION
SEE ABANDONMENT; DENIAL; REFUSAL

REJOINDER
SEE RETORTS

RENEWING
SEE RESUMPTION

ONE HAND WASHES THE OTHER

REPRIMAND

See also CRITICISM

bawl out—To scold someone in a loud voice; to berate; to reprimand, especially thoroughly and severely; to shout out at the top of one's voice. Although this phrase is generally considered an American slang expression, the word *bawl*, meaning to cry out in a loud or rough voice, has been in use in England since at least the early 15th century.

"I will fling you out the window . . . ," bawled out Mr. Pendennis. (William Makepeace Thackeray, *Pendennis*, 1850)

It is believed that the American phrase, meaning to scold or berate, evolved independently on the ranches of the western United States by cowboys, who applied it to the bawling of angry cattle.

If you'll go back on your word like this, you'll bawl me out before the priest. (Rex Beach, *The Barrier*, 1908)

box [one's] ears—To cuff one on the side of the head; to strike sharply about the ears; to reprimand or chastise; to admonish. This expression, dating from about 1600, implies that someone is striking another about the ears and side of the head as one would strike a punching bag or an opponent in boxing. However, the term is most often heard as a figure of speech to warn a youngster that punishment is impending if he doesn't discontinue his present actions. The phrase is also used figuratively to indicate disapprobation or admonishment.

cast in [someone's] teeth—To upbraid or reproach a person; to throw back at a person something he has said or done. Some say the phrase, popular in Shakespeare's time, is an allusion to knocking someone's teeth out by casting stones. It may be an earlier form of the current expression *throw in [someone's] face*.

He casteth the Jews in the teeth that their fathers served strange Gods. (Thomas Timme, tr., *Commentary of John Calvin upon Genesis*, 1578)

chew out—To reprimand, scold, or give someone a tongue-lashing. This American slang expression dates from the middle of this century.

A verbal admonishing from a superior would be recorded by the victim with "I just got eaten out" or "I just got chewed out." (J. B. Roulier, *New York Folk Quarterly*, IV, 1948)

curtain lectures—A wife's nighttime naggings; a shrew's bedtime harangues. The *curtains* refers to drapes on old four-posters; the *lectures* to a wife's supposed practice of showering her husband with sermons when he least wants to listen, i.e., when he wants to fall asleep. The expression, in use since the early 17th century, gained popularity when the English humorist Douglas William Jerrold published his fictional "Mrs. Caudle's Curtain-lectures" in *Punch* in 1846.

don't hurry, Hopkins—Said to one who is late in his payment; a reproof to a person who is working too slowly. The story is told of a Kentuckian named Mr. Hopkins who, when he borrowed money from a friend, wrote upon the note:

The said Hopkins is not to be hurried in paying the above.

This American expression dates from the 1860s, but a similar British expression, *as hasty as Hopkins*, dating from the 17th century, carries an implication that one shouldn't be too hasty. The British expression seemingly derives from the unfortunate experience of a man named Hopkins, legendary since he came to jail one night and was hanged the next morning.

dressing down—A severe, formal reprimand or reproof; a tongue-lashing; a sharp censure. *Dress* 'to treat someone with deserved severity, to give a thrashing or beating to' (*OED*) dates from the 15th century, and *dressing down* from the 19th century. However, the two theories which have been proffered to explain the origin of *dressing down* do not take this long-obsolete use of *dress* into account. The first theory relates to the preparation of fish.

The order was given [to]... fall to splitting and salting [fish]. This operation which is known as "dressing down," is performed on hogshead tubs or boards placed between two barrels. (*Harper's Magazine*, March 1861)

The second theory claims that the phrase derives from the practice of *dressing down* in ore mines which involves breaking up the ore and crushing and powdering it in the stamping mill. It is plausible that either image—of splitting and cutting up fish or breaking up and crushing ore—could have given rise to the figurative *dressing down*.

get the stick—To be severely rebuked or reprimanded, to be called on the carpet. This expression is British slang and apparently derived from the former practice of birching or caning, i.e., beating misbehaving schoolchildren with sticks. With the demise of corporal punishment in schools, the phrase has become figurative in meaning and now refers only to verbal punishment.

give [one] down the banks—To reprimand, chastise, or tongue-lash someone; to give someone a dressing down; to haul over the coals. The origin of this expression, which has been attributed to Irish sources, is unclear. It appeared as early as 1884, when Mark Twain utilized the term in *Huckleberry Finn*.

He give me down the banks for not coming and telling him.

give [someone] Jesse—To punish or scold; to reprimand or castigate. In this expression, *Jesse* may refer to the father of David (Isaiah 11:1,10), a righteous and valiant man. It is more likely, however, that the reference is

271

to the sport of falconry in which a *jess,* or *jesse,* 'a strap used to secure a bird by its leg to a falconer's wrist,' was used as a punishment for poor performance.

> Just as soon as I go home I'll give you jessie. (Alice Cary, *Married,* 1856)

give [someone] the length of one's tongue—To speak one's mind, especially in verbally abusive terms; to give someone a piece of one's mind. A citation from the *OED* dates the phrase from the turn of the 20th century.

haul over the coals—To reprimand or scold; to censure, to take to task. Current figurative use of this expression derives from the former actual practice of dragging heretics over the coals of a slow fire. In a 16th-century treatise, St. Augustine was described as knowing best "how to fetch an heretic over the coals." No longer is the phrase used literally as in the above quotation. Today *haul* or *rake* or *drag* or *fetch over the coals* refers at worst to severe criticism or censure.

> If the Tories do not mend their manners, they will shortly be hauled over the coals in such a manner as will make this country too hot to hold them. (James C. Ballagh, ed., *The Letters of Richard Henry Lee,* 1911)

have [one's] ears slapped back—To be punished either verbally or physically; to suffer defeat; to be put in one's place. This expression, which dates from the late 1800s, probably alludes to actually slapping someone about the ears as a form of punishment. In modern usage, the term is heard only in its figurative sense, 'to suffer a setback of some kind.'

> You're bound to get your ears slapped back. (McKnight Malmar, *Never Say Die,* 1943)

Two common variants of this term are often heard, *pin [someone's] ears back* and *have [one's] ears pinned back,* each connoting the teaching of a lesson.

> Pine was a flip-lipped bastard who should have had his ears pinned back long ago. (John Evans, *Halo in Blood,* 1946)

kale through the reek—Bitter language; unpleasant treatment; severe punishment. The allusion here is to the unpalatableness of the smoky kale broth which once was a mainstay of meals in Scotland. The kale was cooked over an open fire, and the resulting reek created a most disagreeable atmosphere.

> When my mither and him forgathered they set till the sodgers, and I think they gae them their kale through the reek. (Sir Walter Scott, *Old Mortality,* 1816)

a lash of scorpions—An extremely severe punishment; an unusually harsh, vituperative, or vitriolic chastisement or criticism. Though now used figuratively, this expression was once literal, the *scorpion* being an ancient instrument of punishment, a whip or lash with four or five "tails," each set with steel spikes and lead weights. The allusion to the arachnoid scorpion with its venomous, stinging tail is obvious. Needless to say, a scourging with a scorpion was a heinous ordeal which inflicted intense pain and, in many cases, permanent injury or even death.

> My father hath chastised you with whips, but I will chastise you with scorpions. (I Kings 12:11)

lay out in lavender—To chastise harshly and in no uncertain terms; to give someone a dressing down; to knock someone down or unconscious; to kill someone. Although the derivation of *lavender* in this expression is uncertain, *lay someone out* has long meant 'to strike someone so hard as to knock him to the ground.' One source suggests that since both *lavender* and *livid* are derived from the Latin *lividula* 'a purplish-blue plant,' there may be the common theme of intense anger. A more plausible explanation is that branches of the lavender plant were once used to beat freshly washed clothes, and that *lay out in lavender* alludes to this physical act of beating. In contemporary usage, however, this expression usually refers to a verbal beating rather than a physical one.

> If that woman gets the Republican nomination, . . . I will lay her out in lavender. (Vivian Kellems in a syndicated newspaper column, September 15, 1952)

a lick with the rough side of the tongue—See **use the rough side of [one's] tongue,** below.

on the carpet—Summoned before one's superiors for a reprimand; called to account; taken to task; usually in the phrase *call on the carpet.* Although this expression did not appear in this sense until 1900, both the verb *carpet* 'call someone in to be reprimanded, to censure someone' and the phrase *walk the carpet* date from the early 1800s. Both were said of a servant called into the parlor (a carpeted area) before the master or mistress in order to be reprimanded.

rap on the knuckles—A sharp reprimand or rebuff; an admonishment; a dressing down. The allusion in this phrase is to a type of punishment formerly meted out in the classroom to students who had misbehaved, a *rap on the knuckles* from the teacher's ruler. The practice has been discontinued in most school systems, but the figurative use of the term continues.

> I received a sharp rap on my moral knuckles from my conscience. (Mary Kingsley, *Travels in West Africa,* 1897)

read the riot act—To reprimand or chastise vehemently and vociferously; to issue an ultimatum, an or-else; to threaten with drastic punishment. The expression derives from Britain's Riot Act of 1715, which provided that a given number of assembled persons perceived to be causing a disturbance were liable to arrest as felons if they refused to disperse on command. Such command or warning was given by formal reading of the Riot Act.

skin [someone] alive—To reprimand harshly; to abuse verbally or browbeat; to humble or subdue, especially in a venomous, cruel, or merciless manner. The figurative implications of this expression are obvious. Also, *flay alive*.

talk to [someone] like a Dutch uncle—To rebuke or reprove someone with unsparing severity and bluntness. Although an adequate explanation as to why the uncle in this expression is Dutch as opposed to any other nationality has yet to be found, a possible derivation has been proposed in regard to the term *uncle* itself. Apparently, in Roman times, an uncle was a strict guardian given to administering severe reproofs if his charge stepped out of line. The following passage from Joseph C. Neal's *Charcoal Sketches* (1838) illustrates the use of the phrase:

If you keep a-cutting didoes, I must talk to you both like a Dutch uncle.

tell [someone] where to get off—To rebuke, to accuse someone of being presumptuous or stepping on toes; to take down a peg, to tell off. This slang expression of U.S. origin dates from the turn of the century. It may have derived by analogy with the forced ejection of unruly passengers from streetcars or trains. The expression implies that the person who tells another *where to get off* has reached the limits of his endurance and is in effect saying, "You've gone far enough."

He said he was a gentleman, and that no cheap skate in a plug hat could tell him where to get off. (Ade, *More Fables*, 1900)

tongue-lashing—A severe scolding or reprimand; a stinging rebuke or censure; a verbal whipping. Current since the 1880s, this phrase is a modernization of *tongue-banging* which was popular throughout the 1800s. An Anglo-Irish variation is *slap of the tongue*.

use the rough side of [one's] tongue—To bawl out; to give a severe reprimand; to spread derisive gossip. Another form of the expression is *a lick with the rough side of the tongue*. William Ellis relates, in *The Housewife's Companion* (1750), that people, like cows, have a rough side as well as a smooth side to their tongues, and the gossiping sort like to use the rough side. *Rough side* connotes unpleasantness, as well, with allusion to the discomfort a lick from it causes.

Your average welfare administrator would have used the rough side of his tongue on him, giving fresh grounds for complaint. (Mary McCarthy, *House and Garden*, December 1983)

RESIGNATION
See also SUBMISSION

give her the bells and let her fly—To acquiesce to the inevitable, regardless of cost; to acknowledge reality or failure before risking further loss; to make the best of an unalterable situation. This expression originated in the sport of falconry, in which a worthless bird was released without bothering to remove the valuable bells attached to it.

like it or lump it—To accept and put up with; to resign oneself to the inevitable; to make the best of an undesirable situation. The exact origin of this informal expression is difficult to determine. The most plausible suggestion is that *lump it* originally meant 'gulp it down' and was probably said in reference to distasteful medicine. Figurative use of the expression appeared in print by the early 1800s.

> I'll buy clothes as I see fit, and if anybody don't like it, why they may lump it, that's all. (Harriet Beecher Stowe, *Poganuc People*, 1878)

Sometimes *lump it* means simply 'dislike' as in the following quotation:

> Whether we like him or lump him, he [the Interviewer] is master of the situation. (Grant Allen in *Interviews*, 1893)

Like it or lump it is usually heard in situations where no actual choice exists.

take [one's] medicine—To submit oneself to punishment; to submit to something disagreeable or unpleasant; to accept the consequences of one's act. The allusion in this phrase is to the unpleasant taste that accompanied most medicines in the past. In fact, certain extremely bitter medicines were administered by parents to their children as punishment for misbehaving.

> Princess, inscribe beneath my name:
> "He never begged, he never sighed,
> He took his medicine as it came."
> For this the poets lived—and died.
> (Sir John C. Squire, *Ballade of the Poetic Life: Envoi*, 1918)

that's the way the ball bounces—That's life; that's the way it goes; there's nothing to be done about it. Just as one cannot determine ahead of time how a ball will bounce, so too no one can predict or prevent the twists and turns of fate. This expression and the analogous *that's the way the cookie crumbles* are usually said in resignation to a fait accompli.

RESOLVE
SEE PERSEVERANCE

RESTARTING
SEE RESUMPTION

RESTLESSNESS
SEE IMPATIENCE

RESUMPTION

Resumption

go on with your birds' egging—Continue what you were saying or doing. This 19th-century New England jocular expression is seldom heard today. Its origin is obscure, but apparently lies in the situation of a stranger interrupting a man gathering birds' eggs to ask for directions or some other information. After receiving his information, the stranger urged the man to *go on with your bird's egging.*

> So now go on with your bird's egging, and make your Christmas as fast as you please. (Seba Smith, *Way Down East*, 1854)

A related term, *none of one's bird's egging*, means 'none of one's business.'

return to our muttons—Return to the business at hand; back to the subject. In Pierre Blanchet's play, *La Farce de Maistre Pierre Patelin*, first staged about 1460, a cloth dealer employs an attorney, M. Patelin, to prosecute a shepherd for stealing the dealer's sheep. While testifying, the cloth dealer suddenly becomes aware that M. Patelin is wearing a suit made of cloth which had been stolen from him. Utterly confused by this turn of events, the dealer constantly digresses from the stolen sheep to the stolen cloth. The judge frequently has to remind the dealer, "*Revenons à ces moutons,* " or 'Let us return to these sheep.' The phrase was much quoted by Rabelais, which may account for its wider currency. Somehow the phrase became corrupted to *revenons à nos moutons*, which British wags translated as 'let us stick to our muttons' or as F. E. Smedley in *Frank Fairlegh* (1850) quips:

> To return to my mutton, as the Mounseers have it.

RETALIATION

Retaliation

an eye for an eye—A law which sanctions revenge; to repay in kind. This line from Exodus 21:24 is part of a longer passage in which the Lord sets forth the judgments and laws according to which the people are instructed to live. However, this expression may be even older if, as some speculate, it was part of the Code of Hammurabi (approx. 1800 B.C.). The noted resemblances between Hammurabi's laws and ancient Mosaic laws make this theory plausible.

fight fire with fire—To argue or fight with an opponent using his tactics or ground rules; to counter an attack with one of equal intensity. This expression refers to the method used to fight a rapidly spreading forest or grass fire. To control such a fire, a firebreak (an area cleared of trees, grass, and other flammable material) is often created some distance in front of the advancing flames. A backfire may then be set to burn the area between the major fire and the firebreak, thereby containing the fire within a limited area where it can be doused with water or dirt. Thus, fire is literally fought with fire in order to defeat it. In its figurative sense, *to fight fire with fire* is to contend with someone on his level, using his tactics to defeat him. The expression usually implies a lowering or abandonment of one's principles.

fix [someone's] wagon—To get even with, avenge; to prevent, interfere with, or destroy another's success, reputation, or expectations; to injure or kill. This expression may stem from the days of the covered wagons when a person's entire family, possessions, and livelihood could be contained in one of these vehicles. An unscrupulous and vindictive enemy might *fix the wagon* in such a way as to assure that it would break down, causing injury to and possible destruction of both the wagon and its contents. The related expression *fix [someone's] little red wagon* is an updated version, and all the more insidious in its implication of harming a child.

give [someone] a dose of [his/her] own medicine—To treat someone as he has treated others; to give someone something unpleasant or distasteful; to get revenge upon someone. Since *medicine* carries a connotation of something disagreeable or bad- tasting, the intent of this expression is quite evident. It dates from about 1890. Varients include *treat [someone] with a dose of [his/her] own medicine, give [someone] a taste of [his/her] own medicine*, and *get a dose* (or *taste) of [one's] own medicine*.

> "He snubbed me," ... explained Miss DeVoe, smiling slightly at the thought of treating Peter with a dose of his own medicine. (Paul Leicester Ford, *The Honorable Peter Stirling*, 1894)

guts for quarters—Originally this threat was proclaimed seriously, indicating that the speaker meant to unseam his opponent with his sword.

> I'll make quarters of thy guts, thou villain. (Robert Greene, *The Scottish History of James IV*, 1592)

In modern usage the term is employed humorously to indicate that one is in serious trouble.

> If this doesn't work, then I think Parkinson will, as they say, "have my guts for quarters." (Tim Heald, *Deadline*, 1975)

heap coals of fire on [someone's] head—To repay hostility with kindness; to answer bad treatment with good, supposedly in order to make one's enemy repent. The allusion is Biblical:

277

If thine enemy be hungry, give him bread to eat; and if he be thirsty, give him water to drink: For thou shalt heap coals of fire upon his head, and the Lord shall reward thee. (Proverbs 25:21–22)

The usual explanation is that the *coals of fire* supposedly melted a person's "iciness."

pay in [one's] own coin—To retaliate in like fashion; to give tit for tat. The first written use of this phrase is attributed to Plautus, the Roman playwright. The implication of the expression is negative, indicating that one can expect equivalent treatment for one's dishonesty.

Glad that he had given her a sop of the same sauce, and paid her his debt in her own coin. (Robert Greene, *Tullies Love*, 1589)

pound of flesh—Vengeance; requital. This expression derives from Shakespeare's *Merchant of Venice,* in which Shylock agrees to lend money to Antonio only on condition that, if the sum is not repaid on time, he be allowed a pound of Antonio's flesh in forfeit.

The pound of flesh which I demand of him is dearly bought, 'tis mine, and I will have it. (IV,i)

The expression implies that, while the demanded retribution is justified, the yielding of it would incapacitate or destroy the giver, just as the yielding of a pound of one's own flesh would certainly have deleterious consequences.

All the other Great Powers want their pound of flesh from Turkey. (*Fortnightly Review,* January 1887)

[a] Roland for an Oliver—An eye for an eye, a blow for a blow; retaliation in kind. Roland and Oliver, two of Charlemagne's paladins, had adventures which were so extraordinarily similar that it was all but impossible to determine which was the more chivalrous. Eventually, the two men met face to face in combat on an island in the Rhine, where, for five days they fought fiercely, with neither gaining an advantage. The bout climaxed when both men met simultaneous untimely deaths.

We resolved to give him a Roland for his Oliver, if he attacked us. (*The Life of Neville Frowde,* 1773)

serve the same sauce—To retaliate in like fashion; to fight fire with fire; to repay in kind.

They serve them with like sauce, requiring death for death. (Richard Eden, *The Decade of the New World or West India,* 1555)

Variations are *serve a sop* or *taste of the same sauce.*

tit for tat—Blow for blow, an eye for an eye and a tooth for a tooth, reciprocal retaliation.

Fair Traders, Reciprocity men, or believers in the tit-for-tat plan of dealing with other nations. (*Daily News,* July 1891)

According to the *OED* this expression is probably a variation of the earlier *tip* 'light blow' for *tap* 'light blow.'

> Much greater is the wrong that rewards evil for good, than that which requires tip for tap. (George Gascoigne, *Works*, 1577)

Other conjectures claim that *tit for tat* came from the French *tant pour tant* 'so much for so much' or the Dutch *dit vor dat* 'this for that.' Use of the phrase dates from at least 1556.

RETORTS

all round my hat—Nonsense; that doesn't make sense. This derisive British retort to another's statement probably derives from an old music hall ballad, *All Round My Hat I Wears a Green Willow*, which first appeared in 1834 according to the *Modern Music Cata-logue* in the British Museum Library. The expression is seldom heard today.

> "Well done!" exclaimed Mr. Jorrocks, patting the orator's back. . . . "All round my hat!" squeaked Benjamin in the crowd. (Robert S. Surtees, *Handley Cross*, 1854)

Dick Tracy—A mildly sarcastic retort to one who makes an obvious observation as if from penetrating insight. This expression derives from the popular comic strip *Dick Tracy* which features a police detective of that name. *Dick Tracy* is analogous to such rhetorical comments as *Is the Pope Catholic?* and *No kidding!* and *You don't say?*

the Dutch have taken Holland—An obvious statement, this expression is used sarcastically to put down someone who tells a piece of stale news as though it were new and exciting. "If my aunt had been a man she'd have been my uncle" is a similar British retort to someone who has laboriously explained the obvious.

famous last words—A phrase expressing the speaker's conviction that the person so addressed is about to engage in an activity that will lead to dire results. The phrase refers to the practice of recording the *famous last words* of distinguished people. It achieved its popularity from its frequent use by U.S. Army Air Corps and RAF personnel during World War II. It was used as a jocular rejoinder to such comments as "This is sure to be a milk run today." Another context might be: "I'm going to tell the boss what I think of her ... famous last words."

> "If you had any sense, you'd ask me to stick around until you whistled up some reinforcements." "No need for that. Sergeant Goslin will be back soon." "Famous last words," I said. (Hartley Howard, *Million Dollar Snapshot*, 1971)

the Greeks had a word for it—A comment whose basic sense is that an idea or fact has been known about for a very long time. This expression, frequently used as a denigrating sarcasm, was apparently coined in 1929 by Zoë Akins in her play *The Greeks Had a Word for It*. In a letter to Burton Stevenson, which is included in *The Home Book of Proverbs, Maxims and Familiar Phrases* (1948), she explains how the phrase grew naturally out of the dialogue.

> In the play there was a conversation which was cut out as the two characters speaking were cut out. One was a photographer who had come to the wedding in the last act, and had had a glass too much, the other his plain little woman assistant. He is speaking rather floridly about the grandeur of Rome and the glory of Greece. He says, "Girls like the bride—her sort—the Greeks had a word for it."
> "Even the Anglo-Saxons have a word for her sort," the assistant acidly comments.
> "And it's usually spelt with a dash."
> "But the Greeks had a special word for it," he contends. "*Hetaera*, plural *hetaerae*."
> "Meaning tarts," she says.
> "Oh no, meaning free souls—in the days when wives were slaves and slaves were wives."
> You will see by this explanation that the phrase is original and grew out of the dialogue.

The phrase caught on shortly after the play opened on Broadway and is occasionally heard today as a sarcastic retort to another's comment.

have another think coming—A disapproving remark to indicate that one is mistaken and needs to reconsider an opinion or intention. This expression is ordinarily used when one is throwing another's words back in his teeth, frequently out of anger or as an act of provocation, as in: "Well, if you think that, let me tell you, you have another think coming."

I can hardly wait—This American expression, dating from the late 1920s, is usually heard as an ironic retort to one who has just reminded the speaker of an impending encounter with an undesirable person or with a disagreeable situation, or as a rebuff to another's ego trip.

> "And what's so special about you?"
> "I might tell you one of these fine days," I winked at her. "That is, if you play your cards right."
> "I can hardly wait," she parried. (Frank Norman, *Much Ado about Nuffink*, 1974)

The British seem to prefer the variant, *I can't wait*, using it, however, in an identical fashion to its American counterpart.

> FRED: She's coming to the station tomorrow morning to see us off, you don't mind, do you?
> GARRY: I can't wait. (Noel Coward, *Present Laughter*, 1943)

lareovers to catch meddlers—Francis Grose, in *A Dictionary of the Vulgar Tongue* (1785), lists this phrase as:

... an answer frequently given to children, or young people, as a rebuke for their impertinent curiosity, in enquiring what is contained in a box, bundle, or other closed conveyance.

However, *Halliwell's Dictionary of Archaic and Provincial Words* (1847) lists *lareovers* as whips, or instruments of chastisement and adds:

Therefore lareovers for meddlers equals a punishment for meddlers; hence, something not to be meddled with.

In either case, the figurative sense indicates a sharp rebuke to indicate that one has inquired about something that is none of his business. Chiefly dialectal today, and used only in the figurative sense, the phrase has been in use since at least 1698. Variants of the expression are *layovers to catch meddlers* and *larrows to catch meddlers*.

milking ducks as my mother bade me—A facetious answer to a prying question about one's whereabouts or activities. This expression apparently was in common use at the time it appeared in a 15th-century poem.

My master looketh as he were mad:
"Where hast thou been, my sorry lad?"
"Milking ducks as my mother bade."

A variation is *milking geese.*

"Well, little corduroys, have they milked the geese today?"
"Milked the geese! Why they don't milk the geese, you silly."
"No? Dear heart, how do the goslings live then?"
(George Eliot, *Scenes of Clerical Life*, 1857)

Queen Anne is dead—A sarcastic remark made to the bearer of stale news. A similar, current American phrase is *So what else is new?* Anne was Queen of Great Britain and Ireland from 1702–14. The expression dates from the 18th century.

touché—Literally French for 'touched,' *touché* is a fencing term indicating a hit or score. In verbal fencing or argumentation the parry *touché* acknowledges accuracy and truth in an opponent's remark or retort frequently with the implication that the point of the remark was deserved or well said.

zinger—A witty retort; a clever punchline. This term is derived from the verb *zing*, meaning 'to make a sharp, shrill sound' as that made by a swiftly passing object such as a bullet. The definition carries even further, for a *zinger* hits with the impact of a bullet, quick and hard, and usually unexpectedly.

Cavett's wit is his moat.... In casual chatter the zingers are just as fast and frequent as they are on the show. (*Life*, October 30, 1970)

RETRIBUTION
SEE RETALIATION

REVENGE
SEE RETALIATION

REVERSAL

Reversal

back water—To retreat from a position; to reverse one's stance on a subject; to withdraw from a situation. This American expression, dating from the early 1800s, has been attributed to the action of paddlewheel steamboats when they were thrown into reverse. However, it seems more likely that the phrase resulted from the action of a man using his canoe paddle or boat oars to avoid a snag or some other damaging obstacle which presented itself in the water; thus withdrawing from a situation or reversing himself.

> I don't see why we can't rig it up. How many want to back water? (Louise Rich, *We Took to the Woods*, 1942)

bite a file—To bite something that bites back; to try something that can only end in misfortune; to suffer an unexpected and serious rebuff. Aesop tells a fable of a viper that found a file and, thinking it edible, bit it. To his surprise he found it not only unpalatable but also injurious, for it wounded his mouth. The file informed the snake that a file's function is to bite, not to be bitten. The expression has been in figurative use in English since the Middle Ages and is occasionally heard as *gnaw a file*.

> He bit the file of English obstinacy, and broke his teeth. (William Cory, *Modern English History*, 1880)

catch a tartar—To experience a reversal of expectations, particularly in dealing with another person; to find intractable one anticipated to be docile; to meet one's match, often specifically to marry a shrew.

> What a Tartar have I caught!
> (John Dryden, *Kind Keeper*, 1678)

By extension the phrase may mean to have a bargain backfire, an advantage prove a liability, a gift becomes a curse, and similar reversals.

Frankenstein monster—An invention or other creation that eventually works against or kills its creator; something that backfires or boomerangs. The expression comes from Mary Shelley's famous work *Frankenstein* (1818), in which the notorious monster turned against and destroyed its maker, Dr. Frankenstein. The phrase is used figuratively to describe a project or undertaking begun with good intentions, but which ultimately develops into an uncontrollable agent of destruction or evil.

> Is Great Britain creating for herself something of a Frankenstein monster on the Nile? (*Saturday Review*, April 1907)

from Delilah's lap to Abraham's bosom—From evil to good; from sin to salvation. This expression, usually heard in the proverb *there is no leaping from Delilah's lap to Abraham's bosom*, connotes that one can't live a life of sin and then expect to go to heaven upon his death. Delilah, of course, is the notorious sinner of Biblical fame, the mistress of Samson, and Abraham was the chosen of the Lord.

hoist with [one's] own petard—To be defeated by a plan that backfires; to be caught in one's own trap. In this expression, *petard* refers to an ancient, short-fused time bomb or grenade. Obviously, a soldier who placed the charge was endangered not only by enemy fire, but also by the exploding petard if he did not get away soon enough or if the fuse were faulty. So many soldiers were killed by exploding petards that the expression came into widespread literal, and later, figurative, use.

> Let it work;
> For tis sport, to have the engineer
> Hoist with his own petard; and it shall go hard
> But I will delve one yard below their mines,
> And blow them at the moon ...
> (Shakespeare, *Hamlet*, III,iv)

man bites dog—A surprising turn of events; a reversal of the usual order of things. This phrase first appeared in written form in the *New York Sun* about 1880. Charles A. Dana, then editor of the paper, is usually credited with the article that contained the phrase. However, Edward Mitchell, assistant editor to Dana for a good many years, attributes it to John B. Bogart, the City Editor at the time of the phrase's appearance. The connotation of a reversal that causes surprise is self-evident in Bogart's original sentence.

> When a dog bites a man that is not news, but when a man bites a dog that is news.

the shoe is on the other foot—The situation is reversed. This expression, with its obvious allusion, is most often used in reference to a certain poetic justice that results from the exchange or reversal of disparate roles: the controller becomes the controlled, the oppressor becomes the oppressed, the critic becomes the criticized, and so on.

> Recently, much to British chagrin, the shoe was on the other foot. (*The Nation*, March 17, 1945)

the tables are turned—The situation is completely reversed, roles have been switched, positions interchanged; the exact opposite is now the case. The *tables* in this expression refers to the playing boards which, in certain games, are fully turned round, so that the relative positions of the adversaries are reversed. The phrase often implies that one now enjoys (or suffers) the perspective formerly held by an opponent. The following citation shows both figurative application and literal derivation:

> Whosoever thou art that dost another wrong, do but turn the tables: imagine thy neighbour were now playing thy game, and thou his. (Bishop Robert Sanderson, *Sermons*, 1634)

It also illustrates the active use of the phrase, somewhat less common today, *turn tables* or *turn the tables on*.

turn the cat in the pan—To change sides out of self-interest; to reverse things so cleverly that they appear the opposite of what they really are; to be a traitor. Although the origin of this term is unknown, a number of explanations have been forwarded. Dr. Samuel Johnson in his *Dictionary* (1755) lists two possibilities:

> the term should be *catipan*, from Catipania, or it is a corruption of *Cate in the pan*.

However, modern philologists have dismissed both of Johnson's suppositions as erroneous. The most plausible explanation ascribes it to the French *tourner côté en peine* 'to turn sides in trouble'. Whatever the case, the expression has continued in use since at least the 14th century. A variant is *cat-in-pan*.

> You are a Villain, have turned Cat-in-pan and are a Tory. (John Crowne, *City Politiques*, 1675)

turn the tide—To reverse the current trend of events, especially from one extreme to the other; to turn the tables. *Tide* (literally the ebb and flow of the ocean waters) is used here figuratively to represent the course or direction in which any matter or concern is moving.

ugly duckling—A homely or unpromising child who blossoms into a beautiful or accomplished adult; anything appearing to lack redeeming qualities that subsequently proves worthy of respect and notice. This expression comes from Hans Christian Andersen's *Ugly Duckling*, in which the title character, after struggling through a year of ridicule and hardship, develops into a glorious white swan. While the expression retains its human applications, it is also used for an inanimate object that is initially thought to be worthless but later proves to be a windfall. This figurative use of the phrase was illustrated by W. O. Douglas, as cited in *Webster's Third*:

> From the beginning Alaska was treated pretty much as our ugly duckling.

[my] Venus turns out a whelp—An expression formerly used on experiencing a reversal of expectations, a failure instead of the anticipated success. The expression comes from dice: the highest roll, three sixes, was called a *Venus*; the lowest, three aces, a *canis* (dog). The aptness was

MAN BITES DOG

reinforced by the association of *Venus* with beauty and divinity, and of *whelp* with cur and mongrel.

REWARD
See also PAYMENT

catch the gold ring—To gain a prize or a bonus; to win a premium as the result of a gamble; also *catch the brass ring*. Merry-go-rounds and carousels offer free rides to those who are willing to gamble and try to grab a gold ring, which usually sits in a slot at shoulder height about two feet outside the revolving platform.

> The thing with kids is, if they want to grab for the gold ring, you have to let them do it, and not say anything. If they fall off, they fall off … (J. D. Salinger, *The Catcher in the Rye*, 1951)

The origin of the expression dates back to the days of jousting when participants at tournaments would try to pick off a small ring on the points of their lances, thus *winning the ring*. Those who were successful in a *ride at the ring* or a *run at the ring* were allowed to carry off the prize.

> After which they ran at the Ring, and the Marquis de la Chastre got the prize. (*The London Gazette*, 1686)

wooden spoon—A booby prize; a consolation prize; the lowest on a list. This expression originated with the practice of awarding a *wooden spoon* to the student who finished last on the mathematics tripos test at Cambridge University, the tripos list being a ranking of those who qualified for mathematical honors. Also a *wooden spoon* was originally presented to the person who received the last appointment in the Junior Exhibition at Yale University; more recently it has been presented to the most popular student in the class. Since originally the last person on the list received the *wooden spoon*, the term has assumed a figurative meaning of booby prize in both America and England.

> The international matches … have now all been played … Ireland, who won the championship last year … have only 1 point and take the "wooden spoon." (*Westminster Gazette*, March 19, 1900)

RIDICULE
SEE INSULT

RISK
SEE DANGER; VULNERABILITY

RUINATION
SEE DOWNFALL

SAMENESS
SEE EQUIVALENCE

SANCTION
SEE AUTHORITATIVENESS

SCOLDING
SEE REPRIMAND

SECRECY
See also SILENCE

behind the scenes—In private; not in public; behind what the ordinary spectators see; in a position to see the hidden or secret functioning. The allusion in this phrase is to the business that occurs backstage at a theater, so important in creating many of the illusions of the drama for the audience. The term has been used metaphorically since the mid 17th century.

> I . . . have been behind the scenes, both of pleasure and business. (Lord Chesterfield, *Letters*, February 18, 1748)

between you and me and the bed-post—In secrecy; between ourselves only. This expression, often an indication that a bit of choice gossip is about to be exchanged, has been in use since at least 1832. Common to both the United States and Great Britain, the term is used also when advising a friend of some impending business deal where some fast money can be made.

> Between you and me and the bedpost—as the old ladies say—I don't want Jack to have her. (R.D. Blackmore, *Christowell*, 1882)

Many variations exist: *between you and me and the gatepost, between you and me and the doorpost, between you and me and the lamppost,* and *between you and me and the barn.*

> Between you and I and the barn, as we say out west, I am no friend of such folks as these over here. (Oliver Optic, *In Doors and Out*, 1876)

button [one's] lip—To keep quiet or silent; to keep a secret; also *button up* and *button up [one's] face* or *lip.* The expression has been in use since 1868.

close as a Kentish oyster—Close-mouthed; tight- lipped; secretive; difficult to get information from. The reference here is to the superior quality generally attributed to oysters from Kent. Since the best oysters are those that are tightly sealed, one who is *close as a Kentish oyster* is one who can be trusted with any secret.

huggermugger—Covert or clandestine behavior, secrecy, furtiveness; confusion or disarray. This expression, possibly derived from the Middle English *mokeren* 'to conceal,' appeared in Shakespeare's *Hamlet* regarding the manner of Polonius' burial:

> And we have done but greenly
> In hugger mugger to inter him. (IV,v)

Although the expression maintains its furtive connotation, *huggermugger* now more frequently carries the meaning of jumbled confusion or disorganization, a meaning it assumed because clandestine activity is often hurried and haphazard.

> You find matters . . . so clumsily set out, that you fare in the style called hugger-mugger. (William Jerdan, *Autobiography*, 1853)

in petto—Undisclosed, kept secret; private, in one's own thoughts or contemplation. This expression is Italian for 'in the breast.' Citations dating from the 17th century indicate that *in petto* is applied almost exclusively to affairs of church or state.

> There are seven cardinals still remaining in petto, whose names the Pope keeps secret. (*London Gazette*, 1712)

little pitchers have big ears—An exhortation or reminder to guard one's tongue because children may overhear words not intended for their ears. The handle of a pitcher is sometimes called its *ear*. Thus, *pitchers have ears* is a pun on *ears*, and is analogous in meaning to *walls have ears*. This expression appeared in print by the mid 1500s; the later addition of *little* limits the kind of listeners to children.

> Surely Miss Gray, knowing that little pitchers have ears, would have corrected the mistake. (Sarah Tytler, *Buried Diamonds*, 1886)

mum's the word—Remain silent; do not breathe a word of what was just said. Shakespeare conveyed this meaning in *Henry VI, Part II*:

> Seal up your lips, and give no word but—mum. (I,ii)

This expression may have derived from the *m-* sound, which can be produced only with closed lips. The phrase is particularly commonplace in Great Britain.

> As to Cornwall, . . . between you and me, Mrs. Harper, mum's the word. (Dinah Mulock, *Agatha's Husband*, 1852)

on the q.t.—Secretly, surreptitiously, covertly, clandestinely, on the sly. *Q.t.* is simply an abbreviation of the word *quiet* in the original expression *on the quiet*.

> It will be possible to have one spree on the strict q.t. (George Moore, *A Mummer's Wife*, 1884)

skeleton in the closet—A family secret or scandal kept concealed to avoid public shame and disgrace; any confidential matter which, if revealed, could be a source of embarrassment, humiliation, or abasement. Though popularized in the writings of William Thackeray (1811–63), *skeleton in the closet* is reputedly based on an earlier legend that tells of a search for a truly happy person, one free from cares and woes. After such a person had apparently been found, she opened a closet and exposed a human skeleton. "I try to keep my troubles to myself," she explained, "but every night my husband compels me to kiss that skeleton." The skeleton, it seems, was that of a former paramour whom her husband had killed.

> Some particulars regarding the Newcome family . . . will show us that they have a skeleton or two in their closets. (William Thackeray, *The Newcomes*, 1855)

A British variation is *skeleton in the cupboard*.

sub rosa—Latin for "under the rose"—in secret, privately, confidentially. Attempts have been made to trace the origin of this phrase to classical times; however, the *OED* states that it has Germanic origins. In Germany, and later in England and Holland, it was a common practice to paint or sculpture roses on the ceilings of banquet halls. The rose was a symbol reminding the revelers to watch their words. The phrase appeared in print by the mid 16th century. The English version *under the rose* is also heard.

> Being all under the Rose they had privilege to speak all things with freedom. (James Howell, *Parables Reflecting Upon the Times*, 1643)

under [one's] hat—Secret, private, confidential; between you, me, and the lamppost; usually *keep something under [one's] hat*.

> I'd be very grateful . . . if you'd keep the whole affair under your hat. (N. Marsh, *Dead Water*, 1963)

Although the exact origin of this expression is not known, perhaps at one time the space under a person's hat was literally used to conceal things. Use of the phrase dates from the late 19th century.

walls have ears—An admonition to be discreet in speech, implying that privacy is never certain and that no one is to be trusted. The expression is often linked with the so-called *auriculaires* of the Louvre Palace, tubes within the walls by means of which Catherine de Médicis reputedly learned of state secrets. There is no evidence, however, that the phrase actually owes its origin to these contrivances. A variant is *even the walls have ears*.

SELF-RELIANCE

carry a message to Garcia—To accomplish one's assigned task in an independent, resourceful, self-sufficient manner; to do one's job without making a fuss. This Americanism alludes to Elbert Hubbard's article "A Message to Garcia," written during the Spanish-American War. The piece addressed itself to the inability of most people to act without quibbling and procrastinating, citing Major Andrew S. Rowan of the U.S. Army as an exemplary model for his behavior in carrying out the order to find and deliver a message to the Cuban General Garcia. The expression was popular in the early part of this century but is now less frequently heard.

What you have to do, young man, is to carry a message to Garcia. That's your task. You go back to the Research Laboratory and do it! (*American Mercury*, July 1924)

A common variant is *take a message to Garcia.*

cottage industry—A business which is partly or wholly carried out in the home, often based upon the family unit as a labor force. The connection between *cottage* and home and family is self-evident.

For generations now the sewing of gloves has been conducted largely as a cottage industry. (B. Ellis, *Gloves,* 1921)

do off [one's] bat—To accomplish by one's own efforts; to make by oneself, independently. This Briticism is another of the many terms adopted from cricket. The allusion is to the score a player makes from his own hits. The expression dates from the 1840s.

You make, I suppose, ten pounds a night off your own bat. (George Bernard Shaw, *Misalliance,* 1910)

Two related terms, derived from Cockney rhyming slang for *on [one's] own,* are: *on [one's] Pat Malone* reduced to *on [one's] pat;* and *on [one's] Tod Sloan,* reduced to *on [one's] tod,* the latter derived from the name of a famous English jockey.

every tub must stand on its own bottom—Every man for himself, everyone must take care of himself, everyone must paddle his own canoe; sometimes *every tub on its own black bottom.* The *tub* of this expression may mean a vat or cask, or a slow, clumsy ship. *Bottom* may mean either the underside of a barrel or cask or of a ship. Depending on which of these alternative senses one chooses a case can be made for either a nautical or a more general origin for this phrase. Either way the expression is said to have first become popular among southern Blacks before being adopted and reassigned by Black jazzmen to describe complete improvisation. The phrase dates from the early 18th century. Another similar expression is *stand on one's own bottom* 'to be independent, to act on one's own or for oneself,' dating from the early 17th century.

hoe [one's] own row—To make one's own way, to do one's own work, to be independent, to take care of oneself. This self-evident American expression dates from the first half of the 19th century.

Our American pretender must, to adopt an agricultural phrase, "hoe his own row," ... without the aid of protectors or dependents. (*The Knickerbocker,* 1841)

paddle [one's] own canoe—To shift for oneself, to be self-reliant, to handle one's own affairs, to manage independently. This expression, which dates from at least 1828, appeared in a bit of doggerel published in *Harper's Magazine* in May 1854. The first stanza is as follows:

Voyager upon life's sea,
To yourself be true,
And, whate'er your lot may be,
Paddle your own canoe.

It is sometimes facetiously rendered as *Pas de lieu Rhône que nous,* in macaronic French.

pull oneself up by [one's] own boot straps—To better oneself by one's own efforts and resources; to improve one's status without outside help; to start at the bottom and work one's way up. A *bootstrap* is a loop sewn on the side of a boot to help in pulling it on. The expression is a jocular reference to the impossibility of hoisting oneself into the air, even by dint of the mightiest effort.

> I had no money, I could have got some by writing to my family, of course, but it had to be the bootstraps or nothing. (Doris Lessing, *In Pursuit of English,* 1960)

Also current are the variants *lift* or *raise oneself up by [one's] own bootstraps.*

> A poet who lifted himself by his own boot-straps from an obscure versifier to the ranks of real poetry . . . (Kunitz and Haycraft, *British Authors of the 19th Century,* 1922)

rowing crosshanded—Self-reliant; independent; by oneself; without assistance. This Canadian Maritime expression, which has been adopted in parts of eastern Maine, is traced to a 19th-century practice of rowing crosshanded when one rowed his boat alone. In time *crosshanded* came to signify the ability to accomplish something independently, as *Century Magazine* (September 1882) cites in the case of the self-sufficient wives of Nova Scotia.

> The gaunt women bring their stuff to trade at the village stores, rowing crosshanded.

scratch for [one]self—To take care of oneself, to be self-reliant; to look out for one's own best interests. This American colloquialism appeared in print by the mid 19th century.

> Shaking off the other child, [she] told him to scratch for hisself a time, while she began to prepare the supper. (Alice Cary, *Married, not Mated,* 1856)

Scratch for [one]self is infrequently heard today.

SELF-SUFFICIENCY
SEE SELF-RELIANCE

SELLING

under the hammer—Put up for sale at auction. In this expression, dating from the early 1700s, *hammer* refers to the small wooden mallet that an auctioneer raps to indicate an item has been sold.

> He threatened . . . to sell the house under the hammer. (Charles Reade, *It Is Never Too Late to Mend*, 1856)

An earlier form, *under the spear*, arose from the Roman custom of thrusting a spear into the ground to indicate a sale was closed.

> Their houses and fine Gardens are given away,
> And all their goods, under the spear.
> (Ben Jonson, *Catiline*, 1611)

SEMBLANCE
SEE PRETENSE

SERVILITY
SEE OBSEQUIOUSNESS

SHOWINESS
SEE OSTENTATIOUSNESS

SHREWDNESS
SEE PERCEPTIVENESS

SICKNESS
SEE ILL HEALTH

SILENCE
See also SECRECY

lose [one's] tongue—To lose temporarily the power of speech, to be struck dumb. Such speechlessness is usually attributed to emotions such as shyness, fear, or surprise.

mumchance—A person who is silent and glum; one who has nothing to say; a dummy; one who sits mute. In early 16th-century England the silence which was required in a dicing game called *mumchance* led to the coining of the proverb *don't sit there like mumchance who was hanged for saying nothing.* By the 1550s the term had been transferred to the stage to refer to one who acts in a dumb show. The term remains current for one who is silent.

> What an unreasonable thing 'tis to make me stand like mumchance at such a time as this. (Author Unknown, *Terence Made English*, 1694)

The origin of *mumchance* can be traced to *mum*, ultimately from Dutch *mommen* 'to act the part of a mummer; to act in pantomime' combined with *chance*, referring to dice as a game of chance. It appears elsewhere in

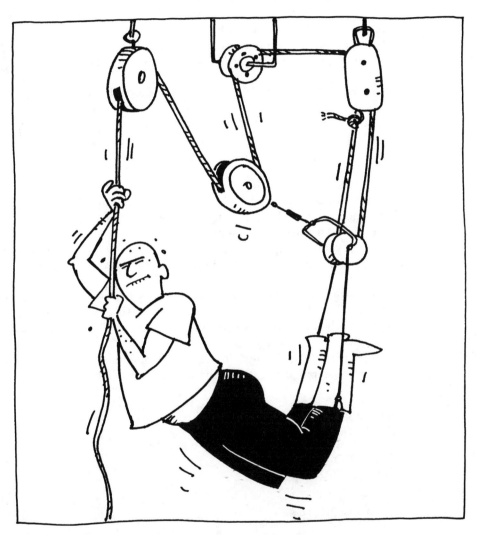

PULL ONESELF UP BY ONE'S OWN BOOTSTRAPS

Modern English as *to keep mum* 'to be silent' and *mum's the word* 'silence is the order of the day.'

pipe down—To become quiet or mute; to cease talking. In this expression, *pipe* may carry any of its numerous sound-related meanings, ranging from a shrill noise to the vocal cords themselves. In contemporary usage, the phrase is most often imperative.

> "Pipe down," replied the husband. "What do you expect for a $10 paint job, grand opera?" (*Kansas City Star*, March 1932)

put a sock in it—Be quiet; shut up; pipe down; to become quiet; to cease talking. The allusion in this Briticism is to stuffing a sock in one's mouth to act as a gag. It is usually used as an exclamation.

> "Oh, put a sock in it!" she invited him scornfully. (R. C. Ashby, *The Plot Against the Widow*, 1932)

see a wolf—To lose one's voice temporarily, to become tongue-tied. The phrase expresses the old belief that if a man saw a wolf before the wolf saw him, the man would temporarily lose the power of speech. The expression dates from the late 16th century.

> Our young companion has seen a wolf, ... and has lost his tongue in consequence. (Sir Walter Scott, *Quentin Durward*, 1823)

you could hear a pin drop—Extremely quiet; said of a state of utter silence. This phrase, in use since the early 19th century, is obvious in its allusion. The French equivalent is *on aurait entendu voler une mouche*, 'one could have heard a fly take wing.'

> Sheridan was listened to with such attention that you might have heard a pin drop. (Samuel Rogers, *Table Talk*, 1855)

SILLINESS
SEE FATUOUSNESS

SIMILARITY
SEE EQUIVALENCE

SINCERITY
SEE CANDIDNESS

SKEPTICISM
SEE SUSPICIOUSNESS

SNOBBISHNESS
SEE HAUGHTINESS

SOLICITATION
SEE PAYMENT

SPONTANEITY

off the cuff—Extempore, on the spur of the moment, spontaneously, impromptu; offhandedly, informally, unofficially. The allusion is to speakers whose only preparation is notes jotted on their shirt cuffs. Of U.S. origin, this expression dates from at least 1938.

> In that scene, shot off the cuff in a shockingly bad light, there leapt out of the screen...something of the real human guts and dignity. (*Penguin New Writing*, 1944)

off the top of [one's] head—Offhandedly, unofficially, informally, without notes or preparation, extemporaneously. In this expression, *the top of the head* represents the superficial nature of the information being given. *Webster's Third* cites Goodman Ace's use of the expression:

> Countless conferences at which everyone talked off the top of their heads.

on the spur of the moment—Impulsively, impetuously; spontaneously, extemporaneously; suddenly, without deliberation. In this expression, *spur* implies speed, alluding to the sharp, U-shaped device strapped to the heel of a boot and used by a rider to prod a horse.

> A speaker who gives us a ready reply upon the spur of the moment. (Robert Blakely, *Freewill*, 1831)

wing it—To undertake anything without adequate preparation, usually with connotations of bluffing one's way through. The term originated in the theater, with reference to actors who would go on stage without knowing their lines, relying on the prompters in the wings to get them through. This literal usage appears as early as 1886 in *Stage Gossip*.

STARTING
See also INITIATION

get a move on—To get going, to proceed; to move speedily or efficiently. This original U.S. expression dates from the late 1800s.

> Come on! Come on!...Get a move on! Will you hurry up! (C. E. Mulford, *Bar-20 Days*, 1911)

A more picturesque variant is the American slang *get a wiggle on*, current since the turn of the century. This expression plays on the image of one's posture while running or walking quickly, a more defined image than tha. conjured up by the word *move* in the former expression.

get cracking—To get moving, to get started on; to hustle, hurry. Although the origin of this slang expression is unknown, it may be related to a relatively uncommon meaning of *crack* 'to move or travel speedily, to whip along,' which dates from the early 19th century. The phrase *get cracking* itself, however, appears to be of fairly recent origin.

> Come on, let's get cracking, we're late now. (S. Gibbons, *Matchmaker*, 1949)

get on the stick—To get on the ball, to get started or going, to get a move on. Although the meaning of *stick* in the expression is not clear, the phrase nevertheless enjoys widespread popularity. It is often used as an imperative.

get the show on the road—To get any undertaking under way, but most often to start off on a trip of some kind; to hit the road; usually used in reference to a group of people and their belongings. This expression probably derives from traveling shows, such as theatrical troupes, circuses, etc., which regularly toured the countryside giving performances along the way.

let her go, Gallagher!—Let's go; let's get started without delay. The *Gallagher* to whom this advice is given may be one or none of the legendary people cited in various folklore explanations. He may have been a cab driver in Australia, a hangman in Galveston (Texas), a warden in St. Louis, the owner of a broken-down nag (horse) in Texas, a streetcar operator in New Orleans, St. Louis, Chicago, Galveston, or Camden, New Jersey; or any of an almost endless list of folk heroes named Gallagher. Most likely, *Gallagher* was chosen because it is close in sound to *let 'er go*. In spite of the amorphous nature of this *Gallagher*, the expression has enjoyed international popularity for more than a hundred years.

pull [one's] socks up—To get on the stick or on the ball, to get a move on, to shape up, to show more stuff. This British colloquialism apparently had the earlier sense of bracing oneself for an effort, probably in reference to the way runners pull up their socks before starting off on a race. Or the expression may simply refer to making oneself presentable in appearance.

put [one's] hand to the plow—To undertake a task, to get down to business; to embark on a course of action.

> It was time . . . to set his hand to the plow in good earnest. (George Hickes and Robert Nelson, *Memoirs of the Life of John Kettlewell*, 1718)

The allusion is to Jesus' admonishment of a man who said he would follow Him but only after bidding his family farewell.

And Jesus said unto him, No man, having put his hand to the plough, and looking back, is fit for the kingdom of God. (Luke 9:62)

shake a leg—To get a move on, to get going, to hurry up; to dance. This expression meaning to 'dance' dates from the 17th century. Currently, the other meanings are more common.

> ... if you shake a leg and somebody doesn't get in ahead of you ... (John Dos Passos, cited in *Webster's Third*)

step on the gas—To speed up; also, *step on it*. This expression alludes to the speeding up of a car by depressing the accelerator. The phrase enjoys widespread use in the United States and Great Britain.

> Jazz it up. Keep moving. Step on the gas. (Aldous Huxley, *Jesting Pilate*, 1926)

The phrase is often used imperatively, directing a slothful or sluggish performer to increase his pace.

stir [one's] stumps—To get a move on, to get into action; to shake a leg. In this expression, *stumps* alludes to the legs, or to the wooden prosthetic attachment fastened to a stump or mangled limb. Use of this rather indelicate phrase has declined since the 19th century.

> Come, why don't you stir your stumps? I suppose I must wait on myself. (Baron Edward Lytton, *Ernest Maltravers*, 1837)

STATUS

above the salt—Among the distinguished or honored guests at a dinner; of high rank, important. Formerly a large saltcellar, i.e., a saltshaker or salt mill, was customarily placed in the middle of dining tables. The higher-ranking guests were seated at the upper or master's end of the table, *above the salt*, while those of lesser rank were seated at the lower end of the table, *below the salt*. The phrase has been in use since the late 16th century.

> Though of Tory sentiments, she by no means approved of those feudal times when the chaplain was placed below the salt. (James Payn, *The Luck of the Darrells*, 1885)

bacon and rice aristocracy—Well-to-do, but boorish landowners; uncouth, prosperous farmers; nouveau riche. This disparaging term from the mid 1800s is seldom heard today. Once popular, especially among the landowners of the South, the term originally signified anyone who had made his money through the production or distribution of the commodities pork or rice. Shortly after the phrase's inception, it took on a pejorative sense which it has retained, perhaps as the traditionally wealthy looked with disdain upon those with commercially acquired riches.

Thomas Smith bought his brother's lot, and remained in Charleston, S.C. to build up the 'bacon and rice aristocracy.' (Elizabeth Poyas, *A Peep into the Past*, 1853)

blueblood—An aristocrat or noble; a thoroughbred. Fair-skinned Spaniards prided themselves on their pure stock, without Moorish or Jewish admixture. Their extremely light complexions revealed a bluish cast to their veins, which they consequently believed carried blue blood, as opposed to the supposed black blood of Moors and Jews.

born to the purple—Of royal or exalted birth. Purple has long been associated with royalty because of its former scarcity and consequent costliness. It was obtainable only by processing huge quantities of a certain mollusk, which was harvested at Tyre, an ancient seaport of Phoenicia, and was called Tyrian purple. *Born in the purple* is a literal translation of *Porphyrogenitus*, a surname of the Byzantine Emperor Constantine VII (905–959) and his successors, most accurately applied only to those born during their father's reign; it was customary for the Empress to undergo childbirth in a room whose walls were lined with purple—possibly porphyry. Today *born to the purple* is more commonly heard.

born with a silver spoon in [one's] mouth—Born to wealth and high station. It was formerly customary for godparents to give spoons as christening gifts. The child born to wealth could anticipate a silver one from the moment of his birth.

born within the sound of Bow bells—A British expression denoting a Londoner, especially of the lower classes; a native of the East End district; a Cockney. The church of St. Mary-le-Bow, so called because of the bows or arches that supported its steeple, was known for the peal of its bells, which could be heard throughout the city. The phrase has been used to denote a Cockney since the early 17th century.

Brahmin—A person from a long-established, highy cultured family, especially one from an old New England family; a member of an aristocratic social class. The allusion in this term is to the priestly, or the highest, caste in Hinduism. Oliver Wendell Holmes is credited with the birth of the expression in his novel *Elsie Venner* (1861):

> That is exactly what the young man is. He comes of the Brahmin caste of New England. This is harmless, inoffensive, untitled aristocracy to which I have referred, and which I am sure you will at once acknowledge.

In modern use, the word is most commonly heard satirically as a synonym for a supercilious intellectual or a snob.

He took delight, too, in shocking his Brahmin relatives, who belong to one of the oldest and richest families in Massachusetts. (*American Weekly*, November 2, 1947)

brown-bagger—A person of inferior status or social standing. In the United States, the term derives from the practice of the less affluent, to carry their lunches in brown paper bags. In Britain, a *brown-bagger* is a nonresident student at public school or university; his brown bag is the attaché case in which he carries his books. Such students are usually looked upon with a degree of disdain or condescension by those in residence.

bush league—Of inferior status; mediocre; second-rate; unprofessional; unsophisticated. This American expression arose about 1900, roughly the time that major league baseball teams began to subsidize the minor leagues. Since most minor league teams were in small cities and towns, they became associated with the *bush*, i.e., the backwoods and rural areas of America. Hence, these so-called *bush leagues* represented a lower level of baseball than the major leagues. The transition into everyday speech as a synonym for second-rate, or unsophisticated, followed shortly thereafter. The frequently used noun form is *bush leaguer*.

You may think Sherlock Holmes was pretty good, but he is just a bush leaguer compared to the modern detective. (*Chicago Daily News*, June 27, 1945)

codfish aristocracy—A disparaging appellation for the nouveau riche, originally those Massachusetts aristocrats who made their money from the codfishing industry; also *the codfish gentility*. This expression, which dates from 1849, was the title of a poem written in the 1920s by American journalist Wallace Irwin. The first stanza reads as follows:

Of all the fish that swim or swish
In ocean's deep autocracy,
There's none possess such haughtiness
As the codfish aristocracy.

country club set—A disparaging term for the fashion-conscious, affluent social group who often consider themselves the elite of a community.

the Four Hundred—The social elite; the wealthy, refined people generally regarded as "high society." This term dates from 1889 when Ward McAllister, a prominent New York socialite, was given the task of deciding who should be invited to a centenary celebration of the inauguration of George Washington. His list included the names of four hundred people whom he considered to be the true elite, the crème de la crème, as it were. The list received rapid acceptance and the term *the Four Hundred* became an overnight sensation and came to be established in the language.

To social strivers she is the Queen of the 400. (*Coronet*, August 1948)

In 1904 Mrs. William Astor, grande dame of New York society, increased the number of the class to 800, but *the Eight Hundred* has never gained great currency.

gallery gods—Those members of a theater audience occupying the highest, and therefore the cheapest, seats; those persons sitting in the balcony or gallery of a theater. The *OED* attributes this expression to the fact that persons occupying gallery seats are on high, as are the gods. However, another source credits the painting on the ceiling over the gallery in London's Drury Lane Theatre as the inspiration for this expression. The ceiling in question is painted to resemble a cloudy blue sky peopled by numerous flying cupids. Thus, it is in reference to the cupids painted on the ceiling above their heads that persons sitting in the gallery first became known as *gods* or *gallery gods*. The term dates from the latter half of the 18th century.

gentleman of the four outs—A man without manners, wit, money, or credit—the four marks of a true gentleman. This subtle expression used by Englishmen to denote an upstart has been in use at least since the late 18th century. Sometimes the expression varies according to whether the "essentials" are considered more or less than four in number.

> A gentleman of three outs—"out of pocket, out of elbows, and out of credit." (Edward Lytton, *Paul Clifford*, 1830)

grass roots—The common people, the working class; the rank and file of a political party; the voters. At the beginning of this century the term was used to mean 'source or origin,' the fundamental or basic level of anything. This figurative extension of literal *grass roots* later acquired the political dimension denoting the people of rural or agricultural sections of the country as a factional, economic, or social group. Finally, *grass roots* was extended to include not just farmers and inhabitants of rural areas but the common people in general, or the rank and file of a political party or social organization.

> "No crisis so grave has confronted our people" since the Civil War, Mr. Lowden told the grassroots convention at Springfield. (*Nation*, June 1935)

the great unwashed—The general public, the masses; hoi polloi. Although its coinage has been attributed to Edmund Burke (1729–97), this phrase has been in print only since the early 19th century.

> Gentlemen, there can be but little doubt that your ancestors were the Great Unwashed. (William Makepeace Thackeray, *The History of Pendennis*, 1850)

hoi polloi—The many; the common people; the masses. This expression, taken directly from the Greek, translates literally as 'the many.' Language purists disdain its use as *the hoi-polloi*, literally 'the the many.' However, such distinguished writers as Lord Byron and John Dryden rendered it that way. Its literal connotation has disappeared almost completely, and, in today's usage, the term conveys condescension on the part of the speaker.

Hoi-polloi trampled, hustled, and crowded him. (O. Henry, *Brickdust Row*, 1907)

in the van—In the foremost position in an army or fleet; in the lead; in the forefront of a movement. This phrase is derived from an old military term, *vanguard* or *van*, which designates those troops who are in advance of the main body of the army. Both terms are adaptations of the French *avant-garde*, which translates literally 'before the guard'; however, *avant-garde* has been adopted directly into English, and today usually connotes those young artists, painters, writers, composers who lead the way in experimenting in the fine arts. The phrase, *in the van*, in use since the early 17th century, is seldom heard today in its literal sense.

God and Nature together shaped him to lead in the van,
In the stress of the wildest weather, when the nation needed a man.
(Margaret Sangster, *Abraham Lincoln*)

knight bachelor—The title of a knight who does not belong to one of the special orders; a knight of the lowest order. The *knight bachelor* is a gentleman who has been awarded a nonhereditary title by the monarch. The honor carries with it a place in the Table of Preference, immediately above County Court Judge and immediately below Knight Commander of the Order of the British Empire, and the honorific *Sir*.
The term has been in use since about 1300.

knight banneret—A knight created on the battlefield. Originally a *knight banneret* ranked above other knights and enjoyed the privilege of being allowed to bring his company of vassals onto the battlefield under his own banner. He ranked just below a baron. Eventually the term came to designate any knight who had had his knighthood conferred upon the battlefield for deeds of bravery. Apparently the first such conferring of the honor was to Sir John de Copeland, who captured King David Bruce at Neville's Cross in 1346. When the first baronets were established in 1611, the order of *knight banneret* was allowed to lapse into extinction.
A variant is *knight of the square flag*.

low man on the totem pole—The lowest in rank, the least important or experienced person; a neophyte. A *totem pole* is a tree trunk with symbolic carvings or paintings one above the other. North American Indians placed such poles in front of their homes. The apparent hierarchical arrangement of the symbols may have given rise to the current meaning of *totem pole*, which retains only the idea of 'hierarchy.' Thus, the *low man on the totem pole* refers to one who is at the bottom in the ordering of rank. Its popularity is undoubtedly partly owing to a comic novel, *Low Man on the Totem Pole*, by humorist H. Allen Smith. The following citation from *Webster's Third* shows the corresponding use of a variant phrase for one of superior rank:

... entertain top men on the political totem pole. (Mary Thayer)

pecking order—Hierarchy; the levels of authority within a group of people or an organization; one's relative degree of predominance, aggressiveness, or power in comparison to others. This expression alludes to dominance hierarchy—a zoological term for the instinctive vertical ranking among birds and social mammals, in which the stronger animals assert their dominance over the smaller, weaker ones. Among domestic fowl, particularly chickens, the hierarchy is virtually uncontested; thus, the bird highest on the barnyard totem pole can peck at the dominated without worry of retaliation. Hence, avian dominance hierarchy came to be known as *pecking order* and, by extension, *pecking order* developed its figurative application to the hierarchy of authority and domination in human affairs.

prole—A member of the proletariat; one of the poorest class of working people who only serve the state by their labor and by producing children; one who, being without property or capital, relies on his personal labor for a living. This British slang term was coined during the mid 1800s, but did not gain common use until its use, in 1949, in George Orwell's futuristic novel, *1984*, which depicted 85?% of the population as consisting of proles.

American "class" behavior may be even more complicated than Mr. Fussell gives it credit for being, what with low proles sometimes engaging in upper behavior and vice versa all along the scale. (Christopher Lehmann-Haupt, *The New York Times*, November 18, 1983)

ragtag and bobtail—The rabble, the riffraff, the masses; also, everyone collectively, the whole lot, every man Jack, every Tom, Dick, and Harry. The term, of British origin, was originally *tag*, then *tag and rag*; later the two words were reversed; still later the addition of *bobtail* (credited by some to Samuel Pepys) completed the term as we know it. Its component words all relate to worthless shreds, tatters, remnants, etc. The expression is sometimes extended to indicate comprehensiveness—every last one—as it was in this passage from T. A. Trollope's *What I Remember* (1887):

He shall have them all, rag, tag, and bobtail.

the rank and file—The general membership of an organization, as distinct from its leaders or officers; the lower echelons; the common people in general, hoi polloi. The origin of the term is military, *rank and file* being used to denote common soldiers (privates and corporals as opposed to commissioned officers) since the 18th century; for these were the men commonly required to line up in such formation: *rank* 'a number of soldiers drawn up in line abreast'; *file* 'the number of men constituting the depth from front to rear of a formation in line' (*OED*). By the 19th century the term was popular in government and political circles, as it still is today.

> One of the mere rank and file of the party. (John Stuart Mill, *Considerations on Representative Government*, 1860)

run-of-the-mill—Average, common, routine; mediocre, ordinary, no great shakes. This commonly used adjective is derived from its application to lots of manufactured goods which have not been inspected and consequently not sorted and graded for quality. By extension the term describes persons lacking in originality or individuality, those who through blandness blend in with the masses.

salt of the earth—A person or group of persons epitomizing the best, most noble, and most admirable elements of society; a paragon; the wealthy aristocracy. For centuries, salt has been used in religious ceremonies as a symbol of goodness, purity, and incorruptibility. Thus, it was praise of the highest order when, after preaching the Beatitudes at the Sermon on the Mount, Christ called His disciples the "salt of the earth."

> You are the salt of the earth; but if salt has lost its taste, how shall its saltness be restored? It is no longer good for anything except to be thrown out and trodden underfoot by men. (Matthew 5:13)

top billing—Stardom; a phrase describing the most prominent or important in a group of persons, events, etc. In theater advertisements and billboards, *billing* is the relative position in which a person or act is listed. *Top billing,* then, is the most prominent position, usually above the name of the play, and is reserved for an actor or actress who has attained stardom, one whose name is readily recognized by the public.

> He made his Broadway debut as Lancelot in Camelot, with billing below the title; now, he is returning to Broadway, with top billing. (*Globe & Mail* [Toronto], January 13, 1968)

Although still most commonly used in reference to the theater, the scope of *top billing* has been expanded to include application in other contexts as well.

to the manner born—Destined by birth to observe certain patterns of behavior, usually those associated with good breeding and high social status; also, innately or peculiarly suited for a particular position. This latter use is becoming increasingly common. One *to the manner born* is a natural with an instinctive ability in a given area. The former meaning is still the more accurate, however. Shakespeare's Hamlet gave us the expression when he criticized Claudius' and Denmark's drinking customs:

> But to my mind, though I am native here
> And to the manner born, it is a custom
> More honored in the breach than the observance.

Status

upper crust—The highest social stratum; the wealthy; the aristocracy. This expression originated from the former custom of serving the upper crust of a loaf of bread to the most distinguished guests. As used today, the phrase often carries a suggestion of snobbery.

> He took a fashionable house and hobnobbed lavishly with Washington's tight-ringed upper crust. (*Newsweek*, July 1946)

STUPIDITY
SEE FATUOUSNESS; IGNORANCE; NONSENCE

Submission

SUBMISSION
See also RESIGNATION

acknowledge the corn—To admit or confess to the truth about a matter; to acknowledge losing an argument; to concede one has made a mistake.

> The *Evening Mirror* very naively comes out and acknowledges the corn. (*New York Herald*, June 27, 1846)

This expression, of American origin, dates from the early 19th century. Its first recorded use appears in a Congressional exchange between two members on the floor of the House of Representatives in 1828.

cry barley—To call or cry out for a truce, especially in children's games; to wave the white flag, to surrender. This Scottish and Northern English dialectal expression, which has been in use since the early 19th century, is thought to be a corruption of *parley*.

cry uncle—To admit defeat, to surrender, to give up; also *say uncle*. Although the precise origin of this expression is unknown, an often repeated story claims that an early Roman, finding himself in trouble, cried out *patrue mi patruissime* 'uncle, my best of uncles.' The phrase first appeared in print early in this century.

draw in [one's] horns—To retract an opinion or take a less belligerent stand; to restrain oneself, to hold or pull back; to repress one's feelings of pride, righteousness, or pretension. In use since the 14th century, this expression alludes to the snail's habit of pulling in its tentacles when disturbed.

knuckle under—To submit or yield, to give in, to acknowledge defeat. The origin of this expression has been linked to the obsolete *knuckle* 'knee joint'; hence *knuckle under*, meaning to 'bend the knee before, to bow down to.'

> They must all knuckle under to him. (Mary E. Braddon, *Mount Royal*, 1882)

A similar expression with the same meaning is *knock under*, an abbreviated form of the obsolete *knock under board* or *under the table*. Rapping against the underside of a table with the knuckles was apparently once a sign of submission or defeat as illustrated by the following citation:

> He that flinches his glass, and to drink is not able,
> Let him quarrel no more, but knock under the table.
> (*Gentleman's Journal*, March 1691)

pass under the yoke—To make a humiliating submission; to be forced to acknowledge one's defeat humbly. In ancient Rome vanquished enemies were forced to pass under an arch formed by two spears placed upright in the ground, with a third resting on them. This was a symbol of the even older practice of placing a yoke on the neck of a captive. The expression is little heard today, although *yoke* is often used figuratively for 'servitude, restraint, or humiliation.'

> Jugurtha grants the Romans life and liberty but upon condition that they should pass under the yoke. (John Ozell, tr., *Aubert de Vertot's History of the Revolutions*, 1720)

raise the white flag—To surrender, to indicate one's willingness to make peace; to ask for a truce, to declare an end to hostilities. A white flag, also called the flag of truce, has been the symbol of submission for centuries, perhaps because of its associations with cowardice, or with innocence and goodness.

strike [one's] colors—To lower one's flag as a sign of submission or as a salute; to surrender. This expression is derived from the nautical use of the verb *strike* 'lower,' as in "a ship strikes sail." A related term is *strike [one's] flag*.

strike sail—To acknowledge defeat; to surrender; to eat humble pie; to defer or pay respect to. It was long a naval custom for a defeated ship to *strike* 'lower' its sails or flag as a sign of surrender or submission. Also, friendly ships, upon meeting each other at sea, often lowered their topsails to halfmast as a salute and sign of respect. In the following quotation from Shakespeare's *Henry VI, Part III*, Queen Margaret of England is responding to a request by King Lewis of France that she join him at the royal dinner table.

> No, mighty King of France. Now Margaret
> Must strike her sail and learn a while to serve
> Where kings command.
> (III,iii)

throw in [one's] hand—To give up, to drop out of the proceedings, to cease work on a project. This expression is derived from card games in which a player who is dealt poor cards or who realizes at some point during the game that winning is impossible has the option of turning in his *hand* 'cards' and dropping out of the game.

throw in the sponge—To admit defeat, to give up, to surrender, to say uncle. In boxing, a manager has the option of ending a fight if he determines that his contestant has no chance of winning, and is suffering unnecessary physical abuse. The manager signals his desire to stop the bout by throwing his fighter's sponge or towel into the air. This slang Americanism and the variant *throw in the towel* are used figuratively of any surrender or acknowledgment of defeat.

SUBMISSIVENESS
SEE DEFERENCE; OBSEQUIOUSNESS; SUBMISSION

SUBORDINATION
SEE STATUS

SUBSERVIENCE
SEE OBSEQUIOUSNESS

SUBSISTENCE
SEE POVERTY

SUCCESS

bring down the house—To elicit a vigorous and lengthy ovation from an audience; to be a smash or great success; sometimes *bring down the gallery*. The image created by this expression, in which *house* means 'theater' or 'playhouse,' is one of such loud, sustained applause as to bring about the collapse of the building. The phrase was in use as early as 1754.

build a better mousetrap—This famous expression was first uttered by Ralph Waldo Emerson in April 1871, in Oakland, California. The words never appeared in written form in any of his works, but a Mrs. Sarah S. B. Yule recorded them in a notebook which she was keeping of Emerson's Bay Area addresses. According to Mrs. Yule's transcription, Emerson's exact words were:

If a man can write a better book, preach a better sermon, or make a better mousetrap than his neighbor, though he builds [*sic*] his home in the woods, the world will make a beaten path to his door.

Not all people see the invention of some improved device as a benefit, however.

If a man builds a better mousetrap than his neighbor, the world will not only beat a path to his door, it will make newsreels of him and his wife in beach pajamas, it will discuss his diet and his health, it will publish heart-throb stories of his love life. (Newman Levy, "The Right to Be Let Alone," *American Mercury*, June 1935)

come down on the right side of the fence—To be on the side of the winner; to make a proper moral choice. The fence has long been a symbol of moral, legal, or political division. One may *come down on the right side of the fence*:

> They gently decided on the right side of the fence. (*Manchester Guardian*, January 28, 1891)

or *the wrong side of the fence*:

> Only be careful, be very careful, lest in the confusion
> You should shut yourself on the wrong side of the fence.
> (William Dean Howells, *Stops of Various Quills*, 1894)

Someone who *straddles the fence* tries to please those on both sides simultaneously, while someone who *sits on the fence* is guilty of vacillation; he cannot, or will not, choose on which side to come down. Each of these terms is almost always applied in political contexts, and in modern use often jocularly.

> A politician is an animal who can sit on a fence and yet keep both ears to the ground. (H.L. Mencken, *A New Dictionary of Quotations*, 1942)

have the last laugh—To prove ultimately successful after an apparent defeat; to avenge. The idea of having the last laugh is fairly literal, i.e., though others may laugh now, the butt of their humor will laugh later when, in the final analysis, he is victorious. This phrase was popularized in the 1937 song "They All Laughed," by George and Ira Gershwin:

> They all laughed at us and how!
> But Ho, Ho, Ho!
> Who's got the last laugh now?

Related, proverbial expressions are *he who laughs last laughs best*, and *he laughs best that laughs last*. The latter appeared in *The Mistake* (1706) by Sir John Vanbrugh.

land on [one's] feet—To achieve success despite predictable loss; to extricate oneself from a potentially dangerous situation; to escape failure narrowly. This popular expression usually appears in a context implying that the one who *lands on his feet* does so through undeserved luck; he repeatedly gets himself into scrapes but somehow survives. It is apparently based on the notion that one plummeting downward is unlikely to land safely, let alone feet first.

lay them in the aisles—To be a smashing success; to elicit a great emotional response from an audience. The image created by this expression is of a theatrical audience so overwhelmed by the brilliance of a production, especially a comedy, that they fall from their seats into the aisles in laughter. A common variant is *knock them in the aisles*. The term is now used figuratively of any success with the public.

> I was splendid as a public speaker and laid them in the aisles. (Westbrook Pegler, syndicated newspaper column, October 8, 1951)

maiden over—An extraordinary accomplishment; the surviving of an ordeal. This Briticism signifies a bowler's achievement in cricket. The bowler, the equivalent of a pitcher in American baseball, bowls six balls, which constitute an *over*. If he allows no runs, it is called a *maiden over* (cf. sense of *virgin* in *virgin forest*, etc.).

> Half a dozen maiden overs in succession, every ball dead on the middle stump, and yet played steadily back again to the bowler. (*Daily Telegraph*, May 16, 1864)

In a modern connotative sense the term indicates any dramatic achievement or triumph.

make [one's] jack—To make [one's] fortune; to be fortunate in an undertaking; to succeed in one's endeavors. Although it is almost exclusively American today, the roots of this slang expression probably lie in an old British slang term for a card counter, a small, metal coin-shaped object that resembled a sovereign and was used as a chip. If one accumulated enough of these *jacks*, he could amass quite a large sum of money. Furthermore, if one were underhanded and adroit enough, he could often pass these *jacks* off as sovereigns, thereby increasing his profits a hundredfold. Such a practice was probably responsible for the connotation of dishonesty that seems to accompany *make one's jack* today.

> He made plenty of jack while they were being dull boys. (Stanley Walker, "The Uncanny Knacks of Mr. Doherty," *The New Yorker*, July 12, 1941)

make the grade—To achieve success; to reach a goal; to accomplish one's desire or ambition; to come up to the proper standard. The source of this expression is uncertain. Some attribute it to a team of horses trying to reach the top of a hill; others to the grading system used in school: A, B, C, etc.; and others to the standard rating that is used in classifying things, as in *Grade A milk*. Whatever the case, the phrase has been employed as a figure of speech since the late 1920s.

> Many thousands of veterans can continue to find new opportunities and make the grade in businesses of their own. (*Great Falls Tribune*, September 27, 1948)

pan out—To succeed; to yield results, especially favorable ones; to occur. This expression alludes to panning for gold, a method of prospecting in which a shallow pan is used to scoop a small amount of gravel and sand from a stream. Any gold present settles to the bottom of the pan as the gravel and sand are washed away. *Pan out*, then, originally indicated a successful prospecting venture. As the California gold rush that spawned this expression began to subside, *pan out* became more figurative, and has remained in widespread usage since the late 19th century.

> Socialism . . . may pan out as a new kind of religion. (Sinclair Lewis, *Our Mr. Wrenn*, 1914)

pay dirt—Any desired result or goal, especially one related to wealth or success; a fortunate discovery. Literally, *pay dirt* is a mining term that refers to an area of land that contains enough valuable metals or other resources to merit excavation. After its introduction in the 1870s, *pay dirt* soon became more figurative, commonly being applied to any success, especially in the phrase *hit pay dirt*.

> I didn't hit pay dirt until near the bottom of the second box of discarded telephone directories. (John Evans, *Halo in Blood*, 1946)

In recent years, *pay dirt* has been used frequently to describe the end zone (goal area) of a football field.

ring the bell—To succeed, to make a hit; to be the best. The *bell* of this expression may be that attached to the strength-testing machine at carnivals which rings when a player is successful. Or it may be the bell in target shooting that rings when the bull's-eye is hit.

strike oil—To have good luck or success, especially financial; to discover a source of potential personal aggrandizement; to strike it rich; to hit pay dirt. This expression alludes to oil as an entity which inevitably leads to wealth and success, a concept strengthened in recent years by the increasing prominence of Middle East oil barons. Though still used literally to describe the locating of underground oil, *strike oil* is commonly applied figuratively in contexts directly or indirectly related to money or other personal good fortune.

> He has certainly "struck oil" in the Costa Rica and Honduras loans. (*Punch*, March 6, 1875)

sweep the board—To win everything in a card game; to win all the prizes or awards at a meeting. The denotation of *board* in this expression is a table where games are played; hence, to *sweep the board* is to *clean up* and win everything. The expression has been in use since the 17th century.

> Spadillo first, unconquerable lord!
> Led off two captive trumps and swept the board.
> (Alexander Pope, *The Rape of the Lock*, 1711)

turn up trumps—To prove successful; to turn out well despite negative expectations. This expression, dating from at least the 1850s, refers to the trump suit in a game of cards and especially to a situation where the unexpected appearance of a trump card helps save the day. The term originated in England but soon found its way to the United States. It is still in everyday use in both countries.

> Instances ... of short courtships and speedy marriages, which have turned up trumps—I beg your pardon—which have turned out well, after all. (Wilkie Collins, *No Name*, 1862)

A variant phrase is *come up trumps*. The allusion is to drawing or playing a winning trump card. See **trump card**, PLOY.

with flying colors—Victoriously, triumphantly, successfully; handily, easily; superbly, in extraordinary fashion. This phrase, usually in expressions such as *come off with flying colors* and *come out of it with flying colors*, alludes to a triumphant fleet of ships sailing into home port with their colors (i.e., flags) proudly displayed on the mastheads. Used figuratively, *with flying colors* often implies that one has not only survived a potentially precarious predicament but has been victorious to boot.

SUFFERANCE
SEE ENDURANCE

SUITABILITY
SEE WORTHINESS

SUPERFLUOUSNESS
SEE ABUNDANCE; EXCESSIVENESS

SUPERSTITION

beware the ides of March—A warning of impending danger, rarely heard today. This expression alludes to the words of the soothsayer who warned Julius Caesar to "Beware the ides of March." Caesar ignored the advice, only to be killed on that very day, the 15th of March, in 44 B.C. According to the ancient Roman calendar, the ides falls on the 15th day of March, May, July, and October, and on the 13th day of the other months.

burning ears—If one's ears burn (or ring), it is commonly believed that someone else is talking about him. This ancient superstition dates from at least the 1st century. In *Natural History*, Pliny wrote:

> It is acknowledged that the absent feel a presentiment of remarks about themselves by the ringing of their ears.

This citation suggests the frequent variant *ringing in the ears.* Erasmus, in *Adagia* (1500), explains the burning sensation as stimulating the right ear if the talk is complimentary and the left ear if uncomplimentary. Sir Thomas Browne (d. 1682) agrees with Erasmus but ascribes the action to a guardian angel. Jonathan Swift, in *Polite Conversation* (1738), seems to believe the reverse:

> Lord Sparkish: Miss, did your left ear burn last night?
> Miss Notable: Pray why, my lord?
> Lord Sparkish: Because I was then in some company where you were extolled to the skies, I assure you.

cross [one's] fingers—To make a mental reservation; to wish for success; to hope for protection from bad luck or from evil. Since the death of Jesus Christ upon the cross, people have made the sign of the cross as an affirmation of faith. Crossing one's fingers is simply a private way of asking for protection through Christ's intervention. There are two popular methods of crossing the fingers: one involves the St. Andrew's Cross, placing the middle finger of the right hand atop the index finger of the same hand; the other involves the Greek Cross, placing the index finger of one hand atop the index finger of the other hand at right angles.

A variant expression *keep [one's] fingers crossed*, which dates from the first half of this century, may be connected with the old superstition that making the sign of the cross kept bad luck away. Today, although the superstition is still practiced by adults, it is most commonly practiced by children, who are led to believe that a lie doesn't count if one's fingers are crossed.

> We'll ... duck when we hear a mortar, and keep our fingers crossed. (*Penguin New Writing*, 1945)

cut [one's] nails on Sunday—To assure oneself of bad luck; to invite evil; to tempt the devil; to practice wickedness and depravity. This phrase is predicated upon a superstition dating to at least the Middle Ages. Although originally the day of the week appeared variously as Sunday or Friday, the superstition finally settled upon Sunday for evil and Friday for sorrow. Robert Forby, in *The Vocabulary of East Anglia* (1830), recorded an East Anglian poem designed as a mnemonic device for what befalls one for cutting his nails upon any given day of the week.

> Cut them on Monday, you cut them for health;
> Cut them on Tuesday, you cut them for wealth,
> Cut them on Wednesday, you cut them for news;
> Cut them on Thursday, a new pair of shoes;
> Cut them on Friday, you cut them for sorrow;
> Cut them on Saturday, see your true-love tomorrow;
> Cut them on Sunday, the devil will be with you all week.

dead man's hand—A pair of aces and a pair of eights in a poker hand; bad luck; misfortune; at a disadvantage when entering a contest. This superstition came into existence shortly after August 2, 1876, the day Jack McCall shot Wild Bill Hickok in the back in Deadwood, South Dakota, while Hickok was holding such a poker hand. Some controversy exists as to whether Hickok held aces and eights:

> Throughout the West the combination of aces and eights is known as the *dead man's hand*. (Ramon Adams, *Western Words*, 1944)

or jacks and eights:

> Dead man's hand, in poker, two pairs, jacks and eights. (*The Century Dictionary, Supplement*, 1909)

Most authorities agree that it was the former.

elf locks—Tangled hair; hair that is matted and knotted supposedly because of the work of elves. This superstition dates back to at least the time of Shakespeare, who made use of the term, or alluded to it, in many of his plays. The creation of these locks was supposedly one of Queen Mab's favorite amusements.

> This is that very Mab
> That plats the manes of horses in the night;
> And bakes the elf-locks in foul sluttish hairs.
> (*Romeo and Juliet*, I, iv)

The expression has remained in use although the superstition has been dead for many years.

> Their hair remains matted and wreathed in elves-locks. (*Gentlemen's Magazine*, 1810)

jinx—A person or thing supposed to bring bad luck; an unlucky charm or spell; a hex. This word, spelled *jynx* by the British, alludes to the unusual nesting practice of the jinx, or wryneck, (the woodpecker *Jynx torquilla*.) The bird lays its eggs on bare wood without padding its nest. Such an unusual practice led people in the Middle Ages to assign special magical powers to the jinx. As such, its feathers were treasured for the manufacture of potions, talismans, and all types of elixirs, especially by the practitioners of black magic, hence its connotation of bad luck.

> Dave Shean and Peaches Graham . . . have not escaped the jinx that has been following the champions. (*Chicago Daily News*, September 19, 1911)

knock on wood—A phrase uttered to avoid a reversal of good fortune about which one has just boasted; spoken with the hope of escaping a misfortune which one has thus far averted and to keep away ill fortune or evil spirits. The origin of this phrase lies in superstition, but where the superstition had its roots is anybody's guess. Of the many explanations the knocking on a tree trunk to invoke the spirits who live within seems to be the most popular. Nora Archibald Smith in her poem, "Knocking on Wood" defines the process:

> They'd knock on a tree and would timidly say
> To the Spirit who might be within there that day;
> "Fairy fair, Fairy fair, wish thou me well;
> 'Gainst evil witcheries weave me a spell!" . . .
> An' e'en to this day is the practice made good
> When, to ward off disaster, we knock upon wood.

Other theories refer to the touching of wood to be free from capture, as in the children's game of tag, and the turning of one's thoughts to the wooden cross of Jesus Christ to beseech His assistance. The British equivalent and probably the older phrase is *touch wood*. An old British proverb tells us: "Touch wood; it's sure to come good."

old wives' tale—A foolish or nonsensical story; a traditional but inaccurate concept or superstition. This expression is derived from the fanciful yarns often related by elderly women.

These are the sort of old wives' tales which he sings and recites to us. (Benjamin Jowett, *The Dialogues of Plato*, 1875)

Today the expression usually describes a superstitious notion still adhered to by many people even though it has been discredited by modern science.

third time's the charm—A desired end will be attained, after previous failures, following a third attempt to achieve it. This expression of superstition goes back to at least the 13th century. Although its exact origin is unknown, most scholars agree that the *charm* refers to a magical effect or spell, and the *third time* alludes to the traditionally mystical associations of the number *three*. An Associated Press release of October 29, 1981, shortly after the Los Angeles Dodgers had defeated the New York Yankees in the 1981 World Series, reveals that the term continues to retain its bewitching connotation:

"Our feeling after Sunday was there was a certain amount of destiny," Garvey said. "The third time's the charm," a reference to the fact that this was the third World Series for many of the current Dodgers against the Yankees.

three on a match—Any practice which reputedly brings ill luck, but most often the specific and literal practice of lighting three cigarettes with one match. The superstition supposedly arose among soldiers in wartime who believed that the glow from a match kept alive long enough to light three cigarettes would give the enemy time for careful aim at them as targets, thus quite possibly bringing about their death.

SURPASSING
SEE OUTDOING

SURRENDER
SEE SUBMISSION

SUSPICIOUSNESS

bug under the chip—Something suspected as an ulterior motive or hidden cause; an undisclosed fact. The allusion here is to the paranoiac bent of some people's minds, people who can be so suspicious as to believe that something is concealed beneath a wood chip. Although the expression has been in use since the 1880s, it is particularly appropriate in today's world of electronic eavesdropping, for it is possible that there is a *bug* 'miniature microphone' under a chip.

To those uneasy over the alliance, he gave his word that there are 'no such bugs under the chips.' (*Newsweek*, July 15, 1946)

nigger in the woodpile—Something suspicious, such as an undisclosed fact, hidden element, or ulterior motive. This expression sprang up during the era of slavery in the United States, most specifically in regard to the Underground Railroad, a system whereby abolitionists aided runaway slaves, often concealing them through any expedient—one of which was a woodpile. The phrase first appeared in print in 1852, but the offensiveness of the word *nigger* inhibits the phrase's use in contemporary speech and writing and may well signal its demise.

> Like a great many others ignorant of facts, he finds "a nigger in the wood pile" when there is neither wood pile nor nigger. (*Congressional Record*, February 1897)

smell a rat—To instinctively sense evil, treachery, or wrongdoing; to be suspicious. A cat has a keen sense of smell which enables it to detect an unseen rat; whether this or another everyday image is at the origin of the expression, the fact is that it has been in use since at leat the 17th century, Samuel Butler employing it in *Hudibras*, part I (1663). The phrase is still quite common in the United States and Great Britain.

> I asked her so many questions, that, though a woman ignorant enough, she began to smell a rat. (William R. Chetwood, *Voyages of W.O.G. Vaughan*, 1736)

something rotten in Denmark—An expression used to describe a suspected problem which cannot be pinpointed; something of a questionable or suspicious nature; anything that disconcerts and instills anxiety. In Shakespeare's *Hamlet*, Marcellus is uneasy because the ghost of Hamlet's father had appeared to him. He sees this as a portent and conjectures to Horatio:

> Something is rotten in the state of Denmark. (I,iv)

SUSTENANCE
SEE FOOD AND DRINK

SWINDLING
SEE TRICKERY

TALENT
SEE ABILITY

TEMPORIZING

Fabian tactics—A policy of delay; running away to harass one's enemy; fighting and running away to live and fight another day. This expression is derived from the policy of Quintus Fabius Maximus, the Roman general who defeated Hannibal in the Second Punic War (218–201 B.C.). Recognizing the superior strength of the attacking force, Fabius avoided major pitched battles, engaged the Carthaginians in minor skirmishes, and subverted their supply lines. Eventually his tactics succeeded, and he achieved victory for the Roman Empire and the cognomen Cunctator. The phrase gained great popularity in the late 19th century when William Morris founded a society to bring socialism to Great Britain. Adopting the name, Fabian Society, Morris in 1884 defined the society's policy:

> We must do what we can . . . and like Quintus Fabius, who was never defeated, reform the government, not overthrow it . . . . We must take the present social order and build upon it.

filibuster—The use of irregular or obstructive tactics, such as long speeches or trivial objections, by a minority legislator to prevent or hinder the passage or consideration of legislation generally favored by the majority; the use of such tactics to force the passage of unpopular legislation; to waste time for the purpose of obstruction. The filibuster, long a staple of U.S. Congressional politics, derives from the French *fribustier* 'pirate' and the British *flibuster* 'rover, traveler.' The French pirates terrorized the Spanish West Indies in the 17th century. The name *filibusters* was later applied to illegal bands of Americans and Texans who, in the 1850s, entered Central America to foment revolution. Soon the term was applied to anyone who took part in illegal or irregular warfare or other obstructionist activity against a government. The transition to its current meaning was then but a short jump.

> A filibuster was indulged in which lasted . . . for nine continuous calendar days. (*Congressional Record*, February 11, 1890)

hold at bay—To fend off one's literal or figurative assailant by taking the offense, thereby bringing about a standstill as both parties are poised and ready to attack. This expression is said to derive from the modern French *être aux bois* 'to be at close quarters with the barking dogs.' Originally a hunting phrase dating from the 16th century, *hold at a bay* or *keep at a bay* refers to a situation in which a hunted animal, unable to flee further, turns to defend itself at close quarters. Figurative use, also dating from the 1500s, is now heard more frequently than the literal.

> By riding . . . keep death as it were at a bay. (Francis Fuller, *Medicina Gymnastica*, 1711)

mark time—To await developments; to be active without progressing; to keep time by moving the feet alternately, as in marching, but without advancing; to pause in action temporarily. This expression, its figurative sense adopted from an original, martial application, has been in use since the early 19th century. It is still used in its literal sense by the military, but is always heard as a figurative expression otherwise.

> The agnostic's appeal to us is to halt and mark time. (Frederick W. H. Myers, *Human Personality*, 1903)

play for time—To employ dilatory tactics to stave off defeat; to postpone making a decision, to drag out negotiations. This expression probably derives from those sports in which one team monopolizes control in the remaining minutes of a game in order to prevent a last-minute turnaround and victory by the opposing team.

stonewall—To obstruct or block legislation; to delay or impede an activity. This term was applied to the Civil War General Thomas J. Jackson, in honor of his steadfastness at the Battle of Bull Run. The expression is also a cricket term for an exclusively defensive or delaying strategy. Its meaning was subsequently extended to include stubborn blocking and delaying tactics on a government level.

> Obstruction did not merely consist in stonewalling Government business. (*Contemporary Review*, November 1916)

As a result of its use in the Watergate hearings, *stonewall* took on the more specific meaning of the obstruction of or the resistance to government inquiry or investigation, as through vagueness and noncooperation.

TENACITY
SEE PERSEVERANCE

TERMINATION
See also COMPLETION

all over but the shouting—This expression conveys the idea that things have become so one-sided that one knows what the outcome will be before the contest has ended. In common use in both Great Britain and the United States, the term first appeared in the mid-19th century. Occasional variations are *all over except the shouting* and, in England, *all over bar the shouting*.

> The Englishman would say the back of a job was broken, or all is over but the shouting. (Kipling, *Man and Beast*, 1891)

at close of play—At the time of termination; when all is said and done. This Briticism is used to express the end of something or the termination of a cycle. Its root, like that of so many British expressions, lies in the game of cricket, and the term probably had its origin in the late 18th century.

> Let me have the memorandum by close of play on Wednesday. (Norman W. Schur, *English English*, 1980)

A related term *at the end of the day* is roughly the equivalent of the American *when all is said and done*.

> Large housing units may be more efficient, but at the end of the day people want their separate homes. (Norman W. Schur, *English English*, 1980)

bitter end—A difficult or disagreeable conclusion; the last or ultimate extremity; death; often in the phrase *to the bitter end*. According to Captain John Smith's *A Sea Grammar* (1627):

> A bitter is but the turn of a cable about the bits, and wear it out by little and little. And the bitters end is that part of the cable doth stay within board.

William Henry Smyth in *The Sailor's Word-book* (1867) elaborates further:

> A ship is "brought up to a bitter" when the cable is allowed to run out to that stop . . . . When a chain or rope is paid out to the bitter-end, no more remains to be let go.

A variation of the phrase *bitter end* appears in the Bible (Proverbs 5:4) and some conjecture this usage, rather than the nautical, to be its origin.

> But her end is bitter as wormwood.

The phrase gave rise to the term *bitter-ender* 'a diehard,' in use since 1850.

curtains—The end, usually a disastrous or unfortunate one; most often, death itself. This slang term, of obvious theatrical derivation, is often used to indicate the end of some illegitimate enterprise, and as such is similar to expressions such as *the jig is up* (see below).

> It looked like curtains for Ezra then and there. But just that moment he saw a chance of salvation. (Jesse Lilienthal, *Horse Crazy*, 1941)

[one's] days are numbered—See ILL HEALTH.

dead letter—The end of the line; an unfortunate conclusion; the termination of usefulness; no longer in force. In postal terminology a *dead letter* is one which cannot be delivered or returned to the sender. Therefore, it sits in the dead letter office for a period of time before it is finally destroyed. In legal terminology a *dead letter* is a law that is no longer acted upon, a statute or ordinance that is no longer enforced, although not formally repealed. Each of these definitions contributes to the figurative intent of the expression, to come to an ill-fated end.

> Many a treaty of marriage became a dead letter almost as soon as it was signed. (Edward Freeman, *The History of the Norman Conquest*, 1869)

draw stumps—To leave; to terminate a situation; to clear out. This British expression can be ascribed to the game of cricket; when the game is over, the stumps are pulled from the ground and everybody departs. Since the stumps are an integral part of the equipment, the term has come to signify absolute termination. The phrase has been in use since the early 19th century.

> When the stumps and the match also were drawn, four wickets were down for 96 runs. (*The Field*, July 4, 1868)

A variant is *up stumps*.

in the homestretch—In the final stages; nearing the completion of a project, ordeal, activity, or other matter; the denouement. In racing terminology, the homestretch is the last leg of a race, i.e., the straight part of a racecourse from the last turn to the finish line. Figurative use of this Americanism was recorded as early as the mid 19th century. It usually suggests some degree of relief because *in the homestretch*, the end is in sight. A variant is *n the homestretch*.

> Already we see the slave states . . . on the homestretch to become free. (*Congressional Globe*, March 12, 1864)

the jig is up—This is it, it's all over, this is the end of the line; usually used in reference to being caught or discovered in some wrongdoing. This slang or dialectal expression, which dates from the late 1700s, derives from the obsolete 'prank, joke, trick' meaning of *jig*.

John Audley it—To bring a theatrical performance to a close; to conclude whatever one is doing; to hurry. This expression supposedly arose because of the actions of a travelling theatrical producer named Shuter. He would station an assistant outside the theater, and when enough customers had purchased tickets for the next performance the assistant would enter the rear of the theater and inquire in a loud voice, "Is John Audley here?" Upon this prearranged signal, the production would be concluded as quickly as possible so that the new paying audience might enter. Thus, to *John Audley* anything came to mean to finish up hurriedly. In the United States the phrase has become a circus slang term meaning 'hurry.' A variant is *John Orderly it*.

nip in the bud—To terminate a project, plan, or other matter in its early stages; to prevent or stop something before it has had a chance to develop. A bud is an undeveloped part of a plant which, if nipped by frost, pests, or a zealous gardener, does not grow to fruition; hence the expression.

> Dost thou approach to censure our delights, and nip them in the bud? (Sir Aston Cokaine, *Masque*, 1639)

ring down the curtain—To terminate or bring to an end. In the theater, the person responsible for raising or lowering the stage curtain once received his cue from the stage manager who would ring a bell at the appropriate moment.

> The curtain had to be rung down before the play was ended. (*The Times*, August 31, 1887)

While still used in the theater, *ring down the curtain on* is applied figuratively in other contexts as well. A variation is the shortened *ring down*.

> The functionary whose business it is to "ring down" had satisfied himself that nobody wanted any more of it. (*Daily News*, October 2, 1882)

stem the tide—To stop, terminate, end; to squash, quell, check; to block or stifle; to nip in the bud. The most plausible conjecture is that *stem* in this expression is derived from the Icelandic *stemma* 'to stop the flow of'; attempts to relate it to the stem of an ocean-going vessel defy logic. *Tide* implies a flow of events.

> Aristophanes evidently saw the tide that was strongly in favour of the new candidate for scenic supremacy, and he vainly tried to stem it by the barrier of his ridicule. (Fred Paley, *The Tragedies of Aeschylus*, 1855)

TEST

baptism of fire—See INITIATION.

dry run—A trial; a rehearsal; something done for practice only. The origin of this term is obscure, but it probably came from the military, where *dry run* is frequently used of any simulated situation in which skills are practiced in preparation for use in actual combat. Perhaps the term came from dry-land simulations of troop landings from boats, wherein the soldiers would not get their feet wet as they would in a real landing.

> She had to locate his pulse, get her watch ready, and make a couple of dry runs. (*Saturday Evening Post*, November 27, 1943)

go through fire and water—See DESIRE.

have [one's] work cut out—See DIFFICULTY.

ordeal by fire—A severe test of character; a very distressing situation. In ancient Britain, an ordeal was a type of trial in which divine intervention was considered the only proof of a suspect's innocence. These ordeals took many brutal forms, ranging from having one's arm immersed in boiling water to being bound and tossed into an icy river. In both cases, an unscathed survivor was proclaimed innocent. The harshest ordeals, however, involved fire. The accused was forced either to grasp a red-hot iron in his hand or to walk barefooted through sizzling rocks and embers. Again, a suspect who emerged uninjured was considered guiltless. Although these cruel trials were abolished shortly after the Norman conquest of Britain, the expression has retained its meaning of an exceedingly agonizing experience undergone to test one's worth.

put through [one's] facings—To require another to exhibit his skill for purposes of scrutiny; to make a person perform to the utmost of his capabilities. Literal *facings* are military maneuvers.

> Grace, not at all unwillingly, was put through her facings. (Anthony Trollope, *The Last Chronicle of Barset*, 1867)

The expression usually carries connotations of being badgered or harassed, as in the following bit of doggerel by F. Egerton.

We were scarcely wed a week
When she put me through my facings.
And walloped me—and worse;
She said I did not want a wife,
I ought to have had a nurse.

put through [one's] paces—To require another to display the full range of his abilities; to test another's resources to the utmost. *Paces* here refers to the training steps or gaits of horses. The equestrian phrase was first extended to persons called upon to perform at their maximum potential, and subsequently to inanimate objects as well.

> The captain affirmed that the ship would show us in time all her paces. (Ralph Waldo Emerson, *English Traits*, 1856)

> The test pilots...put the new planes through their paces. (H. H. Arnold and I. C. Eaker, cited in *Webster's Third*)

quiz—An oral or written examination; an eccentric; a practical joke; to give a test; to kid another person. The origin of this word is questionable; however, it is oftentimes attributed to a Dublin theater manager named Daly, who, it seems, about 1780, wagered with a friend that, within twenty-four hours, he could introduce a meaningless word into the language. The wager was accepted, and that evening Mr. Daly sent his theatrical employees to the streets of Dublin to chalk the letters *Q-U-I-Z* on all available building sides, walls, anyplace where the general populace might see them on the next morning. By the evening of the next day all Dublin was inquiring the meaning of the strange new word. Mr. Daly was said to have won his wager. The word, whatever its origin, acquired a number of meanings and has remained in the language. Today, it is most commonly heard as a noun meaning 'short, quick test,' or as a verb meaning 'question,' or 'give a test.' During the 1930s an American radio show, entitled "Quiz Kids," was introduced and achieved such popularity that the term *quiz kid* is still heard to indicate a precocious youngster. A type of television program that has gained considerable popularity since World War II is the *quiz show* in which contestants win money or prizes for answering pre-determined questions presented by the host. Another related term is *quizzing glass*, meaning 'monocle,' probably from the fact that it can aid one in examining something more closely.

take the measure of—To judge the character of, to size up, to ascertain the good and bad points. *Measure* in this expression refers literally to the dimensions of a body, information necessary to a tailor who needs exact *measurements* to fit someone for clothes. Figuratively the term refers not to size, but to character.

> Our hostess...bustled off... to take the measure of the newcomer. (Sir A. Conan Doyle, *Micah Clarke*, 1889)

Even further removed from the literal use is the application of this expression to organizations or institutions.

> The people have taken the measure of this whole labor movement. (*Nations*, January 5, 1893)

test of the boar's head—A test with rigid requirements; a test of cuckoldry. The story is told that a boy walked into King Arthur's court and, placing a boar's head upon the famous round table, remarked that no cuckold's knife could cut it. Of all the knights in Arthur's court only Sir Cradock's could sever the flesh. A variant is *test of the brawn's head*.

weigh in the balance—The allusion in this expression is to the scales upon which Fortune or Justice decides the fates of men; hence, to *weigh in the balance* implies a figurative placing of someone or an idea in one tray of the scales and actions or principles in the other, in order to determine how the two measure up. The term appears in the Bible when Daniel interprets the vision of Belshazzar and informs him:

> Thou art weighed in the balances, and art found wanting. (Daniel 5:27)

The phrase has been in use in England since at least the Middle Ages.

THOROUGHNESS
SEE INCLUSIVENESS; TOTALITY

THWARTING
SEE IMPEDIMENT; TERMINATION

TIME
See also OPPORTUNENESS

before [one] had nails on [one's] toes—Before one was born; long ago, in the distant past. This expression refers to the fact that a baby's toenails develop prenatally. Thus, an event or other matter that occurred before a person's toenails developed occurred before he was born. In its most common usage, the expression cites a younger person's age as the basis for denigrating his status, experience, ideals, or philosophies.

> There's Ulysses and old Nestor, whose wit was moldy ere your grandsires had nails on their toes. (Shakespeare, *Troilus and Cressida*, II,i)

between dog and wolf—Neither day nor night; dusk. The dog is a domesticated animal and therefore associated with all that is civilized and ordered, such as the day. On the other hand, the wild and mysterious wolf is associated with the night, from the image of a wolf baying at the moon. Although they are of the same family, dogs and wolves are as different as day and night. And *between dog and wolf*, or day and night, is dusk.

blind man's holiday—Dusk; neither day nor night. This phrase, used as early as 1599, is said to refer to the time just before candles are lighted when it is too dark to work or read—a fitting time to rest, or take a *holiday*. However, this explanation does not account for the use of *blind man* in the phrase. Perhaps dusk is a holiday for a blind man because it offers him a brief respite from his aloneness. He has company because everyone is in the same state of semidarkness until the candles are lit. In fact, being accustomed to the darkness, a blind man can enjoy an advantage. The phrase is rarely heard today.

D-day—A deadline, the last hour, the moment of truth; a date established for any significant event, originally for a secret military operation. During World War II, the Allied invasion of Normandy was set for June 5, 1944. To avoid referring to the date, for security reasons, the code word *D-day* was adopted. Hostile weather conditions, however, forced the postponement of this famous D-day until the next day. The term is currently used in a similar way, especially in the academic world, where students refer to the due date for the submission of work as *D-day*.

gandermonth—The month during which a wife is confined after giving birth to a child. This old British term, dating from about 1600, refers to that time after a wife gives birth when her husband supposedly wanders about perhaps even enjoying the company of other women. Such aimless wandering is known as *gandermooning*, and during that period the husband is known as a *gandermooner*. The allusion in all of these terms is apparently to the capricious rambling of the gander while the goose is sitting on the nest.

> I'll keep her at the least this gandermonth,
> While my fair wife lies in.
> (Richard Brome, *The English Moor*, 1652)

graveyard shift—A work shift usually from twelve midnight until eight in the morning; any late-night shift; also the *graveyard watch*. Factories running 24 hours a day employ three shifts of workers—day, afternoon or swing, and midnight or graveyard. The expression gained currency during World War II when so many factories were operating around-the-clock. The phrase, American slang and dating from the early part of this century, is an allusion to the late hour of the shift, which works in the dead of night when it is quiet and still as a graveyard.

> A month later he and his fellows went on "graveyard" shift. (*The Saturday Evening Post*, November 1908)

since Hector was a pup—A long lapse of time; for ages. This expression, which has been in common use since the Middle Ages, is of uncertain origin. There has been great speculation through the years as to the identity of *Hector*, but a positive identification has never been made. A plausible explanation may be that the phrase refers to the early childhood of the hero of ancient Troy, Hector, and thus implies a very long time ago.

> He has been here for ages—since Hector was a pup. (Anne Rowe, *The Little Dog Barked*, 1942)

St. Tib's Eve—Never; when two Sundays meet; the second Tuesday of next week. Since St. Tib never existed, there is, of course, no *St. Tib's Eve*.

> He would return and claim her hand on "Tib's Eve" an Irish festival which is stated to occur "neither before nor after Christmas." (William H. Maxwell, *The Bivouac*, 1837)

A related term, *Greek calends*, also means 'never,' *calends* being a term from the Roman system of marking the days of the month.

> But, quoth Pantagruel, when will you be out of debt? At the next ensuing term of the Greek calends, answered Panurge. (François Rabelais, *Pantagruel*, 1545)

zero hour—Deadline; an anticipated stressful or critical period of time; the precise time established for the commencement of a military operation. This phrase originated and was widely used during World War I. It was for the most part replaced by the analogous term *H-hour* during World War II. As currently used, the expression often carries an implication of dread.

TIMELINESS
SEE OPPORTUNENESS; TIME

TIMIDITY
SEE FEAR

TIPPLING
SEE DRUNKENNESS; FOOD AND DRINK

TOIL
SEE EXERTION

TOTALITY
See also INCLUSIVENESS

hook, line, and sinker—Entirely, completely; without reservations. The allusion is to a fish so hungry that it swallows not only the bait but the fishhook, the lead weight (sinker), and some of the fishing line as well. The expression appeared as early as 1838 in T. W. Barnes' *Memoir of T. Weed*. It most often describes the naïveté or gullibility of an accepting, unquestioning attitude, and implies that a person can be easily duped.

ins and outs—All the details of a subject, occurrence, etc.; all there is to know about something, including nuances and subtle particulars. Some say *ins* originally referred to the party in government, and *outs* to the opposition. However, the meaning of *ins and outs* suggests wholeness and entirety because of the conjunction of opposites, regardless of what each opposite signifies. A somewhat literal application of this phrase is in reference to the windings and turnings in a road, and, by extension, to less concrete things, such as a plan or course of action.

love me, love my dog—A proverbial way of saying "If you love me, you must accept my faults along with my good qualities." *Dog* stands for an unpleasant or undesirable but intrinsic part of a person's character, one that cannot be ignored or avoided. John Heywood used this expression in his *Proverbs* (1546). It is also said to have been a popular 12th-century Latin proverb from the writings of Saint Bernard: *Qui me amat, amet et canem meum.*

thread and thrum—A whole, a totality; anything taken in its entirety, particularly when such is seen as embracing both positive and negative elements; the good and the bad, the wheat and the chaff, the virtues and the vices. *Thread and thrum* represents the entire length of warp yarn, including the tuft which fastens it to the loom and which remains so attached when the web is cut off. In Shakespeare's *A Midsummer Night's Dream*, Bottom as Pyramus discovers the bloodstained mantle of his beloved Thisbe and presumes her dead, whereupon he asks the Fates to make the destruction complete:

> O Fates! come, come,
> Cut thread and thrum,
> Quail, crush, conclude, and quell!
> (V,i)

The above use also plays on the notion that the Fates determine man's life by spinning, measuring, and cutting its thread at whim.

whole ball of wax—Any entity taken as a totality; any matter or concern together with its ramifications, implications, and consequences; its components, particulars, and details, etc. No satisfactory explanation or origin for this very common expression has yet been found.

whole schmear—The entire story; anything taken in its totality; the whole ball of wax; all there is to know about something. This American slang expression is simply an adaptation of a Yiddish verb meaning to smear or to spread. Its date of origin as a figurative term is uncertain.

> Tommy, I want a complete list of everyone who lives in the place or who works there.... Names, ages, business they're in, daily schedules—the whole schmear. (Lawrence Sanders, *The Anderson Tapes*, 1970)

whole shebang—All one's worldly possessions; everything in its entirety; the whole nine yards; an entire series of actions; a soldier's tent and all his possessions. The origin of this American slang expression is somewhat obscure, but its coinage is generally attributed to Southern farmers sometime prior to the American Civil War. Probably a variation of the Irish word *shebeen*, a low, public house or a temporary habitation where illicit liquor was sold, the expression became popular during the Civil War as a term to denote a Confederate soldier's tent and other personal possessions, all his worldly goods. Union troops, returning from the war, spread the term throughout the North, and it has been common throughout the United States since that time.

> Wade and me claims the whole shebang. (*The Daily Ardmoreite*, May 9, 1948)

TRANSPORTATION
SEE VEHICLES

TRICKERY
See also PLOY

accidentally on purpose—In a sly manner; with the real purpose intentionally obscured; with concealed intent. This American expression, indicating a deliberate action made to appear accidental, has been popular sporadically since the early 1900s.

Amyris plays the fool—This expression is said of a person who appears to be acting crazily, but who is actually acting wisely. Amyris, an inhabitant of Sybaris, a Greek settlement in southern Italy, was sent to consult the oracle at Delphi, where he learned that his country was doomed to destruction. When he informed his countrymen of the prophecy, they laughed at him and called him a fool. He fled to Peloponnesus and saved his life, for the oracle's prediction proved true.

bamboozle—To cheat by trickery; to mystify; to perplex; to practice deception. This colloquial expression, of uncertain derivation, has been in use since about 1700. Rejecting the probability of a Gypsy origin, the *OED* conjectures that the word is probably of cant origin.

> He has been bamboozled by Miss Pat Ward. (Emanuel Trujillo, *I Love You, I Hate You*, 1955)

a dead cat on a line—Something suspicious; a deception or bamboozlement; a carrot on a stick; an allurement; an enticement. This American black slang term is used today to indicate that something is of a suspicious nature, that some unknown trickery is afoot. The term was probably derived from an old practice of dog thieves, or burglars, to lure dogs away from their yards. Mark Twain wrote of the practice, and P. G. Wodehouse in his short story *Ukridge's Dog College* describes the process:

I borrowed a dead cat and tied a string to it, legged it to Old Nickerson's garden after dark, dug a board out of the back of the shed, and shoved my head down and chirruped. The dogs came trickling out, and I hared off, towing old Colonel Cat on his string.... Hounds picked up the scent right away and started off in a bunch at fifty miles an hour.

A less plausible, although highly conceivable, explanation for the connotation of the phrase ascribes it to a voodoo warning: if one awakes in the morning and discovers a dead cat strung up by the neck, one should take it as a signal to pack up and leave.

done with mirrors—Usually expressing a jocular response to some imaginative or clever happening, this phrase, dating from at least World War I, was probably conceived from a trick used in magic acts on stage. Magicians and escape artists have for years used mirrors to create illusions for the audience.

No, no, it isn't. Death's very laughable, such a cunning little mystery. All done with mirrors. (Noel Coward, *Private Lives*, 1933)

elwetritch hunting—The misleading of a person harmlessly as a practical joke; pulling a fast one. This Pennsylvania Dutch expression, dating from the early 1800s, suggests that the victim is naïve and easily misled. The evasive elwetritch, a fictitious bird of Pennsylvania Dutch invention, is known by many other names; *elbedritch* and *elpentrecher* are among them. Reported to be similar to the snipe, the elwetritch is a shy bird; therefore, catching one is a time-consuming process. The novice hunter is taken out into the deep woods on a cold winter's night, positioned at the intersection of two hunting paths, and left with burlap bag in hand. The "drivers" leave to flush the game toward the waiting hunter, and he waits, and waits, and waits ...

Have you ever been taken out to hunt Elwetritches? Have you ever been put out on a cold winter night, in the dark of the moon, to catch this elusive relative of the American snipe? (John Stoudt, *Sunbonnets and Shoofly Pies*, 1973)

Jack Horner—One who gains his own ends by trickery; a cunning cheat.
Little Jack Horner sat in a corner
Eating his Christmas pie.
He stuck in his thumb and pulled out a plum
And said, "What a good boy am I!"
Supposedly the *plum* the real Jack Horner pulled out was the deed to the manor of Mells, which is still owned by his descendants. Horner, who was steward to the Abbot of Glastonbury during the reign of Henry VIII, allegedly delivered the deeds to the king at the dissolution of the monasteries. One version holds that Jack Horner was sent as a courier with the deeds concealed in a pie. He lifted the corner of the crust, and pulled

out his *plum*. A more plausible version reports that he secured the deeds by trickery and delivered them to the king, who rewarded him for his fealty.

play booty—To act as a decoy for confederates in order to victimize another player in a game; to play or act falsely. This expression, dating from the 16th century, refers to the capturing of booty from a victim. Unlike the pirates of old who were outright thieves and plunderers, the person *playing booty* is underhanded and sneaky. The loser is usually unaware that he is a victim, and the conspirators divide the booty after his departure.

> He had scornfully refused a considerable bribe to play booty on such an occasion. (Henry Fielding, *Joseph Andrews*, 1742)

pull a fast one—To trick by doing or saying something clever and unexpected; to gain the upper hand by a sudden show of skill; to swindle or defraud. Perhaps this originally U.S. slang expression first applied to a deft movement, such as in a game of football or some other sport, which caused control of the ball to change hands.

> Brick pulled a fast one in the St. Mary's game. (J. Sayre, *Rackety Rax*, 1932)

However, this expression and the analogous *put one over on* or *put over a fast one* now apply to any remark or action which gives a person unfair advantage.

> The thought that a girl capable of thinking up a fast one like that should be madly throwing herself away on Blair Eggleston...was infinitely saddening. (P. G. Wodehouse, *Hot Water*, 1932)

pull [someone's] leg—To mislead a person harmlessly; to bamboozle or trick in a jocular manner; to tease or kid. This expression may have derived from the "trippers-up," a former group of English criminals who tripped and subsequently robbed their victims. The expression's current reference is to a scheme in which the victim is purposely but humorously hoodwinked.

> I suspected that he was pulling my leg, but a glance at him convinced me otherwise. (F. Scott Fitzgerald, *The Great Gatsby*, 1925)

pull the wool over [someone's] eyes—To deceive or delude, to hoodwink or bamboozle.

> He said his only purpose was to "cite substantial evidence that will show just who is trying to pull the wool over the eyes of the American people." (*St. Paul Pioneer Press*, June 1949)

Attempts to account for the use of *wool* in this expression are unconvincing. This popular Americanism dates from the 19th century.

Rochester rappings—The knocks and rappings heard by spiritualists. This term refers to the supposed rappings heard by two sisters, Margaret and

Kate Fox, in their Hydesville, New York, home in 1848. Kate quite accidently discovered that if she snapped her fingers, some ghostly intelligence in the wall would answer with the identical number of raps. A code was worked out whereby the spirit could answer all manner of questions. From this simple beginning the spiritualistic movement was initiated. Nearby Rochester was the scene of the first demonstration of spiritualism in 1849, and by 1855 the movement had spread across the United States and into Europe, where it was received with great enthusiasm, especially in England. Eventually, the sisters admitted faking the noises, but their admission did little to slow the movement.

rope in—To draw into some scheme or enterprise by deception; to take in, to ensnare or hook. This expression had its origins in the American West when roundups were commonplace and cowboys spent their time roping or lassoing cattle in order to brand them.

He will probably rope the victim into his favorite charity, the Margaret MacMillan Memorial Fund. (*Time*, February 1950)

shucking and jiving—Tricking another by giving a false impression; putting on the demeanor of a simpleton; deceiving another by passing false information. This American Black English phrase was derived from the two verbs, *shuck* and *jive*, both meaning in Black slang 'to deceive' or 'to hoodwink'. The expression, in use since the 1920s, originally implied that, on occasion, a black man would assume a shuffling, "yassuh" attitude around whites in order to avoid trouble or to protect himself from a physical or psychological battering. The guise is used also to eavesdrop to gather information or to mislead authorities.

Harry Belafonte's shucking and jiving preacher in "Buck and the Preacher" was a particularly telling portrayal. (*Newsweek*, October 23, 1972)

sting—A swindling scheme; a fraudulent claim; a small but successful confidence game; to cheat; to swindle; to steal; to overcharge. In the second edition of his *A Classical Dictionary of the Vulgar Tongue* (1788), Francis Grose defines a *stingbum* as a 'niggard, miser,' and from that term the idea of *stinging* someone, overcharging or soaking him so as to improve one's profits, evolved. By 1812 the verb had come to mean 'cheat' or 'rob,' and by the late 1800s the noun form had come to signify, especially in America, a smalltime confidence game. The term became a part of the common vocabulary with the popularity of the movie *The Sting*, starring Paul Newman and Robert Redford, released in 1973. Since the appearance of the film the word has been used to encompass any fraudulent operation whether carried on by underworld figures or by law enforcement officers.

The Drug Enforcement Administration has been running an undercover sting operation for several years using advertisements to lure readers who want to manufacture illegal drugs, a magazine editor says. (*Associated Press Release*, August 11, 1983)

A related term, *wire game*, also refers to a big-time confidence game.

thimblerig—To manipulate data cleverly in order to deceive or confuse; to pull a fast one; to cheat or swindle. *Thimblerigging* was a swindling game popular in the 19th century at race courses and fairs. The game involved three thimbles, one of which had a pea hidden under it. The victim of this swindle would bet on which thimble was hiding the pea. Reference to the trick appeared in print by the early 1800s. Soon after, the term was used figuratively for any deceitful or underhanded manipulation.

> Don't let us have any juggling and thimblerigging with virtue and vice. (William Makepeace Thackeray, *Catherine*, 1839)

throw dust in [someone's] eyes—To mislead or deceive, to dupe; to confuse or bewilder, to prevent someone from seeing the reality of a situation; to throw someone off guard, to render someone temporarily unfit to act. The most popular explanation for this expression is that it derives from the Muhammadan practice of casting dust into the air to confound religious enemies. Apparently Muhammad used this common military expedient on a number of occasions. The following quotation from the Koran alludes to the practice.

> Neither didst thou, O Mahomet, cast dust into their eyes, but it was God who confounded them.

The figurative use of *throw dust in [someone's] eyes* appeared in print as early as the 1600s.

two more, and up goes the donkey—A statement made to mislead people into paying for something not forthcoming. This British expression, which was in use as early as 1830, derives from an old sham practiced at English country fairs. The showman would promise that as soon as enough pennies had been collected, his donkey would balance itself on top of a ladder. Of course, enough pennies were never collected, and the donkey never balanced itself. The statement is occasionally heard today as a statement of derision, usually thrown at some entertainer who is performing poorly or who promises something out of the ordinary.

whip the devil around the stump—To avoid a difficulty by artful excuse or evasion; to achieve illicitly what could be achieved honorably; to dodge a problem successfully but dishonestly. This American expression, dating from the late 18th century, alludes to having such a high degree of guile that one can outmatch the devil himself in a contest of wits. The subject of much conjecture, its derivation remains obscure. It is generally agreed that the phrase was coined in the American South, and it continues to be heard more commonly there than in other parts of the country. Variants are *beat* *the devil around a bush,* most commonly heard in Great Britain, and *whip the devil round a post,* another American form.

> I "whipped the devil round the stump" by hiring a white distiller and calling him "overseer." (J. R. Gilmore [Edmund Kirke], *My Southern Friends,* 1863)

TRIVIALITY
SEE INSIGNIFICANCE

TROUBLESOMENESS
SEE DIFFICULTY

TURNAROUND
SEE REVERSAL

UNCERTAINTY
SEE CONFUSION; VACILLATION

UNCONVENTIONALITY
SEE ECCENTRICITY; FATUOUSNESS

UNFAIRNESS
SEE INJUSTICE; UNSCRUPULOUSNESS

UNIMPORTANCE
SEE INSIGNIFICANCE

UNREST
SEE DISORDER

UNSCRUPULOUSNESS

ambulance chaser—An overly aggressive lawyer who solicits clients in unethical or at best unprofessional ways. The term derives from those who actually made it a practice to arrive at the scene of a disaster in order to capitalize on its potential for their personal gain.

> In New York City there is a style of lawyers known to the profession as "ambulance chasers," because they are on hand wherever there is a railway wreck, or a street-car collision, or a gasoline explosion with . . . their offers of professional service. (*Congressional Record,* July 24, 1897)

blue sky—To deal in unsound stocks or bonds; to make a doubtful investment; to deal in worthless or questionable securities. The allusion in this expression is to the *blue sky laws* that were passed in the United States during the early 1900s to protect the public from buying unsound stocks. One Kansas lawmaker allegedly remarked that some business companies would "capitalize the blue skies" if possible, thus giving birth to the phrase.

"You're operating illegally," he said.
"Either you are selling stock in violation of the blue sky law or you are asking charity." (*Reader's Digest*, September 1946)

cheap shot—A brutal or unsportsmanlike tackle or hit in football; taking unfair advantage of someone. The term developed from its use in American football, coming to be used figuratively in reference to a remark or action that is unneccessarily cruel or unfair.

crafty as a redhead—Unscrupulous; deceitful; cunning; artful. This expression is generally attributed to the guile of Judas Iscariot and his betrayal of Jesus Christ. Since that legendary betrayal, red-haired persons have been unfortunate victims by association with Judas, who is said to have had red hair. The belief was given further impetus during the Middle Ages when the fat of a dead red-haired person was in demand as an ingredient for making poisons. Variants are *cunning as a red-haired person* and *cunning as a redhead*. Shakespeare alludes to the belief in *As You Like It:*
    Rosalind: His hair is of the very dissembling color.
    Celia: Somewhat browner than Judas's.
    (III, iv)
Related terms which carry the same meaning are *cunning as a fox* and *cunning as a serpent*. Both the fox and the serpent have been associated with craftiness for centuries.

crooked as a dog's hind leg—Dishonest; unscrupulous; untrustworthy. This American expression, dating from the late 19th century, alludes to someone who is extremely deceitful. The basis of the simile is obvious. Another term, *dogleg*, is used in golf to denote a fairway designed with a sharp angle between tee and green.

golden handshake—In America this expression refers to a secret understanding between the Department of Defense and a contractor, which is sealed with the so-called *golden handshake*. Such a handshake assures the contractor that, if his costs exceed the specified contract figure, the government will still guarantee him a profit. The phrase has been in use since the early 1950s. See also MONEY.

hit below the belt—To use unfair means; to go against the rules. The Marquis of Queensberry rules of prize fighting, adopted in 1867, prohibit boxers from hitting their opponents below the waist belt. A derivative, commonly used term is *low blow*.

kickback—Money returned unethically for a business favor. This expression refers to an underhanded agreement between two parties for the mutual profit of each; for example, returning part of one's salary to the man who is responsible for getting one a job, or *kicking back* part of one's profits for receiving the contract to do a job.

Longshoremen were finding it tougher than ever to get jobs, even through kick backs of pay, bottles of liquor, and cigars. (Felix Riesenberg, Jr., *Golden Gate*, 1940)

The term has been in use since about 1930, and occasionally is used to imply a simple rebate, or, more ominously, to denote an arrangement whereby a percentage of insurance money will be paid a collaborating thief if he returns stolen goods to the owner after the insurance company has made payment. A related term, *payola,* is used in commercial music circles in reference to a disc jockey who accepts money for playing a particular record frequently to increase its popularity and sales.

knave in grain—An unprincipled, crafty man; a blackguard; a thorough knave. The allusion in this phrase is to another phrase, *dyed in the grain.* The bodies of kermes and cochineal insects, used to create a bright red dye, look like kernels of grain when dried. Since such dye is of a permanent and deep quality, *dyed in the grain* came to mean 'deep-dyed'; hence, a *knave in grain* is a thoroughgoing rogue.

> O maltster! break that cheating peck; 'tis plain
> Whene'er you use it, you're a knave in grain.
> (Benjamin Franklin, *Poor Richard's Almanack,* 1739)

A common variant is *rogue in grain.*

low blow—An unfair or unscrupulous attack, a cheap shot. This term probably derives from *hit below the belt;* in prize fighting, a violation of the Marquis of Queensberry rules. The word is almost always used figuratively, meaning to take unfair advantage by striking where one is most vulnerable.

phone phreak—A cheat who avoids paying for long-distance telephone calls by employing modern technological methods. This expression first appeared in 1972, shortly after the discovery of the original *blue box. Newsweek,* in its February 17, 1975 edition, offered a brief, effective description of this illegal device.

> The blue box—which can actually be any color, but was christened after the first one found—beeps electronic imitations of Bell signals so that users can "seize" lines to make free calls all over the world.

Phone phreak, an alternate spelling of *freak* to conform with *phone,* is the name given to anyone who makes use of these illegal devices. A rather loose brotherhood of these *phone phreaks,* who seem to delight in their devious ways, has been put together and is referred to as *phone phreakdom.*

> Placing the signals related to a call on separate circuits . . . will also increase greatly the difficulty that so-called "phone phreaks" have in placing long-distance calls without paying toll charges. (*The New York Times,* January 18, 1976)

shyster—An unscrupulous person, especially an attorney; a pettifogger. The origin of this American slang term is uncertain. In use since the mid 19th century, the expression has been attributed to a variety of sources: from the German word *Scheisse* 'excrement'; from a New York attorney named *Scheuster*, who during the 1840s was repeatedly reprimanded in court for pettifoggery; from an extension of *shy* in the sense of 'disreputable'; from a corruption of the word *shicer* a 'worthless individual.' Whatever the case, in today's figurative use the word invariably refers to a person, especially an attorney, who will take advantage of people or a situation to gain his own ends.

> Next we come to his Excellency, the Prime Minister...a lawyer of shyster caliber. (Mark Twain, *Roughing It*, 1872)

thumb of gold—The allusion in this phrase is to the unscrupulous practice of some merchants, especially millers. Since the Middle Ages, millers have been notorious for applying additional weight to the scales by means of the thumb. In the *Prologue* to the *Canterbury Tales*, Chaucer writes of the miller who is making the pilgrimage:

> Wel coude he stelen corn and tollen thries, And yet he hadde a thombe of gold, pardee.

The practice was not resticted to the Middle Ages, for even today many a butcher or greengrocer is accused of having a *thumb of gold*.

two-faced—Double dealing; false; deceitful; unscrupulous; pretending to be religious when one is actually evil. This expression is derived from the Roman god Janus, who is depicted as having two faces, giving him the power to see backward as well as forward at the same time. Sometime during the 1600s the term came to connote dishonesty or insincerity.

> "I grant you that he's not two-faced," I said. "But what's the use of that when the one face he has got is so peculiarly unpleasant." (C.P. Snow, *The Affair*, 1960)

Variants are *have two faces* and *keep two faces under one head*.

USELESSNESS
SEE FUTILITY

VACILLATION

back and fill—To vacillate, tergiversate; to blow hot and cold, to be wishy-washy. *Back and fill* is a nautical phrase describing a method of maneuvering a sailboat in which the sails are trimmed so that the wind strikes them first on the forward and then on the aft side, so as to reduce forward movement. The figurative U.S. informal use of the phrase plays on the idea of the alternating forward and backward motion as opposed to a significant movement in any one direction. It is used to describe any lack of commitment to a particular point of view.

blow hot and cold—To accept first, then reject; to seesaw, shilly-shally. This phrase stems from Aesop's fable of a traveler who was entertained by a satyr. The traveler blew his fingers to warm them, then, with the same breath, blew his broth to cool it. Apparently the satyr was appalled to meet one who could blow both hot and cold, and said:

> If you have gotten a trick of blowing hot and cold out of the same mouth, I've e'en done with ye. (R. Lestrange, *Fables of Aesop*, 1694)

As commonly used, *blow hot and cold* smacks less of hypocrisy than *back and fill*; it seems more natural and less manipulative.

Box and Cox—Alternately sharing the same position, serving the same function or occupying the same space. *Box and Cox*, an 1847 farce by J. M. Morton, features two men—John Box and James Cox—who occupied the same apartment without being aware of each other's existence, as one worked the day shift and the other worked at night. The *OED's* earliest citation for the phrase is from 1881.

> Representing mind and body as playing a perpetual game of Box and Cox. (C. E. Raven, *Creator Spirit*, 1927)
>
> The French Community... shares, Box-and-Coxwise, the Luxembourg Palace with the French Senate. (*Spectator*, August 14, 1959)

chop and change—To vacillate; to change frequently; to vary from moment to moment; to barter; to buy and sell. This alliterative British phrase, which dates back to the 1500s, originally dealt with bargaining. However, the *OED* explains that early in the phrase's history *chop* lost its force in the expression, and the emphasis passed from *barter* to *change*.

> O, who would trust the world... That... chops and changes every minute. (Francis Quarles, *Emblems*, 1635)

Delphic sword—A two-edged sword; an argument that works two ways; an ambiguity. In ancient Greece the Oracle at Delphi was notorious for ambiguous prophecies, such as:

> Thou shalt go thou shalt return never in battle shalt thou perish.

Hence, a Delphic sword is double-edged: it slices on either side. Metaphorically, it alludes to the use of argument that forwards positive and negative issues simultaneously.

> "Your Delphic sword," the panther then replied,
> "Is double-edged and cuts on either side."
> (John Dryden, *The Hind and the Panther*, 1687)

fall between two stools—To be indecisive, to vacillate; to fail because of the inability to make a choice or decision. This expression implies that if someone cannot decide which of two stools to sit upon, he is likely to fall between them.

> The unphilosophical attempt to sit upon two stools. (Joseph C. Neal, *Charcoal Sketches*, 1837)

The French equivalent, *être assis entre deux chaises*, means literally 'to be seated between two chairs.'

hold with the hare and run with the hounds—To straddle the fence; to play both ends against the middle; to get the best of both worlds. This hunting phrase is stronger than *back and fill* or *blow hot and cold*, implying an inability to commit oneself to one point of view, and an attempt to cover up by espousing both sides at once.

in dock, out nettle—Inconstancy, vacillation, changeability, instability. This obsolete expression was originally part of a charm repeated while rubbing leaves of the herb *dock* into nettle stings in order to counteract any ill effects: "Nettle in, dock out, Dock in, nettle out, Nettle in, dock out, Dock rub nettle out." An early figurative use of the expression is found in Nicholas Udall's *Ralph Roister Doister* (1553):

> I can not skill of such changeable mettle,
> There is nothing with them but in dock out nettle.

Jack of both sides—One who tries to favor both parties simultaneously in an antagonistic situation; one who tries to remain neutral; one who sides with first one party and then the other, usually because of ulterior motives. This expression, dating from the mid-1500s, makes use of the omnipresent English *Jack*, a term applied to any man in general, to indicate any person who tries to straddle the fence. Variations are *Jack-o-both-sides* and *Jack-a-both-sides*.

> How often have those men of honor...play'd Jack a both sides, today for and tomorrow against. (Daniel Defoe, *The Complete English Gentleman*, 1729)

Jekyll and Hyde—One whose nature is contradictory—sometimes good and benevolent, other times evil and malevolent; a split personality; anything characterized by the opposition of antagonistic forces. This popular phrase comes from Robert Louis Stevenson's *The Case of Dr. Jekyll and Mr. Hyde* (1886). In this story, Jekyll appears as a kind, respectable character, Hyde as an ugly, despicable figure; however, both personalities belong to one man. The following quotation from *The Times Literary Supplement* (July 2, 1931) shows a current use of this phrase.

> Turner was a case of Jekyll and Hyde in real life and oscillated continuously   between   the   Victorian   respectability   of Bloomsbury...and the Rabelaisian society of the London Docks.

on the fence—Undecided, especially in regard to political issues. This expression alludes to the dilemma of a person atop a wall who must decide which is the safer side to descend. In contemporary usage, this American slang phrase usually describes a politician who waits to see how an issue fares before committing his support in either direction.

> Now all would-but-dare-not-be-politicians who insist in sitting on the fence, will be amerced a penalty for the same. (*Annals of Cleveland*, 1830)

reed shaken by the wind—A spineless, wishy-washy person whose opinions shift with the prevailing political or conventional winds; a tergiversator. As currently used, the image stands on its own; the phrase bears no relationship to the New Testament context in which it was spoken by Jesus regarding John the Baptist.

> What went ye out into the wilderness to see? A reed shaken with the wind? (Matthew 11:7)

shilly-shally—To vacillate between two ways of thinking or acting; to dally with trifles to avoid making a decision. The original phrase was *shall I, shall I*, which was altered to *shill I, shall I*. The present form of *shilly-shally* was used as early as the 1700s. It is an innocuous phrase which, like *blow hot and cold*, suggests no hypocrisy or manipulative behavior.

> To shilly-shally on the matter, to act in one way today and in a different way tomorrow. (F. W. Farrar, *Life and Work of St. Paul*, 1879)

weathercock—A person of wavering principles; an indecisive person; a trend follower. In the 9th century, a papal decree ordered each church to place the likeness of a cock atop its steeple in allusion to St. Peter's triple denial of Jesus before the cock crowed twice. After a time, these cocks were mounted on pivots so that they pointed to the direction from which the wind was blowing. Thus, *weathercock* acquired the sense of something being directed by the fancy of the prevailing wind. The term, used figuratively since the time of Chaucer, still carries its meaning of one of vacillating principles.

> He was...a terrible weathercock in the matter of opinion. (Robert Brough, *Marston Lynch*, 1870)

The expression's figurative meaning has been extended to include a person who quickly adopts the latest styles and fads, suggesting a comparison to the ever-changing directions of the fashion world.

VALIDATION
SEE AUTHORITATIVENESS

VALIDITY
SEE AUTHORITATIVENESS

VALUE
SEE WORTHINESS

VEHICLES

Black Maria—A van for conveying prisoners. This U.S. colloquial term reputedly derives from a Black woman named Maria Lee who ran a lodging house for sailors in Boston. Apparently she was a prodigious woman whom the police called on when they needed extra strength to handle rambunctious prisoners. Eventually her name became associated with the van which rounded up prisoners and carried them to jail or court.

> A new Black Maria, . . . a new wagon for the conveyance of prisoners to and from the courts of justice. (*Boston Evening Traveller*, September 25, 1847)

bone-shaker—A facetious name for early model bicycles; later applied to similarly unsteady automobiles such as the early model Fords. Since the first bicycles lacked rubber tires and other modern cushioning conveniences and few roads were paved, their ride was something less than smooth and comfortable. The term was in use as early as 1874.

bucket of bolts—An irreverent American slang term for an old rundown car that rattles and shakes noisily when moving, producing a sound similar to the rattling of a bucketful of bolts or screws.

flying saucer—A mysterious, disk-shaped flying object; an unidentified flying object; a *UFO*. This term was coined in the late 1940s when large numbers of sightings of *flying saucers* were made. When first brought to the public's attention, these bizarre phenomena were the subject of much fanciful speculation as to their origin.

> Theodore Fitch, author of *Our Paradise inside the Earth*, believes that flying saucers originate within the earth and are piloted by small people who have discovered how to power such vehicles with "free energy." (*The People's Almanac*, 1975)

Originally applied as a general term for all such objects, regardless of shape, in recent years the term has been replaced by *UFO*, for "unidentified flying object," for mysterious aircraft have been sighted not only in the shape of disks but also in the shapes of cigars, cones, and a number of other forms. Shooting across the sky at great speeds, often in formation, they are still reported almost daily by competent observers but remain elusive.

> It was the perfect setting for a UFO landing—a misty, eerie night on a brush-covered hill. (*The People's Almanac*, 1975)

meatwagon—An ambulance. This slang expression alludes to the damaged human flesh transported to hospitals in these emergency vehicles.

We'll need a couple of meatwagons. The minister and two other people were killed and ... there're a lot of injured. (E. McBain, *Hail, Hail, the Gang's All Here*, 1971)

This expression often includes both paddy wagons and hearses.

paddy wagon—A patrol wagon; an enclosed truck or van used by the police to transport prisoners; a Black Maria. *Paddy*, a corruption of the common Irish name Patrick, was once used as a nickname for anyone of Irish descent. Since many police officers in major American cities at the turn of the century were Irish, through association their patrol wagons came to be known as *paddy wagons*. Although the ethnic implications were gradually lost after the 1920s, the expression has remained in widespread use.

> Police who attempted to enforce city segregation rules met with a torrent of jeers, and several tennis players who sat down on the courts had to be carried to paddy wagons. (*Aurora* [Illinois] *Beacon News*, November 7, 1948)

panda car—A police car. This British colloquialism undoubtedly alludes to the appearance of English police cars: white vehicles with a broad horizontal stripe along the middle.

prairie schooner—A large wagon with a high, canvas-covered frame, used by early American settlers of the West to cross the prairies. This expression is simply a fanciful name invented by the pioneers for the Conestoga wagons with which many moved their entire households westward. These wagons were named for the Conestoga valley in Lancaster County, Pennsylvania where they were first manufactured in the 1700s. Many of the wagons were lengthened or widened before the long trek west, for they not only had to transport the household goods but also to serve as a mobile home for an entire family. The term's first known appearance in print is 1858.

> To send produce to market, the [Pennsylvania] Germans invented the Conestoga wagon ... the ancestor of the "prairie schooner" which later carried pioneers to California and Oregon. (Henry Bragdon and Samuel McCutcheon, *History of a Free People*, 1969)

The nickname *stogy* for a cigar derives from Conestoga wagon. The drivers of these wagons, before setting out on a long journey, were known to roll a number of crude cigars from tobacco grown near Conestoga. These cigars were quite strong and became known as *Conestogas* which was quickly shortened to *stogas* and then *stogies*. Today a *stogy* refers to any cheap, strong cigar.

rattletrap—A rickety old car that rattles and clatters and shakes while in motion; a dangerously dilapidated vehicle.

Zulu car—This American railroad slang term was born in the late 1800s when many foreign immigrants, bearing all their worldly possessions, were making their way westward by means of cheap rail transportation. For some reason not entirely clear the railroad workers nicknamed these immigrants *Zulus*, and the cars in which they rode, often meagerly converted boxcars or cattle cars, became known as *Zulu cars*.

> Zulu cars...provided for the transportation of the stock and household effects of the settlers...a weird appearance when loaded with all the impedimenta. (Godfrey Irwin, *American Tramp and Underworld Slang*, 1931)

The term is obsolete today.

VENDING
SEE SELLING

VENGEANCE
SEE RETALIATION

VEXATION
See also ANGER

cross [someone's] bows—To annoy, displease, or offend; to overstep one's bounds and behave inappropriately toward another person. This expression has nautical origins. When one ship passes in front of another, crossing her path, the first is said to *cross the bows* of the second. Such a move is considered dangerous and a breach of the nautical rules of the road. Both the nautical and figurative meanings are in use today.

darken [one's] door—To be an unwelcome visitor; to appear at the door; to enter one's house. This term, employed since the early 1700s, is most frequently applied in a negative sense to indicate that the person doing the darkening is not a welcome caller. The concept behind the phrase is that one's shadow falling upon the door creates a feeling of foreboding or that the blocking of the doorway with one's body causes a degree of uneasiness among those within.

> I never darkened his door in my life. (Jonathan Swift, *Polite Conversation*, 1738)

daughter of the horseleech—Anyone, especially a woman, who is overly demanding, clinging, and critical; an exigent harpy. This expression is based on a Biblical reference:

> The horseleach hath two daughters, crying, Give, give. (Proverbs 30:15)

The horseleech is a large, bloodsucking parasite with a forked tongue. It was sometimes used as a medicinal leech in the medieval practice of bloodletting, i.e., removing blood from a diseased person or animal in the belief that this would effect a cure. Because of its size and voracious appetite, the horseleech was thought to be insatiable. Since each fork of its tongue is called a *daughter,* the expression *daughter of the horseleech* is appropriate in describing someone who acts like a leech, sponging off other people. The word *horseleech* was once used to describe a veterinarian.

dog [some one's] footsteps—To follow another slavishly; to force one's presence upon another; to pester. The allusion here is to a dog following closely at its master's heels, sometimes so persistently that its master tries to rid himself of its constant presence. Metaphorically, the term has come to imply a pertinacious fellow who in trying to collect a debt or to gather information is driving his victim to distraction. The term, dating from about 1500, has acquired a disparaging connotation. Common variants are *dog [some one's] heels* and *hound [some one's] footsteps.*

> Spies and informers dogged his footsteps. (William Dixon, *William Penn,* 1851)

drive up the wall—To plague or badger someone to the breaking point; to drive someone "crazy" by repeated harassment. This slang expression brings to mind the picture of someone literally climbing the wall of an enclosing space to escape the source of annoyance. One so driven is said to *climb the wall.*

get [someone's] back up—To anger or provoke. The reference is to the way a cat arches its back when angered or threatened. This expression appeared as early as 1728 in *The Provok'd Husband* by Sir John Vanbrugh and Colley Cibber.

get [someone's] dander up—To arouse someone's anger or temper. There are two theories as to the origin of the phrase. One hypothesis suggests that *dander* derives from *dandruff* 'the scurf of the scalp.' Another theory is based on the meaning of *dander* as ferment used in making molasses in the West Indies. By extension *ferment* means 'agitation or tumult.' Thus, to get someone's dander up is to provoke and agitate him. This expression dates at least from 1831, when it appeared in the *American Comic Annual* by H. J. Finn.

get [someone's] Dutch up—To arouse someone's ire, to madden; also *get [someone's] Irish* or *Indian up.* Although the exact origins of these expressions are unknown, they would seem to be references to the reputed hotheaded nature of the nationalities in question. Barrere and Leland's *Dictionary of Slang, Jargon and Cant* (1888) offers the following:

> Irish, Indian, Dutch (American), all of these words are used to signify anger or arousing temper. But to say that one has his "Indian up,"

DOG SOMEONE'S FOOTSTEPS

implies a great degree of vindictiveness, while Dutch wrath is stubborn but yielding to reason.

get [someone's] goat—To annoy or irritate; to antagonize or frustrate a person. The expression is synonymous with the French *prendre la chèvre*, to take the goat.' The phrase, in general use since World War I, implies the prodding of someone to anger or irritability.

> "You certainly got my goat" she said in the quaint American fashion, "telling me little No-no was too fat." (H. L. Wilson, *Ruggles of Red Gap*, 1915)

get [someone's] hackles up—To irritate or annoy; to anger, often with pugilistic potential. This expression stems from the sport of cockfighting; *hackles* are the long, shiny feathers on the neck of certain birds such as gamecocks. When confronted by its opponent, a gamecock reacts with a show of strength, causing its hackles to become erect. Through the years, this expression and the related *get [someone's] dander up* (where *dander* may be a corruption of *dandruff*, thus implying hair) have been applied to dogs and cats. When these animals are threatened, the hair on their neck involuntarily stands on end. Eventually, the figurative use to describe a person became common.

> As my hackles were now fairly up, I crept and ran as well as I could after my wounded game. (Clive Phillipps-Wolley, *Sport in the Crimea and Caucasus*, 1881)

get [someone's] monkey up—To anger or provoke. The reference is to the irritable and irascible temperament of monkeys. Used as early as 1863 in *Tyneside Songs*, the expression is originally British and has never been common in the United States.

make [someone's] nose swell—To render someone jealous.

> He heard Lord Altham say ... my wife has got a son, which will make my brother's nose swell. (Thomas B. and Thomas J. Howell, *Cobbett's Complete Collection of State Trials*, 1813)

This expression, dating from the early 1700s, is probably a jocular variation of *put someone's nose out of joint*. At any event, this expression seems to imply that the feeling of jealousy will be manifest in the person experiencing it.

pain in the ass—An obnoxious person; someone who is disliked; one whose behavior is annoying; a disagreeable obligation or duty. The origin of this 20th-century slang expression is unknown. The phrase suggests that someone is so annoying that he causes discomfort in a very sensitive part of the anatomy.

> Connie is supposed to be attractive, vulnerable, funny, and probably a pain in the ass at times. (Michael Leahy, *TV Guide*, April 9, 1983)

Common variants of the term are *pain in the neck* and the euphemistic *pain in the rump*, both more socially acceptable than the original.

> Harcourt without money was just a pain in the neck. (Peter Cheney, *A Trap for Bellamy*, 1941)

penny in the slot—To bait someone; get someone up on his high horse; to tease subtly. This expression is usually heard when one drops a controversial topic into the midst of a conversation, especially when one knows that an ardent proponent of some cause is present. Any snide remark in opposition to the proponent's beliefs usually evokes a tirade of great proportions. It is at this point that the antagonist turns to a nearby friend and says 'penny in the slot,' an allusion to the activity that follows the insertion of money into a coin-operated machine such as a jukebox.

pot-house politician—An obnoxious fellow who hangs about taverns expounding on his political views for all who will listen. He is usually of little knowledge or only half-informed about the issues of which he speaks. The term was coined in America in the late 1700s and is occasionally heard today.

> He was distracted by petitions of 'numerous and respectable meetings' consisting of some half dozen scurvy pot-house politicians. (Washington Irving, *Knickerbocker's History of New York*, 1809)

A variant is *ale-house politician*.

rib [someone]—To tease another person; to make fun of someone; to pull someone's leg; to irritate or vex. This expression is derived from the literal act of poking somebody in the ribs with an elbow or a finger, as some jokesters are prone to do. To *rib someone* and *ribbing* assumed their modern connotations of teasing in the early 1900s. Shortly thereafter, the noun *rib* came to connote a joke or a veiled criticism.

> Wilt said, "He is a parasite." Maybe this was a rib. (Red Smith, *The New York Herald-Tribune*, January 25, 1952)

ruffle feathers—To anger, irritate, annoy; to disturb, upset, agitate. When a bird is threatened or challenged, the feathers on its back and neck become ruffled, that is, erect, in a show of strength and apparent anger. This expression is applied figuratively to describe a manifestation of a person's anger.

> The dean ruffled his plumage, and said with asperity...(Frederic Farrar, *Julian Home*, 1859)

VICTIMIZATION
SEE EXPLOITATION; MANIPULATION

VIRTUOUSNESS
SEE WORTHINESS

VISAGE

See also PHYSICAL APPEARANCE

beetle-browed—Having prominent, shaggy eyebrows; scowling, sullen. Although the exact origin of this expression is unknown, it has been suggested that the reference is to the short-tufted antennae, analogous to eyebrows, protruding at right angles from the head of some types of beetles. The phrase appeared in William Langland's *Piers Plowman*.

fish eye—A blank or quizzical gaze; a hostile stare. The vacuity of piscine eyes is clearly the source of this phrase. The following illustration is cited in *Webster's Third:*

I saw you guys giving me the fish eye . . . so I ran.

gag-tooth—A projecting tooth; a bucktooth. *Gag-toothed* dates from the 16th century and is rarely heard today. The current word for such a condition is *bucktoothed* or *gat–toothed*.

If she be gag-toothed tell her some merry jest to make her laugh. (John Lyly, *Euphues, the Anatomy of Wit,* 1579)

grin like a Cheshire cat—To grin broadly and mysteriously; to be constantly smiling widely for no apparent reason. The phrase usually carries connotations of smugness or vacuousness. The expression, which dates from the late 18th century, gained currency because of the perpetually grinning cat in Lewis Carroll's *Alice's Adventures in Wonderland* (1865). The phrase appeared in response to Alice's question as to why the Duchess' cat grinned so broadly and inscrutably:

"It's a Cheshire cat," said the Duchess, "and that's why."

hangdog look—A browbeaten, abject appearance; a guilty or shamefaced demeanor; a sneaky countenance; having a visage befitting a despicable person. The allusion in this expression was originally to a base, despicable person who was mean enough to hang a dog. However, time has tempered that meaning so that today one with a *hangdog look* is generally said to appear defeated, intimidated, or downcast. The expression has been in use since the mid-17th century.

I can't have the hang-dog look which the unfortunate Theseus has. (Sir Walter Scott, *Journal,* January 7, 1826)

A related term carrying much the same connotation is *hangdog air*.

like an owl in an ivy bush—With a vacant, dumb look; with an empty stare, such as some people have when drunk. This expression plays on the fact that the ivy bush is the favorite haunt of the owl, known for its wisdom and solemnity; it is also the favorite plant of Bacchus, the god of wine. Rarely heard today, this expression dates from the early 17th century.

"Pr'y thee, how did the fool look?" "Look! Egad, he look'd for all the world like an owl in an ivy bush." (Jonathan Swift, *Polite Conversation*, 1738)

Mona Lisa smile—An enigmatic smile; a smile which carries an aura of mystery about it. Known properly as *La Gioconda*, the brilliant portrait of the wife of Francesco del Gioconda known as the *Mona Lisa*, by Leonardo da Vinci (1452–1519), is distinguished by the subject's peculiar smile, a smile whose meaning has been the source of much speculation through the centuries. A common variant is the *Gioconda smile*.

> Here one could be sure that there was some kind of a queer face behind the Gioconda smile and the Roman eyebrows. (Aldous Huxley, *The Gioconda Smile*, 1921)

poker face—An expressionless face; a visage which does not reveal one's thoughts or emotions; a dead pan. In poker, it is essential that a player not tip his hand by showing emotion in his face, lest the other players bet accordingly and thus limit his winnings or increase his losses. Though still applicable to the card game, *poker face* is also used figuratively in many varied contexts.

> He glanced around the circle and found poker faces, but there was a light in Baldy's eyes that warmed him. (Clarence Mulford, *Rustler's Valley*, 1924)

widow's peak—A V-shaped hairline in the middle of the forehead. It was once customary for a widow to wear a black hat which had a *peak*, 'a triangular piece of material that extended down on the forehead,' as if pointing at the nose. A similar-looking hairline came to be known as a *widow's peak* by association.

> She had on her forehead what is sometimes denominated a "widow's peak"—that is to say, her hair grew down to a point in the middle. (Henry Wadsworth Longfellow, *Kavanagh, A Tale*, 1849)

A related expression, *widow's lock*, describes a lock or tuft of hair that grows apart from the rest of the hair on the head. The term alludes to an ancient superstitious belief that a woman with such a stray shock of hair would be widowed soon after marriage.

VULGARITY
SEE PROFANITY

VULNERABILITY
See also DANGER; INDEBTEDNESS

Achilles heel—Any particularly vulnerable area; a weakness; a soft spot. Legend has it that Thetis, mother of the Greek hero Achilles immersed him in the river Styx at birth, in order to make him invulnerable. In doing so, she held him by one heel, which was therefore never touched by the water. Later, as a great warrior in the Trojan war, Achilles went unharmed by his enemies until Paris, to whom Apollo had told the secret of Achilles' heel, mortally wounded him by shooting an arrow into his heel. The first recorded use of the term was in 1810 in Coleridge's *The Friend:*

Ireland, that vulnerable heel of the British Achilles!

The sinew connecting the back of the heel to the calf of the leg is called the Achilles tendon.

between two fires—Under attack from both sides at once; caught in a precarious or dangerous situation with no way out. A soldier who was exposed to gunfire from two or more sides was said to be *between two fires.* This literal usage appeared as early as 1885.

He was about to find himself placed between two fires—viz. the Mahdi and the reinforced garrison of Metammeh. (*The Times,* February 20, 1885)

On the figurative level current today, *fire* refers to any danger which threatens from all sides simultaneously.

between wind and water—In a vulnerable, precarious position; exposed or unprotected, defenseless. Literally, the phrase refers to that part of the ship's side which is alternately exposed and submerged, marking the fluctuation of the water line. Such an area is particularly vulnerable to attack and corrosion. Figuratively, the phrase refers to any vulnerable state or dangerous situation. The literal use appears as early as 1588, the figurative as early as 1652.

Now they have crackt me betwixt wind and water a'most past cure. Stay, let me feel my self. (Arthur Wilson, *Inconstant Ladie,* 1652)

Both levels of meaning remain in use today.

caught bending—Taken by surprise; at a disadvantage; in a vulnerable position. A child bending over is not on his guard and is particularly well-positioned for a kicking or spanking. A 1903 song by George Robey included the line:

My word! I catch you bending!

caught flat-footed—Caught unprepared, unready, by surprise, not on one's toes. This phrase probably derives from baseball or football, and dates from the early 1920s. It refers to someone's being caught (thrown out or tackled) while standing still or flat-footed. A person in such a position reacts less quickly than one on his toes.

caught with [one's] pants down—Taken completely off guard or entirely by surprise; found in a compromising or embarrassing position; hence, also unquestionably guilty; caught in the act, in flagrante delicto. General acceptance of this inelegant expression has been attributed to its appearance in a 1946 issue of *The Saturday Evening Post.*

chink in [one's] armor—A weakness or vulnerability; an area in which one's defenses are inadequate or ineffective; a personality flaw. The phrase alludes to the armor worn by knights. A *chink* 'crack, cleft, or narrow opening' could cost a knight his life. Figuratively, a *chink in one's armor* refers to a personal rather than physical vulnerability. Some modern psychologists have adopted the word *armor* to mean 'character or personality,' emphasizing those aspects of one's character which are formed in defense and serve self-protective functions.

clay pigeon—A person or thing in a vulnerable position; an easy mark; one who can be easily taken advantage of; an easy job or task, a cinch. This American slang expression is an extension of the term *clay pigeon* as used in trapshooting, where it represents a disklike object of baked clay thrown into the air as a target. It has been in literal usage since 1888.

fair game—A legitimate object of attack or ridicule; an easy target of derision. The term originated with wildlife laws limiting the hunting of certain animals to a specific time or season of the year, during which the hunted animals are *fair game.* In its figurative sense, this phrase refers to a person or thing whose manner or appearance makes him a likely victim of mockery.

> In that character it becomes fair game for ridicule. (Jeremy Bentham, *Chrestomathia,* 1816)

gone coon—One who is in bad straits; a person who is on the brink of disaster, whose goose is cooked; a lost soul, a goner. A *coon* (raccoon) which cannot escape from a hunter is a gone coon. A ludicrous fable probably fabricated to explain this expression tells of a raccoon which, trapped in a tree at gunpoint by Davey Crockett, said to the great marksman, "I know I'm a gone coon." The Democratic party was aware of the fable when they applied the label *coon* to the Whigs during the presidential contest of 1840.

gone goose—One who is in a highly vulnerable situation; a hopeless case; a lost cause; one in dire straits. This Americanism, dating from about 1830, is probably an alliterative variation of the older term, *gone coon,* which dates from the days of the American Revolution.

> If he hadn't come just as he did, I'd been a gone coon. (Harold Frederic, *The Deserter,* 1898)

A large number of anecdotes exist which tell of treed coons pleading with the hunter not to shoot for they know they are *gone coons.* Apparently the expression was so satisfying that a number of similar terms arose, *gone chick, gone beaver, gone gander,* and *gone horse,* all conveying the same meaning.

> Two more minutes of her, and I'm a gone goose. (*The Saturday Evening Post*, March 19, 1949)

live in a glass house—To be in a vulnerable position, to be open to attack; to live a public life, to be in the public eye. The expression plays on two well-known properties of glass—its transparency and its brittleness. The phrase is apparently a truncated version of the old proverb *people who live in glass houses shouldn't throw stones,* dating from the early 17th century.

> In the glass house world of commercial publishing, ... Peter Mayer is something of a superstar. (*Saturday Review,* February 1979)

on the rebound—Living through a period of time after an emotional trauma when one is especially vulnerable.

> She caught him on the rebound, i.e., got engaged to him, after he had been refused by someone else. (W. E. Collins, *Contemporary English,* 1927)

The allusion is to grabbing a missed shot in basketball or striking a hockey puck deflected by the goalie and making a goal, implying that the defending team was taken unawares or was in a lax or defenseless attitude. In the game of love, one suffering disappointment from a recently-ended love affair is said to be *on the rebound* and can often be susceptible to another's advances. The term has been in use since the early 20th century.

on the ropes—On the verge of ruin or collapse; at the mercy of whatever forces threaten to overcome one. The metaphor is from the boxing ring. When a prize fighter is on the ropes, he is in a weakened and very vulnerable position. His opponent is in control, and will probably soon be able to finish him off.

open season—A time when persons or ideas in disfavor are subject to attack from all sides. The expression, of American origin, comes from hunting and refers to those periods during which various types of game are legitimate quarry.

out on a limb—In a vulnerable, compromising, or risky position; at a disadvantage. This expression refers to the predicament of a person in a tree who, having climbed out onto one of the branches (limbs), faces the prospect of injury if the limb should not be strong enough to support him. The figurative implications are that a person has espoused an unconventional idea or cause which, if it fails, may precipitate his downfall, resulting in a loss of influence, prestige, and credibility.

> No one is willing to go out on any limb. No one is willing to say yes or no to a proposition. He must always go to someone higher. (John Steinbeck, *Russian Journal,* 1948)

over a barrel—In an embarrassing or uncomfortable position or situation; with one's back against the wall, helpless, in someone else's power. This chiefly U.S. slang expression dates from at least 1939. According to the *OED* the allusion is to the helpless condition of a person who, after having been saved from drowning, is placed over a barrel in order to clear the water out of his lungs.

sitting duck—An easy mark or target, a ripe victim; a person or thing in an open or vulnerable position. The allusion is to the comparative ease of shooting a duck resting on the water as opposed to one in flight.

stick [one's] neck out—To expose oneself to danger or criticism; to take a chance, to risk failure; to invite trouble. This early 20th-century American expression plays with the idea that sticking one's neck out is equivalent to asking to have one's head chopped off. Thus vulnerability, usually nonphysical, is also implicit in the figurative uses of this expression.

> We've stuck our necks out—we're looking for trouble, see ? (H. Hastings, *Seagulls Over Sorrento*, 1950)

turn turtle—To be utterly helpless or defenseless. When turned on their backs, turtles are completely powerless and without defense. *Turn turtle* also means 'to overturn, upset, capsize.'

up a tree—Cornered, trapped, caught; at another's mercy, in another's power. The expression is said to come from coon hunting; once a raccoon is treed by the hounds, he's a gone coon.

> I had her in my power—up a tree, as the Americans say. (William Makepiece Thackeray, *Major Gahagan*, 1839)

where the shoe pinches—The sore spot or vulnerable area; the true source of trouble or distress. This expression purportedly derived from Plutarch's biography of Paulus Aemilius. Questioned as to why he divorced his fair, faithful, and fertile wife, Aemilius removed his shoe and replied, "Is it not handsome? Is it not new? Yet none knows where it pinches, save he that wears it." This expression, equivalents of which exist in most European languages, appeared in English literature as early as the time of Chaucer.

> Subtle enemies, that know... where the shoe pincheth us most. (Gabriel Harvey, *Letterbook*, 1580)

WAVERING
SEE VACILLATION

WHOLENESS
SEE TOTALITY

WORDS
SEE LANGUAGE

WORK
SEE EXERTION

WORSENING
SEE EXACERBATION

WORTHINESS

Worthiness

WORTHINESS

fall of a sparrow—Small events are significant, especially in the eyes of God; do not underestimate the importance of small things. Although there is an allusion to the fall of a sparrow in the New Testament, Matthew 10:29, the phrase in this exact form derives from Shakespeare's *Hamlet*. Hamlet, who has just accepted a fencing challenge from Laertes, a superior swordsman, explains to Horatio why he is willing to face Laertes.

> Not a whit; we defy augury. There's a special providence in the fall of a sparrow. (V, ii)

good wine needs no bush—A worthwhile product doesn't need to be advertised; a thing of quality speaks for itself. An ivy bush, the plant sacred to the Greek god Bacchus, was at one time a common symbol hung outside taverns to indicate that wine was dispensed inside. Although the practice itself has died, one may still see reminders on the sign boards of some taverns and pubs. The implication in this expression is, of course, that if a public-house owner serves good wine, he doesn't need any ivy. The phrase first made its appearance in the 1500s.

> Some ale-houses upon the road I saw, And some with bushes showing they wine did draw. (*Poor Robin's Perambulations*, 1678)

nothing to sneeze at—Not a thing to be ignored or rejected as a trifle; not a person to be treated with derision or contempt; worthy of serious consideration; also *not to be sneezed at*. Now used exclusively in the negative, *to sneeze at* 'to regard as of little value' was common in the 1800s, though precisely how *sneezing at* came to be equated with an estimation of worth is not clear. The expression is most often found with reference to sums of money, as illustrated by the following passage from Lockhart's *Memoirs of Sir Walter Scott*:

> As I am situated, £300 or £400 is not to be sneezed at.

pay [one's] dues—To prove oneself worthy by fulfilling obligations; to start at the bottom, gain experience, and work one's way up. As early as the 1600s, *dues* referred to a fee for membership in an organization. In the United States, during the 1900s, *dues* gained currency as a figurative slang term for nonfinancial obligations; *pay one's dues* means to earn rights or recognition with hard work and perseverance. The expression is current especially among jazz musicians in referring to the years of anonymity and financial hardship devoted to learning and developing an individual style.

SITTING DUCK

Duke, Thad, Mel and myself, we've paid considerable amounts of dues in trying to get this thing off the ground. (*Down Beat*, April 17, 1969)

worth a Jew's eye—Of great value; extremely precious; worth a fortune. The allusion in this phrase is to the medieval practice of torturing Jews by gouging out an eye to extort money from them or to force payment of the exorbitant taxes which were levied upon them. The expression has been in use since about 1200.

Although the journey . . . would cost twice the value of a gold seal, yet, that in the end it might be worth a Jew's eye. (Frederick Marryat, *Peter Simple*, 1833)

worth [one's] salt—To be worthy or deserving of one's wages or pay; to be efficient and hard-working; often used negatively in the phrase *not worth one's salt*. The *salt* of this expression is said to have come from the old Roman practice of paying soldiers their wages in salt, then a rare and precious commodity. When money for the purchase of salt was substituted for the salt itself, it was known as *salārium* 'salt money,' the predecessor of the English *salary*, from Latin *sal* 'salt.' *Worth one's salt* has been in common usage since the early 19th century.

worth the whistle—Worthy, deserving; acceptable, commendable; of value and importance. This expression, implying that a person is worth the effort of whistling for him, is derived from a proverb cited by John Heywood in *Dialogue Containing the Number in Effect of All the Proverbs in the English Tongue* (1546):

It is a poor dog that is not worth the whistling.

Shakespeare uses the phrase in *King Lear* when Goneril implies that at one time she was held in high regard by Albany, but that now she is being treated more poorly and with less respect than one would accord a common cur:

I have been worth the whistle. (IV,ii)

The expression is often used in the negative *not worth a whistle*, frequently to describe a person whose friendship is considered worthless.

WORTHLESSNESS
SEE INSIGNIFICANCE

YIELDING
SEE DEFERENCE

See also AGE

blue on the plum—Freshness; delicate charm; youth. This expression, dating from the late 17th century, alludes to young, newly gathered plums. Figuratively, the term refers to that time in life when one has just achieved the first blush of adulthood. It is often heard negatively to symbolize the loss of youthful beauty and innocence.

> She was handsome in her time ...
> She has quite lost the blue on the plum.
> (Jonathan Swift, *Polite Conversation*, 1738)

A variant of this phrase, *the bloom on the peach*, carries the same connotation.

> The bloom has been off the peach anytime these fifteen years. (Arthur Murphy, *Old Maid*, 1761)

hobbledehoy—Half man, half boy; a name for a youth in the awkward late teen years when he is neither a man nor a boy. The *OED* defines this term as of uncertain origin, with all instances of the use of *hobble* occurring after 1700, except one dated 1540. Prior to 1700 all other citations have *hobber* or a variant of that spelling.

> The first seven years bring up as a child,
> The next to learning, for waxing too wild.
> The next keep under *Sir Hobbard de Hoy,*
> The next a man no longer a boy.
> (Thomas Tusser, *Five Hundred Points of Good Husbandry*, 1573)

The term, although seldom heard today, is still in use.

> Hobbledehoy, neither man nor
>   boy . . .
> There's a god and a devil in Hobbledehoy.
> (Witter Bynner, *Hobbledehoy*, 1930)

latchkey kids—Children who come home from school to an empty house because their parents are still at work. In occasional use since about 1900, this expression came into everyday use during the late 1970s such these children and their plight were brought to the attention of the Amerian public. The term derives from the fact that these children wear house keys on a string around their necks so they may let themselves into their homes when they return from school, there being no one at home since the parent or parents are still working.

> At an inner city school we found about one in three children was a latchkey kid. (Lynette and Thomas Long, *Latchkey Children and Their Parents*, 1983)

salad days—Youth; the time of juvenile inexperience and naivete; the springtime of one's life. This expression may have derived as an analogy between *green* 'inexperienced, immature' and the predominant color of salad ingredients. This comparison was made in Shakespeare's *Antony and Cleopatra* (I,v):

My salad days,

when I was green in judgment.

In addition to the phrase's youthful sense, *salad days* also refers to any period in a person's life or career characterized by callowness and unsophistication.

In directing "The Pride and the Passion" Stanley Kramer created a picture as vast, heavily populated, and downright foolish as anything the Master [C. B. DeMille] confected in his salad days. (*New Yorker,* July 1957)

Index

All references are to page numbers within the text. Items in boldface type are specific entries, while items in *italic type* are to be found within entries.

Aaron's serpent, p. 48
Abe's cabe, p. 201
above-board, p. 32
above the salt, p. 297
Abraham man, p. 249
Abraham men, p. 249
Abraham-sham, p. 249
Abraham ward, p. 249
accidentally on purpose, p. 325
ace in the hole, p. 239
ace up [one's] sleeve, p. 239
Achilles heel, p. 345
acknowledge the corn, p. 304
across-the-board, p. 155
Adam and Eve, p. 174
Adam's Ale, p. 122
add fuel to the fire, p. 97
add insult to injury, p. 97
affable as a wet dog, p. 210
afraid of [one's] own shadow,
    p. 121
after you, my dear Alphonse, p. 59
against the collar, p. 104
aim to please, p. 90
air [one's] lungs, p. 254
airy-fairy, p. 116
alea jacta est, p. 185
ale-house politician, p. 343
All adrift, p. 44
all along the line, p. 155
all around the Wrekin, p. 155
all balled up, p. 44
all down the line, p. 155
alley cat, p. 256
alley-catting around, p. 256

all hollow, p. 218
all is fish that comes to his net,
    p. 106, p. 12
all mops and brooms, p. 79
all over bar the shouting, p. 316
all over but the shouting, p. 316
all over except the shouting, p. 316
all round my hat, p. 279
All Round My Hat I Wears a Green
    Willow, p. 279
all shook up, p. 72
all the fat is in the fire, p. 185
all the king's horses (and all the
    king's men), p. 155
all the world and his wife, p. 156
all thumbs, p. 30
all wet, p. 94
almighty dollar, p. 201
almighty gold, p. 201
alpha and omega, p. 156
alpha to omega, p. 156
ambulance chaser, p. 330
amen corner, p. 23
Amyris plays the fool, p. 325
anchor leg, p. 14
anchor man, p. 14
anise and cumin, p. 167
Anne's fan, p. 176
any more for the Skylark?, p. 61
applaud to the echo, p. 23
apple-polish, p. 210
apple-polisher, p. 210
applesauce, p. 207
arguing in a circle, p. 71
around the mahogany, p. 131

arrive in an armchair, p. 138
arrow of Acestes, p. 27
as a hog does side saddle, p. 143
as hasty as Hopkins, p. 271
to ask for the moon, p. 133
as proud as a dog in a doublet,
 p. 229
ass in a lion's skin, p. 249
ass kisser, p. 210
as wise as Doctor Doddypoll, p. 117
at a fair was dropped, p. 132
at close of play, p. 316
Athanasian wench, p. 256
at loose ends, p. 44
at rack and manger, p. 16
at sea, p. 44
at sixes and sevens, p. 72
at the end of the day, p. 316
Attic figs, p. 140, p. 64
Aunt Edna, p. 262
Austerlitz look, p. 148
avant-garde, p. 301
awkward squad, p. 30
axle grease, p. 201
back and fill, p. 333
back and fill, p. 334, p. 335
backstairs influence, p. 192
back the wrong horse, p. 94
back to square one, p. 110
back to the drawing board, p. 110
back water, p. 282
bacon and rice aristocracy, p. 297
bad-ball hitter, p. 94
bag a brace, p. 113
bag and baggage, p. 156
bag lady, p. 243
bag of bones, p. 234
bag of tricks, p. 239
bail out, p. 61
baker's dozen, p. 100
bald as a coot, p. 234
balderdash, p. 207
ball up, p. 72
bamboo curtain, p. 152
bamboozle, p. 325
banana oil, p. 207
bandy-legged, p. 234
bang on, p. 247
bang on, p. 248

to bang one's head against the wall,
 p. 133
bang on target, p. 247
bang to rights, p. 37
bank-walker, p. 257
banned in Boston, p. 260
banyan days, p. 123
baptism of blood, p. 165
baptism of fire, p. 165, p. 319
baptism of water, p. 165
bare as a barn, p. 100
barfly, p. 79
bark at the moon, p. 132
bark up the wrong tree, p. 94
barmy on the crumpet, p. 84
Baron Münchhausen, p. 196
barrack, p. 176
to barrack for, p. 176
Bartholomew doll, p. 214
bathroom talk, p. 254
bat on a sticky wicket, p. 70
batty, p. 86
bawl out, p. 270
bay at the moon, p. 132
Beach-la-Mar, p. 188
be all things to all men, p. 140
beans are in flower, p. 116
bear's service, p. 30
bear garden, p. 45
beat a dead horse, p. 134
beat all hollow, p. 218
beat around the bush, p. 36
beat Banagher, p. 219
beat generation, p. 263
beatniks, p. 263
beat [one's] head against the wall,
 p. 132
beat the air, p. 133
beat the devil around a bush, p. 329
beat the Dutch, p. 219
beautiful downtown Burbank,
 p. 167
bêche-de-mer, p. 188
beauty is only skin deep, p. 234
be cut for the simples, p. 118
bed of down, p. 163
bed of flowers, p. 163
bed of nails, p. 67
bed of roses, p. 163

be driven round the bend, p. 88
beetle-browed, p. 344
before [one] had nails on [one's] toes, p. 18, p. 321
before you can say "Jack Robinson," p. 174
before you can say "Jack Robinson," p. 174
before you can say "knife", p. 174
beggar's bush, p. 243
behind the scenes, p. 287
be in Dulcarnon, p. 47
Bellerophontic letter, p. 57
belly-timber, p. 123
bent out of shape, p. 20
be on a sticky wicket, p. 70
be out for a duck, p. 112
be put in the pudding club, p. 237
beside [oneself], p. 181
bet dollars to doughnuts, p. 38
bet [one's] boots, p. 37
bet [one's] bottom dollar, p. 37
bet [one's] life, p. 37
between dog and wolf, p. 321
between two fires, p. 346
between wind and water, p. 346
between you and me and the barn, p. 287
between you and me and the bed-post, p. 287
between you and me and the doorpost, p. 287
between you and me and the gatepost, p. 287
between you and me and the lamppost, p. 287
beware of Greeks bearing gifts, p. 249
beware the ides of March, p. 57, p. 310
big eyes, p. 65
billingsgate, p. 254
bindle stiff, p. 243
bite a file, p. 282
bite [one's] thumb at, p. 176
to bite the bridle, p. 150
bite the bullet, p. 89
black as isel, p. 234
black as itchul, p. 234

black as the devil's nutting-bag, p. 234
Black as the knockers of Newgate, p. 238
Black Maria, p. 337
blankety-blank, p. 254
bleed one for his money, p. 157
the blind leading the blind, p. 133
blind man's holiday, p. 322
blockhead, p. 143
blood, sweat, and tears, p. 104
bloody but unbowed, p. 228
bloom on the peach, p. 353
blow hot and cold, p. 334
blow hot and cold, p. 335, p. 336
blow lunch, p. 149
blue around the gills, p. 80
blue blazes, p. 100
blueblood, p. 298
blue box, p. 332
blue gown, p. 257
blue laws, p. 260
bluenose, p. 261
blue-nosed, p. 261
blue on the plum, p. 353
blue-pencil, p. 52
Blue peter, p. 63
blues, p. 261
blue sky, p. 330
blue sky laws, p. 330
blush like a black dog, p. 235
blush like a blue dog, p. 235
body English, p. 49
bollixed up, p. 72
bombast, p. 186
bone-shaker, p. 337
boodle, p. 201
bootlick, p. 211
bore four holes in the blue, p. 133
born in the purple, p. 298
born to the purple, p. 298
born with a silver spoon in [one's] mouth, p. 298
born within the sound of Bow bells, p. 298
borrowed plumes, p. 250
bosom buddy, p. 130
bosom buddy, p. 130
bosom chum, p. 130

bosom friend, p. 130
bottlearse, p. 235
bottleass, p. 235
bottleneck, p. 152
bottom of the bag, p. 239
Box and Cox, p. 334
box [one's] ears, p. 270
boy scout, p. 24
Boy Scouts, p. 24
Brahmin, p. 298
brain drain, p. 108
brain drain, p. 11
brain gain, p. 11
brainwashing, p. 192
brand-new, p. 18
bran-new, p. 7
break a butterfly on a wheel,
    p. 100
break for tall timber, p. 64
break his duck, p. 113
breaking his slump, p. 113
break the egg in [someone's]
    pocket, p. 152
break the ice, p. 165
brick in [one's] hat, p. 79
bridle, p. 140
bridle back, p. 140
bridle up, p. 140
bring down the gallery, p. 306
bring down the house, p. 306
broken reed, p. 110
Bronx cheer, p. 179
brown-bagger, p. 299
brownie points, p. 211
brown-nose, p. 211
brown nose, p. 211
brush fire, p. 264
brush-fire war, p. 264
bucket of bolts, p. 337
buckle down, p. 105
buckle down to, p. 105
buckle oneself to, p. 105
buckle to, p. 105
bug house, p. 84
bug under the chip, p. 313
build a better mousetrap, p. 306
bull in a china shop, p. 30
bumf, p. 186
bum fodder, p. 186

buncombe, p. 208
bunk, p. 208
bunkum, p. 208
burning ears, p. 310
bush, p. 299
bush league, p. 299
bush leaguer, p. 299
bush leagues, p. 299
butter-fingered, p. 31
butterfingers, p. 31
button [one's] lip, p. 287
button up, p. 287
button up [one's] face, p. 287
buzz word, p. 186
cabbages and kings, p. 199
[one's] cake is dough, p. 110
call a spade a spade, p. 32
call one uncle, p. 161
call on the carpet, p. 273
cambric tea, p. 123
candidate for Berkshire, p. 147
candle-holder, p. 25
cap in hand, p. 59
cap in hand, p. 60
card up one's sleeve, p. 239
carpe diem, p. 109
carrelure de ventre, p. 123
carry a message to Garcia, p. 289
carry a torch for, p. 190
carry it hollow, p. 218
carry the ball, p. 49
Carthaginian peace, p. 101
Casanova, p. 257
cash on the barrelhead, p. 222
cast in [someone's] teeth, p. 270
cast stones against the wind,
    p. 133
cat, p. 149
cat's cradle, p. 167
catcall, p. 178
catch a crab, p. 31
catch a tartar, p. 282
catch the brass ring, p. 286
catch the gold ring, p. 286
cat ice, p. 57
cat-in-pan, p. 284
caught bending, p. 346
caught dead to rights, p. 37
caught flat-footed, p. 346

caught with [one's] pants down, p. 346

cauliflower ear, p. 235

chair days, p. 19

champ at the bit, p. 150

chapter and verse, p. 27

charley horse, p. 146

cheap-Jack, p. 168

cheap-John, p. 168

cheap shot, p. 331

chew out, p. 270

chi-chi, p. 216

chicken feed, p. 202

Chinese ace, p. 45

Chinese fire drill, p. 45

Chinese landing, p. 45

Chinese national anthem, p. 45

Chinese three-point landing, p. 45

chink in [one's] armor, p. 347

chip basket, p. 200

to choke Caligula's horse, p. 101

choke-pear, p. 152

chop and change, p. 334

chronicle small beer, p. 168

chronikers, p. 127

civic illiteracy, p. 186

claptrap, p. 186

clay eater, p. 243

clay pigeon, p. 347

clean up, p. 309

climb the wall, p. 340

climb up May Hill, p. 146

clockwork orange, p. 192

close as a Kentish oyster, p. 287

close as the bark to the tree, p. 130

cloud of witnesses, p. 16

cockamamie, p. 116

cock and bull story, p. 208

cock a snook, p. 176

cock a snook, p. 178

cockeyed, p. 85

Cock Lane ghost story, p. 197

codfish aristocracy, p. 299

the codfish gentility, p. 299

cold as a cucumber, p. 261

collar-work, p. 104

collywobbles, p. 147

come a cropper, p. 77

come a purler, p. 77

come down on the right side of the fence, p. 307

come from Wigan, p. 168

come hell or high water, p. 229

come home by Weeping Cross, p. 137

to come in pudding-time, p. 214

come off with flying colors, p. 310

come-outer, p. 264

come out flat-footed, p. 32

come out of it with flying colors, p. 310

come to bat for, p. 25

come unglued, p. 45

come unhinged, p. 45

comstockery, p. 260

confusion worse confounded, p. 72, p. 97

cool as a cucumber, p. 261

cooling card, p. 152

cool [one's] heels, p. 150

coop-happy, p. 181

cork-brained, p. 143

corner the market, p. 49

corn in Egypt, p. 16

cottage industry, p. 290

Cotton mouth, p. 70

cotton mouth thirst, p. 70

count noses, p. 156

country club set, p. 299

County Clare payment, p. 222

courteous as a dog in the kitchen, p. 60

cowtown, p. 173

Coxey's Army, p. 73

crack-brained, p. 85

crackpot, p. 85

cradlesnatch, p. 191

crafty as a redhead, p. 331

cramp [someone's] style, p. 153

cratch-cradle, p. 167

crazy as a bedbug, p. 181

crazy as a coot, p. 118

crazy as a loon, p. 181

a creaking cart goes long on its wheels, p. 89

creaking gate hangs long on its hinges, p. 89

the creeps

the creeps, p. 121
crooked as a dog's hind leg, p. 331
cross as two sticks, p. 20
crosshanded, p. 291
cross [one's] fingers, p. 310
cross [someone's] bows, p. 339
cry all the way to the bank, p. 202
cry barley, p. 304
cry for the moon, p. 133
cry [one's] eyes out, p. 137
cry over spilt milk, p. 184
cry uncle, p. 304
cry wolf, p. 197
cunning as a fox, p. 331
cunning as a red-haired person, p. 331
cunning as a redhead, p. 331
cunning as a serpent, p. 331
cupped, p. 67
curry a short horse, p. 174
to curry Favel, p. 211
curry favor, p. 211
curtain lectures, p. 270
curtains, p. 317
Custer's last stand, p. 78
cut a crab, p. 31
cut and run, p. 61
cut a swath, p. 214
cut off [one's] nose to spite [one's] face, p. 97
to cut one's lucky, p. 61
cut [one's] nails on Sunday, p. 311
cut [one's] stick, p. 61
cut out of whole cloth, p. 198
cut out work for, p. 68
damn with faint praise, p. 52
Damocles' sword, p. 58
damp squib, p. 110
dance attendance on, p. 211
dance like a trooper, p. 256
darken [one's] door, p. 339
dar la higa, p. 178
daughter of the horseleech, p. 339
[one's] days are numbered, p. 147
D-day, p. 322
dead as Chelsea, p. 11
a dead cat on a line, p. 325
dead duck, p. 110

dead letter, p. 317
dead man's hand, p. 311
dead men's shoes, p. 66
deadpan, p. 235
dead ringer, p. 252
dead to rights, p. 37
Delenda est Carthago, p. 101
Delphic sword, p. 334
derby dog, p. 153
derby duck, p. 112
devil's dozen, p. 93
dickens, p. 254
the dickens take you, p. 254
Dick Tracy, p. 279
did not lay a finger on, p. 61
die for want of lobster sauce, p. 101
diehard, p. 229
the die is cast, p. 185
ding-a-ling, p. 117
dingbat, p. 117
dip into the blue, p. 254
dip [one's] pen in gall, p. 52
dirty word, p. 187
dirty work at the crossroads, p. 57
dit vor dat, p. 279
do a Dunkirk, p. 62
do a moonlight flit, p. 64
do a Nelson, p. 229
Doctor Doddypoll, p. 117
doddypoll, p. 117
doesn't amount to a hill of beans, p. 170, p. 170
does not know beans about, p. 170
dog's body, p. 168
dog in a doublet, p. 229
a dog in one's doublet, p. 229
dogleg, p. 331
dogs in dough, p. 67
dog [some one's] footsteps, p. 340
dog [some one's] heels, p. 340
dolce far niente, p. 163
dollars to doughnuts, p. 38
don't come the uncle over me, p. 53
don't give up the ship, p. 230
don't hurry, Hopkins, p. 271

don't sit there like mumchance who was hanged for saying nothing, p. 292

done with mirrors, p. 326

Don Juan, p. 257

Don Juan, p. 257

do off [one's] bat, p. 290

Doolally tap, p. 85

dot [one's] *i*s **and cross [one's]** *t*s, p. 247

double dip, p. 106

double dippers, p. 107

Double dipping, p. 107

double in brass, p. 14

Do unto others as you would have them do unto you, p. 266

down-at-the-heel, p. 244

down in the boondocks, p. 168

down the drain, p. 112

down the pipe, p. 112

down the tube, p. 112

down the tube, p. 112

down the tubes, p. 112

draw a red herring across the trail, p. 240

draw in [one's] horns, p. 304

draw stumps, p. 317

dressing down, p. 271

dress the house, p. 197

drink like a fish, p. 79

drive round the bend, p. 183

drive up the wall, p. 340

a drop in the bucket, p. 169

a drop in the ocean, p. 169

drop like a hot potato, p. 68

drown the miller, p. 128

drown the miller, p. 244

drug on the market, p. 101

drugstore cowboy, p. 214

drunk as a fiddler, p. 79

drunk as a lord, p. 80

drunk as David's sow, p. 80

drunk as Davy's sow, p. 80

dry run, p. 319

duck egg, p. 112

Duke of Exeter's daughter, p. 40

dumb Dora, p. 143

dunce, p. 143

dunderhead, p. 144

the Dutch have taken Holland, p. 279

dyed in the grain, p. 332

eating crow, p. 38

eating [one's] words, p. 38

eat [one's] hat, p. 38

eat [someone's] salt, p. 130

eavesdropper, p. 56

an elephant in the moon, p. 117

eggs is eggs, p. 38

eisenen Vorhang, p. 153

elbow grease, p. 105

elf locks, p. 311

elwetritch hunting, p. 326

empty nester, p. 11

empty nest syndrome, p. 11

to end up in smoke, p. 113

English, p. 215

English leave (filer à l'anglaise), p. 62

enough [something] to choke Caligula's horse, p. 101

escape the bear and fall to the lion, p. 98

être assis entre deux chaises, p. 335

être aux bois, p. 315

être sur un grand pied dans le monde, p. 131

even steven, p. 92

even the walls have ears, p. 289

everybody and his brother, p. 156

every man Jack, p. 157

every mother's son, p. 156

everything but the kitchen sink, p. 157

everything but the kitchen sink, p. 157

everything but the kitchen stove, p. 157

everything from soup to nuts, p. 158

everything that opens and shuts, p. 157

every tub must stand on its own bottom, p. 290

every tub on its own black bottom, p. 290

ex cathedra, p. 28

an eye for an eye, p. 276

eye opener, p. 124

Fabian tactics, p. 314

faire la figue, p. 178
fair game, p. 347
fall between two stools, p. 334
fall by the way, p. 112
fall by the wayside, p. 112
fall of a sparrow, p. 350
famous last words, p. 279
fanfaron, p. 216, p. 216
fanfaronade, p. 216
fanfarrado, p. 216
far and away, p. 38
far from the mark, p. 96
fast buck, p. 202
fast food, p. 124
the fat's in the fire, p. 185
fat city, p. 16
feather [one's] nest, p. 107
feed the fishes, p. 147
feel a draft, p. 226
**feel as if a cat has kittened in
    [one's] mouth,** p. 80
feel the draught, p. 226
fetch over the coals, p. 272
fiddlesticks, p. 208
field day, p. 213
fight fire with fire, p. 277
to fight fire with fire, p. 277
the fig of Spain, p. 178
filibuster, p. 315
filthy lucre, p. 202
find a giggles' nest, p. 117
find bones in, p. 34
fine feathers make fine birds,
    p. 215
fine kettle of fish, p. 74
finishing touch, p. 42
fire-new, p. 19
firewater, p. 124
fish eye, p. 344
fish in troubled waters, p. 107
fishy about the gills, p. 80
fit to be tied, p. 21
*fit your hand exactly in the place
    where your marble lies,* p. 105
fix [someone's] little red wagon,
    p. 277
fix [someone's] wagon, p. 277
flag down, p. 49
flag station, p. 49

flag stop, p. 49
flake, p. 85
flat as a pancake, p. 236
flat-footed, p. 32
flat hat, p. 215
flat hatter, p. 215
flay alive, p. 274
flip [one's] lid, p. 182
flip out, p. 182
flog a dead horse, p. 133
flourish of trumpets, p. 215
flutter the dovecotes, p. 45
fly in amber, p. 169
flying, p. 82
flying saucer, p. 337
fly in the face of, p. 264
to fly in the face of danger, p. 264
to fly in the face of providence,
    p. 264
fly in the ointment, p. 153
fly on the wall, p. 56
fofaraw, p. 216
foofaraw, p. 216
foot the bill, p. 223
forbidden fruit, p. 65
force [someone's] hand, p. 41
forgotten man, p. 169
fork out, p. 223
fork over, p. 223
fork the fingers, p. 178
fork up, p. 223
forty acres and a mule, p. 17
four-flusher, p. 250
the Four Hundred, p. 299
fox's sleep, p. 250
Frankenstein monster, p. 282
freak out, p. 182
freak out, p. 182
freckled as a turkey's egg, p. 236
Fred Karno's army, p. 73
French leave, p. 62
a frog in [one's] throat, p. 147
from A to Izzard, p. 157
from China to Peru, p. 158
from Dan to Beersheba, p. 158
**from Delilah's lap to Abraham's
    bosom,** p. 283
**from Land's End to John o' Groat's
    [House],** p. 158

from soda to hock, p. 158
from soup to nuts, p. 158
from stem to stern, p. 159
from the horse's mouth, p. 28
from the teeth outward, p. 197
froufrou, p. 216
full as a bull, p. 80
full as an egg, p. 80
full as a tick, p. 80
full of beans, p. 117
full of beans, p. 94
full of crap, p. 94
full of hops, p. 94
full of prunes, p. 94
full of shit, p. 94
Fu Manchu mustache, p. 236
fun city, p. 17
funny house, p. 84
fuss and feathers, p. 216
gag-tooth, p. 344
gallery gods, p. 300
gallery gods, p. 300
gall of bitterness, p. 53
the game is up, p. 112
gandermonth, p. 322
gandermooner, p. 322
gandermooning, p. 322
gay Lothario, p. 257
geezer, p. 19
gentleman of the four outs, p. 300
get a bang out of, p. 90
get a charge out of, p. 90
get a dose (or taste) of [one's] own
    medicine, p. 277
get a duck, p. 112
get a move on, p. 295
get away with murder, p. 166
get a wiggle on, p. 295
get cracking, p. 296
to get down off one's high horse,
    p. 141
get hold of the wrong end of the
    stick, p. 95
get [one's] feet wet, p. 165
get [one's] kicks, p. 90
get [one's] teeth into, p. 105
get on the stick, p. 296
get on tick, p. 223
get [someone's] back up, p. 340

get [someone's] dander up, p. 340
get [someone's] dander up, p. 342
get [someone's] Dutch up, p. 340
get [someone's] goat, p. 342
get [someone's] hackles up, p. 342
get [someone's] Irish, p. 340
get [someone's] monkey up, p. 342
get something off [one's] chest,
    p. 33
get the ball rolling, p. 165
get the deadwood on, p. 49
get the hang of, p. 14
get the nod, p. 24
get the show on the road, p. 296
get the stick, p. 271
get the whetstone, p. 198
get the wrong bull by the tail, p. 95
get the wrong pig by the ear, p. 95
get the wrong sow by the ear,
    p. 95
get under way, p. 166
the ghost walks, p. 223
ghost word, p. 187
gild refined gold, p. 103
gild the lily, p. 103
ginger, p. 88
ginger beer, p. 88
gingerbread, p. 101
Gioconda smile, p. 345
girl in every port, p. 259
give a leg up, p. 25
give her the bells and let her fly,
    p. 275
give [one's] eyeteeth, p. 65
give [one's] right arm, p. 65
give [one] down the banks, p. 271
give [someone] a dose of [his/her]
    own medicine, p. 277
give [someone] a taste of [his/her]
    own medicine, p. 277
give [someone] Jesse, p. 271
give [someone] the finger, p. 179
give [someone] the length of one's
    tongue, p. 272
give the bird, p. 178
to give the fico, p. 178
give the fig, p. 178
give the goose, p. 178
give the nod, p. 24

give the raspberry, p. 179
give the raspberry, p. 180
give the sack, p. 178
give the wall, p. 60
give the whetstone, p. 198
gnaw a file, p. 282
go above (or beyond) one's latchet,
   p. 198
go bananas, p. 182
gobbledegook, gobbledygook,
   p. 187
go beyond one's latchet, p. 198
go by beggar's bush, p. 243
**God writes straight with crooked
   lines,** p. 46
gofer, p. 168
go gandering, p. 56
go haywire, p. 182, p. 73
go home by beggar's bush, p. 243
golden handshake, p. 202, p. 331
gone beaver, p. 348
gone chick, p. 347
gone coon, p. 347
gone coon, p. 347
gone gander, p. 348
gone goose, p. 347
gone horse, p. 348
gone to my uncle's, p. 161
good buddy, p. 131
good ole boy, p. 130
good Samaritan, p. 25
good wine needs no bush, p. 350
Goody Two Shoes, p. 262
go off the deep end, p. 182
go off the deep end, p. 182
go on tick, p. 223
go on with your bird's egging, p. 276
go on with your birds' egging,
   p. 276
goose bumps, p. 121
goose egg, p. 112
goose egg, p. 113
goose flesh, p. 121
the goose hangs high, p. 213
the goose honks high, p. 213
goose pimples, p. 121
go overboard, p. 102
to go over like a lead balloon, p. 113
go round the bend, p. 183

go round the bend, p. 88
gospel truth, p. 28
go through fire and water, p. 65,
   p. 319
go through-stitch, p. 43
go through the roof, p. 102
go to bat for, p. 25
go to Bath, p. 208
go to Battersea, p. 117
**go to Battersea, to be cut for the
   simples,** p. 117
go to Putney, p. 179
go to Putney on a pig, p. 179
go to the bat, p. 25
go to the dickens, p. 254
go to the well once too often,
   p. 78
go up in smoke, p. 113
go whistle, p. 268
to go woolgathering, p. 164
grandstand, p. 216
grandstand finish, p. 216
grandstand play, p. 216
grass roots, p. 300
graveyard shift, p. 322
graveyard watch, p. 322
*great cry and little wool as the devil
   said when he sheared the hogs,*
   p. 134
the great unwashed, p. 300
Greek calends, p. 323
the Greeks had a word for it,
   p. 279
green around the gills, p. 80
green fingers, p. 14
green thumb, p. 14
grin like a Cheshire cat, p. 344
grist for the mill, p. 107
grit your teeth, p. 89
Gros-Jean comme devant, p. 119
group grope, p. 258
gunner's daughter, p. 40
guts for quarters, p. 277
guttersnipe, p. 244
had it up to here, p. 102
hairdown, p. 33
a hair in the butter, p. 67
a hair of the dog that bit you,
   p. 124

half-cocked, p. 80
half in the bag, p. 82
half seas over, p. 81
ham, p. 216
hamfat man, p. 217
handsome is as handsome does,
   p. 236
handsome is that handsome does,
   p. 236
hangdog air, p. 344
hangdog look, p. 344
hang in there, p. 230
hang loose, p. 33
hang tough, p. 230
happy warrior, p. 230
hard as the knockers of Newgate,
   p. 238
a hard nut to crack, p. 67
hard row to hoe, p. 68
hard up, p. 244
harp shilling, p. 202
haste makes waste, p. 151
hat in hand, p. 60
hat in hand, p. 60
hat to a halfpenny, p. 38
haul over the coals, p. 272
have a handle on, p. 50
have a jag on, p. 81
have a moonflaw in the brain,
   p. 85
have an ax to grind, p. 230
have another think coming, p. 280
have a package on, p. 81
have a screw loose, p. 86
have a tile loose, p. 86
have bats in [one's] belfry, p. 86
to have been in the sun, p. 81
have been to Barking Creek,
   p. 147
have but a mile to midsummer, p. 86
have eyes for, p. 65
have it hollow, p. 218
have [one's] ears pinned back, p. 272
have [one's] ears slapped back,
   p. 272
have [one's] heart in [one's] mouth,
   p. 121
have [one's] work cut out, p. 319,
   p. 68

have one foot in the grave, p. 147
have scissors to grind, p. 230
have some marbles missing, p. 183
have [someone's] number, p. 226
*have [someone] around one's little
   finger,* p. 195
have someone dead to rights, p. 37
have [something] up [one's] sleeve,
   p. 240
have their simples cut, p. 118
have the last laugh, p. 307
have the sun in [one's] eyes, p. 81
have two faces, p. 333
have two left feet, p. 31
have windmills in [one's] head,
   p. 118
*having both feet planted on the
   ground,* p. 82
head of wax, p. 118
heap coals of fire on [someone's]
   head, p. 277
heap Pelion upon Ossa, p. 98
heartthrob, p. 190
he laughs best that laughs last,
   p. 307
a hell of a way to run a railway,
   p. 73
help a lame dog over a stile, p. 26
He must be cut of the simples,
   p. 118
here lies the rub, p. 154
hewers of wood and drawers of
   water, p. 105
he who laughs last laughs best,
   p. 307
*he who rides a tiger is afraid to
   dismount,* p. 59
hick, p. 144
hick town, p. 144, p. 173
higgledy-piggledy, p. 73
high, p. 82
high-hat, p. 140
high in the instep, p. 140
high-kilted, p. 258
high road to Needham, p. 244
hightail it, p. 62
hill of beans, p. 169
Hippocratic countenance, p. 147
Hippocratic face, p. 148

hippy movement, p. 263
hit a blot, p. 95
hit below the belt, p. 331
hit below the belt, p. 332
to hit one's head against the wall,
    p. 132
hit the nail on the head, p. 247
hit the sauce, p. 82
hob and nob, p. 131
hobbledehoy, p. 353
hobnob, p. 131
hobos, p. 243
hodge in armor, hodge, p. 31
hodgepodge, p. 200
hoe [one's] own row, p. 290
hog in armor, p. 31
hog shearing, p. 134
hoi polloi, p. 300
hoist the blue peter, p. 62
hoist with [one's] own petard,
    p. 283, p. 78
hoity-toity, p. 140
hold an eel by the tail, p. 68
hold at a bay, p. 315
hold at bay, p. 315
hold [one's] ground, p. 232
hold [one's] heart in [one's] hand,
    p. 190
hold the fort, p. 50
hold the line, p. 50
hold the purse strings, p. 50
hold with the hare and run with
    the hounds, p. 335
homely as a hedge fence, p. 237
homely as a mud fence, p. 236
hooch, p. 124
hook, line, and sinker, p. 323
Hooverville, p. 245
hopping mad, p. 22
hop the twig, p. 63
hot corner, p. 68
hot-dog, p. 217
to hot-dog it, p. 217
hot potato, p. 68
hot under the collar, p. 21
hound [some one's] footsteps, p. 340
huggermugger, p. 73, p. 287
humbug, p. 250
hung on the nail, p. 161

hunker down, p. 237
hurly-burly, p. 74
hurrah's nest, p. 74
hush puppy, p. 125
I can't wait, p. 280
I can hardly wait, p. 280
*If your head is wax, stay away from
    the fire*, p. 118
I knew him when!, p. 53
*I knew him when he was only a cab
    driver*, p. 53
*il faut battre le fer pendant qu'il est
    chaud*, p. 109
ils s'entendent comme larrons en foire,
    p. 132
in a jiffy, p. 174
in a pig's whisper, p. 174
in a snit, p. 21
in a tiff, p. 21
in bed with [one's] boots on, p. 81
in black and white, p. 28
in Carey Street, p. 245
Indian up, p. 340
in dock, out nettle, p. 335
in for a penny, in for a pound,
    p. 43
inkhorn term, p. 187
in low water, p. 245
in one's birthday suit, p. 237
in [one's] books, p. 24
in [one's] cups, p. 81
in one's good books, p. 24
in petto, p. 288
in Queer Street, p. 161
in sackcloth and ashes, p. 138
ins and outs, p. 323
in [someone's] pocket, p. 194
in spades, p. 39
in spite of hell or high water, p. 229
in the altitudes, p. 82
in the bag, p. 39, p. 82
in the bag, p. 83
in the black, p. 162
in the buff, p. 237
in the driver's seat, p. 50
in the hole, p. 161
in the homestretch, p. 318
in the homestretch, p. 318
in the ketchup, p. 162

in the market, p. 101
in the ozone, p. 118
in the ozone, p. 82
in the pudding club, p. 237
in the red, p. 162
in the red, p. 162
in there pitching, p. 105
in the saddle, p. 50
in the straw, p. 148
in the twinkling of a bed post, p. 174
in the twinkling of a bed staff, p. 174
in the twinkling of an eye, p. 174
in the van, p. 301
in the wrong box, p. 95
in two shakes of a lamb's tail, p. 175
iron curtain, p. 152
iron curtain, p. 153
iron hand in a velvet glove, p. 250
itching palm, p. 66
I wasn't born yesterday, p. 226
Jack-a-both-sides, p. 335
Jack-a-Dandy, p. 170
jack-a-dandyism, p. 170
Jack at a pinch, p. 26
Jack Horner, p. 326
Jack-in-office, p. 141
Jack-o-both-sides, p. 335
Jack-o-Dandy, p. 170
jack of all trades, p. 15
Jack of both sides, p. 335
Jamie Duff, p. 138
a jaundiced eye, p. 248
jawbone, p. 41
jawbreaker, p. 187
Jekyll and Hyde, p. 335
Je ne le connais ni d'Eve ni d'Adam, p. 145
jerk the cat, p. 149
jerkwater town, p. 173
the jig is up, p. 317
the jig is up, p. 318
jinx, p. 312
Job's comforter, p. 98
John Audley, p. 318
John Audley it, p. 318
John Orderly it, p. 318
join the pudding club, p. 237

jug-bitten, p. 82
jump down [someone's] throat, p. 53
jynx, p. 312
Jynx torquilla, p. 312
Kafkaesque, p. 134
kale through the reek, p. 272
ka me, ka thee, p. 26, p. 266
keep a stiff upper lip, p. 232
keep at a bay, p. 315
to keep mum, p. 294
keep [one's] chin up, p. 232
keep [one's] fingers crossed, p. 311
keep [one's] hand in, p. 15
keep [one's] nose to the grindstone, p. 232
keep [one's] pecker up, p. 232
keep something under [one's] hat, p. 289
keep the ball rolling, p. 165
keep the pot boiling, p. 89
keep two faces under one head, p. 333
Kentish fire, p. 24
kettle of fish, p. 74
kick against the pricks, p. 134, p. 264
kickback, p. 331
kicking back, p. 331
kick over the traces, p. 265
a king's ransom, p. 203
kith and kin, p. 159
knave in grain, p. 332
knave in grain, p. 332
knight bachelor, p. 301
knight banneret, p. 301
knight banneret, p. 301
knight of the square flag, p. 301
knobstick wedding, p. 41
knock for a loop, p. 46
knock one's head against the wall, p. 133
knock [one's] socks off, p. 219
knock on wood, p. 312
knock someone's block off, p. 219
knock them in the aisles, p. 307
knock the spots out of, p. 219
knock under, p. 305
knock under board, p. 305

know a hawk from a handsaw, p. 227

know chalk from cheese, p. 227

Know-Nothing, p. 144

knuckle down, p. 105

knuckle down to your taw, p. 105

knuckle under, p. 304

knuckle under, p. 304

L. L. Whisky, p. 125

laced mutton, p. 258

ladies of Barking Creek, p. 240

land on [one's] feet, p. 307

lareovers to catch meddlers, p. 281

larrows to catch meddlers, p. 281

a lash of scorpions, p. 272

last leaf, p. 19

last licks, p. 106

latchkey kids, p. 353

laterem lavare, p. 137

Latet anguis in herba, p. 58

Lawrence bids him high wages, p. 163

lay an egg, p. 113

lay [one's] nuts aside, p. 19

lay out in lavender, p. 273

layovers to catch meddlers, p. 281

lay someone out, p. 273

lay them in the aisles, p. 307

lazy as Lawrence, p. 163

lazy as Lawrence's dog, p. 163

lazy as Ludlam's dog, p. 163

lead balloon, p. 113

lead-pipe cinch, p. 39

the Left, p. 265

Left-handed, p. 179

left-handed, p. 180

left-handed compliment, p. 179

left-handed compliment, p. 180

left-handed marriages, p. 179

left high and dry, p. 12

left in the basket, p. 12

left in the lurch, p. 12

left wing, p. 265

left-wing, p. 265

left-wingers, p. 265

lemon, p. 114

let her go, Gallagher!, p. 296

let it all hang out, p. 33

let it all hang out, p. 33

let [one's] hair down, p. 33

Letter to Stella, p. 92

let the dead bury the dead, p. 185

lick [one's] chops, p. 91

to lick [someone's] boots, p. 211

lickspittle, p. 211

a lick with the rough side of the tongue, p. 273

a lick with the rough side of the tongue, p. 274

lie for the whetstone, p. 197

lie in one's beard, p. 198

lie in one's teeth, p. 198

lie in one's throat, p. 198

lie through [one's] teeth, p. 198

lie with a latchet, p. 198

life of Riley, p. 91

like an owl in an ivy bush, p. 344, p. 82

like it or lump it, p. 275

line one's nest, p. 107

little old lady from Dubuque, p. 262

little old lady from Dubuque, p. 262

little pitchers have big ears, p. 288

little pot is soon hot, p. 21

live at rack and manger, p. 16

live in a glass house, p. 348

loaves and fishes, p. 17, p. 203

locker-room talk, p. 254

logrolling, p. 266

Lolita, p. 258

long in the tooth, p. 19

a long row to hoe, p. 68

look as if butter wouldn't melt in [one's] mouth, p. 251

look babies in the eyes, p. 191

look beneath the surface, p. 227

look down [one's] nose, p. 141

look through a millstone, p. 227

look through blue glasses, p. 248

loose ends, p. 43

loosen up, p. 33

loose screw, p. 86

lose in hake, gain in herring, p. 94

lose [one's] bearings, p. 46

lose one's breakfast, p. 149

lose [one's] head, p. 183

lose one's lunch, p. 149

lose [one's] marbles, p. 183

lose [one's] shirt, p. 114, p. 162
lose [one's] tongue, p. 292
lose the handle, p. 50
lost sheep, p. 258
lotus-eater, p. 163
love me, love my dog, p. 324
love-tooth in the head, p. 191
low blow, p. 331
low blow, p. 332
low man on the totem pole, p. 301
lump it, p. 275, p. 275
lynx-eyed, p. 15
mad as a baited bear, p. 22
mad as a baited boar, p. 22
mad as a baited bull, p. 21
mad as a hatter, p. 183, p. 22
mad as a March hare, p. 183
mad as a marsh hare, p. 184
mad as an atter, p. 183
mad as a tup, p. 22
mad as a tup in a halter, p. 22
mad as a wet hen, p. 22
mad as hops, p. 22
made a blot, p. 95
mad money, p. 203
the mahogany, p. 131
maiden over, p. 308
make a blot, p. 95
make a boner, p. 96
make a clean breast, p. 33
make a hash of, p. 74
make a moonlight flitting, p. 64
make bones about, p. 34
make bricks without straw, p. 134
make fair weather, p. 212
make hay while the sun shines,
    p. 107
make heavy weather of, p. 70
make horns at, p. 180
make no bones about, p. 34
make one's jack, p. 308
make [one's] jack, p. 308
make [one's] mouth water, p. 66
make [one's] pile, p. 203
make [someone's] nose swell,
    p. 342
make the grade, p. 308
make the hair stand on end,
    p. 121

make three bites of a cherry, p. 102
make time, p. 258
make time with, p. 258
make tracks, p. 63
make two bites of a cherry, p. 102
mal à propos, p. 188
malapropism, p. 188
malt above the meal, p. 82
man bites dog, p. 283
many words will not fill a bushel,
    p. 135
to march out [with] bag and baggage,
    p. 156
mare's nest, p. 75
mark time, p. 315
Mary Jane cookies, p. 125
masher, p. 258
mean as hungry Tyson, p. 22
meatwagon, p. 337
meet [one's] Waterloo, p. 78
Memoir of T. Weed, p. 323
Meriden audience, p. 170
method in [one's] madness, p. 251
Mexican breakfast, p. 125
Mickey Finn, p. 125
Mickey Mouse, p. 170
Midas touch, p. 203
midsummer madness, p. 86
milk, p. 107
milking ducks as my mother bade
    me, p. 281
milking geese, p. 281
to milk [someone] for all he is worth,
    p. 108
to milk the bull, p. 135
milk the ram, p. 135
miller's eye, p. 128
to mince matters, p. 34
mishmash, p. 200
Miss Goody Two Shoes, p. 262
a miss is as good as a mile, p. 114
Miss Nancy, p. 86
miss the boat, p. 114
to miss the bus, p. 114
miss the cushion, p. 95
mom and pop, p. 170
Mona Lisa smile, p. 345
money burns a hole in [one's]
    pocket, p. 150, p. 203

*money burns a
hole in [one's]
pocket*

money burns a hole in [one's] purse, p. 150

money doesn't grow on trees, p. 204

money is the root of all evil, p. 205

monkey's allowance, p. 204

monkey's money, p. 204

Montezuma's revenge, p. 148

Montezuma's revenge, p. 148

Montgomery's division, all on one side, p. 166

moonshine, p. 126, p. 210

morganatic marriages, p. 179

mountain dew, p. 126

mountain oysters, p. 126

mount the high horse, p. 141

Mrs. Grundy, p. 262

Mrs. Malaprop, p. 188

mum's the word, p. 288

mum's the word, p. 294

mumchance, p. 292

Murphy's law, p. 70

music to the ears, p. 91

mutton dressed as lamb, p. 251

muzzle the ox, p. 51

my cup runneth over, p. 17

my kingdom for a horse!, p. 66

My Lord Tomnoddy, p. 119

nail [one's] colors to the mast, p. 233

naked ape, p. 238

naked truth, p. 34

Nancy boy, p. 88

the natives are restless, p. 75

neck and crop, p. 77

neck and neck, p. 93

need it yesterday, p. 150

nest egg, p. 204

the never-never plan, p. 223

never waste powder on a dead duck, p. 94

Newgate frill, p. 238

Newgate fringe, p. 238

Newgate knocker, p. 238

the New Left, p. 265

nice kettle of fish, p. 74

nice Nelly, p. 262

Nice Nellyism, p. 263

nickel and dime to death, p. 224

nigger in the woodpile, p. 313

nightcap, p. 126

nimble ninepence, p. 204

a nimble ninepence is better than a slow shilling, p. 204

nineteen bites to a bilberry, p. 102

nineteen bits to a bilberry, p. 102

nineteenth hole, p. 127

nineteenth hole, p. 127

nip and chuck, p. 93

nip and tack, p. 93

nip and tuck, p. 93

nip and tuck, p. 93

nip in the bud, p. 318

no bed of roses, p. 163

noddies, p. 119

no dice, p. 267

a nod is as good as a wink to a blind horse, p. 135

no eyes, p. 65

no great shakes, p. 171

no-man's-land, p. 75

no money, no mistress, p. 224

no money, no Swiss, p. 224

none of one's bird's egging, p. 276

Norman blood, p. 141

nose of wax, p. 194

no soap, p. 267

not a shot in the locker, p. 206

notch in his tail, p. 58

not have all [one's] buttons, p. 118

not have the foggiest (idea), p. 46

nothing like leather, p. 248

nothing to sneeze at, p. 350

no tickee, no shirtee, p. 224

no tickee, no washee, p. 224

not just another pretty face, p. 15

not know A from a windmill, p. 144

not know B from a battledore, p. 145

not know from Adam, p. 145

not know from Adam, p. 146

not know from Adam's off ox, p. 145

not know if [one] is afoot or on horseback, p. 47

not know if [one] is coming or going, p. 146

not know [one's] ass [or Brit. arse] from [one's] elbow, p. 145
not know shit from shinola, p. 146
not know which end is up, p. 146
not to be sneezed at, p. 350
not to know if [one] is coming or going, p. 47
not to know which end is up, p. 47
not to mince the matter, p. 34
not worth a hill of beans, p. 170
not worth a jot, p. 171
not worth an h, p. 171
not worth an iota, p. 171
not worth a whistle, p. 352
not worth one's salt, p. 352
nourish a snake in [one's] bosom, p. 58
Nunky pays for all, p. 132
Occam's razor, p. 247
off base, p. 95
off [one's] feed, p. 148
off one's rocker, p. 88
off [one's] trolley, p. 88
off the beam, p. 96
off the cuff, p. 295
off the top of [one's] head, p. 295
old buddy, p. 130
an old ewe dressed lamb-fashion, p. 251
old wives' tale, p. 312
olla podrida, p. 200
on a good footing, p. 131
on a good footing with [someone], p. 131
on aurait entendu voler une mouche, p. 294
one fell swoop, p. 175
one hand washes the other, p. 267
one-horse town, p. 171
one-horse town, p. 173
one-night stand, p. 259
one over the eight, p. 82
one swell foop, p. 175
on [one's] beam-ends, p. 245
on [one's] high horse, p. 141
on one's hunkers, p. 237
on [one's] last legs, p. 149
on [one's] own, p. 290

on [one's] pat, p. 290
on [one's] tod, p. 290
on [one's] uppers, p. 245
on the blink, p. 149
on the button, p. 247
on the button, p. 248
on the carpet, p. 273
on the cuff, p. 224
on the double, p. 175
on the fence, p. 336
on the fritz, p. 149
on the high ropes, p. 141
on the home stretch, p. 293
on the money, p. 248
on the nail, p. 224
on the nod, p. 225
on the nose, p. 248
on the q.t., p. 288
on the quiet, p. 288
on the rebound, p. 348
on the rocks, p. 162
on the ropes, p. 348
on the sauce, p. 82
on the spur of the moment, p. 295
open season, p. 348
oppose Preston and his mastiffs, p. 135
ordeal by fire, p. 319
out at elbows, p. 245
out Herod Herod, p. 102, p. 220
out in left field, p. 96
out in space, p. 118
out in the sun too long, p. 88
out of countenance, p. 22
out of joint, p. 75
out of kilter, p. 76
out of the frying pan into the fire, p. 98
out of the red, p. 162
out of the straw, p. 148
out of whole cloth, p. 198
out on a limb, p. 348
outrageous fortune, p. 54
out to lunch, p. 146
over a barrel, p. 349
overshoot the mark, p. 102, p. 96
over the hill, p. 20
over the mahogany, p. 131
oyster part, p. 171

P. A. Y. E.

P. A. Y. E, p. 225
p. d. q., p. 175
paddle [one's] own canoe, p. 290
paddy wagon, p. 338
pad in the straw, p. 58
pain in the ass, p. 342
pain in the neck, p. 343
pain in the rump, p. 343
painted cat, p. 256
painted cat, p. 259
paint the lily, p. 103
panda car, p. 338
pan out, p. 308
paper the house, p. 197
pardon my French, p. 254
Parthian fight, p. 180
Parthian glance, p. 180
Parthian shaft, p. 180
Parthian shot, p. 180
parting shot, p. 180
party pooper, p. 267
pas de lieu Rhône que nous, p. 291
pass the bottle of smoke, p. 251
pass the bottle of smoke, p. 251
pass under the yoke, p. 305
patch the lion's skin with the fox's tail, p. 240
patrue mi patruissime, p. 304
Paul's man, p. 164
Paul's walkers, p. 164
pay as you go, p. 225
pay dirt, p. 309
pay in [one's] own coin, p. 278
payola, p. 332
pay [one's] dues, p. 350
pay [one's] scot, p. 225
pay scot and lot, p. 225
pay someone in washers, p. 225
pay [someone] peanuts, p. 225
pay through the nose, p. 156
peanut gallery, p. 172
peanut gallery, p. 53, p. 172
pebble on the beach, p. 172
pecking order, p. 302
pelican crossing, p. 26
penny-ante, p. 172
penny in the slot, p. 343
people who live in glass houses
    shouldn't throw stones, p. 348

phone phreak, p. 332
phone phreakdom, p. 332
pick-me-up, p. 124
pick [someone's] brains, p. 108
pidgin English, p. 188
pie-eyed, p. 82
pilgarlic, p. 238
pinch-hit, p. 26
pinch-hitter, p. 16
pin money, p. 204
pin [someone's] ears back, p. 272
pipe down, p. 294
pitchers have ears, p. 288
a plague on both your houses,
    p. 180
play a straight bat, p. 15
play booty, p. 327
play both ends against the middle,
    p. 194
play fast and loose, p. 194
play footsie, p. 172
play for fun, p. 91
play for grins, p. 91
play for love, p. 91
play for time, p. 315
playing booty, p. 327
play like a trooper, p. 256
play possum, p. 251
play the bird with the long neck,
    p. 56
Play the dickens, p. 254
play the field, p. 108
play to the gallery, p. 217
play to the grandstand, p. 217
pleasure bent, p. 91
plow the sands, p. 135
Podunk, p. 172
Podunk, U.S.A, p. 168
point-blank, p. 34
point of no return, p. 185
poker face, p. 345
polish up the apple, p. 210
to poop out, p. 267
poor as a churchmouse, p. 246
poor as Job, p. 246
poor as Job's cat, p. 246
poor as Job's turkey, p. 246
portmanteau word, p. 188
posh, p. 217

potboiler, p. 89
Potemkin village, p. 252
pot-house politician, p. 343
pot likker, p. 127
pot liquor, p. 127
potluck, p. 127, p. 200
pot shot, p. 53
pound of flesh, p. 278
prairie schooner, p. 338
praise the Lord, and pass the
    ammunition, p. 233
pratfall, p. 154
preggers, p. 237
preggy, p. 237
prego, p. 237
prendre la chèvre, p. 342
pretty kettle of fish, p. 74
pretty pennies, p. 205
pretty penny, p. 205
prole, p. 302
pudding-time, p. 214
pull a boner, p. 96
pull a fast one, p. 327
pull bacon, p. 176
pull devil, pull baker, p. 93
pull for tall timber, p. 64
pull [one's] socks up, p. 296
pull oneself up by [one's] own
    boot straps, p. 291
pull [someone's] chestnuts out of
    the fire, p. 195
pull [someone's] leg, p. 327
pull strings, p. 195
pull the wool over [someone's]
    eyes, p. 327
pull up stakes, p. 63
to pull wires, p. 195, p. 195
pumping iron, p. 106
pump iron, p. 106
punch-drunk, p. 119
punchy, p. 119
punk and plaster, p. 127
punk and plaster John, p. 127
punk and plaster route, p. 127
put a bold face on, p. 51
put a rope to the eye of a needle,
    p. 136
put a sock in it, p. 294
put in [one's] best licks, p. 106

put on a bold front, p. 51
put [one's] hand to the plow,
    p. 296
put [one's] shoulder to the wheel,
    p. 106
put one over on, p. 327
put out the miller's eye, p. 127
put over a fast one, p. 327
put someone's nose out of joint,
    p. 342
put [someone] in the hole, p. 161
put the screws to, p. 41
put the shutters up, p. 114
put the squeeze on, p. 41
put through [one's] facings, p. 319
put through [one's] paces, p. 320
putting the miller's eyes out, p. 128
put to bed with a shovel, p. 83
quacksalver, p. 252
quake in one's boots, p. 122
Quaker bargain, p. 34
Quaker guns, p. 252
queen, p. 88
Queen Anne's fan, p. 176
Queen Anne is dead, p. 281
Queen of the May, p. 88
queer, p. 88
queer as a clockwork orange, p. 192
queer in the attic, p. 83, p. 88
quench [one's] thirst at any dirty
    puddle, p. 259
Qui me amat, amet et canem meum,
    p. 324
quiz, p. 320
quiz kid, p. 320
quiz show, p. 320
quizzing glass, p. 320
Ragamoffyn, p. 246
ragamuffin, p. 246
Ragman Roll, p. 189
rag on every bush, p. 259
ragtag and bobtail, p. 159, p. 302
raise [one's] screw, p. 205
*raise oneself up by [one's] own
    bootstraps,* p. 291
raise the dickens, p. 254
raise the white flag, p. 305
ram down [someone's] throat, p. 41
the rank and file, p. 302

rap on the knuckles, p. 273
rare kettle of fish, p. 74
rattle [one's] cage, p. 47
rattletrap, p. 338
razzle-dazzle, p. 47
read between the lines, p. 227
read [someone] like a book, p. 228
read the riot act, p. 273
ready rhino, p. 205
red-eye, p. 128
red-flag term, p. 188
red herring, p. 240
reed shaken by the wind, p. 336
representative for Berkshire, p. 147
return one's breakfast, p. 149
return one's lunch, p. 149
return to our muttons, p. 276
revenons à ces moutons, p. 276
revenons à nos moutons, p. 276
rhinocerical, p. 205
rhino fat, p. 205
ribbing, p. 343
rib [someone], p. 343
ride at the ring, p. 286
to ride the high horse, p. 141
right and left, p. 159
right down the line, p. 155
the right hand doesn't know what
    the left hand is doing, p. 76
right off the bat, p. 175
right off the reel, p. 175
right on the button, p. 247
right on the money, p. 248
rigmarole, p. 189
rigmarole, p. 189
ring down, p. 318
ring down the curtain, p. 318
ringer, p. 252
ringing in the ears, p. 310
ring the bell, p. 309
ring up, p. 166
ring up the curtain on, p. 166
rip and tuck, p. 93
roast snow in a furnace, p. 136
robber barons, p. 108
rob the cradle, p. 191
Rochester rappings, p. 327
rogue in grain, p. 332
[a] Roland for an Oliver, p. 278

roll with the punches, p. 89
Romeo, p. 257
roorback, p. 240
root of all evil, p. 205
rope in, p. 328
rotgut, p. 128
roué, p. 259
rough side, p. 274
round the bend, p. 86
round the bend, p. 88
rowing crosshanded, p. 291
rubber check, p. 205
rubber chicken, p. 128
rubber chicken circuit, p. 128
rubber chicken syndrome, p. 128
rubberneck, p. 56
rub it in, p. 98
rub salt in a wound, p. 98
rub shoulders, p. 131
ruffle feathers, p. 343
run a tight ship, p. 51
run at the ring, p. 286
run into the ground, p. 103
run-of-the-mill, p. 303
run rings around, p. 220
run riot, p. 76
the runs, p. 149
run the gamut, p. 159
saddler of Bawtry, p. 63
sad sack, p. 115
sad sack of shit, p. 115
sail under false colors, p. 253
Saint Audrey's lace, p. 217
salad days, p. 353
salt of the earth, p. 303
sand-hiller, p. 244
sand-lapper, p. 244
say uncle, p. 304
scare the daylights out of
    [someone], p. 122
Scavenger's daughter, p. 40
scot and lot, p. 225
scratch for [one]self, p. 291
Scratch my back, I'll scratch yours,
    p. 266
*se couper le nez pour faire dépit à
    son visage*, p. 98
secretary's breakfast, p. 125
see a wolf, p. 294

see far in(to) a millstone, p. 228
see through a brick wall, p. 228
see through a millstone, p. 228
see through [someone], p. 228
seize the day, p. 109
sell smoke, p. 251
send to Dulcarnon, p. 47
serve a sop, p. 278
serve the same sauce, p. 278
set on cinque and sice, p. 72
set one's face, p. 51
set on six and seven, p. 72
shack up, p. 260
a shadow of [one's] former self,
    p. 149, p. 238
shadow of oneself, p. 238
shake a leg, p. 297
shake in one's boots, p. 122
shake in [one's] shoes, p. 122
shake like an aspen leaf, p. 122
shake the daylights out of someone,
    p. 122
shake the dust from [one's] feet,
    p. 63
shall I, shall I, p. 336
sham Abraham, p. 249
shambles, p. 76
shanghai, p. 42⁻
shanghaiing, p. 42
shell out, p. 226
shill I, shall I, p. 336
shilly-shally, p. 336
shine up the apple, p. 210
shit on a shingle, p. 129
the shoe is on the other foot,
    p. 283
shoe the goose, p. 136
shoo-in, p. 39
shook up, p. 72
shoot deer in the balcony, p. 172
shooting the tube, p. 112
shoot moose in the theater, p. 173
shoot one's breakfast, p. 149
shoot [one's] cookies, p. 149
shoot [one's] cuffs, p. 218
shoot one's dinner, p. 149
shoot one's linen, p. 218
shoot one's lunch, p. 149
shoot one's supper, p. 149

shoot the cat, p. 149, p. 83
shoot the daylights out of someone,
    p. 122
shoot the moon, p. 64
shoot the tube, p. 112
shopping bag lady, p. 243
short horse is soon curried, p. 174
short of the mark, p. 96
shotgun marriage, p. 42
shotgun wedding, p. 42
a shot in the locker, p. 206
shot in the locker, p. 206
the show must go on, p. 233
shucking and jiving, p. 328
shyster, p. 333
sick as a cat, p. 149
side winder, p. 58
sign off, p. 43
silly as a coot, p. 118
similia similibus curantur, p. 124
simple Jack, p. 119
simple Jack, p. 119
simple Jack as before, p. 119
since Hector was a pup, p. 322
sing like a trooper, p. 256
sink one's teeth into, p. 105
Sir Hobbard de Hoy, p. 353
sit like a bump on a log, p. 164
sits on the fence, p. 307
sitting duck, p. 349
sit upon hot cockles, p. 151
sit up with a sick friend, p. 240
Skeffinger's daughter, p. 40
skeleton at the feast, p. 154
skeleton in the closet, p. 288
skeleton in the cupboard, p. 289
skim milk masquerading as cream,
    p. 253
skin [someone] alive, p. 274
skin the bear at once, p. 34
slaphappy, p. 119, p. 47
a slap in the face, p. 180
slap of the tongue, p. 274
sleep with one eye open, p. 250
sleeveless errand, p. 136
sleeveless reason, p. 136
sleeveless words, p. 136
slings and arrows, p. 54
sling the bat, p. 189

slip one's trolley, p. 88
the slippery slope, p. 78
slip someone a Mickey, p. 126
slush fund, p. 206
small potatoes, p. 173, p. 206
smart Alec(k), p. 142
smart alecky, p. 142
smell a rat, p. 314
to smell of the inkhorn, p. 187
snake in the grass, p. 58
sneaky pete, p. 128
to sneeze at, p. 350
snow job, p. 198
social butterfly, p. 119
social ladder, p. 119
social whirl, p. 119, p. 119
Sod's law, p. 70
soft fire makes sweet malt, p. 151
something rotten in Denmark,
    p. 314
Sooner, p. 151
SOS, p. 129
So what else is new, p. 281
sow [one's] wild oats, p. 103,
    p. 260
spacey, p. 82
Spanish fan, p. 176
speak by the card, p. 36
speak for Buncombe, p. 208
speak to Buncombe, p. 208
spiff one's biscuits, p. 149
spit cotton, p. 70
spot on, p. 247, p. 248
springes to catch woodcocks, p. 241
spring up like mushrooms, p. 17
square meal, p. 129
square the circle, p. 136
St. Bernard's soup, p. 241
St. Tib's Eve, p. 323
stalking horse, p. 241
stand one's ground, p. 232
stand on one's own bottom, p. 290
stand sam, p. 132
stand the gaff, p. 90
to stand to one's gun(s), p. 233
starkers, p. 239
stark naked, p. 239
starko, p. 239
start the ball rolling, p. 165

steal the show, p. 220
steer, p. 50
stem the tide, p. 319
Stepin Fetchit, p. 212
step on it, p. 297
step on the gas, p. 297
stick [one's] neck out, p. 349
stick to [one's] guns, p. 233
sticky wicket, p. 70
sting, p. 328
stingbum, p. 328
stir-crazy, p. 184
stir [one's] stumps, p. 297
stolen sweets, p. 91
stone soup, p. 241
stonewall, p. 316
stop-watch critic, p. 54
storm in a teacup, p. 104
straddles the fence, p. 307
straight from the horse's mouth, p. 28
straight from the shoulder, p. 36
to strain at the leash, p. 150
strike a balance, p. 93
strike for tall timber, p. 64
strike oil, p. 309
strike [one's] colors, p. 305
strike [one's] flag, p. 305
strike sail, p. 305, p. 60
strike while the iron is hot,
    p. 109, p. 214
string [someone] along, p. 253
stripped to the buff, p. 237
stuffed shirt, p. 142
stupid as a coot, p. 118
sub rosa, p. 289
sudden death, p. 175
Suffolk milk, p. 253
sugar and honey, p. 206
sure as eggs is eggs, p. 38
sure as shooting, p. 39
sur l'ongle, p. 224
swear like a trooper, p. 256
sweep the board, p. 309
swings and roundabouts, p. 93
sword of Damocles, p. 58
the tables are turned, p. 283
tag and rag, p. 302
take a bath, p. 115, p. 162
take a deep breath, p. 89

take a gander, p. 56
take a gander, p. 57
take a message to Garcia, p. 290
take a powder, p. 64
take a run-out powder, p. 64
take a shine to, p. 191
to take a sight, p. 178
take for gospel, p. 28
take in water, p. 96
take it in snuff, p. 22
take it on the chin, p. 90
take [one's] medicine, p. 275
take the bit between [one's] teeth,
  p. 265
take the bit in one's teeth, p. 265
take the cake, p. 220
take the measure of, p. 320
take the rag off the bush, p. 259
take the wall, p. 60
take time by the forelock, p. 109
take to the tall timber, p. 64
talk for Buncombe, p. 208
talk the bark off a tree, p. 256
talk to Buncombe, p. 208
talk to [someone] like a Dutch
  uncle, p. 274
talk turkey, p. 36
tank town, p. 173
Tantony pig, p. 212
tant pour tant, p. 279
tarred with the troppo brush,
  p. 184
taste of the same sauce, p. 278
telling noses, p. 157
tell [someone] where to get off,
  p. 274
tempest in a teacup, p. 104
tempest in a teapot, p. 103
ten acres and a mule, p. 17
tender trap, p. 191
test of the boar's head, p. 321
test of the brawn's head, p. 321
that's flat, p. 39
that's music to my ears, p. 91
that's the way the ball bounces,
  p. 275
that's the way the cookie crumbles,
  p. 275
that's water over the dam, p. 185

that's water under the bridge, p. 185
that ain't hay, p. 206
that went better in Wigan, p. 168
there's the rub, p. 154
there is no leaping from Delilah's lap
  to Abraham's bosom, p. 283
thick as thieves, p. 132
thimblerig, p. 329
third time's the charm, p. 313
this is not my pidgin, p. 188
thread and thrum, p. 324
threads and thrums, p. 201
three acres and a cow, p. 17
three acres and a cow, p. 17
Three Acres and a Cow Collings,
  p. 18
three blue beans in a blue
  bladder, p. 173
three-martini lunch, p. 129
three on a match, p. 313
three sheets in the wind, p. 83
three sheets to the wind, p. 83, p. 83
throw a curve or a curve ball,
  p. 242
throw a tub to the whale, p. 242
throw dust in [someone's] eyes,
  p. 329
throw for a loop, p. 46
throw in [one's] hand, p. 305
throw in [someone's] face, p. 270
throw in the sponge, p. 306
throw in the towel, p. 306
throw out the baby with the bath
  water, p. 104
throw straws against the wind,
  p. 136
thumb of gold, p. 333
thumb one's nose, p. 178
thumb [one's] nose, p. 180
thumbs down, p. 267
tickle [one's] fancy, p. 92
to tie a bag on, p. 81, p. 82, p. 83
tiebreaker, p. 176
tie one on, p. 83
tie up the loose ends, p. 43
tiger's milk, p. 129
tiger by the tail, p. 59
tinhorn gambler, p. 218
tirl at the latch, p. 151

tirl at the pin, p. 151
tit for tat, p. 278
toad-eater, p. 212
to a T, p. 248
tobacco road, p. 246
toffee-nosed, p. 142
Tom, Dick, and Harry, p. 159
tommyrot, p. 210
Tom Noddies, p. 119
Tom Noddy, p. 119
Toms o' Bedlam, p. 249, p. 249
Tom Tiddler's ground, p. 214
tongue-lashing, p. 274
top billing, p. 303
topsy-turvy, p. 77
torch-bearer, p. 190
torch singer, p. 190
torch song, p. 190
torpedo juice, p. 129
toss one's cookies, p. 149
totem pole, p. 301
to the bitter end, p. 317
to the manner born, p. 15, p. 303
touché, p. 281
touch wood, p. 312
tough customer, p. 71
a tough nut to crack, p. 67
towering ambition, p. 104
towering rage, p. 23
treat [someone] with a dose of [his/her] own medicine, p. 277
Trojan horse, p. 242
the trots, p. 149
trump card, p. 242
trump up, p. 199
tube it, p. 112
tuft-hunter, p. 212
turn a deaf ear, p. 268
turn [someone] around [one's] little finger, p. 195
turn tables, p. 284
turn the cat in the pan, p. 284
turn the tables on, p. 284
turn the tide, p. 284
turn turtle, p. 349
turn up trumps, p. 309
twist [someone's] arm, p. 41
twist [someone] around [one's] little finger, p. 195

two-faced, p. 333
two more, and up goes the donkey, p. 329
UFO, p. 337
ugly as a mud fence, p. 237
ugly customer, p. 70
ugly duckling, p. 239, p. 284
Uncle Tom Cobleigh and all, p. 160
under [one's] hat, p. 289
underprivileged man, p. 169
under [someone's] thumb, p. 195
under the hammer, p. 292
under the rose, p. 289
under the spear, p. 292
under the table, p. 305
under the table, p. 83
under the weather, p. 149, p. 83
under way, p. 166
unvarnished tale, p. 36
unvarnished truth, p. 37
up a stump, p. 48
up a tree, p. 349
upper crust, p. 304
upstage, p. 222
up stumps, p. 317
up to the gills, p. 83
urban cowboy, p. 215
use the rough side of [one's] tongue, p. 274
venom is in the tail, p. 71
vent [one's] spleen, p. 23
[my] Venus turns out a whelp, p. 114, p. 284
vicious circle, p. 71
vie et bagues sauves, p. 156
vin de lyon, p. 84
vin de mouton, p. 84
vin de pourceau, p. 84
vin de singe, p. 84
vouloir prendre la lune avec les dents, p. 133
wait for dead men's shoes, p. 66
walls have ears, p. 288
walls have ears, p. 289
ward heeler, p. 213
warm the cockles of the heart, p. 92
warts and all, p. 37

wash a brick, p. 136
washed out, p. 115, p. 162
wash [one's] hands of, p. 268
a watched pot never boils, p. 151
to wave the red flag, p. 188
wear different hats, p. 16
wearing sackcloth and ashes, p. 138
wear [one's] heart on [one's] sleeve, p. 191
wear the willow, p. 138
wear two hats, p. 16
weasel words, p. 189
weathercock, p. 336
weigh in the balance, p. 321
wet blanket, p. 154
wet blanket, p. 94
We wuz robbed, p. 166
what one loses on swings, he gains on roundabouts, p. 93
what the dickens, p. 114, p. 254
when all is said and done, p. 316
when push comes to shove, p. 42, p. 98
when the dust settles, p. 48
where the shoe pinches, p. 349
where to get off, p. 274
whip a dead horse, p. 134
whip the cat, p. 149
whip the devil around the stump, p. 329
whip the devil round a post, p. 330
whistle for it, p. 268
whistling for the wind, p. 268
a white lie, p. 199
whole ball of wax, p. 324
the whole boodle, p. 160
the whole caboodle, p. 160
the whole kit, p. 160
the whole kit and biling, p. 160
the whole kit and boodle, p. 160
the whole kit and caboodle, p. 157, p. 202
the whole kit and caboodle, p. 160
whole schmear, p. 324
whole shebang, p. 324
the whole shooting match, p. 160
whole shtick, p. 160
[the one] who pays the piper calls the tune, p. 51

why the dickens, p. 254
wide of the mark, p. 96
widow's cruse, p. 18
widow's lock, p. 345
widow's peak, p. 239, p. 345
wild as a March hare, p. 184
wild-goose chase, p. 137
willing to give one's ears, p. 65
wimp, p. 120
window dressing, p. 199
wind [someone] around [one's] little finger, p. 195
wine of ape, p. 84
wing it, p. 295
winning the ring, p. 286
wire game, p. 329
wise men of Gotham, p. 120
wish for the moon, p. 133
wither on the vine, p. 115
with flying colors, p. 310
with one's feet under the mahogany, p. 131
a wolf in a lamb's skin, p. 253
wolf in sheep's clothing, p. 253
wooden spoon, p. 286
woolgathering, p. 164
work both sides of the street, p. 109
work the oracle, p. 196
work-to-rule, p. 265
work up to the collar, p. 104
work up to the collar, p. 106
the world's [one's] oyster, p. 196
worship the golden calf, p. 207
worth a Jew's eye, p. 352
worth [one's] salt, p. 352
worth the whistle, p. 352
wowser, p. 263
write off, p. 43
write [someone] down, p. 54
write the book on, p. 28
wrong side of the fence, p. 307
yellow dog under the wagon, p. 96
yen, p. 66
yeoman service, p. 27
you could hear a pin drop, p. 294
young Turk, p. 266
zebra crossing, p. 26
zero hour, p. 323

zero hour

zing

zing, p. 281
zinger, p. 281
zoot suit, p. 218

zoot suiter, p. 218
Zulu car, p. 339